BIOPOLITICS

A John Hope Franklin Center Book

BIOPOLITICS

A READER

Timothy Campbell and Adam Sitze, editors

Duke University Press *Durham and London* 2013

Designed by George T. Whipple

Typeset in 10/14 Minion Pro by Westchester Publishing Services

Library of Congress Cataloging-in-Publication Data

Biopolitics : a reader / Timothy Campbell and Adam Sitze, editors.

    pages cm

  "A John Hope Franklin Center Book."

  Includes bibliographical references and index.

  ISBN 978-0-8223-5332-4 (cloth : alk. paper)—

  ISBN 978-0-8223-5335-5 (pbk. : alk. paper)

  1. Biopolitics—Philosophy.   I. Campbell, Timothy C.

II. Sitze, Adam.

  JA80.B547 2013

  320.01—dc23

                         2013032321

CONTENTS

1.

There comes a moment in the history of a concept when, looking back, one recognizes a break, an event, something that appears to have set in motion everything that comes after; when what was impossible to see before presents itself, now seemingly without complication, as the origin that provides the lens with which the lines of future pasts can be glimpsed. As a result, not only do the earlier contexts by which the concept was understood shift, but so too does the horizon of meaning shared with other concepts—the moment when living contexts, as Walter Benjamin might say, are transformed into the origin of the concept itself.

No such singular moment comes to mind when charting the history of biopolitics. No defining interval offers itself as the lens able to superimpose the past and the future, allowing us to look back and say, "ah, yes, it was precisely then that biopolitics was born, exactly then that politics gave way to biopolitics, power to biopower, and life to *bios*, *zoē*, and the forms of life that characterize our present." Part of the reason for the missing origin of biopolitics may be simply a question of time—or better, not enough time, as not enough time has passed for a complete accounting of biopolitics, biopower, and for their possible genealogies and archaeologies to have been written. Indeed, it is only today, at a moment that seems both belated and too soon, that a codification of the biopolitical is underway. For many years now, in a process that is more automatic than one would hope, we have been witnessing the seemingly inescapable selection of authors and texts, the exclusion of others, the catalogue of genres that characterize the field of study—in a word, the writing of a canon. Given that such a project remains incomplete, competing versions, not only of the origins of biopolitics, but also of the question of its principal subject and object, will continue to spark debates, transatlantic and transpacific exchanges, and struggles for conceptual dominance. This is a salutary part of the codification currently underway; it is essential for coming to terms with why biopolitics continues to be featured so prominently in contemporary ontologies of the present. To be sure, this means that no point for observing the totality of biopolitics is available to us: there exists no perspective that would allow us to survey and measure the lines that together constitute the concept's theoretical circumference. But this also means that what at first appears to be an endless process—debating the endlessly blurred boundaries of biopolitics—is at one and the same time something else as well: an occasion for thinking. It is an opportunity to free ourselves from any one map for navigating the rough seas of the biopolitical, be it the straightforwardly historical and empirical, the phenomenological, the existentialist, the post-Marxist, or the posthuman. What to some might feel like a missing ground thus evokes for us a different response: an invitation to be creative; a call to ask impertinent questions that one normally might be too embarrassed or too afraid to ask; a solicitation to bring other methodologies, practices, and interpretive keys to bear on the study of biopolitics so as to mark, with all necessary caveats, where we stand in relation to it.

With this in mind, the following pages have been written not merely under the sign of biopolitics, its emerging limits, paradoxes, and increasing theoretical weight, but also its recesses, folds, and shifting contours. To do so we have opted to dramatize biopolitics as the expression of a kind of predicament involving the intersection, or perhaps reciprocal incorporation, of life and politics, the two concepts that together spell biopolitics. The problem at the core of that meeting—the task, perplexing yet also inescapable, of coming up with a theory to make sense of the encounter between the concepts of "life" and "politics"—also lies at the very heart of some of the most exciting and difficult developments in scholarship today.

The reasons for this centrality are, in one sense, not hard to understand. So many of the crises that force themselves upon our present, after all, seem to pivot on the very same axis. Today, for example, we witness the resurgence of neo-Malthusian anxieties that overpopulation and high birth rates in "undeveloped" regions will push the earth's various agricultural "carrying capacities" beyond their breaking point. We participate in debates over healthcare, social security, retirement ages, abortion, and immigration that are so chronic, bitter, and entrenched that in many countries they have led to violence and the breakdown of longstanding political institutions. We engage in struggles over the unequal global distribution of essential medicines and medical technologies, manifested most visibly in the HIV/AIDS pandemic. We observe a constantly morphing "War on Terror" (or, as it is now called, "Overseas Contingency Operations") whose security tactics range from drone strikes to racial profiling to the normalization of exceptional juridical spaces such as indefinite detention in Guantanamo Bay to the massive surveillance of all forms of electronic communication. We discover the emergence of a global trade in human organs, with body parts excised from the healthy bodies of the poor in impoverished regions of the earth, and then transported and transplanted into the sick bodies of the rich. We experience the development of new technologies whose innovative potentialities strain, to the point of rupture, against established codes of intellectual property rights, not to mention longstanding traditions of morals and ethics, producing not only what seem to be unprecedented possibilities for a new mode of political economy—a "commons" that is neither private nor public—but also the conditions for a redoubled return of old fantasies of "immortality": whereas the modern subject dreamed of becoming a "prosthetic God," the contemporary subject wants to use technology to overcome mortality itself, once and for all, whether through a gradual, generalized "negation of death" or through the achievement of a sudden, rapturous "singularity."[1]

The examples could be multiplied, but our point by now should be clear: taken together, these crises have produced a context in which there is a demand for scholarly theories that illuminate the relations between life and politics. To this demand there's been at least one particularly strong response: the reactivation of an account of life and politics offered some thirty years ago by a French philosopher named Michel Foucault. Foucault's first analysis of "biopolitics" appeared in a short piece, more an appendix than anything else, titled ominously enough "Right of Death and Power over Life," which forms the final part of his 1976 book, *La volonté de savoir*.[2] That this little text eventually would launch its own share of articles and books was not at all clear in 1978, when the text first appeared in English as Part III of *The History of Sexuality, Volume 1*. Those of us old enough to remember reading it nearly upon publication will recall that early scholarly attention initially focused on Foucault's finding that sexuality was a problem for the Victorians—a then shocking discovery that today is more likely to elicit shrugs than anything else—and on the implications of Foucault's concept of power for Freudianism and Marxism.[3] The text's concluding passages on biopolitics, by contrast, seemed anomalous if not aberrant: apparently unconnected to the pages that preceded them, these passages also would seem disconnected from the two further volumes of *The History of Sexuality* Foucault would publish before his untimely death in 1984. Consequently, it seems, Foucault's short remarks on biopolitics would be received by Anglophone scholars in a most symptomatic manner, with a silence all the more pronounced for appearing at a moment when Foucault's work otherwise was becoming influential in almost every discipline in the humanities and social sciences.[4]

Over time, however, these other pages of the *La volonté de savoir* began to gain traction. Certainly, feminist readings of Foucault's biopolitics, especially Donna Haraway's 1989 essay on postmodern bodies, played an early and important role in pushing forward biopolitics as a central category in postmodernity.[5] The same could be said for readings set forth by Étienne Balibar, Paul Gilroy, Agnes Heller, and Anne Laura Stoler, each of whom, albeit in very different ways, singled out the term in the 1990s as a decisive horizon for studies of the politics of race.[6] Yet it was not until 1998, with the English translation of Giorgio Agamben's provocative rereading of Foucault's "Right of Death and Power over Life" in *Homo Sacer: Sovereign Power and Bare Life*,[7] that Foucault's long-dormant text on biopolitics was reactivated in its current form. With the appearance of Agamben's controversial commentary on Foucault, which in 2000 was followed by the very different but equally controversial appropriation of Foucault by Michael Hardt and Antonio Negri in their book *Empire*,[8] the concept of "biopolitics" began to migrate from philosophy to not-so-distant shores, including but not limited to the fields of anthropology, geography, sociology, political science, theology, legal studies, bioethics, digital media, art history, and architecture.

The result is what might be called a "biopolitical turn": a proliferation of studies, claiming Foucault as an inspiration, on the relations between "life" and "politics." As part of the voracious intellectual appetite for everything biopolitical, a slew of related neologisms has entered into circulation. In addition to bioethics, biotechnology, biopower, and biohistory—"bio-"terms that were all, in one way or another, already in circulation prior to the biopolitical turn—scholars now proposed to study bioculture, biomedia, biolegitimacy, bioart, biocapital, biolabor, bioscience, biohorror, bioeconomics, bioinformatics, biovalue, biodesire, biocomputing, biotheology, biosociety, and biocentrism, among others. Working in the best experimental spirit of the philosophic traditions of empiricism and nominalism, the inventors of these neologisms seemed to have wanted to shed light on what's new or unprecedented about the present. And yet even as the content of these terms seemed fresh and new, their form remained familiar, even traditional. It's odd, after all, that the standard nouns of disciplinary reason—art, culture, science, society, economics, capital, and so on—should so consistently repeat themselves at and as the root of these inventions, as if the old objects of existing academic disciplines would somehow be transformed simply through the piecemeal addition of the prefix "bio-." Indeed, interpreted as a general phenomenon that exceeds the consciousness of any single scholar, the compulsion to reinterpret everything today in terms of biopolitics appears to repeat a similar inflationary tendency that began nearly two decades ago, when during the "cultural turn" of the early 1990s it seemed like everything could and should be reinterpreted with reference to "culture." If it's the case that today's biopolitical turn is warranted by some sort of desire to comprehend the new, something unprecedented in our present, it's thus curious that the neologisms through which this desire has expressed itself nevertheless silently obey a disciplinary grammar that is anything but new.

Other scholars, reacting with irritation to the compulsive novelty that seems to drive the biopolitical turn, have written it off as nothing more than a mere fad. For these scholars, biopolitics is little more than a passing trend of academic fashion, and a particularly insidious one at that. Not least because the biopolitical turn has brought with it renewed attention to the sort of ontological problems to which the empiricist social sciences have long been allergic, these critics have tended to denounce the emerging discourse on biopolitics for its neglect of historical and cultural contextualization, for its monolithic, reductive, and homogenizing claims, and for its embrace of a theological lexicon that seems to be mystifying and vague, if not also politically regressive. The brusque tone of this criticism notwithstanding, it's far from clear that dismissals of this sort allow any escape whatsoever from the full thrust of biopolitical questioning. Some skeptics of biopolitics, for example, seem to believe it possible to disregard the claims that characterize the biopolitical turn simply by pointing out its incommensurability with the redemptive energy of the existing principles of modern democracy. These same critics, however, often fail to ask what it means that these very same principles derive their energy precisely from the secularized assumption—thanatopolitical to the core, if Agamben is correct[9]—that every human life is and must remain sacred. These scholars seem to want a secular, egalitarian politics that improves the living standards of the world's populations; but they cannot account for the genesis and basis of their own sense of urgency (or, as Hannah Arendt might put it, for the way they experience the "necessity" of their own political commitments). In the end, it seems to us, the tendency to dismiss biopolitics as "mere fashion" is not only premature (since so often the very premises of these same dismissals, unexamined as they are, testify to their failure to fully digest the conceptual challenge of biopolitics). It's also, ultimately, just as symptomatic as is the tendency to turn biopolitics into the very synecdoche of "the new": neither approach, in our view, is able to understand why it is that biopolitical inquiries into the relation between life and politics should turn out to require, with such unusual regularity, a fundamental rethinking of one of the basic categories of the philosophy of history, namely, *the event*.[10]

2.

This anthology offers the reader a chance to produce a much different response to the biopolitical turn. We think there's a more difficult, but also more rewarding, way to think about the demands of a world in which the couplet of life and politics seems to reappear as the innermost interior of every fresh crisis. Rather than *enthusiastically affirm* biopolitics as the newest, latest, and most obvious theoretical response to these crises, *hastily reject* biopolitics as nothing more than the newest, latest, and most passing of academic fads, or *defensively reify* biopolitics into yet another empiricist and historicist research agenda, we propose an *attentive re-reading* of the texts that today have become the source of so much dispute, in so many languages and regions, and that as such have come to constitute something like a "paradigm" of biopolitics.[11] This will be a rereading that doesn't pretend, as do the various declensions of the biopolitical turn, that there's a coherent concept of biopolitics that can be extracted intact from *La volonté de savoir*, as the prior condition for its straightforward affirmation, rejection, or application. Put differently, we don't suppose that Foucault's brief remarks on biopolitics, whether in his little 1976 book or, especially, in the lectures concurrent with that book, can be interpreted as though they are consistent, transparent, and fully worked-through.

In our view, Foucault's foray into biopolitics was anything but straightforward. Filled with doubts and second thoughts, Foucault's writings on biopolitics involve shifts, feints, changes in focus and direction—perhaps even, as Foucault's most ungenerous critic has put it, "deceptions."[12] What appear to be explicit conceptual innovations thus turn out to be, on reflection, implicit returns to problems Foucault had thought through earlier in his intellectual itinerary. What looks like a coherent path for thought, mapped out in detail and in advance by this "new cartographer," reveals itself instead to be a trail that fades away into the conceptual wilderness. Conversely, what seem to be explicit rejections of research on biopolitics, turn out on second thought to be intensified engagements with biopolitics, only now on a new plane and in different terms. All of this implies a very definite reader of Foucault: one who is alive not only to what Foucault *said* in these pages but also, and much more importantly, to what Foucault left *unsaid*. This will be a reader who is less concerned with affirming, rejecting, or applying Foucault's "biopolitics," than with understanding precisely the *turbulence* of Foucault's text—its "hesitations, doubts, and uncertainties."[13] She will understand not only how these generative opacities *enable* the various declensions of the biopolitical turn but also, and, again, much more importantly, retain the potential *to exceed it from within*.

Supposing a reader of this sort, we want to begin the task of rereading by returning now to the text that seems to so many to have been the birthplace of biopolitics: the final pages of *La volonté de savoir*. We reopen this text with the intention of preparing the reader, in turn, to take a fresh look at the more recent texts on biopolitics—the texts that, together, have recursively constituted *La volonté de savoir* as a sort of *Urtext*, an original score that seems to have guided the way the relation between politics and life has been understood in the biopolitical turn. Our aim is to linger with the reader, in particular, over a set of utterances that, precisely in their repetition over the last three decades, seem to have materialized into what Foucault himself would call "statements"— the nuclei, as it were, around which discourses form.[14] Our desire is neither to praise or blame this refrain, nor to chant or march along with it. We instead want to enjoin the reader to hear with us in these statements a different set of repetitions, a set of silences that seems to us to be arhythmic and aberrant, but to that same degree inviting and even provocative. This is a rereading that begins to unfold only once the reader first becomes alert to *the impasses* Foucault encountered when he tried to work through the relations of life and politics in the closing passages of *La volonté de savoir*.[15] There are at least four: *species living, the power of life, the new millennial animal,* and *the resolution to live.* Scored together, these impasses allow us to take a step back from our common sense about the relation of life and politics, in order to inquire into its meaning, conditions, and goals. Taken together, in other words, they allow for the encounter between life and politics to be "problematized," and as such, to be thought anew.[16]

Species Living

The first impasse in Foucault's account of life and politics involves the introduction of what Foucault in other venues refers to as knowledge-power. In *La volonté de savoir*, Foucault relates this particular form of knowledge-power not only to the emerging field of biology, but also to the development of "different fields of knowledge concerned with life in general," agricultural techniques among them.[17] The period of European history in question is one to which Foucault will return repeatedly in his discussions of biopolitics: the period immediately preceding the French Revolution. The overall effect of these changes was a relaxation of death's grip over life; not absolutely, he notes, but relatively. He writes:

> In the space for movement thus conquered, and in its organization and expansion, methods of power and knowledge assumed responsibility for the life processes and undertook to control and modify them. Western man was gradually learning what it meant to be a living species in a living world, to have a body, conditions of existence, individual and collective health, forces that could be modified, and a space in which they could be distributed in optimal manner. For the first time in history, no doubt, biological existence was reflected in political existence; the fact of living was no longer an inaccessible substrate that only emerged from time to time, amid the randomness of death and its fatality; part of it passed into knowledge's field of control and power's sphere of intervention.[18]

In this passage, Foucault locates a junction for life's future enmeshment with politics. As death withdraws, however slightly, gains are made in knowledge about the "substrates" of life that have now become accessible. With this shift, in turn, we witness the emergence of a "space"—a year earlier in his lectures at the Collège de France collected in *Security, Territory, Population*, as well as in the last text he would ever author, he will prefer to speak of a "milieu"[19]—in which "Western man" attends to the significance of being part of a species that lives while at the same time living in a world that is alive. In making this claim, Foucault seems to assume that before the confluence of life and politics that emerges thanks to the development of these life-producing techniques, "Western man" *did not* fully apprehend life in terms of "species," nor that the world in which "Western man" lived actually merited the qualifier "living." Foucault will give to this history a curious name—"biohistory"—that is, at present, just as neglected as "biopolitics" was a decade ago. With this term, Foucault proposes to mark those moments of pressure "in which the movements of life and processes of history interfere with one another," and which, in turn, parallel an intensification of biopower.[20] Foucault will place a caesura at the moment of life's greatest interference with history, distinguishing a period prior to their encounter that in his essay (as well as across his lectures at the Collège de France from 1975–1976 in *"Society Must Be Defended"*) he will call "sovereignty." Before death's respite, Western man, when not dead, was, according to Foucault, less alive than he later became.

We can well imagine why: when the risks of death appeared imminent through epidemics or war, the possibility of feeling alive was much more limited. And yet such a division between history and biohistory proper raises a question, one that informs so many of the essays collected here. What really does it mean to say that life has a history? Life—the very paradigm, it would seem, of novelty and renewal itself[21]—seems constitutively opposed to "the past" that history cannot but take as its object, as well as to "the future" history for which cannot help but to prepare us. What sort of "events" would this biohistory consider, and how, if at all, would those "events" differ from the sort of "events" that contemporary philosophers, most notably Deleuze and Alain Badiou, propose to consider? In what ways, for example, might our very experience of "life" or "flesh" today itself, precisely in its immediacy and novelty, derive its implicit schema from a long-past event (such as the secularization and immanentization of the Christian notion of the afterlife, or the emergence of modern democracy in and through the beheading of the king)?[22] What meaning can "life" have in an epoch when life itself is no longer outside of history, if it ever was, but is now simply an effect of history itself, one of its variables and contingencies? What meaning can living have when no element of life is outside the domain of politics, and no political interest can be found that does not in the last analysis concern life? Conversely, how might certain concepts of life—pertaining to mortality and immortality, necessity and urgency, newness and the old—inscribe themselves into historiography itself? How might certain presuppositions about life govern the very field within which historical knowledge then comes to be valuable for life? For some of the thinkers who appear in this anthology, the best response to this question will be to retranslate it into new and different terms—displacing "aliveness" with "immortality," or redirecting "species" toward "multitude." Others will respond by radicalizing the trope of the organism as machine that has governed modern philosophy since at least Descartes and Hobbes.[23] For these thinkers, the task of biohistory is to imagine a future that does not so much anxiously question as embrace the enframing of "bare life" (or what Agamben calls *zoē*) by *technē*—whether those be the bio-engineered humans of the sort imagined by Peter Sloterdijk, the "materially immortal" beings theorized by Nishitani Osamu, or the sort of cyborg lives for which Donna Haraway called in 1989.[24] And for still others, it signals a defense of linguistic virtuosity or the advantages of hybridity as a model for an affirmative biopolitics.

Foucault's own perspective in "Right of Death and Power over Life" on "species living" will move across different registers, but as the text comes to a close he will settle on an important shift in focus: from law to norm. In a series of earlier lectures, of course, Foucault had devised an archaeology of the abnormal, and so in a sense his return to the conceptual axis of the norm isn't surprising (even if it is, as Roberto Esposito notes, much more opaque than Foucault's commentators have acknowledged[25]). In *La volonté de savoir*, by contrast, Foucault's shift from law to norm takes place alongside a homologous shift from history to biohistory, with each shift in its turn being spurred by a specific event: the emergence of population as an object of knowledge and power. With the advent of biohistory, sovereignty wanes and with it the law as the primary means by which sovereign power is exercised. Often the suggestion in these pages is that in a post-sovereign milieu, populations are less subjected to sovereign power than they are governed through norms.[26] The result is that living as part of a species for Foucault entails learning to live with norms. Whereas before the advent of biohistory, Western man did not know how alive he was (just that he was not dead), once the self-evidence of death withdraws, we witness the emergence of contingent standards for what qualifies as living. No timeless, transcendent life and death laws determine the destiny of this species, only changing, immanent measures that allow for the evaluation of varying degrees and kinds of living. Knowing these norms forms a pedagogical imperative for Foucault. Just as laws, Foucault tells us, become norms, so too do institutions give way to the odd ensembles he calls "*dispositifs*" or "apparatuses."

Foucault's use of the term "*dispositif,*" which is much more central to *La volonté de savoir* than the English translation allows us to perceive,[27] has increasingly become the subject of interest on the part of those writing today in a biopolitical key.[28] As such, it will be helpful to dwell here on some of what's at stake in Foucault's use of the word. In an interview from 1977, Foucault sets out a number of meanings for the term. The concept of "apparatus," Foucault says, names "a thoroughly heterogenous ensemble" of elements such as institutions, architectural forms, regulatory, decisions, administrative measures, and laws; it is also a "formation" which responds strategically to "an urgency," which is why apparatus has a dominant strategic function; it is also "a set of strategies of the relations of force supporting, and supported by, certain types of knowledge."[29] When read against the narrative of life and politics sketched thus far, it rapidly becomes clear why the concept of "apparatus" dominates so much recent reflection. This concept serves as a bridge between life and politics; it is one of the ways in which their chiasmic intersection is measured, effected, and felt as a strategic "urgency." The result is not that "law fades into the background or that the institutions of justice tend to disappear but rather that the law operates more and more as a norm, and that the judicial institution is increasingly incorporated into a continuum of apparatuses (medical, administrative, and so on) whose functions are for the most part regulatory."[30] In this "prologue" to biopolitics, jurisprudence cedes the stage to the apparatus, which aims at regulating life with reference to norms instead of laws, and which discharges this aim with an intensity derived from the newly strategic "necessity" of life for politics.

These apparatuses have a second function as well. Not only do they remind us that we are alive in a living world or that together they separate history from biohistory, separating species that are more alive from those that are less alive; they also represent what Foucault calls "a biological threshold of modernity": "But what might be called a society's 'biological threshold of modernity' has been reached when the life of the species is wagered on its own political strategies."[31] To describe this encounter, Foucault will use a curious turn of phrase, one that is by no means self-evident, but one whose implications are worth dwelling on and explicating. Biopolitics, in his phrasing, involves a sort of "game" in which nothing less than the species itself, the species as a living entity, is "at play" or "at stake" [*enjeu*].[32] Given these stakes, it would be a mistake to underestimate the seriousness of this game. It is in fact a "wager," a most high-stakes gamble. The impression one gets reading "Right of Death and Power over Life" as well as *The Birth of Biopolitics* and *Security, Territory, Population* is of a game in which life, which before was one among a number of stakes, begins to drift to another in which life has now become the only stake. Some of the reasons for such a drift surely concern the increasing efficiency with which risk is calculated, such that calculations lead to a form of wagering over life. Another reason may well be that the increasing material valuations of life, which were less possible when life was held at bay by death, begin to make it easier for a staking of life in a context of wagering to take place (as long as the knowledge-power on which the operation of apparatuses was premised was insufficient to coalesce as a normalizing power around its object, life).[33] Whatever the reason, an increasingly high-stakes "speculation" about the status of life and living begins. Knowledge of biopolitics entails risky propositions: death's slight withdrawal for living opens up the space for a knowledge of life that is irreducibly probabilistic in form, such that understanding life's enmeshment with politics always involves some roll of the dice about the future of both life and politics. In this sense, knowing the story of how life and politics come together means asking how it has come to be that collective life has assumed the form of a massive bet—a deadly serious game of chance in which the population is at once *the central player* and *the main prize*, at once *the subject of politics* and *the objective of politics itself.*[34]

Power of Life

The wagering on life by politics that sets the scene for the birth of biopolitics at the end of the eighteenth century isn't only focused on a living species. As knowledge-power takes life as its object, and as the norm inflects the law toward it, the body becomes available in ways that it hadn't before for power. It is at the level of the body that the conjunction of life and politics will be felt precisely because where life before was infinite in Foucault's account—Foucault will name it "classical being" in his 1966 book *Les mots et les choses*, translated into English as *The Order of Things*—life is soon contained by the body. It is when the body has been opened up and opened by power that we have a *Kehre* or "pivot" that will spell the birth of biopolitics in Foucault's story.

> Power would no longer be dealing simply with legal subjects over whom the ultimate dominion was death, but with living beings, and the mastery [*la prise*]

it would be able to exercise over them would have to be applied at the level of life itself; it was the taking charge of life [*la prise en charge de la vie*] more than the threat of death, that gave power its access even to the body.[35]

Here, much as we saw above, the story of the encounter between life and politics is marked by a *chiasmus*. Now, however, the chiasmus is not between life and history, but between the body and power. This taking charge of life through the body by power is one that informs as well a number of readings collected here—the immunitary declensions of biopolitics in Donna Haraway and Roberto Esposito in particular.[36] So too Alain Badiou, who will subtly shift the wager from life to life's boundaries, that is to its ostensible container, the body.[37] This focus on the body in biopolitics as cause and effect for its emergence as a category indicates too that there is a mode of feeling, of being aware of the body, that would make clearer just how often life is wagered across a body's duration or time, or a subject's experience. Yet we should also note, as many do here, that the taking charge of life set in motion by a certain regime of knowledge-power (which we might call the "non-teleological" natural sciences[38]), also includes another kind of holding that isn't merely on the side of power. Such a possibility of grabbing hold of life "all the way to the body" is not limited to the state or the institution, but is enacted as well by the subject of this new knowledge-power. That possibility is of course at the heart of Foucault's reading of neoliberalism two years later in *The Birth of Biopolitics*.

We note something else in the encounter between life and politics, which concerns precisely Foucault's bringing together living beings with how they are seized. This notion of the seizing or the holding of living beings is one that will reappear in the decades following the publication of *La volonté de savoir*, as well as in his lectures from the 1980s. Foucault's insight is that a power that seizes living beings differs from an earlier power that exercised power over life without also being able to take hold of it. We know the name of such a power: sovereignty. Sovereignty with all its laws didn't fundamentally "seize" life. The knowledge-power of life, however, does—and it does so in the precise degree that scientific knowledge "grasps" the processes internal to the body. This "hold" over living beings through and across their bodies that precedes the advent of biopolitics is one Foucault spoke about in terms slightly different from sovereignty in *The Order of Things*. There Foucault, in lieu of speaking of sovereignty per se, prefers to describe what he calls the "classical period of being."

Classical being was without flaw [*sans défaut*]; life, on the other hand, is without edges or shading [*sans frange ni dégradé*]. Being was spread out over an immense table; life isolates forms that are bound in upon themselves. Being was posited in the perpetually analyzable space of representation; life withdraws into the enigma of a force inaccessible in its essence; apprehendable only in the efforts it makes here and there to manifest and maintain itself.[39]

Soon after he notes: "Biological being becomes regional and autonomous; life, on the confines of being, is what is exterior to it and also what manifests itself within it."[40] These passages precede Foucault's reading of biopolitics, but they are helpful in making clear the place of the body. One of the ways that "life isolates forms that are bound in upon themselves" will be through the body. We might well conclude then that the body provides "the edge" that power grasps with its new knowledge of life. With this reading in hand, biopolitics, rather than resolving the opposition between life and politics, attempts to solve "the enigma of a force inaccessible in its essence" by isolating life in its corporeal form. The impasse that emerges here pertains to something like a missing chronology. "Classical being" is succeeded by "the enigma" of the force of life, which the conjunction of *bios* and politics in biopolitics answers. In other words, biopolitics is the explicit solution to an inexplicit problem: power's inability to fully access life. The more that knowledge-power grows in intensity, the more the scene is set for the question of life to be answered by apparatuses that focus, in particular, on the body. As the prior condition for this access, we must call attention to a detail that other readings tend to overlook: in a biopolitical horizon, life becomes representable once again. The analyzable space of representation that before characterized *being* now, thanks to power's seizure of the body, shifts toward *life*.

The Millennial Animal

Once life encounters the political thanks both to the lessening of death's felt presence and science's mastery of life through the body, bets on life begin to be placed at the level of the population. Modern man is born. But here Foucault's story veers unexpectedly. Rather than simply examining the ways in which politics and life come together across bodies in what Foucault calls an "anatomo-politics," he returns to the earlier theme of "species living" and reframes it now as an antimetabole. It is this reframing that continues to grab the attention of so many. The passage: "For millennia, man remained what he was for Aristotle: a living animal with the additional capacity for a political existence; modern man is an animal whose politics places his existence as a living being in question."[41] Let's linger over the passage for a moment by first noting again the rhetorical move that will characterize so much of Foucault's reflection and those writing in a biopolitical key more generally. In Foucault's transposition, the adjective "living" moves from qualifying the noun "animal" to qualifying a much different noun: "being." The result is that "life" takes up the place of "politics" and "politics" the place of "life." The reason for this reversal, Foucault argues, is that something has changed with regard to politics. Here there are two moments the reader should register. First, crossing the "biological threshold of modernity," for millennia "political" had qualified existence, marking an addition to living. Once the biological threshold for modernity has been crossed, by contrast, politics is shorn of its qualifying status. Politics is no longer about addition; no longer does it qualify existence. It now appears to have become *autonomous* from existence. The impression is that in some way this autonomy of politics is the condition for problematizing what before was not a problem. The move from "addition" to "autonomy," from the "political" to "politics," suggests not only that politics lacks a mooring, but also that one of the main effects of this newly unmoored politics is to confer upon life an unprecedented position. Modern man is no longer a living animal but an animal who has somehow been separated from living being. Where before man was a living animal under conditions of sovereignty, which is to say under the classical episteme, now man is an animal whose living has migrated to being. Only when politics has separated the animal from his living can the very status of living be called into question. The living animal is replaced by an animal whose *living* is in some sense separable from its *existing*—without, we might say with recourse to the etymology of the word "existence" itself, the ability to "stand outside" the living being he discovers himself to be (*ex-sistēre*, "to stand outside"). Modern man, in other words, exists in ways that the pre-modern animal did not thanks to a freeing of politics from its mere status as capacity or addition. Power's "grasp" of life (in the double sense of grip and understanding) does not allow us to stand outside of our own lives, to project ourselves, to devise narratives able to change the conditions of our living non-existence. We are the animal whose politics place that existence—note "existence," not "life"—in question.

Second, let's also note that Foucault's introduction of the animal whose existence is put into question isn't really all that surprising. As he notes in *The

Order of Things, when speaking of Georges Cuvier and the science of living beings, "if living beings are a classification, the plant is best able to express its limpid existence; but if they are a manifestation of life, the animal is better equipped to make its enigma perceptible."[42] Once the animal comes to manifest life, that is "to show us the incessant transition from inorganic to the organic by means of respiration or digestion, and the inverse transformation brought about by death," death enters the frame once again. It is this swerving of life toward the animal in biopolitics that re-introduces death, but now from the inside, transforming the organic into the inorganic.[43] The animal in question, it bears remarking, is not Aristotle's "political animal," but rather an animal who enframes a specific episteme (to remain with Foucault's terminology) characterized by a cohabitation of death and life that will be named "living."[44] We recall that earlier Foucault had described the slackening of death's hold over life which set the scene for Western man's opening to species living. Here, however, death appears to return through the backdoor via the animal, which Foucault reminds us was not the case with plants: "The plants held sway on the frontiers of movement and immobility, of the sentient and the non-sentient; whereas the animal maintains its existence on the frontiers of life and death. Death besieges it on all sides; furthermore, it threatens it also from within, for only the organism can die, and it is from the depth of their lives that death overtakes living beings." The outcome of this change in course of life toward the animal is decisive for biopolitics: "The animal appears as the bearer of that death to which it is, at the same time, subjected; it contains a perpetual devouring of life by life. It belongs to nature only at the price of containing within itself a nucleus of anti-nature."[45] The intensification of the death-bearing attributes of the animal appears as one possible outcome of the encounter between *bios* and *politika*.

What are we to make of this millennial animal who exists but perhaps does not live and what mode of being is appropriate to the man and woman who have crossed over the threshold of modernity into the crucible that repeatedly sutures life and politics? What kind of chiasmic knowledge is consistent with such an animal? To what kind of problems does such an existential animal respond? These questions are a deeply important part of the following reader. Indeed we might say that all of the writers here are attempting to work through what this state of existential animality ultimately means. In that sense, this reader is directed to the animal that we have become, or are becoming—and this is not just any animal, but the animal whose biopolitics pose a threat to itself. This is not to say that the authors collected here are in agreement with Foucault's diagnostic. Clearly they are not, but all do respond to it. For our part, we think it worthwhile to reflect on the consequences of the story Foucault tells about life and politics, especially in relation to Foucault's stunning phrase: "a biological threshold for modernity." Even a quick glance at the anthology of readings collected here suggests that the biological threshold for modernity has shifted since Foucault wrote. Where will it be found today?

By way of response, let's return to an earlier moment in "Right of Death and Power over Life" in which Foucault, again in the language of wager and gambling, speaks of another staking of life that occurs thanks to the possibility of nuclear annihilation: "The principle underlying the tactics of battle—that one has to be capable of killing in order to go on living—has become the principle that defines the strategy of states. But the existence in question is no longer the juridical existence of sovereignty: at stake is the biological existence of a population."[46] For Foucault, decisions about the existence of those populations are "increasingly informed by the naked question of survival."[47] Here to survive means crossing the biological threshold of modernity, to become part of a population whose existence is the object of a political wager. Although Foucault will have little to say about the pedagogical effects of this shift, surely one such effect will be learning what it means to be staked collectively—what it means, in other words, to survive, to desire that one's individual existence be sustained through some sort of wager on collective life. Today these gambles would seem to be at the very heart of contemporary existence. In casino capitalism and other assorted forms of neoliberalism, entire populations (of donors, of consumers, of persons) come into an existence whose effect is to send its members scurrying to learn how to survive individually. We survive without existing—or, better, we survive individually having forgotten how to exist collectively (given that there is no longer any outside left to view, let alone to stand on).

And yet this existing as part of a population and surviving solely as an individual undoubtedly has another effect, namely to heighten, for a privileged few, the pleasures of being alive. Paradoxically, the more that populations become "unnecessary" or "superfluous" for capitalism, the more capitalism reifies the sensation of aliveness itself as a "scarce commodity" that's "in demand." The more that certain populations are made the object of political strategies that call their very existence into question, in other words, the more euphorically alive other populations feel—not despite, but because of, the planetary gambles in which they're involved. This reader asks you to consider this vertiginous wager—this dizzying spiral of pleasure and power—as a third impasse we inherit from the analysis of the "mastery" of life we find analyzed in *La volonté de savoir*.[48]

Resolved to Live

Overcoming classical being and sovereignty, politics now reaches into the interior recesses of life through the body, making life itself both the subject and the object of politics. Life's dramatic need to maintain itself and manifest itself as Foucault describes it finds its ally in a form of politics that no longer manifests itself only within the traditional institutions, practices, and discourses of modern politics. We see such a new politics liberated from the traditional political spaces of old everywhere we look: in courts, in Western parliaments, in metropolitan public spaces, and in families in which the political is nowhere to be found.[49] And yet, the very return of the animal no longer moored to the political raises questions about the direction that biopolitics will take from this point forward. This because in Foucault's analysis the animal carries death within it, setting the stage for the final act in the narrative of life's chiasmatic exchange with politics. How can life manage to manifest and maintain itself when one result of the emergence of biopolitics is precisely to have intensified the mortifying features of the subject of biopolitics, namely the animal? Another way of saying this would be to note that in the birth of biopolitics, an antinomy with regard to life can be sensed: the increase in the space for living creates an opening for politics, which in turn alters the former relation between death and life. The earlier questions we raised about species living and grabbing hold of life merge into a more fundamental question: what part does politicized death play in the suturing of life and politics?

Here Foucault has little to tell us directly in "Power of Death and Right over Life." We can glean a number of possibilities from Foucault's other works. In a seminar that appeared in 1976 as part of the lectures at the Collège de France as *"Society Must Be Defended,"* which is included here, Foucault will link the increasingly significant role of death in biopolitics to racism which reaches paroxysmic levels in the twentieth century during Nazism. In that setting, biopolitics appears deeply homologous to thanatopolitics. There, the living of a certain self-identified "race" of human beings becomes identical with the goal of excluding another "race" from life itself, as if the death internal to life could be avoided not by deferring it, but by displacing it, by creating a stark new caesura internal to species-being. The form of racism Foucault here invites us to consider is very different from the sort of racism that now has been reified into a "lens" for social scientific research.[50] The racism we experience in the biopolitical field can't be reduced either to the "biological essentialism" that some complacent critics of racism have come to identify with racism as such, or to the "neo-racism"—the emphasis on fixed and immutable "cultural differences"—that is the dialectical counterpart of this complacent critical dependency on the authority of the natural sciences. It is a paradoxical form of racism, a racism that sorts out and hierarchizes populations without also seeking support either in "theoretical racism" (such as social Darwinism, Malthusian economics, or eugenics) or "spontaneous racism" (the sort that focuses on phenotype, and derives from hatred, ignorance, or irrationality).[51] In the strict Foucauldian sense, in fact, biopolitical racism produces its thanatopolitical effects in populations without any explicit reference to "race" whatsoever. It's a racism that, instead of referring to "race," now refers, thanks precisely to the universalist tendencies of contemporary biology, only to ambiguous caesuræ internal to a single "species." It doesn't seek to exclude certain populations from the institutions of civil and political life; it explains why, despite so many painstaking attempts at inclusion, certain populations nevertheless seem permanently incapable of achieving flourishing lives within those institutions. Speaking now in the name not of a "master race," but on behalf of the entire human species, it helps us understand why enduring disproportions in unemployment, imprisonment, crime, and disease are not matters for political dispute or political resistance, but simply ongoing statistical anomalies and pathologies the available political and juridical remedies for which have been—tragically—exhausted.[52] The result is a racism that is proper to *laissez-faire* capitalist economy: a racism that explains, without open hostility, why the current unequal distribution of biopower— the distribution of the globalized world into "life zones" (where citizens are protected by a host of techniques of health, security, and safety) and "death zones" (where "wasted lives" are exposed to disease, accident, and war, and left to die)[53]—regrettably could not be otherwise.

Foucault, of course, was not content simply to let biopolitics drift to the thanatopolitical. As the recent publication of Foucault's later seminars suggests (not only the "political" lectures collected together under the titles *Security, Territory, Population* and *The Birth of Biopolitics*, but also his later "ethical" courses on the Greeks), the intensification of death across populations is only one among many iterations of the biopolitical. In these other texts, Foucault directs the reader toward governmentality as another possible response to the "power over life." Such an outlet for biopolitics in governmentality, toward the governing of self and others, is one that Foucault will find in "the production of the collective interest through the play of desire," leading him to speak of "the naturalness of population and the possible artificiality of the means one adopts to manage it." At the same time, however, it's far from clear exactly what sort of politics is implied in Foucault's writings from this period.[54] For a reader like Jacques Rancière, Foucault's problematization of "social security" during the late 1970s leaves Foucault's thought on biopolitics constitutively exposed to an appropriation of a Reaganite sort, where "government is not the solution to our problems, but the problem itself." Although, on Rancière's read, Foucault may not be the "technocrat" his earlier critics supposed him to be, the ambiguities of his late books on ethics and politics nevertheless permanently admit the possibility of finding in Foucault the exemplary claims of neoliberal thought.[55]

To be sure, Foucault's apparent abandonment of the project he outlined in *La volonté de savoir* did take place under conditions defined by the rise to power of neoliberal theories and practices in Deng Xiaopeng's China, Margaret Thatcher's England, and Ronald Reagan's America.[56] Not least, however, because Foucault during this same period focused his attention on the question of what it means for a philosopher to relate to the events of the living present, we would be off the mark were we to consent to this reading too quickly. During these eight incredibly pregnant years of lectures and inquiry—these lectures whose genius is inseparable precisely from their incompleteness, their open and exposed relation to their own present, their "courage" to "think out loud"[57]—Foucault revealed how, among other things, neoliberalism can accomplish the political aims it inherits from pastoral power—its attempts, that is to say, to provide for the "salvation" of both one and all—only on condition that it *first* produce a subject who conducts himself as an "entrepreneur of himself."[58] Neoliberalism governs by metaphorizing the market as a game, by metaphorizing the state as its umpire, and by metaphorizing individuals and populations as players for whom all choices are in principle possible—with the one exception of the choice not to play the game of the market at all.

Given the way that neoliberalism not only totalizes but also individualizes us, Foucault's famous "ethical turn" at the close of the 1970s—his shift from the analysis of modern apparatuses of "power-knowledge" to a set of close studies of ancient Greek practices for the "care of the self"—may not be the solipsistic retreat or apology for neoliberalism that some scholars today suppose it was. Not only do these critics of Foucault seem to forget that all of Foucault's ostensibly "modern" studies of "power-knowledge" during the 1970s amounted, in effect, on Foucault's own terms, to an extended interrogation of the genealogy of another ancient Greek figure (namely, *Oedipus Tyrannos*, who in 1973 Foucault situated as a "founding instance" of a relation between power and knowledge "from which our civilization is not yet emancipated"[59]); they also appear to leave in silence the sense in which Foucault's final lectures marked the beginnings of a manifestly philosophical act to cut against the definitive events of his present, to create a political and theoretical lexicon that would be up to the unprecedented task of bringing about the first "anti-pastoral revolution."[60] Under biopolitical conditions, in other words—these conditions in which subjects are "herded" or "shepherded" by the neopastoral practices of deregulation, privatization, incentivization, and marketization to survive only insofar as one and all manage to conduct their lives in a sufficiently entrepreneurial way—Foucault's "ethical turn" may be understood to yield nothing less than a paradigm of political resistance to the specific mode of pastoral power that confronted him in his own present.

On this read, we would be obliged to think again about the politics implied in the practice of philosophical truth-telling Foucault rediscovered, in the last years of his life, in the works of Euripides and Plato. This risky practice of courageous performative statements—the principled *carelessness* of the self the Greeks called *parrēsia*—consisted of speech unadorned by any rhetorical *technē*, political speech the utterance of which, Foucault noted, had the potential to place into question the very life of the speaker himself.[61] In these final lectures of his life, it would thus seem, the courage to tell the truth was already emerging within Foucault's thought as the name of a death-defying biopolitics—a counter-*dispositif* to the *thanatos* that is internal to and constitutive of neoliberalism, a mode of seriousness that could serve as a counterpoint to the compulsory play of the market. Truth-telling, that is to say, qualifies as one of many techniques that could link the care for the polity directly and essentially to the ethical task of living well.[62] Ethics, thought biopolitically, would not then be reducible to a matter of individual choice; it would make the political once again a qualifier of being. Especially if one rereads

Foucault's *La volonté de savoir* alongside his earlier work, and his *oeuvre* as such within the horizon of the Marxist critique of capitalism,[63] Foucault's thought on biopolitics doesn't then exemplify neoliberalism, so much as provide an interpretive key for its deciphering and dissolution.

3.

Without pretending this rereading of *La volonté de savoir* is in any way complete, let's nevertheless set down Foucault's book for a moment, in order to return to and clarify the premise of this exegesis. What we hope to have presented to the reader by tarrying with Foucault's text in this way is the unusual dynamic that seems to be at play in *La volonté de savoir*. In the very text that the biopolitical turn has converted into an *Urtext* for clarifying the relations between life and politics, the encounter between life and politics reveals itself not as *a relation* but as *a series of non-relations*. In *La volonté de savoir*, it seems to us, life and politics encounter one another mainly in and through a set of *generative aporias*—impasses that aren't merely "negative," but that in each case double as productive spaces, blind spots the very opacity of which doubles, paradoxically, as a source of insight. It's this strangely inviting unreadability that, in our view, helps explain the sheer repetition of the story Foucault tells, indeed the story's capacity, as it were, to get a "grip" or "hold" on Foucault's readers. In particular, we think it no accident that Foucault's text would incite so many readers to recite the story of biopolitics using the terms and tropes of theatre—in the form of what Foucault himself might have called a *theatrum philosophicum*.[64] Not least because the encounter between politics and life is, in genealogical terms, derived in part from the relation between the mask and the body,[65] it's understandable that Foucault's remarks on biopolitics should have been so consistently interpreted within the biopolitical turn with reference to the terms of familiar dramatic genres (such as tragedy, comedy, epic, and horror). For Aristotle, remember, poetics is the study of *plot*—it's the analysis of narrative twists and turns, of ironic reversals, of sudden recognitions and fateful mistakes and errors, and above all of events.[66] Impasses of the sort we have outlined in *La volonté de savoir* seem to us to provide the prior condition on which Foucault's text may be converted into a plot so defined: they seem to us to operate as so many hollow joints and empty sockets, so many open pivot points, the main function of which is, in turn, to allow readers to narrativize, using the familiar and recognizable terms of existing genres, an encounter that's otherwise unrecognizable, that indeed has no genre of its own. It's with this in mind that we have collected the following readings. Each elaborates some element of Foucault's story; none exhausts it.

The first reading comes from that political philosopher who Foucault always seems to have read, who sometimes even seems to have read Foucault, and whose writings on life and politics are "biopolitical" in all but name.[67] Foucault's 1976 reflections on biopolitics, remember, taper off in an incomplete meditation on the strange way that life and law interrelate in modern politics. In modernity, Foucault argues, human needs, human potential, and human possibility became juridified: they became the rallying cry for a new revolutionary politics grounded in "the rights of man and of the citizen." But, Foucault observes, this happened at the same time that biopower was beginning to consolidate its mastery of the body through new regimes of power/knowledge. At the center of the "rights of man," Foucault suggests, is thus a curious impasse. The modern concept of life refers less to a single, stable essence, than to a set of continuously shifting norms (pertaining to health and welfare, safety and security) that measured a set of intrinsically limitless demands (you can never have enough safety or health, after all).[68] Because these norms and demands eluded the juridical forms that proposed to protect life (and, classically, law operated through stable definitions of clear limits), the "rights of man" could not materialize in the absence of very specific administrative apparatuses—apparatuses whose structures needed to be just as variable and expansive as the life they proposed to govern was unpredictable and unbounded. The result was that human life entered into law at the very moment that biopower "grasped" life as a series of indefinite, enigmatic processes, and handed life over to apparatuses of governmentality whose operation then quickly began to exceed law from within. The "rights of man," in other words, were declared at the precise moment when law lost touch with life.

As we know, Foucault would proceed to study this aporia from the interior of politics, by inquiring into the way that power gained access to life through the problematization of sexuality. Thirty years earlier, by contrast, Arendt already had studied a similar aporia—only from the exterior of politics. Writing in the midst of the refugee crisis that emerged in the wake of the Second World War, Arendt inquired into the aporia of human rights from the standpoint of the masses of "stateless people" who had been excluded from all legal protections except those of human rights. Originally published in 1951, a year after the Universal Declaration of Human Rights, Arendt's reflections on "The Perplexities of the Rights of Man" circle around an insoluble impasse internal to that Declaration. The "stateless people" who at that time clearly were most in need of the protections of human rights were also those who were least likely to be protected by human rights. Because no right can be enforced outside of the horizon of an established political community, human rights were all but meaningless for populations who no longer belonged to any political community. And this, in turn, gave rise to the aporia that provoked Arendt's thought. At the very moment that the loss of their home qualified "stateless people" as "pure humans" (as humans in general, rather than as members of this or that particular political community, as "English" or "French"), their "human rights" no longer could be effectively invoked. The one subject to whom human rights in principle *ought to* apply—the abstract and naked human, the human being conceived in its most basic existential givenness—was therefore also the one subject to whom human rights *did not* and *could not* apply at all. The community of those who belonged to no other community except humanity as such, and who in principle should have been at the very center of all human rights, were therefore paradoxically excluded from any human rights. Like the declaration of the "rights of man" analyzed by Foucault, the human rights analyzed by Arendt were declared at the precise moment when law lost touch with life. In the thinking of both Foucault and Arendt (though in very different ways, and with much different corollaries[69]), *the inclusion of life within law* thus coincides with *the exclusion of life from law.*

In the selection from *The Human Condition* we reproduce here, meanwhile, Hannah Arendt inquires into another of the problematics of life and politics that Foucault would take up only much later. Her point of departure is a conceptual reversal that anticipates one of Foucault's own, but without also being reducible to it. For Arendt, the distinctive character of modern politics is exemplified by its productive mistranslation of Aristotle's formulation of the human: for the moderns, the human is not a "political animal" but rather a "social animal."[70] In Arendt's view, modern thought transposes to the political domains of action and work the concept of "necessity" that, for Aristotle, was the hallmark of the reproduction of life (through household labor and the labor of childbirth itself) and that, as such, was very antithesis of both action and work. The symptoms of this transposition of life onto politics, in Arendt's telling, include the disappearance of persuasion and freedom from politics, the displacement of immortality by mortality as the central form for political historiography, and the emergence of violent techniques of government dictated by the "necessity" of defending society against its own potentialities of mortality and natality. In some ways, Arendt's anxieties over modern politics seem to lead her to narrate the encounter of life and politics in the genre of a "horror story": "life," in Arendt's rendering, often seems like a "blob" that is about to attack politics.[71] In other ways, however, Arendt's criticisms of the modern reduction of politics to the safeguarding of life, her studies of the introduction of mortality into historiography, her inquiry into the concept of "sacred human life" as the residue of the secularization of salvation, and above all her thinking on the problems of birth and natality—all today seem to be so many oblique heralds of Foucault's later, comparable inquiries. Understood in this manner, Arendt's *Human Condition* provides a complementary response to the same general event—the same general problematization of life and politics—to which Foucault responded in *La volonté de savoir*: whereas Foucault's text considers the problematization of life by politics, *The Human Condition* takes up the problematization of politics by life. And in this sense, the birth of biopolitics takes place in a way and at a site that—in true genealogical fashion—cuts against the origin stories that govern the biopolitical turn.

Following Arendt is a series of texts from the greatest contemporary divulgator of Foucault's biopolitical narrative, and devoted reader of Arendt, Giorgio Agamben.[72] For Agamben, biopolitics is less a plotting of life and politics than a clue that points to the secret, inner link between modern democracy and its constitutive double: the totalitarian state. In Agamben's rendering, the story of biopolitics is actually a continuing story about sovereignty, of "bare life" produced by the state of exception. More tragic than epic, the biopolitical for Agamben is not at all synonymous, as it is not only for Foucault but also for Arendt, with the emergence of modernity in and through the *overturning* of Aristotle. Rather it is coterminous with the whole of Western metaphysics *beginning with* Aristotle. Reworking Foucault's reversals and chiasmic sleights of hand, Agamben offers the reader a single narrative of the adventures and misadventures of a single conceptual personæ: *homo sacer*, which Agamben, using precisely the language of classical poetics, calls "the protagonist" of his book.[73] This requires Agamben to appropriate Foucault's text in a way that cuts sharply against Foucault's answer to the question of precisely how, why, and when it was that life happened to become the object of politics. Here, as elsewhere, the attentive reader shall have to be vigilant about the risk that unexamined assumptions derived from some or another unstated philosophy of history might predetermine our thinking about biopolitics. Indeed, as Jacques Derrida, among others, has shown, any rigorous inquiry into biopolitics can, and should, throw into question the basic concepts of the philosophy of history itself—up to and including the concept of the event.[74]

What goes for time holds for space as well. If, as Carlo Galli argues, every "political thought" is both grounded in and riven by an implicit "political space" that remains inaccessible to it,[75] then exactly what "political space" is it that stirs within Foucault's remarks on biopolitics? Is it the European city, into which and out of which grain flows? The territory of the sovereign European state, as Foucault himself seems to suppose? The concentration camp, as Agamben proposes?[76] The "milieu" of Jean-Baptiste Lamarck and Jakob von Uexküll?[77] Or is Foucault's thinking on biopolitics most notable for the way it seems to abandon any thought of space whatsoever?[78] How, in any case, might explicit reflection on that political space change the way we think of "biopolitics" itself? Taking up the figure of sovereignty and bare life produced by the state of exception, but now in the political space of the postcolony, Achille Mbembe merges Foucault's right to take life and let live and Agamben's discussion of *homo sacer*. The result is a distressing account of a new and different dimension to contemporary biopower: its function as *necropower*. Extending and intensifying Foucault's arguably incomplete meditations on biopolitics and racism, Mbembe directs the reader's attention to the way in which necropower functions to destroy persons by creating the rigidly striated spaces he calls "death-worlds." This reading of biopolitics, which depends crucially on the thought of Georges Bataille, reveals an intolerable "expenditure of life" that becomes apparent when "death reveals the human subject's animal side." In that reference to the animal, Mbembe also gestures to a possible resolution of the massive negativity of necropower in trickery in ways that some readers may find deeply troubling. Mbembe's text is followed by Warren Montag's response in "Necro-economics: Adam Smith and Death in the Life of the Universal." Montag too takes up Agamben's figure of *homo sacer* as the subject of biopower to make an argument about the role of the negative in the market theology of Adam Smith. But where Mbembe focuses on savage and animal life in political spaces of siege and occupation, Montag moves the narrative of biopolitics up slightly to a moment in the thought of

Adam Smith, in order to rethink the concept now within the smooth space of the world market. His answer, despite its differences from Mbembe, is equally distressing. "The subsistence of a population may, and does in specific circumstances, require the death of a significant number of individuals; to be precise it requires that they be allowed to die so that others may live."[79] Regardless of what the reader concludes from her examination of the Mbembe–Montag dispute, she should not fail to note something else: the way biopolitics functions in this dispute as a spur for the rereading of the foundational texts of modern political thought, in order to draw out their specifically biopolitical valences and sculpt them into optics for understanding our present.[80] This, we would submit, is another iteration of the remarkable way that biopolitics is the name for a certain technique of retelling. Not only is it the case that energy implicit in Foucault's narrative spurs its own retelling; it is also the case that the energy from Foucault's narrative spurs the retelling of certain familiar stories, such as the history of political thought.

For its part, Michael Hardt and Antonio Negri's rereading of Foucault stands at the polar opposite of Agamben's. In the first of their texts we include here, a selection titled "Biopolitical Production" from their 2000 book *Empire*, Hardt and Negri interpret "the biopolitical nature of the new paradigm of power," as a form of power "that regulates social life from its interior." To do so they decisively shift the ultimate horizon for biopolitics and biopower to society and the social space in which life and politics encounter each other. As compelling as Foucault's account is for a contemporary ontology of ourselves, they argue that Foucault failed to consider that the true shared object of biopolitics and disciplinarity is precisely society. By appropriating Deleuze's notion of "societies of control" along with Foucault's linking of biopower with capitalist subsumption at the end of the *ancien régime* as well as Agamben's paradigm of biopolitics, Hardt and Negri believe they can account for the "intensification and generalization of the normalizing apparatuses of disciplinarity that internally animate our common and daily practices" in ways that Foucault, Deleuze, and Félix Guattari cannot.[81] The name they give to this new society of biopolitical control and right and paradigm of power is "Empire," which they term "a milieu of the event." Ten years later Hardt and Negri return to Foucault in a context of subjectivization and event by following out a distinction between biopolitics and biopower. In their account the intersection of life and politics is less a chiasmic encounter than an event that folds inside and outside. Biopolitics, as they read it, is a disruptive force that arrives from the outside rupturing the continuity of history. At the same time the event on the inside appears as innovation and creation. Emphasizing the concept of "event" allows Hardt and Negri to shift the angle of vision away from the separation of life and politics, and to accentuate existence as an affirmative horizon for biopolitics today—a horizon that becomes especially clear once we achieve full theoretical self-consciousness about the kernels and fragments of secularized theological traditions that never ceased to animate the basic concepts of modern political reason in the first place. From this view, biopolitics is not then the name for a tragic plot according to which liberalism is permanently fated to retain the potential to revert to totalitarianism; it is narrativizable, to the contrary, as the experience of a new form of communism, one that bears almost no relation to the old bureaucratic communism of the twentieth century, and that, existing as it does in a state of permanent incipience, is utopian or even messianic in character.

Alongside these selections, we have included two texts, "Labor, Action, Intellect" and "An Equivocal Concept: Biopolitics" from Paolo Virno. Here we see Virno grappling with the ambiguity of Foucault's story, especially the emphasis on modern man as animal by focusing on the linguistic experience of human beings. Elaborating a model of virtuosity as a response to biopower or what he prefers to call "labor-power," Virno winds up focusing on the multitude's "potential to produce, in which labor-power marks a future capacity for virtuosity, in language." The difference between Hardt and Negri's perspective on biopolitics and Virno's really concerns their poetics. For Hardt and Negri, the general ground for their reading of biopolitics is a world in which the laughter of the multitude is meant to dissolve biopower, which ends, as most comedies do, with victory, in this case of the multitude's fully extended subjectivization in the common. Virno's outlook too is primarily comic with his emphasis on the self-assuredness of the virtuoso who keeps the upper hand over labor power. Often though the impression is something slightly more tragic, given the ease with which the general intellect manifests itself as a "hierarchical system, as a pillar of the production of surplus value."[82]

The third section of readings opens with Donna Haraway's classic essay "The Biopolitics of Postmodern Bodies: Determinations of Self in Immune System Discourse." Haraway shows how deeply riven Foucault's narrative is by what she sees as traditional forms of European humanism. In her posthuman response, she finds solace in imagining a biopolitical body whose immune system allows for increasing levels of contamination and hybridization.

Of particular interest is her notion that the immune system is a kind of practice that informs "the dialectics of western biopolitics," one that operates as a Foucauldian apparatus able to produce bodies at the interstices of the normal and the pathological. This is no Agambenian production of the sacred or the profane given that any component in immune systems can be interfaced with any other. And yet despite the seemingly Dionysian overtones with which she writes of immunization, Haraway is less than sanguine about the ultimate possibilities for immunized, semi-permeable selves to overcome the "impossibilities of individuation and identification."

German philosopher Peter Sloterdijk takes up Haraway's immunized semi-permeable selves and extends them to the decadence of collective forms of life today. Associating the advent of biopower and biopolitics to what he calls the elaboration of modus vivendi under globalization, his reading of biopolitics is less a defense of communal forms of life and more a symptomology of the dissolution of self and place that has occurred under neo-liberalism. Sloterdijk offers what might be described as a biohistory of contemporary society in which ethnic definitions of nation-states function less and less as containers for collective life. In their place a wager ensues on the development of immunological designs capable of creating within these societies "permeable" or "thin" walls. Individuals are tasked with designing their own forms of immunity within these "societies." Sloterdijk's reading of biopower and globalization shares a number of points of contact with his earlier essay titled "Rules for the Human Zoo," especially in his superimposition of forms of immunity with forms of habitation and domestication. Here though Sloterdijk more forcefully commemorates the end of communal life, while casting his gaze across the present future landscape of thin walls, empty places, and selves absented from social and personal identity.

Roberto Esposito also takes up immunity as a way of coming to terms with contemporary biopolitics, but rather than turning to the cyborg, he introduces the figures of incorporation and flesh as "the way of being in common of that which seeks to be immune." The result is to show how the establishment of a biopolitical language across a number of different disciplines cannot be thought apart from that language's explicitly communitarian connotations. In the second selection, Esposito sketches a genealogy of immunity in classic liberalism. On Esposito's read immunization emerges as deeply constitutive of a liberal, political lexicon, which includes sovereignty, property, and liberty. Esposito doesn't upend Foucault's account of how life becomes the object of the political so much as complement it; immunization is seen as the means by which biopolitics both protects and in some cases negates a commonly held life. In the second of two texts from Esposito, the Italian philosopher details further how biopolitics may be situated within the horizon of immunization. Of special importance is the role of the body for both sovereign power and biopower. Building on Foucault's ambiguous reading of the norm sketched in "Right of Power and Life over Death," Esposito argues that immunity and biopower in modernity have become co-terminous to the degree that immunization of living bodies often turns into self-destruction (of the body, but also of the body politic). Yet that isn't the entire story. Another narrative can be found in immunity's opening to community and to community's untapped power to produce norms in living bodies in such a way that non-normative norms appear. Esposito's notion of the common is clearly less indebted to political theology than that of Agamben to the degree it emerges out of a conflict that takes place between individual bodies and life itself. Such a conflict becomes the site on Esposito's read out of which newly emerging forms of life held in common become visible. Immunization, biopower, and the preservation of the body's borders become in Esposito's reading the mere specular image of a common capable of composing immanent singularities that do not move to protect or negate life.

The final group of readings is dedicated to those who either contest fundamentally Foucault's enjambment of life and politics, or who are attempting to shift our understanding of biopolitics as a way of returning to prior models of political action. Drawing out a much different Aristotle than the one illuminated by Arendt, Foucault, Agamben, or Virno, Alain Badiou rethinks the death in life that biopower instrumentalizes, treating it not as the mirror double of life, but as a positive principle, immortality. Here as elsewhere, Badiou moves beyond Nietzsche not by ignoring him but by turning Nietzschean thought against itself, pushing it past its own immanent horizon.[83] If for Nietzsche the problem of politics is how to breed an animal with the right to make promises,[84] for Badiou the problem of politics is how to make a promise—how to maintain a "fidelity"—in a way that carries the animal beyond any and all possible regimes of breeding.[85] For Badiou, the relation of life and politics entails a much different wager than the one named by Foucault. In his text "What Is It to Live?," which we include here, Badiou grapples with the migration of the qualifier "living" that we noted from the passage in "Power over Life." But rather than choosing to focus on the living being, Badiou turns to the other reversal, namely "living worlds." Here though Badiou concentrates on the temporal conditions under which a subject may be said to live, not in terms of reaction to some prior trauma, but rather a wager on the present and the subject's possibility of incorporating the present into its own conditions of appearance: "Ultimately life is the wager, made on a body that has entered into appearing, that one will faithfully entrust this body with a new temporality, keeping at a distance the conservative drive (the ill-named 'life' instinct) as well as the mortifying drive (the death instinct)."[86] For Badiou, the relation of life and politics will be written in the present on the body as fragments of infinite truths.

Readers who are surprised to find Badiou's text included in this anthology no doubt also will be surprised to find our next reading, a little piece by Gilles Deleuze called "Immanence: A Life. . . ." Both texts are, to be sure, improbable selections: whereas Badiou's essay polemicizes against everything that seems to be even remotely associated with "biopolitics," Deleuze's essay seems not to address the question at all, devoting itself instead to an elaboration of what it means to live a life worthy of its events.[87] And yet despite the very different ways in which each text appears to swerve away from the biopolitical, both texts, especially when taken together, in fact cut to the very quick of the problem of biopolitics. To begin, both texts seek to emphasize the prior conditions on which it is possible to think "life" at all, anterior to its grasp by the non-teleological natural sciences, its politicization by *dispositifs* ancient and modern, or even its ontological capture in and by *technē*. Both texts then assert that "life" can only really emerge as a problem for thought within a horizon where the epistemological dyad of the subject and the object of knowledge—or, in Foucauldian language, the "transcendental-empirical couplet"—has dissolved, leaving in its place an experience that is precisely "impersonal." Both texts show, furthermore, how "life" as we usually experience and think it is non-identical with itself, so that it is almost impossible to think "life itself" without recourse to terms other than "life" (such as, for example, "*technē*" or "politics"). And both, finally, bring to the absolute center of philosophic inquiry a problem—the event—that otherwise stirs only latently in all writing on biopolitics. For all of these reasons, the mere absence of the word "biopolitics" from these texts should not distract us from perceiving the much more fundamental sense in which each text *radicalizes* the problematization of life and politics that silently animated Foucault's *La volonté de savoir*. Indeed, if these texts do not appear, at least on first glance, to be concerned with "biopolitics," this is simply because each takes the thought of biopolitics to such an extreme that each ends up exceeding "biopolitics" from within, passing beyond it on its own terms. To be sure, both Badiou and Deleuze do this in directions that are fundamentally opposed to one another—with Deleuze trying to think life on its own terms, in its absolute immanence, without any recourse to any exteriority whatsoever, and Badiou attempting to think life from the standpoint of a pure exteriority, an infinity and immortality so absolute that its essence can be grasped only with reference to mathematics. But for this very reason, these are two texts that are essential for any and all problematizations of life and politics. Precisely in the extremity of their opposition, the selections by Deleuze and Badiou bring into full view just how difficult, and yet also how indispensable, it has become, after Foucault, to answer a classical philosophic question: What does it mean to live? Read side by side, as a single disjunctive synthesis, these texts demarcate the outermost antipodes that together define the interior of the biopolitical field.

In Slavoj Žižek's reading, meanwhile, much as in the reading we have already summarized by Rancière, the biopolitical stands in for a particularly resistant form of postpolitics, which appears as nothing other than a new form of master (and mastery) in which any "higher causes" of the political are made subservient to only one: life as transcendence. Žižek's essay is both a devastating critique of capitalist ethics, which tries to hide its rapacity and homicidal work under cover of a discourse of human rights, as well as a broadside against Foucault and, more specifically, Agamben's biopolitical paradigm. Of particular interest in the story of the life's encounter with the political is Žižek's insistence that the subject produced by apparatuses of knowledge-power also produces a remainder that evades and resists the very apparatuses that produce the subject. The power of biopolitics can be found according to Žižek in its ability to produce a subject that holds within the "agent of its own containment," and hence is able to block an opening to the political as a negative. Such an operation of containment for Žižek must be resisted. Sharing points of contact with Hardt and Negri's perspective on production along with Badiou's on immortality, Žižek's essay reminds us of the effects of the biopolitical on the autonomy of the political.

Even, especially, in this third group of readings, however, the relation of life and politics remains a problem for thought: not despite but because of the way these texts seek to expose the limits of the Foucaultian problematization of "biopolitics," they are worthy of the reader's close and careful attention. If, as Hegel argues, the essence of a thing can only be understood with reference to its limit, then no account of "biopolitics" will be complete until it encounters these texts.[88] These texts too, after all, as Badiou's reference to Aristotle shows, derive from the same problematic that concerned Foucault. Speaking of the good, Aristotle writes:

> Will not the knowledge of it [the good] then have a great influence on life [*bion*]? Shall we not, like archers who have a mark to aim at, be more likely to hit upon what is right? If so, we must try, in outline at least, to determine what it is, and of which of the sciences or capacities it is object. It would seem to belong to the most authoritative art and that which is most truly the master art. And politics appears to be of this nature; for it is that ordains which of the sciences should be studied in a polity.[89]

From start to finish, the texts gathered together here allow for study of just this sort—but with an essential twist. The point of re-reading biopolitics today is not, of course, to master or resolve the opacities of these texts. It's to adjust your eyesight to the darkness of the opacities themselves, so as to take aim yourself at the mark whose absence is the common feature of each and all of them. Life, politics—to dwell on this encounter today is to discern that strangest of marks, this mark that is intimately yours without also being yours alone, this question mark that governs the one who lives, but who has not yet learned how to live.

Notes

The authors wish to thank Kevin Attell, Courtney Berger, Bruno Bosteels, Charles Bourjaily, Dean Greg Call, Dean Walter Cohen, Jonathan Culler, Lorenzo Fabbri, David Rojas, Nica Siegel and Meghna Sridhar for their support and contributions to this project.

1. On modern man as a "prosthetic God," see Sigmund Freud, "Civilization and Its Discontents," *The Standard Edition of the Complete Works of Sigmund Freud*, vol. 21, ed. J. Strachey et al. (London: Hogart Press, 1953–74), 91–92. On the "negation of death," see Nishitani Osamu, "The Wonderland of 'Immortality,'" in *Contemporary Japanese Thought*, ed. Richard Calichman (New York: Columbia University Press, 2005), 131–156. On the "singularity," see Ray Kurzweil, *The Singularity Is Near: When Humans Transcend Biology* (New York: The Viking Press, 2005).

2. Michel Foucault, *The History of Sexuality*, vol. 1: *An Introduction*, trans. Robert Hurley (New York: Vintage Books, 1978); Michel Foucault, *Histoire de la sexualité*, tome 1: *La volonté de savoir* (Paris: Éditions Gallimard, 1976). We draw a distinction between

Foucault's first analysis of biopolitics and his first utterance of the word "biopolitics." The latter took place in his October 1974 lecture on "the birth of social medicine." See, on this point, Marc Schuilenburg and Sjoerd van Tuinen, "Michel Foucault: Biopolitiek en Bestuurlijkhied," *Krisis: Tijdschrift voor actuele filosofie* 3:1 (2009), 3.

3. See, for example, Leo Bersani, review of *The Subject of Power*, *diacritics* 7:3 (Autumn 1977), esp. 3–6; Edith Kurzweil, review of *The History of Sexuality, Volume 1: An Introduction*, *Theory and Society* 8:3 (November 1979), 422–425; Marcus Rediker, review of *The History of Sexuality, Volume 1: An Introduction*, *The William and Mary Quarterly* 36:4 (October 1979), 637–640.

4. In his 1993 summary of *La Volonté de savoir*, for example, Foucault's biographer David Macey remains almost completely silent on "biopolitics," focusing instead on the "repressive hypothesis" and on the concept of the *dispositif*, which he calls "the text's major theoretical innovation." See David Macey, *The Lives of Michel Foucault: A Biography* (New York: Vintage Books, 1995), 354–358.

5. Donna Haraway, "The Biopolitics of Postmodern Bodies: Determinations of Self in Immune System Discourse," *differences: A Journal of Feminist Cultural Studies* 1:1 (1989), 3–43; Donna Haraway, "The Bio-politics of a Multicultural Field," *Primate Visions: Gender, Race, and Nature in the World of Modern Science* (New York: Routledge, 1989), 244–275.

6. Étienne Balibar, "Foucault and Marx: The Question of Nominalism," in *Michel Foucault, Philosopher*, trans. Timothy J. Armstrong (New York: Routledge, 1992), 38–56; Paul Gilroy, "'After the Love Has Gone': Bio-Politics and Etho-Poetics in the Black Public Sphere," *Public Culture* 7 (1994), 49–76; Anne Laura Stoler, *Race and the Education of Desire: Foucault's History of Sexuality and the Colonial Order of Things* (Durham, NC: Duke University Press, 1995); and *Biopolitics: The Politics of the Body, Race and Nature*, ed. Agnes Heller, Sonja Puntscher Riekmann, and Ferenc Fehér (Aldershot: Avebury, 1996).

7. Giorgio Agamben, *Homo Sacer: Sovereign Power and Bare Life*, trans. Daniel Heller-Roazen (Stanford, CA: Stanford University Press, 1998).

8. Michael Hardt and Antonio Negri, *Empire* (Cambridge, MA: Harvard University Press, 2000).

9. Agamben, *Homo Sacer*, 9–10.

10. Balibar, "Foucault and Marx," 55. Nowhere is this symptom more acute than in the response to the biopolitical turn found in Paul Rabinow and Nikolas Rose, "Biopower Today," *BioSocieties* 1:2 (2006), 195–217.

11. See, for example, *La biopolitica: Il potere sulla vita e la costituzione di soggettività*, ed. Pierandrea Amato (Milan: Associazione Culturale Mimesis, 2004); *Biopolitica: storia e attualità di un concetto*, ed. Antonella Cutro (Verona: Ombre Corte, 2005); Laura Bazzicalupo, "Biopolitica," in *Enciclopedia del pensiero politico: autori, concetti, dottrine*, ed. Roberto Esposito and Carlo Galli (Roma-Bari: Gius, Laterza, and Figli, 2005), 79–81; Gabriel Giorgi and Fermín Rodríguez, *Ensayos sobre biopolítica: excesos de vida* (Buenos Aires: Paidós, 2007); Thomas Lemke, *Gouvernementalität und Biopolitik* (Wiesbaden: VS Verlag für Sozialwissenschaften, 2007); Francesco D'Agostino, *Introduzione alla biopolitica: Dodici voci fondamentali* (Rome: Aracne Editrice, 2009); Schuilenburg and van

Tuinen, "Michel Foucault: Biopolitiek en Bestuurlijkheid," 1–5; Laura Bazzicalupo, *Biopolitica: Una Mappa Concettuale* (Rome: Carocci Editore, 2010); Thomas Lemke, *Biopolitics: An Advanced Introduction*, trans. Eric Trump (New York: New York University Press, 2011).

12. Jacques Rancière, "The Difficult Legacy of Michel Foucault," *Chronicles of Consensual Times*, trans. Steven Corcoran (New York: Continuum Press, 2010), 127. With this criticism of Foucault, we note, Rancière is not far from the polemic directed against Foucault by Jean Baudrillard in his March 1977 response to *La Volonté de savoir*. There Baudrillard speaks of the "seduction" of Foucault's writing, which in Baudrillard's view "mirrors" the very powers it purports to describe. See Jean Baudrillard, *Forget Foucault*, trans. Phil Beitchman et al. (Cambridge, MA: Semiotext[e], 2007), 29–30.

13. Warren Montag, "Toward a Conception of Racism without Race: Foucault and Contemporary Biopolitics," *Pli* 13 (2002), 124.

14. Gilles Deleuze, *Foucault* (Paris: Les Éditions de Minuit, 1986), 11.

15. Ibid., 96.

16. Michel Foucault, "Polemics, Politics and Problematizations: An Interview with Michel Foucault," *Ethics: Subjectivity and Truth; Essential Works of Michel Foucault 1954–1984*, vol. 1, ed. Paul Rabinow, trans. Robert Hurley et al. (New York: The New Press, 1998), 117.

17. Foucault, *The History of Sexuality*, vol. 1, 142.

18. Ibid., 142, translation modified.

19. Michel Foucault, *Security, Territory, Population: Lectures at the Collège de France, 1977–1978*, trans. Graham Burchell (New York: Palgrave, 2007), 20–30, 60–1, 77–78; Foucault, "La vie: l'expérience et la science," *Dits et écrits, 1954–1988, Tome IV: 1980–1988*, eds. Daniel Defert and François Ewald (Paris: Gallimard, 1994), 774. Compare Gilles Deleuze, "L'immanence: une vie . . . ," *Deux régimes de fous: textes et entretiens, 1975–1995*, ed. David Lapoujade (Paris: Les Éditions de Minuit, 2003), 363.

20. Foucault, *The History of Sexuality*, vol. 1, 143.

21. Gil Anidjar, "The Meaning of Life," *Critical Inquiry* 37:4 (Summer 2011), 701, 710.

22. Hannah Arendt, *The Human Condition* (Chicago: The University of Chicago Press, 1958), 313–20; Eric Santner, *The Royal Remains: The People's Two Bodies and the Endgames of Sovereignty* (Chicago: University of Chicago Press, 2011).

23. On the organism as machine, see Martin Heidegger, *The Fundamental Concepts of Metaphysics: World, Finitude, Solitude*, trans. William McNeill and Nicholas Walker (Bloomington: Indiana University Press, 1995), 212–236; Roberto Esposito, *Immunitas. La protezione e negazione della vita* (Torino: Einaudi, 2002), 136 (translated into English by Zakiya Hanafi as *Immunitas: The Protection and Negation of Life* [London: Polity Press, 2011]).

24. See, in general, Donna Haraway, "A Cyborg Manifesto," in *Simians, Cyborgs, and Women: The Reinvention of Nature* (New York: Routledge, 1991), 149–182; and, more generally, *The Cyborg Handbook*, ed. Chris Hables Gray (New York: Routledge, 1995).

25. Esposito, *Immunitas*, 170–172.

26. In such a view biohistory "would no longer be the unitary and mythological history of the human species through time" since population emerges as a collection of

genetic variations (Michel Foucault, "Bio-histoire et bio-politique," in *Dits et écrits, 1954-1988, Tome III: 1976-1979*, ed. Daniel Defert and François Ewald [Paris: Gallimard, 1994], 97).

27. Part Four of *La volonté de savoir*, which is rendered in English as "The Deployment of Sexuality," is in French, titled "Le dispositif de sexualité."

28. On the notion of dispositif, see Gilles Deleuze, "What is a *Dispositif?*," in *Michel Foucault: Philosopher*, trans. Timothy J. Armstrong (New York: Routledge, 1992), 159–169; Giorgio Agamben, *What Is an Apparatus? and Other Essays*, trans. David Kishik and Stefan Pedatella (Stanford: Stanford University Press, 2009), 1–24; Roberto Esposito, "The *Dispositif* of the Person," trans. Timothy Campbell, *Law, Culture and the Humanities* 8:1 (February 2012), 17–30.

29. Michel Foucault, "Confessions of the Flesh," in *Power/Knowledge: Selected Interviews and Other Writings, 1972–1977*, ed. Colin Gordon (New York: Pantheon Books, 1980), 194–196.

30. Foucault, *The History of Sexuality*, vol. 1, 144.

31. Ibid., 143. The English translation of *La volonté de savoir* elides the term "biological" as a descriptor of threshold.

32. "*Enjeu*," it is worth noting, is the French title of the chapter in *La volonté de savoir* that in *The History of Sexuality* is translated simply as "Objective."

33. See, on this point, the conclusion to Foucault's first lecture on the abnormal: "I would like to try to study this appearance, this emergence of techniques of normalization and the powers linked to them by taking as a principle . . . that these techniques of normalization . . . are not simply the effect of the combination of medical knowledge and judicial power, of their composition or their plugging of each into the other, but a certain type of power—distinct from both medical and judicial power . . . It is a type of power that finally ends up in the courtroom" (Michel Foucault, *Abnormal: Lectures at the Collège de France 1974–1975*, trans. Graham Burchell [New York: Picador, 2003], 25–26).

34. Put differently, biopolitics does not exist as a simple "object" of knowledge or action. Its mode of existence is rather that of a subject relating its life to itself as the central objective of any possible life in common. See, on this point, Emilio Raimondi, "Sei frammenti aporetici sulla biopolitica (con qualche resto)," in *La biopolitica*, ed. Amato, 184.

35. Foucault, *The History of Sexuality*, vol. 1, 142–143. The translation of "*la prise*" as "mastery" and "taking charge of" is off the mark. The distinction between sovereignty's "transcendent" relation to life "from above," and biopower's "hold" on life "from within" life itself, is lost in translation. An additional problem is presented by the term "mastery," which is close to "sovereignty," and so seems to continue in precisely the domain, biopolitics, that Foucault seems to take as its limit.

36. Esposito's perspective on the limits of Foucauldian biopolitics is useful to keep in mind here. "Precisely because he is able to describe the genealogical mechanisms of modern society so thoroughly and extensively, he runs the risk of remaining hermeneutically imprisoned in its dynamics, and thus losing, or at least failing to fully grasp, the limit point at which modernity comes face to face with its outside: the moment, that is, when

the differential margins that for centuries separated and juxtaposed the domains of the real and the imaginary, the natural and the artificial, the organic and the inorganic, finally explode or implode" (Esposito, *Immunitas*, 175).

37. Alain Badiou, *Logics of Worlds: Being and Event 2*, trans. Alberto Toscano (London: Continuum, 2010), 35.

38. Foucault, *Security, Territory, Population*, 234–238.

39. Michel Foucault, *The Order of Things: An Archaeology of the Human Sciences* (New York: Vintage Books, 1973), 273.

40. Ibid., 273.

41. Foucault, *The History of Sexuality*, vol. 1, 143.

42. Foucault, *The Order of Things*, 277.

43. Compare, on this point, Deleuze's reading of Bergsonism: "Life as *movement* alienates itself in the material form that it creates: by actualizing itself, by differentiating itself, it loses 'contact with the rest of itself.' Every species is thus an arrest of movement" (Gilles Deleuze, *Bergsonism*, trans. Hugh Tomlinson and Barbara Habberjam [New York: Zone Books, 1991], 104).

44. See, on this score, Heidegger's distinction between the essence of animality and the essence of humanity which consists in "the living character of a living being, as distinct from the non-living being," namely the possibility of dying (Heidegger, *Fundamental Concepts of Metaphysics*, 179). Jacques Derrida's gloss of Heidegger's reading is significant: "the animal doesn't die," but "stops living" (Jacques Derrida, *The Animal that Therefore I Am*, trans. David Wills [New York: Fordham University Press, 2008], 154).

45. Foucault, *The Order of Things*, 273.

46. Foucault, *The History of Sexuality*, vol. 1, 137.

47. Ibid., 137.

48. See, on this point, Jacques Derrida, " 'To Do Justice to Freud': The History of Madness in the Age of Psychoanalysis," trans. Pascale-Anne Brault and Michael Naas, *Critical Inquiry* 20:2 (Winter, 1994), 227–266.

49. "Just as the disciplinary type of power existed in medieval societies, in which schemas of sovereignty were nevertheless present, so too, I think, forms of the power of sovereignty can still be found in contemporary society. Where do we find them? Well, I would find them in the only institution . . . that I have not yet spoken about . . . I mean the family. I was going to say that the family is a remnant, but this is not entirely the case. At any rate, it seems to me that the family is a sort of cell within which the power exercised is not, as one usually says, disciplinary, but rather of the same type as the power of sovereignty" (Michel Foucault, *Psychiatric Power: Lectures at the Collège de France*, trans. Graham Burchell [New York: Palgrave, 2006], 79).

50. Étienne Balibar, "Racism Revisited: Sources, Relevance, and Aporias of a Modern Concept," *PMLA* 123:5 (October 2008), 1630.

51. Étienne Balibar, "Racism and Nationalism," in *Race, Nation, Class: Ambiguous Identities* (New York: Verso Books, 1991), 38.

52. Montag, "Racism without Race," 122–124.

53. Étienne Balibar, "Outlines of a Topography of Cruelty: Citizenship and Civility in the Era of Global Violence" in *We, the People of Europe?: Reflections on Transnational Citizenship*, trans. James Swenson (Princeton: Princeton University Press, 2004), 126.

54. See, on this point, Alain Badiou, "Foucault: Continuity and Discontinuity," in *Adventures in French Philosophy*, ed. and trans. Bruno Bosteels (New York: Verso Books, 2012), 99 (arguing that "it is impossible to find in Foucault an affirmative doctrine of politics").

55. See also, on this point, Julian Bourg, *From Revolution to Ethics: May 1968 and Contemporary French Thought* (Montreal: McGill-Queen's University Press, 2007).

56. David Harvey, *A Brief History of Neoliberalism* (Oxford: Oxford University Press, 2005).

57. Montag, "Racism without Race," 124.

58. Michel Foucault, *The Birth of Biopolitics: Lectures at the Collège de France, 1978–1979*, trans. Graham Burchell (New York: Palgrave, 2008), 226.

59. Michel Foucault, "Truth and Juridical Forms," *Power: Essential Works of Michel Foucault 1954–1984*, vol. 3, ed. James D. Faubion. trans. Robert Hurley et al. (New York: The New Press, 2000), 17.

60. As Foucault argued in 1978, "[t]here have been anti-feudal revolutions; there has never been an anti-pastoral revolution. The pastorate has not yet experienced the process of profound revolution that would have definitively expelled it from history" (Foucault, *Security, Territory, Population*, 150).

61. Michel Foucault, *The Government of Self and Others: Lectures at the Collège de France, 1982–1983*, trans. Graham Burchell (New York: Palgrave, 2010), 62, 315, 318.

62. Michel Foucault, "On the Genealogy of Ethics: An Overview of Work in Progress," in *Ethics: Subjectivity and Truth*, 260. Compare Badiou, "Foucault: Continuity and Discontinuity," 89 (arguing that Foucault's genealogical studies of the 1970s were leading him in the direction of "philosophy as wisdom, as leading 'the good life'").

63. See, for example, Melinda Cooper, *Life as Surplus: Biotechnology and Capitalism in the Neoliberal Era* (Seattle: University of Washington Press, 2008), 5–9.

64. Michel Foucault, "Theatrum philosophicum," *Language, Counter-Memory, Practice: Selected Essays and Interviews*, ed. Donald Bouchard (Ithaca: Cornell University Press, 1977), 196.

65. See, for example, Giorgio Agamben, "Comedy," in *The End of the Poem: Studies in Poetics*, trans. Daniel Heller-Roazen (Stanford: Stanford University Press, 1999), 1–22; Roberto Esposito, *Third Person: Politics of Life and Philosophy of the Impersonal*, trans. Zakiya Hanafi (Cambridge, UK: Polity Press, 2012); and Giorgio Agamben, "Identity Without the Person," in *Nudities*, trans. David Kishik and Stefan Pedatella (Stanford: Stanford University Press, 2011), 46–54.

66. Aristotle, "Poetics," trans. I. Bywater, in *The Complete Works of Aristotle,* vol. 2, ed. Jonathan Barnes (Princeton: Princeton University Press, 1984), 2321–2332, esp. 2322–2323 (Book 9).

67. The sense in which Hannah Arendt is a thinker of "biopolitics" is clarified by Miguel Vatter, "Natality and Biopolitics in Hannah Arendt," *Revista de Ciencia Política* 26:2 (2006), 137–159; Kathrin Braun, "Biopolitics and Temporality in Arendt and Foucault,"

Time and Society 16:1 (2007), 5–23; and Claire Blencowe, "Foucault's and Arendt's 'Insider View' of Biopolitics: A Critique of Agamben," *History of the Human Sciences* 23 (2010), 113–130. Foucault's own mentions of Arendt are notably scant. See, for example, Michel Foucault, "Politics and Ethics: An Interview," in *The Foucault Reader*, ed. Paul Rabinow (New York: Pantheon Books, 1984), 378–379.

68. Foucault, "The Politics of Health in the Eighteenth Century," in *Power*, 98–99.

69. Given the limited aims of this introduction, we set aside the intricate problem of Arendt's aporetic declaration that "there is only one human right" (*Es gibt nur ein einziges Menschenrecht*): the "right to have rights." For more on this formulation, the reader may consult the detailed secondary literature focused on it, including but not limited to Étienne Balibar, "(De)Constructing the Human as Human Institution: A Reflection on the Coherence of Hannah Arendt's Practical Philosophy," *Social Research* 74:3 (Fall 2007), 727–738; Christoph Menke, "The 'Aporias of Human Rights' and the 'One Human Right': Regarding the Coherence of Hannah Arendt's Argument," Trans. Birgit Kaiser and Kathrin Thiele, *Social Research* 74:3 (Fall 2007), 739–762; Judith Butler and Gayatri Spivak, *Who Sings the Nation-State? Language, Politics, Belonging* (London: Seagull Press, 2007); and Ayten Gündoğdu, "'Perplexities of the Rights of Man': Arendt on the Aporias of Human Rights," *European Journal of Political Theory* 11:1 (January 2012), 4–24.

70. Arendt, *The Human Condition*, 23; but cf. Vatter, "Natality and Biopolitics," 147.

71. See, on this point, Hanna Pitkin, *The Attack of the Blob: Hannah Arendt's Concept of the Social* (Chicago: University of Chicago Press, 2000). The genre of the horror story is not uncommon among thinkers who write on life. See, on this point, Eugene Thacker, *After Life* (Chicago: University of Chicago Press, 2010), 1–24.

72. For Agamben's expression of gratitude to Arendt, see "Letter from Giorgio Agamben to Hannah Arendt, 21 Feb. 1970," *diacritics* 39:4 (Winter 2009), 111.

73. Agamben, *Homo Sacer*, 6.

74. Jacques Derrida, *The Beast and the Sovereign*, vol. 1, trans. Geoffrey Bennington (Chicago: University of Chicago Press, 2009), 333.

75. Carlo Galli, *Political Spaces and Global War*, trans. Elisabeth Fay, ed. Adam Sitze (Minneapolis: University of Minnesota Press, 2010), 4–8.

76. Agamben, *Homo Sacer*, 166–180.

77. For Jean-Baptiste Lamarck's use of the term "milieu," see his *Zoological Philosophy: An Exposition with Regard to the Natural History of Animals*, trans. Hugh Eliot (London: Macmillian, 1914); cf. Jakob von Uexküll, *A Foray into the Worlds of Animals and Humans with a Theory of Meaning*, trans. Joseph D. O'Neil (Minneapolis: University of Minnesota Press, 2010). A helpful summary of milieu's meanings can be found in Margo Huxley's "Spatial Rationalities: Order, Environment, Evolution and Government," *Social & Cultural Geography* 7:5 (October 2006), 771–787.

78. See, on this point, Stuart Elden, "Governmentality, Calculation, Territory," *Environment and Planning D: Society and Space* 25:3 (2007), 562–580; Raimondi, "Sei frammenti aporetici sulla biopolitica," 186–190.

79. Warren Montag, "Necro-economics: Adam Smith and Death in the Life of the Universal," in *Radical Philosophy* 134 (November–December 2005), 14.

80. See also, for example, Melinda Cooper's rereading of Aristotle in "The Living and the Dead: Variations on *de Anima*," *Angelaki* 7:3 (2002), 81–104; Nishitani Osamu's rereading of Hegel, Heidegger, and Levinas in "The Wonderland of 'Immortality'"; Eugene Thacker's rereading of Aristotle and Kant in *After Life*; and Miguel Vatter's rereading of Nietzsche in "Eternal life and Biopower," *CR: The New Centennial Review* 10:3 (2010), 217–249.

81. Gilles Deleuze, "Postscript on the Societies of Control," *October* 59 (Winter 1992), 3–7.

82. Paolo Virno, *The Grammar of the Multitude: For an Analysis of Contemporary Forms of Life*, trans. Isabella Bertoletti, James Cascaito, and Andrea Casson (New York: Semiotext(e), 2002), 66.

83. See, for example, Alain Badiou, *Manifesto for Philosophy*, trans. and ed. Norman Madarasz (Albany: SUNY Press, 1999), 99–101, 121.

84. Friedrich Nietzsche, *On the Genealogy of Morals*, trans. Walter Kaufmann and R. J. Hollingdale (New York: Vintage Books, 1989), 57–60.

85. See especially Alain Badiou, *Ethics: An Essay on the Understanding of Evil*, trans. Peter Hallward (New York: Verso Books, 2001), 4–7, 40–57.

86. Badiou, *Logics of Worlds*, 589.

87. For the contrary reading, see Giorgio Agamben, "Pure Immanence," in *Potentialities: Collected Essay in Philosophy*, ed. and trans. Daniel Heller-Roazen (Stanford: Stanford University Press, 1999), 220–239; Esposito, *Third Person*, 142–151.

88. G. W. F. Hegel, *Science of Logic*, trans. A. V. Miller (New York: Humanity Books, 1999), 126.

89. Aristotle, "Nicomachean Ethics," trans. W. D. Ross, in *The Complete Works of Aristotle*, vol. 2, p. 1729 (1094a 19), translation modified.

CHAPTER 1

RIGHT OF DEATH AND

POWER OVER LIFE

Michel Foucault

For a long time; one of the characteristic privileges of sovereign power was the right to decide life and death. In a formal sense, it derived no doubt from the ancient *patria potestas* that granted the father of the Roman family the right to "dispose" of the life of his children and his slaves; just as he had given them life, so he could take it away. By the time the right of life and death was framed by the classical theoreticians, it was in a considerably diminished form. It was no longer considered that this power of the sovereign over his subjects could be exercised in an absolute and unconditional way, but only in cases where the sovereign's very existence was in jeopardy: a sort of right of rejoinder. If he were threatened by external enemies who sought to overthrow him or contest his rights, he could then legitimately wage war, and require his subjects to take part in the defense of the state; without "directly proposing their death," he was empowered to "expose their life": in this sense, he wielded an "indirect" power over them of life and death.[1] But if someone dared to rise up against him and transgress his laws, then he could exercise a direct power over the offender's life: as punishment, the latter would be put to death. Viewed in this way, the power of life and death was not an absolute privilege: it was conditioned by the defense of the sovereign, and his own survival. Must we follow Hobbes in seeing it as the transfer to the prince of the natural right possessed by every individual to defend his life even if this meant the death of others? Or should it be regarded as a specific right that was manifested with the formation of that new juridical being, the sovereign?[2] In any case, in its modern form—relative and limited—as in its ancient and absolute form, the right of life and death is a dissymmetrical one. The sovereign exercised his right of life only by exercising his right to kill, or by refraining from killing; he evidenced his power over life only through the death he was capable of requiring. The right which was formulated as the "power of life and death" was in reality the right to *take* life or *let* live. Its symbol, after all, was the sword. Perhaps this juridical form must be referred to a historical type of society in which power was exercised mainly as a means of deduction *(prélèvement)*, a subtraction mechanism, a right to appropriate a portion of the wealth, a tax of products, goods and services, labor and blood, levied on the subjects. Power in this instance was essentially a right of seizure: of things, time, bodies, and ultimately life itself; it culminated in the privilege to seize hold of life in order to suppress it.

Since the classical age the West has undergone a very profound transformation of these mechanisms of power. "Deduction" has tended to be no longer the major form of power but merely one element among others, working to incite, reinforce, control, monitor, optimize, and organize the forces under it: a power bent on generating forces, making them grow, and ordering them, rather than one dedicated to impeding them, making them submit, or destroying them. There has been a parallel shift in the right of death, or at least a tendency to align itself with the exigencies of a life-administering power and to define itself accordingly. This death that was based on the right of the sovereign is now manifested as simply the reverse of the right of the social body to ensure, maintain, or develop its life. Yet wars were never as bloody as they have been since the nineteenth century, and all things being equal, never before did regimes visit such holocausts on their own populations. But this formidable power of death—and this is perhaps what accounts for part of its force and the cynicism with which it has so greatly expanded its limits—now presents itself as the counterpart of a power that exerts a positive influence on life, that endeavors to administer, optimize, and multiply it, subjecting it to precise controls and comprehensive regulations. Wars are no longer waged in the name of a sovereign who must be defended; they are waged on behalf of the existence of everyone; entire populations are mobilized for the purpose of wholesale slaughter in the name of life necessity: massacres have become vital. It is as managers of life and survival, of bodies and the race, that so many regimes have been able to wage so many wars, causing so many men to be killed. And through a turn that closes the circle, as the technology of wars has caused them to tend increasingly toward all-out destruction, the decision that initiates them and the one that terminates them are in fact increasingly informed by the naked question of survival. The atomic situation is now at the end point of this process: the power to expose a whole population to death is the underside of the power to guarantee an individual's continued existence. The principle underlying the tactics of battle—that one has to be capable of killing in order to go on living—has become the principle that defines the strategy of states. But the existence in question is no longer the juridical existence of sovereignty; at stake is the biological existence of a population. If genocide is indeed the dream of modern powers, this is not because of a recent return of the ancient right to kill; it is because power is situated and exercised at the level of life, the species, the race, and the large-scale phenomena of population.

On another level, I might have taken up the example of the death penalty. Together with war, it was for a long time the other form of the right of the sword; it constituted the reply of the sovereign to those who attacked his will, his law, or his person. Those who died on the scaffold became fewer and fewer, in contrast to those who died in wars. But it was for the same reasons that the latter became more numerous and the former more and more rare. As soon as power gave itself the function of administering life, its reason for being and the logic of its exercise—and not the awakening of humanitarian feelings—made it more and more difficult to apply the death penalty. How could power exercise its highest prerogative by putting people to death, when its main role was to ensure, sustain, and multiply life, to put this life in order? For such a power, execution was at the same time a limit, a scandal, and a contradiction. Hence capital punishment could not be maintained except by invoking less the enormity of the crime itself than the monstrosity of the criminal, his incorrigibility, and the safeguard of society. One had the right to kill those who represented a kind of biological danger to others.

One might say that the ancient right to *take* life or *let* live was replaced by a power to *foster* life or *disallow* it to the point of death. This is perhaps what explains that disqualification of death which marks the recent wane of the rituals that accompanied it. That death is so carefully evaded is linked less to a new anxiety which makes death unbearable for our societies than to the fact that the procedures of power have not ceased to turn away from death. In the passage from this world to the other, death was the manner in which a terrestrial sovereignty was relieved by another, singularly more powerful sovereignty; the pageantry that surrounded it was in the category of political ceremony. Now it is over life, throughout its unfolding, that power establishes its dominion; death is power's limit, the moment that escapes it; death becomes the most secret aspect of existence, the most "private." It is not surprising that suicide—once a crime, since it was a way to usurp the power of death which the sovereign alone, whether the one here below or the Lord above, had the right to exercise—became, in the course of the nineteenth century, one of the first conducts to enter into the sphere of sociological analysis; it testified to the individual and private right to die, at the borders and in the interstices of power that was exercised over life. This determination to die, strange and yet so persistent and constant in its manifestations, and consequently so difficult to explain as being due to particular circumstances or individual accidents, was one of the first astonishments of a society in which political power had assigned itself the task of administering life.

In concrete terms, starting in the seventeenth century, this power over life evolved in two basic forms; these forms were not antithetical, however; they constituted rather two poles of development linked together by a whole intermediary cluster of relations. One of these poles—the first to be formed, it seems—centered on the body as a machine: its disciplining, the optimization of its capabilities, the extortion of its forces, the parallel increase of its usefulness and its docility, its integration into systems of efficient and economic controls, all this was ensured by the procedures of power that characterized the *disciplines: an anatomo-politics of the human body.* The second, formed somewhat later, focused on the species body, the body imbued with the mechanics of life and serving as the basis of the biological processes: propagation, births and mortality, the level of health, life expectancy and longevity, with all the conditions that can cause these to vary. Their supervision was effected through an entire series of interventions and *regulatory controls: a bio-politics of the population.* The disciplines of the body and the regulations of the population constituted the two poles around which the organization of power over life was deployed. The setting up, in the course of the classical age, of this great bipolar technology—anatomic and biological, individualizing and specifying, directed toward the performances of the body, with attention to the processes of life—characterized a power whose highest function was perhaps no longer to kill, but to invest life through and through.

The old power of death that symbolized sovereign power was now carefully supplanted by the administration of bodies and the calculated management of life. During the classical period, there was a rapid development of various disciplines—universities, secondary schools, barracks, workshops; there was also the emergence, in the field of political practices and economic observation, of the problems of birthrate, longevity, public health, housing, and migration. Hence there was an explosion of numerous and diverse techniques for achieving the subjugation of bodies and the control of populations, marking the beginning of an era of "bio-power." The two directions taken by its development still appeared to be clearly separate in the eighteenth century. With regard to discipline, this development was embodied in institutions such as the army and the schools, and in reflections on tactics, apprenticeship, education, and the nature of societies, ranging from the strictly military analyses of Marshal de Saxe to the political reveries of Guibert or Servan. As for population controls, one notes the emergence of demography, the evaluation of the relationship between resources and inhabitants, the constructing of tables analyzing wealth and its circulation: the work of Quesnay, Moheau, and Süssmilch. The philosophy of the "Ideologists," as a theory of ideas, signs, and the individual genesis of sensations, but also a theory of the social composition of interests—ideology being a doctrine of apprenticeship, but also a doctrine of contracts and the regulated formation of the social body—no doubt constituted the abstract discourse in which one sought to coordinate these two techniques of power in order to construct a general theory of it. In point of fact, however, they were not to be joined at the level of a speculative discourse, but in the form of concrete arrangements (*agencements concrets*) that would go to make up the great technology of power in the nineteenth century: the deployment of sexuality would be one of them, and one of the most important.

This bio-power was without question an indispensable element in the development of capitalism; the latter would not have been possible without the controlled insertion of bodies into the machinery of production and the adjustment of the phenomena of population to economic processes. But this was not all it required; it also needed the growth of both these factors, their reinforcement as well as their availability and docility; it had to have methods of power capable of optimizing forces, aptitudes, and life in general without at the same time making them more difficult to govern. If the development of the great instruments of the state, as *institutions* of power, ensured the maintenance of production relations, the rudiments of anatomo- and bio-politics, created in the eighteenth century as *techniques* of power present at every level of the social body and utilized by very diverse institutions (the family and the army, schools and the police, individual medicine and the administration of collective bodies), operated in the sphere of economic processes, their development, and the forces working to sustain them. They also acted as factors of segrega-tion and social hierarchization, exerting their influence on the respective forces of both these movements, guaranteeing relations of domination and effects of hegemony. The adjustment of the accumulation of men to that of capital, the joining of the growth of human groups to the expansion of pro-ductive forces and the differential allocation of profit, were made possible in part by the exercise of bio-power in its many forms and modes of application. The investment of the body, its valorization, and the distributive management of its forces were at the time indispensable.

One knows how many times the question has been raised concerning the role of an ascetic morality in the first formation of capitalism; but what oc-curred in the eighteenth century in some Western countries, an event bound up with the development of capitalism, was a different phenomenon having perhaps a wider impact than the new morality; this was nothing less than the entry of life into history, that is, the entry of phenomena peculiar to the life of the human species into the order of knowledge and power, into the sphere of political techniques. It is not a question of claiming that this was the moment when the first contact between life and history was brought about. On the con-trary, the pressure exerted by the biological on the historical had remained very strong for thousands of years; epidemics and famine were the two great dramatic forms of this relationship that was always dominated by the menace of death. But through a circular process, the economic—and primarily agricultural—development of the eighteenth century, and an increase in productivity and re-sources even more rapid than the demographic growth it encouraged, allowed a measure of relief from these profound threats: despite some renewed out-breaks, the period of great ravages from starvation and plague had come to a close before the French Revolution; death was ceasing to torment life so directly. But at the same time, the development of the different fields of knowledge concerned with life in general, the improvement of agricultural techniques, and the observations and measures relative to man's life and sur-vival contributed to this relaxation: a relative control over life averted some of the imminent risks of death. In the space for movement thus conquered, and broadening and organizing that space, methods of power and knowledge as-sumed responsibility for the life processes and undertook to control and mod-ify them. Western man was gradually learning what it meant to be a living species in a living world, to have a body, conditions of existence, probabilities of life, an individual and collective welfare, forces that could be modified, and a space in which they could be distributed in an optimal manner. For the first time in history, no doubt, biological existence was reflected in political existence; the fact of living was no longer an inaccessible substrate that only emerged from time to time, amid the randomness of death and its fatality; part of it passed into knowledge's field of control and power's sphere of intervention. Power would no longer be dealing simply with legal subjects over whom the ultimate dominion was death, but with living beings, and the mastery it would be able to exercise over them would have to be applied at the level of life itself; it was the taking charge of life, more than the threat of death, that gave power its access even to the body. If one can apply the term *bio-history* to the pressures through which the movements of life and the processes of history interfere with one another, one would have to speak of *bio-power* to designate what brought life and its mechanisms into the realm of explicit calculations and made knowledge-power an agent of transformation of human life. It is not that life has been totally integrated into techniques that govern and administer it; it constantly escapes them. Outside the Western world, famine exists, on a greater scale than ever; and the biological risks confronting the species are perhaps greater, and certainly more serious, than before the birth of microbiology. But what might be called a society's "threshold of modernity" has been reached when the life of the species is wagered on its own political strategies. For millennia, man remained what he was for Aristotle: a living animal with the additional capacity for a political existence; modern man is an animal whose politics places his existence as a living being in question.

This transformation had considerable consequences. It would serve no purpose here to dwell on the rupture that occurred then in the pattern of scientific discourse and on the manner in which the twofold problematic of life and man disrupted and redistributed the order of the classical episteme. If the question of man was raised—insofar as he was a specific living being, and specifically related to other living beings—the reason for this is to be sought in the new mode of relation between history and life: in this dual position of life that placed it at the same time outside history, in its biological environment, and inside human historicity, penetrated by the latter's techniques of knowledge and power. There is no need either to lay further stress on the proliferation of political technologies that ensued, investing the body, health, modes of subsistence and habitation, living conditions, the whole space of existence.

Another consequence of this development of bio-power was the growing importance assumed by the action of the norm, at the expense of the juridical system of the law. Law cannot help but be armed, and its arm, *par excellence,* is death; to those who transgress it, it replies, at least as a last resort, with that absolute menace. The law always refers to the sword. But a power whose task is to take charge of life needs continuous regulatory and corrective mechanisms. It is no longer a matter of bringing death into play in the field of sovereignty, but of distributing the living in the domain of value and utility. Such a power has to qualify, measure, appraise, and hierarchize, rather than display itself in its murderous splendor; it does not have to draw the line that separates the enemies of the sovereign from his obedient subjects; it effects distributions around the norm. I do not mean to say that the law fades into the background or that the institutions of justice tend to disappear, but rather that the law operates more and more as a norm, and that the judicial institution is increasingly incorporated into a continuum of apparatuses (medical, administrative, and so on) whose functions are for the most part regulatory. A normalizing society is the historical outcome of a technology of power centered on life. We have entered a phase of juridical regression in comparison with the pre-seventeenth-century societies we are acquainted with; we should not be deceived by all the Constitutions framed throughout the world since the French Revolution, the Codes written and revised, a whole continual and clamorous legislative activity: these were the forms that made an essentially normalizing power acceptable.

Moreover, against this power that was still new in the nineteenth century, the forces that resisted relied for support on the very thing it invested, that is, on life and man as a living being. Since the last century, the great struggles that have challenged the general system of power were not guided by the belief in a return to former rights, or by the age old dream of a cycle of time or a Golden Age. One no longer aspired toward the coming of the emperor of the poor, of the kingdom of the latter days, or even the restoration of our imagined ancestral rights; what was demanded and what served as an objective was life, understood as the basic needs, man's concrete essence, the realization of his potential, a plenitude of the possible. Whether or not it was Utopia that was wanted is of little importance; what we have seen has been a very real process of struggle; life as a political object was in a sense taken at face value and turned back against the system that was bent on controlling it. It was life more than the law that became the issue of political struggles, even if the latter were formulated through affirmations concerning rights. The "right" to life, to one's body, to health, to happiness, to the satisfaction of needs, and beyond all the oppressions or "alienations," the "right" to rediscover what one is and all that one can be, this "right"—which the classical juridical system was utterly incapable of comprehending—was the political response to all these new procedures of power which did not derive, either, from the traditional right of sovereignty.

This is the background that enables us to understand the importance assumed by sex as a political issue. It was at the pivot of the two axes along which developed the entire political technology of life. On the one hand it was tied to the disciplines of the body: the harnessing, intensification, and distribution of forces, the adjustment and economy of energies. On the other hand, it was applied to the regulation of populations, through all the far-reaching effects of its activity. It fitted in both categories at once, giving rise to infinitesimal surveillances, permanent controls, extremely meticulous orderings of space, indeterminate medical or psychological examinations, to an entire micro-power concerned with the body. But it gave rise as well to comprehensive measures, statistical assessments, and interventions aimed at the entire social body or at groups taken as a whole. Sex was a means of access both to the life of the body and the life of the species. It was employed as a standard for the disciplines and as a basis for regulations. This is why in the nineteenth century sexuality was sought out in the smallest details of individual existences; it was tracked down in behavior, pursued in dreams; it was suspected of underlying the least follies, it was traced back into the earliest years of childhood; it became the stamp of individuality—at the same time what enabled one to analyze the latter and what made it possible to master it. But one also sees it becoming the theme of political operations, economic interventions (through incitements to or curbs on procreation), and ideological campaigns for raising standards of morality and responsibility: it was put forward as the index of a society's strength, revealing of both its political energy and its biological vigor. Spread out from one pole to the other of this technology of sex was a whole series of different tactics that combined in varying proportions the objective of disciplining the body and that of regulating populations.

Whence the importance of the four great lines of attack along which the politics of sex advanced for two centuries. Each one was a way of combining disciplinary techniques with regulative methods. The first two rested on the requirements of regulation, on a whole thematic of the species, descent, and collective welfare, in order to obtain results at the level of discipline; the sexualization of children was accomplished in the form of a campaign for the health of the race (precocious sexuality was presented from the eighteenth century to the end of the nineteenth as an epidemic menace that risked compromising not only the future health of adults but the future of the entire society and species); the hysterization of women, which involved a thorough medicalization of their bodies and their sex, was carried out in the name of the responsibility they owed to the health of their children, the solidity of the family institution, and the safeguarding of society. It was the reverse relationship that applied in the case of birth controls and the psychiatrization of perversions: here the intervention was regulatory in nature, but it had to rely on the demand for individual disciplines and constraints *(dressages)*. Broadly speaking, at the juncture of the "body" and the "population," sex became a crucial target of a power organized around the management of life rather than the menace of death.

The blood relation long remained an important element in the mechanisms of power, its manifestations, and its rituals. For a society in which the systems of alliance, the political form of the sovereign, the differentiation into orders and castes, and the value of descent lines were predominant; for a society in which famine, epidemics, and violence made death imminent, blood constituted one of the fundamental values. It owed its high value at the same time to its instrumental role (the ability to shed blood), to the way it functioned in the order of signs (to have a certain blood, to be of the same blood, to be prepared to risk one's blood), and also to its precariousness (easily spilled, subject to drying up, too readily mixed, capable of being quickly corrupted). A society of blood—I was tempted to say, of "sanguinity"—where power spoke *through* blood: the honor of war, the fear of famine, the triumph of death, the sovereign with his sword, executioners, and tortures; blood was *a reality with a symbolic function*. We, on the other hand, are in a society of "sex," or rather a society "with a sexuality": the mechanisms of power are addressed to the body, to life, to what causes it to proliferate, to what reinforces the species, its stamina, its ability to dominate, or its capacity for being used. Through the themes of health, progeny, race, the future of the species, the vitality of the social body, power spoke *of* sexuality and *to* sexuality; the latter was not a mark or a symbol, it was an object and a target. Moreover, its importance was due less to its rarity or its precariousness than to its insistence, its insidious presence, the fact that it was everywhere an object of excitement and fear at the same time. Power delineated it, aroused it, and employed it as the proliferating meaning that had always to be taken control of again lest it escape; it was *an effect with a meaning-value*. I do not mean to say that a substitution of sex for blood was by itself responsible for all the transformations that marked the threshold of our modernity. It is not the soul of two civilizations or the organizing principle of two cultural forms that I am attempting to express; I am looking for the reasons for which sexuality, far from being repressed in the society of that period, on the contrary was constantly aroused. The new procedures of power that were devised during the classical age and employed in the nineteenth century were what caused our societies to go from *a symbolics of blood* to *an analytics of sexuality*. Clearly, nothing was more on the side of the law, death, transgression, the symbolic, and sovereignty than blood; just as sexuality was on the side of the norm, knowledge, life, meaning, the disciplines, and regulations.

Sade and the first eugenists were contemporary with this transition from "sanguinity" to "sexuality." But whereas the first dreams of the perfecting of the species inclined the whole problem toward an extremely exacting administration of sex (the art of determining good marriages, of inducing the desired fertilities, of ensuring the health and longevity of children), and while the new concept of race tended to obliterate the aristocratic particularities of blood, retaining only the controllable effects of sex, Sade carried the exhaustive analysis of sex over into the mechanisms of the old power of sovereignty and endowed it with the ancient but fully maintained prestige of blood; the latter flowed through the whole dimension of pleasure—the blood of torture and absolute power, the blood of the caste which was respected in itself and which nonetheless was made to flow in the major rituals of parricide and incest, the blood of the people, which was shed unreservedly since the sort that flowed in its veins was not even deserving of a name. In Sade, sex is without any norm or intrinsic rule that might be formulated from its own nature; but it is subject to the unrestricted law of a power which itself knows no other law but its own; if by chance it is at times forced to accept the order of progressions carefully disciplined into successive days, this exercise carries it to a point where it is no longer anything but a unique and naked sovereignty: an unlimited right of all-powerful monstrosity.

While it is true that the analytics of sexuality and the symbolics of blood were grounded at first in two very distinct regimes of power, in actual fact the passage from one to the other did not come about (any more than did these powers themselves) without overlappings, interactions, and echoes. In different ways, the preoccupation with blood and the law has for nearly two centuries haunted the administration of sexuality. Two of these interferences are noteworthy, the one for its historical importance, the other for the problems it poses. Beginning in the second half of the nineteenth century, the thematics of blood was sometimes called on to lend its entire historical weight toward revitalizing the type of political power that was exercised through the devices of sexuality. Racism took shape at this point (racism in its modern, "biologizing," statist form): it was then that a whole politics of settlement (*peuplement*), family, marriage, education, social hierarchization, and property, accompanied by a long series of permanent interventions at the level of the body, conduct, health, and everyday life, received their color and their justification from the mythical concern with protecting the purity of the blood and ensuring the triumph of the race. Nazism was doubtless the most cunning and the most naïve (and the former because of the latter) combination of the fantasies of blood and the paroxysms of a disciplinary power. A eugenic ordering of society, with all that implied in the way of extension and intensification of micro-powers, in the guise of an unrestricted state control (*étatisation*), was accompanied by the oneiric exaltation of a superior blood; the latter implied both the systematic genocide of others and the risk of exposing oneself to a total sacrifice. It is an irony of history that the Hitlerite politics of sex remained an insignificant practice while the blood myth was transformed into the greatest blood bath in recent memory.

At the opposite extreme, starting from this same end of the nineteenth century, we can trace the theoretical effort to reinscribe the thematic of sexuality in the system of law, the symbolic order, and sovereignty. It is to the political credit of psychoanalysis—or at least, of what was most coherent in it—that it regarded with suspicion (and this from its inception, that is, from the moment it broke away from the neuropsychiatry of degenerescence) the irrevocably proliferating aspects which might be contained in these power mechanisms aimed at controlling and administering the everyday life of sexuality: whence the Freudian endeavor (out of reaction no doubt to the great surge of racism that was contemporary with it) to ground sexuality in the law—the law of alliance, tabooed consanguinity, and the Sovereign-Father, in short, to surround desire with all the trappings of the old order of power. It was owing to this that psychoanalysis was—in the main, with a few exceptions—in theoretical and practical opposition to fascism. But this position of psychoanalysis was tied to a specific historical conjuncture. And yet, to conceive the category of the sexual in terms of the law, death, blood, and sovereignty—whatever the references to Sade and Bataille, and however one might gauge their "subversive" influence—is in the last analysis a historical "retro-version." We must conceptualize the deployment of sexuality on the basis of the techniques of power that are contemporary with it.

People are going to say that I am dealing in a historicism which is more careless than radical; that I am evading the biologically established existence of sexual functions for the benefit of phenomena that are variable, perhaps, but fragile, secondary, and ultimately superficial; and that I speak of sexuality as if sex did not exist. And one would be entitled to object as follows: "You claim to analyze in detail the processes by which women's bodies, the lives of children, family relationships, and an entire network of social relations were sexualized. You wish to describe that great awakening of sexual concern since the eighteenth century and our growing eagerness to suspect the presence of sex in everything. Let us admit as much and suppose that the mechanisms of power were in fact used more to arouse and 'excite' sexuality than to repress it. But here you remain quite near to the thing you no doubt believe you have gotten away from; at bottom, when you point out phenomena of diffusion, anchorage, and fixation of sexuality, you are trying to reveal what might be called the organization of 'erotic zones' in the social body; it may well be the case that you have done nothing more than transpose to the level of diffuse processes mechanisms which psychoanalysis has identified with precision at the level of the individual. But you pass over the thing on the basis of which this sexualization was able to develop and which psychoanalysis does not fail to recognize—namely, sex. Before Freud, one sought to localize sexuality as closely as possible: in sex, in its reproductive functions, in its immediate anatomical localizations; one fell back upon a biological minimum: organ, instinct, and finality. You, on the other hand, are in a symmetrical and inverse position: for you, there remain only groundless effects, ramifications without roots, a sexuality without a sex. What is this if not castration once again?"

Here we need to distinguish between two questions. First, does the analysis of sexuality necessarily imply the elision of the body, anatomy, the biological, the functional? To this question, I think we can reply in the negative. In any case, the purpose of the present study is in fact to show how deployments of power are directly connected to the body—to bodies, functions, physiological processes, sensations, and pleasures; far from the body having to be effaced, what is needed is to make it visible through an analysis in which the biological and the historical are not consecutive to one another, as in the evolutionism of the first sociologists, but are bound together in an increasingly complex fashion in accordance with the development of the modern technologies of power that take life as their objective. Hence I do not envisage a "history of mentalities" that would take account of bodies only through the manner in which they have been perceived and given meaning and value; but a "history of bodies" and the manner in which what is most material and most vital in them has been invested.

Another question, distinct from the first one: this materiality that is referred to, is it not, then, that of sex, and is it not paradoxical to venture a history of sexuality at the level of bodies, without there being the least question of sex? After all, is the power that is exercised through sexuality not directed specifically at that element of reality which is "sex," sex in general? That sexuality is not, in relation to power, an exterior domain to which power is applied, that on the contrary it is a result and an instrument of power's designs, is all very well. But as for sex, is it not the "other" with respect to power, while being the center around which sexuality distributes its effects? Now, it is precisely this idea of sex *in itself* that we cannot accept without examination. Is "sex" really the anchorage point that supports the manifestations of sexuality, or is it not rather a complex idea that was formed inside the deployment of sexuality? In any case, one could show how this idea of sex took form in the different strategies of power and the definite role it played therein.

All along the great lines which the development of the deployment of sexuality has followed since the nineteenth century, one sees the elaboration of this idea that there exists something other than bodies, organs, somatic localizations, functions, anatomo-physiological systems, sensations, and pleasures; something else and something more, with intrinsic properties and laws of its own: "sex." Thus, in the process of hysterization of women, "sex" was defined in three ways: as that which belongs in common to men and women; as that which belongs, *par excellence,* to men, and hence is lacking in women; but at the same time, as that which by itself constitutes woman's body, ordering it wholly in terms of the functions of reproduction and keeping it in constant agitation through the effects of that very function. Hysteria was interpreted in this strategy as the movement of sex insofar as it was the "one" and the "other," whole and part, principle and lack. In the sexualization of childhood, there was formed the idea of a sex that was both present (from the evidence of anatomy) and absent (from the standpoint of physiology), present too if one considered its activity, and deficient if one referred to its reproductive finality; or again, actual in its manifestations, but hidden in its eventual effects, whose pathological seriousness would only become apparent later. If the sex of the child was still present in the adult, it was in the form of a secret causality that tended to nullify the sex of the latter (it was one of the tenets of eighteenth- and nineteenth-century medicine that precocious sex would eventually result in sterility, impotence, frigidity, the inability to experience pleasure, or the deadening of the senses); by sexualizing childhood, the idea was established of a sex characterized essentially by the interplay of presence and absence, the visible and the hidden; masturbation and the effects imputed to it were thought to reveal in a privileged way this interplay of presence and absence, of the visible and the hidden.

In the psychiatrization of perversions, sex was related to biological functions and to an anatomo-physiological machinery that gave it its "meaning," that is, its finality; but it was also referred to an instinct which, through its peculiar development and according to the objects to which it could become attached, made it possible for perverse behavior patterns to arise and made their genesis intelligible. Thus "sex" was defined by the interlacing of function and instinct, finality and signification; moreover, this was the form in which it was manifested, more clearly than anywhere else, in the model perversion, in that "fetishism" which, from at least as early as 1877, served as the guiding thread for analyzing all the other deviations. In it one could clearly perceive the way in which the instinct became fastened to an object in accordance with an individual's historical adherence and biological inadequacy. Lastly, in the socialization of procreative behavior, "sex" was described as being caught between a law of reality (economic necessity being its most abrupt and immediate form) and an economy of pleasure which was always attempting to circumvent that law—when, that is, it did not ignore it altogether. The most notorious of "frauds," coitus interruptus, represented the point where the insistence of the real forced an end to pleasure and where the pleasure found a way to surface despite the economy dictated by the real. It is apparent that the deployment of sexuality, with its different strategies, was what established this notion of "sex"; and in the four major forms of hysteria, onanism, fetishism, and interrupted coition, it showed this sex to be governed by the interplay of whole and part, principle and lack, absence and presence, excess and deficiency, by the function of instinct, finality, and meaning, of reality and pleasure.

The theory thus generated performed a certain number of functions that made it indispensable. First, the notion of "sex" made it possible to group together, in an artificial unity, anatomical elements, biological functions, conducts, sensations, and pleasures, and it enabled one to make use of this fictitious unity as a causal principle, an omnipresent meaning, a secret to be discovered everywhere: sex was thus able to function as a unique signifier and as a universal signified. Further, by presenting itself in a unitary fashion, as anatomy and lack, as function and latency, as instinct and meaning, it was able to mark the line of contact between a knowledge of human sexuality and the biological sciences of reproduction; thus, without really borrowing anything from these sciences, excepting a few doubtful analogies, the knowledge of sexuality gained through proximity a guarantee of quasi-scientificity; but by virtue of this same proximity, some of the contents of biology and physiology were able to serve as a principle of normality for human sexuality. Finally, the notion of sex brought about a fundamental reversal; it made it possible to invert the representation of the relationships of power to sexuality, causing the latter to appear, not in its essential and positive relation to power, but as being rooted in a specific and irreducible urgency which power tries as best it can to dominate; thus the idea of "sex" makes it possible to evade what gives "power" its power; it enables one to conceive power solely as law and taboo. Sex—that agency which appears to dominate us and that secret which seems to underlie all that we are, that point which enthralls us through the power it manifests and the meaning it conceals, and which we ask to reveal what we are and to free us from what defines us—is doubtless but an ideal point made necessary by the deployment of sexuality and its operation. We must not make the mistake of thinking that sex is an autonomous agency which secondarily produces manifold effects of sexuality over the entire length of its surface of contact with power. On the contrary, sex is the most speculative, most ideal, and most internal element in a deployment of sexuality organized by power in its grip on bodies and their materiality, their forces, energies, sensations, and pleasures.

It might be added that "sex" performs yet another function that runs through and sustains the ones we have just examined. Its role in this instance is more practical than theoretical. It is through sex—in fact, an imaginary point determined by the deployment of sexuality—that each individual has to pass in order to have access to his own intelligibility (seeing that it is both the hidden aspect and the generative principle of meaning), to the whole of his body (since it is a real and threatened part of it, while symbolically constituting the whole), to his identity (since it joins the force of a drive to the singularity of a history). Through a reversal that doubtless had its surreptitious beginnings long ago—it was already making itself felt at the time of the Christian pastoral of the flesh—we have arrived at the point where we expect our intelligibility to come from what was for many centuries thought of as madness; the plenitude of our body from what was long considered its stigma and likened to a wound; our identity from what was perceived as an obscure and nameless urge. Hence the importance we ascribe to it, the reverential fear with which we surround it, the care we take to know it. Hence the fact that over the centuries it has become more important than our soul, more important almost than our life; and so it is that all the world's enigmas appear frivolous to us compared to this secret, minuscule in each of us, but of a density that makes it more serious than any other. The Faustian pact, whose temptation has been instilled in us by the deployment of sexuality, is now as follows: to exchange life in its entirety for sex itself, for the truth and the sovereignty of sex. Sex is worth dying for. It is in this (strictly historical) sense that sex is indeed imbued with the death instinct. When a long while ago the West discovered love, it bestowed on it a value high enough to make death acceptable; nowadays it is sex that claims this equivalence, the highest of all. And while the deployment of sexuality permits the techniques of power to invest life, the fictitious point of sex, itself marked by that deployment, exerts enough charm on everyone for them to accept hearing the grumble of death within it.

By creating the imaginary element that is "sex," the deployment of sexuality established one of its most essential internal operating principles: the desire for sex—the desire to have it, to have access to it, to discover it, to liberate it, to articulate it in discourse, to formulate it in truth. It constituted "sex" itself as something desirable. And it is this desirability of sex that attaches each one of us to the injunction to know it, to reveal its law and its power; it is this desirability that makes us think we are affirming the rights of our sex against all power, when in fact we are fastened to the deployment of sexuality that has lifted up from deep within us a sort of mirage in which we think we see ourselves reflected—the dark shimmer of sex.

"It is sex," said Kate in *The Plumed Serpent*. "How wonderful sex can be, when men keep it powerful and sacred, and it fills the world! like sunshine through and through one!"

So we must not refer a history of sexuality to the agency of sex; but rather show how "sex" is historically subordinate to sexuality. We must not place sex on the side of reality, and sexuality on that of confused ideas and illusions; sexuality is a very real historical formation; it is what gave rise to the notion of sex, as a speculative element necessary to its operation. We must not think that by saying yes to sex, one says no to power; on the contrary, one tracks along the course laid out by the general deployment of sexuality. It is the agency of sex that we must break away from, if we aim—through a tactical reversal of the various mechanisms of sexuality—to counter the grips of power with the claims of bodies, pleasures, and knowledges, in their multiplicity and their possibility of resistance. The rallying point for the counterattack against the deployment of sexuality ought not to be sex-desire, but bodies and pleasures.

"There has been so much action in the past," said D. H. Lawrence, "especially sexual action, a wearying repetition over and over, without a corresponding thought, a corresponding realization. Now our business is to realize sex. Today the full conscious realization of sex is even more important than the act itself."

Perhaps one day people will wonder at this. They will not be able to understand how a civilization so intent on developing enormous instruments of production and destruction found the time and the infinite patience to inquire so anxiously concerning the actual state of sex; people will smile perhaps when they recall that here were men—meaning ourselves—who believed that therein resided a truth every bit as precious as the one they had already demanded from the earth, the stars, and the pure forms of their thought; people will be surprised at the eagerness with which we went about pretending to rouse from its slumber a sexuality which everything—our discourses, our customs, our institutions, our regulations, our knowledges—was busy producing in the light of day and broadcasting to noisy accompaniment. And people will ask themselves why we were so bent on ending the rule of silence regarding what was the noisiest of our preoccupations. In retrospect, this noise may appear to have been out of place, but how much stranger will seem our persistence in interpreting it as but the refusal to speak and the order to remain silent. People will wonder what could have made us so presumptuous; they will look for the reasons that might explain why we prided ourselves on being the first to grant sex the importance we say is its due and how we came to congratulate ourselves for finally—in the twentieth century—having broken free of a long period of harsh repression, a protracted Christian asceticism, greedily and fastidiously adapted to the imperatives of bourgeois economy. And what we now perceive as the chronicle of a censorship and the difficult struggle to remove it will be seen rather as the centuries-long rise of a complex deployment for compelling sex to speak, for fastening our attention and concern upon sex, for getting us to believe in the sovereignty of its law when in fact we were moved by the power mechanisms of sexuality.

People will be amused at the reproach of pansexualism that was once aimed at Freud and psychoanalysis. But the ones who will appear to have been blind will perhaps be not so much those who formulated the objection as those who discounted it out of hand, as if it merely expressed the fears of an outmoded prudishness. For the first, after all, were only taken unawares by a process which had begun long before and by which, unbeknown to them, they were already surrounded on all sides; what they had attributed solely to the genius of Freud had already gone through a long stage of preparation; they had gotten their dates wrong as to the establishment, in our society, of a general deployment of sexuality. But the others were mistaken concerning the nature of the process; they believed that Freud had at last, through a sudden reversal, restored to sex the rightful share which it had been denied for so long; they had not seen how the good genius of Freud had placed it at one of the critical points marked out for it since the eighteenth century by the strategies of knowledge and power, how wonderfully effective he was—worthy of the greatest spiritual fathers and directors of the classical period—in giving a new impetus to the secular injunction to study sex and transform it into discourse. We are often reminded of the countless procedures which Christianity once employed to make us detest the body; but let us ponder all the ruses that were employed for centuries to make us love sex, to make the knowledge of it desirable and everything said about it precious. Let us consider the stratagems by which we were induced to apply all our skills to discovering its secrets, by which we were attached to the obligation to draw out its truth, and made guilty for having failed to recognize it for so long. These devices are what ought to make us wonder today. Moreover, we need to consider the possibility that one day, perhaps, in a different economy of bodies and pleasures, people will no longer quite understand how the ruses of sexuality, and the power that sustains its organization, were able to subject us to that austere monarchy of sex, so that we became dedicated to the endless task of forcing its secret, of exacting the truest of confessions from a shadow.

The irony of this deployment is in having us believe that our "liberation" is in the balance.

Notes

1. Samuel von Pufendorf, *Le Droit de la nature* (French trans., 1734), p. 445.
2. "Just as a composite body can have properties not found in any of the simple bodies of which the mixture consists, so a moral body, by virtue of the very union of persons of which it is composed, can have certain rights which none of the individuals could expressly claim and whose exercise is the proper function of leaders alone." Pufendorf, *Le Droit de la nature*, p. 452.

CHAPTER 2

"SOCIETY MUST BE DEFENDED," LECTURE AT THE *COLLÈGE DE FRANCE*, MARCH 17, 1976

Michel Foucault

It is time to end then, to try to pull together what I have been saying this year. I have been trying to raise the problem of war, seen as a grid for understanding historical processes. It seemed to me that war was regarded, initially and throughout practically the whole of the eighteenth century, as a war between races. It was that war between races that I wanted to try to reconstruct. And last time, I tried to show you how the very notion of war was eventually eliminated from historical analysis by the principle of national universality.* I would now like to show you how, while the theme of race does not disappear, it does become part of something very different, namely State racism. So today I would like to tell you a little about State racism, or at least situate it for you.

It seems to me that one of the basic phenomena of the nineteenth century was what might be called power's hold over life. What I mean is the acquisition of power over man insofar as man is a living being, that the biological came under State control, that there was at least a certain tendency that leads to what might be termed State control of the biological. And I think that in order to understand what was going on, it helps if we refer to what used to be the classical theory of sovereignty, which ultimately provided us with the backdrop to—a picture of—all these analyses of war, races, and so on. You know that in the classical theory of sovereignty, the right of life and death was one of sovereignty's basic attributes. Now the right of life and death is a strange right. Even at the theoretical level, it is a strange right. What does having the right of life and death actually mean? In one sense, to say that the

---

*In the manuscript, the sentence continues: "at the time of the Revolution."

sovereign has a right of life and death means that he can, basically, either have people put to death or let them live, or in any case that life and death are not natural or immediate phenomena which are primal or radical, and which fall outside the field of power. If we take the argument a little further, or to the point where it becomes paradoxical, it means that in terms of his relationship with the sovereign, the subject is, by rights, neither dead nor alive. From the point of view of life and death, the subject is neutral, and it is thanks to the sovereign that the subject has the right to be alive or, possibly, the right to be dead. In any case, the lives and deaths of subjects become rights only as a result of the will of the sovereign. That is, if you like, the theoretical paradox. And it is of course a theoretical paradox that must have as its corollary a sort of practical disequilibrium. What does the right of life and death actually mean? Obviously not that the sovereign can grant life in the same way that he can inflict death. The right of life and death is always exercised in an unbalanced way: the balance is always tipped in favor of death. Sovereign power's effect on life is exercised only when the sovereign can kill. The very essence of the right of life and death is actually the right to kill: it is at the moment when the sovereign can kill that he exercises his right over life. It is essentially the right of the sword. So there is no real symmetry in the right over life and death. It is not the right to put people to death or to grant them life. Nor is it the right to allow people to live or to leave them to die. It is the right to take life or let live. And this obviously introduces a startling dissymmetry.

And I think that one of the greatest transformations political right underwent in the nineteenth century was precisely that, I wouldn't say exactly that sovereignty's old right—to take life or let live—was replaced, but it came to be complemented by a new right which does not erase the old right but which does penetrate it, permeate it. This is the right, or rather precisely the opposite right. It is the power to "make" live and "let" die. The right of sovereignty was the right to take life or let live. And then this new right is established: the right to make live and to let die.

This transformation obviously did not occur all at once. We can trace it in the theory of right (but here, I will be extraordinarily rapid). The jurists of the seventeenth and especially the eighteenth century were, you see, already asking this question about the right of life and death. The jurists ask: When we enter into a contract, what are individuals doing at the level of the social contract, when they come together to constitute a sovereign, to delegate absolute power over them to a sovereign? They do so because they are forced to by some threat or by need. They therefore do so in order to protect their lives. It is in order to live that they constitute a sovereign. To the extent that this is the case, can life actually become one of the rights of the sovereign? Isn't life the foundation of the sovereign's right, and can the sovereign actually demand that his subjects grant him the right to exercise the power of life and death over them, or in other words, simply the power to kill them? Mustn't life remain outside the contract to the extent that it was the first, initial, and foundational reason for the contract itself? All this is a debate within political philosophy that we can leave on one side, but it clearly demonstrates how the problem of life began to be problematized in the field of political thought, of the analysis of political power. I would in fact like to trace the transformation not at the level of political theory, but rather at the level of the mechanisms, techniques, and technologies of power. And this brings us back to something familiar: in the seventeenth and eighteenth centuries, we saw the emergence of techniques of power that were essentially centered on the body, on the individual body. They included all devices that were used to ensure the spatial distribution of individual bodies (their separation, their alignment, their serialization, and their surveillance) and the organization, around those individuals, of a whole field of visibility. They were also techniques that could be used to take control over bodies. Attempts were made to increase their productive force through exercise, drill, and so on. They were also techniques for rationalizing and strictly economizing on a power that had to be used in the least costly way possible, thanks to a whole system of surveillance, hierarchies, inspections, bookkeeping, and reports—all the technology that can be described as the disciplinary technology of labor. It was established at the end of the seventeenth century, and in the course of the eighteenth.[1]

Now I think we see something new emerging in the second half of the eighteenth century: a new technology of power, but this time it is not disciplinary. This technology of power does not exclude the former, does not exclude disciplinary technology, but it does dovetail into it, integrate it, modify it to some extent, and above all, use it by sort of infiltrating it, embedding itself in existing disciplinary techniques. This new technique does not simply do away with the disciplinary technique, because it exists at a different level, on a different scale, and because it has a different bearing area, and makes use of very different instruments.

Unlike discipline, which is addressed to bodies, the new nondisciplinary power is applied not to man-as-body but to the living man, to man-as-living-being; ultimately, if you like, to man-as-species. To be more specific, I would say that discipline tries to rule a multiplicity of men to the extent that their multiplicity can and must be dissolved into individual bodies that can be kept under surveillance, trained, used, and, if need be, punished. And that the new technology that is being established is addressed to a multiplicity of men, not to the extent that they are nothing more than their individual bodies, but to the extent that they form, on the contrary, a global mass that is affected by overall processes characteristic of birth, death, production, illness, and so on. So after a first seizure of power over the body in an individualizing mode, we have a second seizure of power that is not individualizing but, if you like, massifying, that is directed not at man-as-body but at man-as-species. After the anatomo-politics of the human body established in the course of the eighteenth century, we have, at the end of that century, the emergence of something that is no longer an anatomo-politics of the human body, but what I would call a "biopolitics" of the human race.

What does this new technology of power, this biopolitics, this biopower that is beginning to establish itself, involve? I told you very briefly a moment ago; a set of processes such as the ratio of births to deaths, the rate of reproduction, the fertility of a population, and so on. It is these processes—the birth rate, the mortality rate, longevity, and so on—together with a whole series of related economic and political problems (which I will not come back to for the moment) which, in the second half of the eighteenth century, become biopolitics' first objects of knowledge and the targets it seeks to control. It is at any rate at this moment that the first demographers begin to measure these phenomena in statistical terms. They begin to observe the more or less spontaneous, more or less compulsory techniques that the population actually used to control the birth rate; in a word, if you like, to identify the phenomena of birth-control practices in the eighteenth century. We also see the beginnings of a natalist policy, plans to intervene in all phenomena relating to the birth rate. This biopolitics is not concerned with fertility alone. It also deals with the problem of morbidity, but not simply, as had previously been the case, at the level of the famous epidemics, the threat of which had haunted political powers ever since the early Middle Ages (these famous epidemics were temporary disasters that caused multiple deaths, times when everyone seemed to be in danger of imminent death). At the end of the eighteenth century, it was not epidemics that were the issue, but something else—what might broadly be called endemics, or in other words, the form, nature, extension, duration, and intensity of the illnesses prevalent in a population. These were illnesses that were difficult to eradicate and that were not regarded as epidemics that caused more frequent deaths, but as permanent factors which—and that is how they were dealt with—sapped the population's strength, shortened the working week, wasted energy, and cost money, both because they led to a fall in production and because treating them was expensive. In a word, illness as phenomena affecting a population. Death was no longer something that suddenly swooped down on life—as in an epidemic. Death was now something permanent, something that slips into life, perpetually gnaws at it, diminishes it and weakens it.

These are the phenomena that begin to be taken into account at the end of the eighteenth century, and they result in the development of a medicine whose main function will now be public hygiene, with institutions to coordinate medical care, centralize information, and normalize knowledge. And which also takes the form of campaigns to teach hygiene and to medicalize the population. So, problems of reproduction, the birth rate, and the problem of the mortality rate too. Biopolitics' other field of intervention will be a set of phenomena some of which are universal, and some of which are accidental but which can never be completely eradicated, even if they are accidental. They have similar effects in that they incapacitate individuals, put them out of the circuit or neutralize them. This is the problem, and it will become very important in the early nineteenth century (the time of industrialization), of old age, of individuals who, because of their age, fall out of the field of capacity, of activity. The field of biopolitics also includes accidents, infirmities, and various anomalies. And it is in order to deal with these phenomena that this biopolitics will establish not only charitable institutions (which had been in existence for a very long time), but also much more subtle mechanisms that were much more economically rational than an indiscriminate charity which was at once widespread and patchy, and which was essentially under church control. We see the introduction of more subtle, more rational mechanisms: insurance, individual and collective savings, safety measures, and so on.[2]

Biopolitics' last domain is, finally—I am enumerating the main ones, or at least those that appeared in the late eighteenth and early nineteenth centuries; many others would appear later—control over relations between the human race, or human beings insofar as they are a species, insofar as they are living beings, and their environment, the milieu in which they live. This includes the direct effects of the geographical, climatic, or hydrographic environment: the problem, for instance, of swamps, and of epidemics linked to the existence of swamps throughout the first half of the nineteenth century. And also the problem of the environment to the extent that it is not a natural environment, that it has been created by the population and therefore has effects on that population. This is, essentially, the urban problem. I am simply pointing out some of biopolitics' starting points, some of its practices, and the first of its domains of intervention, knowledge, and power: biopolitics will derive its knowledge from, and define its power's field of intervention in terms of, the birth rate, the mortality rate, various biological disabilities, and the effects of the environment.

In all this, a number of things are, I think, important. The first appears to be this: the appearance of a new element—I almost said a new character—of which both the theory of right and disciplinary practice knew nothing. The theory of right basically knew only the individual and society: the contracting individual and the social body constituted by the voluntary or implicit contract among individuals. Disciplines, for their part, dealt with individuals and their bodies in practical terms. What we are dealing with in this new technology of power is not exactly society (or at least not the social body, as defined by the jurists), nor is it the individual-as-body. It is a new body, a multiple body, a body with so many heads that, while they might not be infinite in number, cannot necessarily be counted. Biopolitics deals with the population, with the population as political problem, as a problem that is at once scientific and political, as a biological problem and as power's problem. And I think that biopolitics emerges at this time.

Second, the other important thing—quite aside from the appearance of the "population" element itself—is the nature of the phenomena that are taken into consideration. You can see that they are collective phenomena which have their economic and political effects, and that they become pertinent only at the mass level. They are phenomena that are aleatory and unpredictable when taken in themselves or individually, but which, at the collective level, display constants that are easy, or at least possible, to establish. And they are, finally, phenomena that occur over a period of time, which have to be studied over a certain period of time; they are serial phenomena. The phenomena addressed by biopolitics are, essentially, aleatory events that occur within a population that exists over a period of time.

On this basis—and this is, I think, the third important point—this technology of power, this biopolitics, will introduce mechanisms with a certain number of functions that are very different from the functions of disciplinary mechanisms. The mechanisms introduced by biopolitics include forecasts, statistical estimates, and overall measures. And their purpose is not to modify any given phenomenon as such, or to modify a given individual insofar as he is an individual, but, essentially, to intervene at the level at which these general phenomena are determined, to intervene at the level of their generality. The mortality rate has to be modified or lowered; life expectancy has to be increased; the birth rate has to be stimulated. And most important of all, regulatory mechanisms must be established to establish an equilibrium, maintain an average, establish a sort of homeostasis, and compensate for variations within this general population and its aleatory field. In a word, security mechanisms have to be installed around the random element inherent in a population of living beings so as to optimize a state of life. Like disciplinary mechanisms, these mechanisms are designed to maximize and extract forces, but they work in very different ways. Unlike disciplines, they no longer train individuals by working at the level of the body itself. There is absolutely no question relating to an individual body, in the way that discipline does. It is therefore not a matter of taking the individual at the level of individuality but, on the contrary, of using overall mechanisms and acting in such a way as to achieve overall states of equilibration or regularity; it is, in a word, a matter of taking control of life and the biological processes of man-as-species and of ensuring that they are not disciplined, but regularized.[3]

Beneath that great absolute power, beneath the dramatic and somber absolute power that was the power of sovereignty, and which consisted in the power to take life, we now have the emergence, with this technology of biopower, of this technology of power over "the" population as such, over men insofar as they are living beings. It is continuous, scientific, and it is the power to make live. Sovereignty took life and let live. And now we have the emergence of a power that I would call the power of regularization, and it, in contrast, consists in making live and letting die.

I think that we can see a concrete manifestation of this power in the famous gradual disqualification of death, which sociologists and historians have discussed so often. Everyone knows, thanks in particular to a certain number of recent studies, that the great public ritualization of death gradually began to disappear, or at least to fade away, in the late eighteenth century and that it is still doing so today. So much so that death—which has ceased to be one of those spectacular ceremonies in which individuals, the family, the group, and practically the whole of society took part—has become, in contrast, something to be hidden away. It has become the most private and shameful thing of all (and ultimately, it is now not so much sex as death that is the object of a taboo). Now I think that the reason why death had become something to be hidden away is not that anxiety has somehow been displaced or that repressive mechanisms have been modified. What once (and until the end of the eighteenth century) made death so spectacular and ritualized it so much was the fact that it was a manifestation of a transition from one power to another. Death was the moment when we made the transition from one power—that of the sovereign of this world—to another—that of the sovereign of the next world. We went from one court of law to another, from a civil or public right over life and death, to a right to either eternal life or eternal damnation. A transition from one power to another. Death also meant the transmission of the power of the dying, and that power was transmitted to those who survived him: last words, last recommendations, last wills and testaments, and so on. All these phenomena of power were ritualized.

Now that power is decreasingly the power of the right to take life, and increasingly the right to intervene to make live, or once power begins to intervene mainly at this level in order to improve life by eliminating accidents, the random element, and deficiencies, death becomes, insofar as it is the end of life, the term, the limit, or the end of power too. Death is outside the power relationship. Death is beyond the reach of power, and power has a grip on it only in general, overall, or statistical terms. Power has no control over death, but it can control mortality. And to that extent, it is only natural that death should now be privatized, and should become the most private thing of all. In the right of sovereignty, death was the moment of the most obvious and most spectacular manifestation of the absolute power of the sovereign; death now becomes, in contrast, the moment when the individual escapes all power, falls back on himself and retreats, so to speak, into his own privacy. Power no longer recognizes death. Power literally ignores death.

To symbolize all this, let's take, if you will, the death of Franco, which is after all a very, very interesting event. It is very interesting because of the symbolic values it brings into play, because the man who died had, as you know, exercised the sovereign right of life and death with great savagery, was the bloodiest of all the dictators, wielded an absolute right of life and death for forty years, and at the moment when he himself was dying, he entered this sort of new field of power over life which consists not only in managing life, but in keeping individuals alive after they are dead. And thanks to a power that is not simply scientific prowess, but the actual exercise of the political biopower established in the eighteenth century, we have become so good at keeping people alive that we've succeeded in keeping them alive when, in biological terms, they should have been dead long ago. And so the man who had exercised the absolute power of life and death over hundreds of thousands of people fell under the influence of a power that managed life so well, that took so little heed of death, and he didn't even realize that he was dead and was being kept alive after his death. I think that this minor but joyous event symbolizes the clash between two systems of power: that of sovereignty over death, and that of the regularization of life.

I would now like to go back to comparing the regulatory technology of life and the disciplinary technology of the body I was telling you about a moment ago. From the eighteenth century onward (or at least the end of the eighteenth century onward) we have, then, two technologies of power which were established at different times and which were superimposed. One technique is disciplinary; it centers on the body, produces individualizing effects, and manipulates the body as a source of forces that have to be rendered both useful and docile. And we also have a second technology which is centered not upon the body but upon life: a technology which brings together the mass effects characteristic of a population, which tries to control the series of random events that can occur in a living mass, a technology which tries to predict the probability of those events (by modifying it, if necessary), or at least to compensate for their effects. This is a technology which aims to establish a sort of homeostasis, not by training individuals, but by achieving an overall equilibrium that protects the security of the whole from internal dangers. So, a technology of drilling, as opposed to, as distinct from, a technology of security; a disciplinary technology, as distinct from a reassuring or regulatory technology. Both technologies are obviously technologies of the body, but one is a technology in which the body is individualized as an organism endowed with capacities, while the other is a technology in which bodies are replaced by general biological processes.

One might say this: it is as though power, which used to have sovereignty as its modality or organizing schema, found itself unable to govern the economic and political body of a society that was undergoing both a demographic explosion and industrialization. So much so that far too many things were escaping the old mechanism of the power of sovereignty, both at the top and at the bottom, both at the level of detail and at the mass level. A first adjustment was made to take care of the details. Discipline had meant adjusting power mechanisms to the individual body by using surveillance and training. That, of course, was the easier and more convenient thing to adjust. That is why it was the first to be introduced—as early as the seventeenth century, or the beginning of the eighteenth—at a local level, in intuitive, empirical, and fragmented forms, and in the restricted framework of institutions such as schools, hospitals, barracks, workshops, and so on. And then at the end of the eighteenth century, you have a second adjustment; the mechanisms are adjusted to phenomena of population, to the biological or biosociological processes characteristic of human masses. This adjustment was obviously much more difficult to make because it implied complex systems of coordination and centralization.

So we have two series: the body-organism-discipline-institutions series, and the population-biological processes-regulatory mechanisms-State.* An organic institutional set, or the organo-discipline of the institution, if you like, and, on the other hand, a biological and Statist set, or bioregulation by the State. I am not trying to introduce a complete dichotomy between State and institution, because disciplines in fact always tend to escape the institutional or local framework in which they are trapped. What is more, they easily take on a Statist dimension in apparatuses such as the police, for example, which is both a disciplinary apparatus and a State apparatus (which just goes to prove that discipline is not always institutional). In similar fashion, the great overall regulations that proliferated throughout the nineteenth century are, obviously enough, found at the State level, but they are also found at the sub-State level, in a whole series of sub-State institutions such as medical institutions, welfare funds, insurance, and so on. That is the first remark I would like to make.

What is more, the two sets of mechanisms—one disciplinary and the other regulatory—do not exist at the same level. Which means of course that they are not mutually exclusive and can be articulated with each other. To take one or two examples. Take, if you like, the example of the town or, more specifically, the rationally planned layout of the model town, the artificial town, the town of utopian reality that was not only dreamed of but actually

*The manuscript has "assuring" in place of "regulatory."

built in the nineteenth century. What were working-class housing estates, as they existed in the nineteenth century? One can easily see how the very grid pattern, the very layout, of the estate articulated, in a sort of perpendicular way, the disciplinary mechanisms that controlled the body, or bodies, by localizing familes (one to a house) and individuals (one to a room). The layout, the fact that individuals were made visible, and the normalization of behavior meant that a sort of spontaneous policing or control was carried out by the spatial layout of the town itself. It is easy to identify a whole series of disciplinary mechanisms in the working-class estate. And then you have a whole series of mechanisms which are, by contrast, regulatory mechanisms, which apply to the population as such and which allow, which encourage patterns of saving related to housing, to the renting of accommodations and, in some cases, their purchase. Health-insurance systems, old-age pensions; rules on hygiene that guarantee the optimal longevity of the population; the pressures that the very organization of the town brings to bear on sexuality and therefore procreation; child care, education, et cetera, so you have [certain] disciplinary measures and [certain] regulatory mechanisms.

Take the very different—though it is not altogether that different—take a different axis, something like sexuality. Basically, why did sexuality become a field of vital strategic importance in the nineteenth century? I think that sexuality was important for a whole host of reasons, and for these reasons in particular. On the one hand, sexuality, being an eminently corporeal mode of behavior, is a matter for individualizing disciplinary controls that take the form of permanent surveillance (and the famous controls that were, from the late eighteenth to the twentieth century, placed both at home and at school on children who masturbated represent precisely this aspect of the disciplinary control of sexuality). But because it also has procreative effects, sexuality is also inscribed, takes effect, in broad biological processes that concern not the bodies of individuals but the element, the multiple unity of the population. Sexuality exists at the point where body and population meet. And so it is a matter for discipline, but also a matter for regularization.

It is, I think, the privileged position it occupies between organism and population, between the body and general phenomena, that explains the extreme emphasis placed upon sexuality in the nineteenth century. Hence too the medical idea that when it is undisciplined and irregular, sexuality also has effects at two levels. At the level of the body, of the undisciplined body that is immediately sanctioned by all the individual diseases that the sexual debauchee brings down upon himself. A child who masturbates too much will be a lifelong invalid: disciplinary sanction at the level of the body. But at the same time, debauched, perverted sexuality has effects at the level of the population, as anyone who has been sexually debauched is assumed to have a heredity. Their descendants also will be affected for generations, unto the seventh generation and unto the seventh of the seventh and so on. This is the theory of degeneracy:[4] given that it is the source of individual diseases and that it is the nucleus of degeneracy, sexuality represents the precise point where the disciplinary and the regulatory, the body and the population, are articulated. Given these conditions, you can understand how and why a technical knowledge such as medicine, or rather the combination of medicine and hygiene, is in the nineteenth century, if not the most important element, an element of considerable importance because of the link it establishes between scientific knowledge of both biological and organic processes (or in other words, the population and the body), and because, at the same time, medicine becomes a political intervention-technique with specific power-effects. Medicine is a power-knowledge that can be applied to both the body and the population, both the organism and biological processes, and it will therefore have both disciplinary effects and regulatory effects.

In more general terms still, we can say that there is one element that will circulate between the disciplinary and the regulatory, which will also be applied to body and population alike, which will make it possible to control both the disciplinary order of the body and the aleatory events that occur in the biological multiplicity. The element that circulates between the two is the norm. The norm is something that can be applied to both a body one wishes to discipline and a population one wishes to regularize. The normalizing society is therefore not, under these conditions, a sort of generalized disciplinary society whose disciplinary institutions have swarmed and finally taken over everything—that, I think, is no more than a first and inadequate interpretation of a normalizing society. The normalizing society is a society in which the norm of discipline and the norm of regulation intersect along an orthogonal articulation. To say that power took possession of life in the nineteenth century, or to say that power at least takes life under its care in the nineteenth century, is to say that it has, thanks to the play of technologies of discipline on the one hand and technologies of regulation on the other, succeeded in covering the whole surface that lies between the organic and the biological, between body and population.

We are, then, in a power that has taken control of both the body and life or that has, if you like, taken control of life in general—with the body as one pole and the population as the other. We can therefore immediately identify the paradoxes that appear at the points where the exercise of this biopower reaches its limits. The paradoxes become apparent if we look, on the one hand, at atomic power, which is not simply the power to kill, in accordance with the rights that are granted to any sovereign, millions and hundreds of millions of people (after all, that is traditional). The workings of contemporary political power are such that atomic power represents a paradox that is difficult, if not impossible, to get around. The power to manufacture and use the atom bomb represents the deployment of a sovereign power that kills, but it is also the power to kill life itself. So the power that is being exercised in this atomic power is exercised in such a way that it is capable of suppressing life itself. And, therefore, to suppress itself insofar as it is the power that guarantees life. Either it is sovereign and uses the atom bomb, and therefore cannot be power, bio-power, or the power to guarantee life, as it has been ever since the nineteenth century. Or, at the opposite extreme, you no longer have a sovereign right that is in excess of biopower, but a biopower that is in excess of sovereign right. This excess of biopower appears when it becomes technologically and politically possible for man not only to manage life but to make it proliferate, to create living matter, to build the monster, and, ultimately, to build viruses that cannot be controlled and that are universally destructive. This formidable extension of biopower, unlike what I was just saying about atomic power, will put it beyond all human sovereignty.

You must excuse this long digression into biopower, but I think that it does provide us with a basic argument that will allow us to get back to the problem I was trying to raise.

If it is true that the power of sovereignty is increasingly on the retreat and that disciplinary or regulatory disciplinary power is on the advance, how will the power to kill and the function of murder operate in this technology of power, which takes life as both its object and its objective? How can a power such as this kill, if it is true that its basic function is to improve life, to prolong its duration, to improve its chances, to avoid accidents, and to compensate for failings? How, under these conditions, is it possible for a political power to kill, to call for deaths, to demand deaths, to give the order to kill, and to expose not only its enemies but its own citizens to the risk of death? Given that this power's objective is essentially to make live, how can it let die? How can the power of death, the function of death, be exercised in a political system centered upon biopower?

It is, I think, at this point that racism intervenes. I am certainly not saying that racism was invented at this time. It had already been in existence for a very long time. But I think it functioned elsewhere. It is indeed the emergence of this biopower that inscribes it in the mechanisms of the State. It is at this moment that racism is inscribed as the basic mechanism of power, as it is exercised in modern States. As a result, the modern State can scarcely function without becoming involved with racism at some point, within certain limits and subject to certain conditions.

What in fact is racism? It is primarily a way of introducing a break into the domain of life that is under power's control: the break between what must live and what must die. The appearance within the biological continuum of the human race of races, the distinction among races, the hierarchy of races, the fact that certain races are described as good and that others, in contrast, are described as inferior: all this is a way of fragmenting the field of the biological that power controls. It is a way of separating out the groups that exist within a population. It is, in short, a way of establishing a biological-type caesura within a population that appears to be a biological domain. This will allow power to treat that population as a mixture of races, or to be more accurate, to treat the species, to subdivide the species it controls, into the subspecies known, precisely, as races. That is the first function of racism: to fragment, to create caesuras within the biological continuum addressed by biopower.

Racism also has a second function. Its role is, if you like, to allow the establishment of a positive relation of this type: "The more you kill, the more deaths you will cause" or "The very fact that you let more die will allow you to live more." I would say that this relation ("If you want to live, you must take lives, you must be able to kill") was not invented by either racism or the modern State. It is the relationship of war: "In order to live, you must destroy your enemies." But racism does make the relationship of war—"If you want to live, the other must die"—function in a way that is completely new and that is quite compatible with the exercise of biopower. On the one hand, racism makes it possible to establish a relationship between my life and the death of the other that is not a military or warlike relationship of confrontation, but a biological-type relationship: "The more inferior species die out, the more abnormal individuals are eliminated, the fewer degenerates there will be in the species as a whole, and the more I—as species rather than individual—can live, the stronger I will be, the more vigorous I will be. I will be able to proliferate." The fact that the other dies does not mean simply that I live in the sense that his death guarantees my safety; the death of the other, the death of the bad race, of the inferior race (or the degenerate, or the abnormal) is something that will make life in general healthier: healthier and purer.

This is not, then, a military, warlike, or political relationship, but a biological relationship. And the reason this mechanism can come into play is that the enemies who have to be done away with are not adversaries in the political sense of the term; they are threats, either external or internal, to the population and for the population. In the biopower system, in other words, killing or the imperative to kill is acceptable only if it results not in a victory over political adversaries, but in the elimination of the biological threat to and the improvement of the species or race. There is a direct connection between the two. In a normalizing society, race or racism is the precondition that makes killing acceptable. When you have a normalizing society, you have a power which is, at least superficially, in the first instance, or in the first line a biopower, and racism is the indispensable precondition that allows someone to be killed, that allows others to be killed. Once the State functions in the biopower mode, racism alone can justify the murderous function of the State.

So you can understand the importance—I almost said the vital importance—of racism to the exercise of such a power: it is the precondition for exercising the right to kill. If the power of normalization wished to exercise the old sovereign right to kill, it must become racist. And if, conversely, a power of sovereignty, or in other words, a power that has the right of life and death, wishes to work with the instruments, mechanisms, and technology of normalization, it too must become racist. When I say "killing," I obviously do not mean simply murder as such, but also every form of indirect murder: the fact of exposing someone to death, increasing the risk of death for some people, or, quite simply, political death, expulsion, rejection, and so on.

I think that we are now in a position to understand a number of things. We can understand, first of all, the link that was quickly—I almost said immediately—established between nineteenth-century biological theory and the discourse of power. Basically, evolutionism, understood in the broad sense—or in other words, not so much Darwin's theory itself as a set, a bundle, of notions (such as: the hierarchy of species that grow from a common evolutionary tree, the struggle for existence among species, the selection that eliminates the less fit)—naturally became within a few years during the nineteenth century not simply a way of transcribing a political discourse into biological terms, and not simply a way of dressing up a political discourse in scientific clothing, but a real way of thinking about the relations between colonization, the necessity for wars, criminality, the phenomena of madness and mental illness, the history of societies with their different classes, and so on. Whenever, in other words, there was a confrontation, a killing or the risk of death, the nineteenth century was quite literally obliged to think about them in the form of evolutionism.

And we can also understand why racism should have developed in modern societies that function in the biopower mode; we can understand why racism broke out at a number of privileged moments, and why they were precisely the moments when the right to take life was imperative. Racism first develops with colonization, or in other words, with colonizing genocide. If you are functioning in the biopower mode, how can you justify the need to kill people, to kill populations, and to kill civilizations? By using the themes of evolutionism, by appealing to a racism.

War. How can one not only wage war on one's adversaries but also expose one's own citizens to war, and let them be killed by the million (and this is precisely what has been going on since the nineteenth century, or since the second half of the nineteenth century), except by activating the theme of racism? From this point onward, war is about two things: it is not simply a matter of destroying a political adversary, but of destroying the enemy race, of destroying that [sort] of biological threat that those people over there represent to our race. In one sense, this is of course no more than a biological extrapolation from the theme of the political enemy. But there is more to it than that. In the nineteenth century—and this is completely new—war will be seen not only as a way of improving one's own race by eliminating the enemy race (in accordance with the themes of natural selection and the struggle for existence), but also as a way of regenerating one's own race. As more and more of our number die, the race to which we belong will become all the purer.

At the end of the nineteenth century, we have then a new racism modeled on war. It was, I think, required because a biopower that wished to wage war had to articulate the will to destroy the adversary with the risk that it might kill those whose lives it had, by definition, to protect, manage, and multiply. The same could be said of criminality. Once the mechanism of biopower was called upon to make it possible to execute or isolate criminals, criminality was conceptualized in racist terms. The same applies to madness, and the same applies to various abnormalities.

I think that, broadly speaking, racism justifies the death-function in the economy of biopower by appealing to the principle that the death of others makes one biologically stronger insofar as one is a member of a race or a population, insofar as one is an element in a unitary living plurality. You can see that, here, we are far removed from the ordinary racism that takes the traditional form of mutual contempt or hatred between races. We are also far removed from the racism that can be seen as a sort of ideological operation that allows States, or a class, to displace the hostility that is directed toward [them], or which is tormenting the social body, onto a mythical adversary. I think that this is something much deeper than an old tradition, much deeper than a new ideology, that it is something else. The specificity of modern racism, or what gives it its specificity, is not bound up with mentalities, ideologies, or the lies of power. It is bound up with the technique of power, with the technology of power. It is bound up with this, and that takes us as far away as possible from the race war and the intelligibility of history. We are dealing with a mechanism that allows biopower to work. So racism is bound up with the workings of a State that is obliged to use race, the elimination of races and the purification of the race, to exercise its sovereign power. The juxtaposition of—or the way biopower functions through—the old sovereign power of life and death implies the workings, the introduction and activation, of racism. And it is, I think, here that we find the actual roots of racism.

So you can understand how and why, given these conditions, the most murderous States are also, of necessity, the most racist. Here, of course, we have to take the example of Nazism. After all, Nazism was in fact the paroxysmal development of the new power mechanisms that had been established since the eighteenth century. Of course, no State could have more disciplinary power than the Nazi regime. Nor was there any other State in which the biological was so tightly, so insistently, regulated. Disciplinary power and biopower: all this permeated, underpinned, Nazi society (control over the biological, of procreation and of heredity; control over illness and accidents too). No society could be more disciplinary or more concerned with providing insurance than that established, or at least planned, by the Nazis. Controlling the random element inherent in biological processes was one of the regime's immediate objectives.

But this society in which insurance and reassurance were universal, this universally disciplinary and regulatory society, was also a society which unleashed murderous power, or in other words, the old sovereign right to take life. This power to kill, which ran through the entire social body of Nazi society, was first manifested when the power to take life, the power of life and death, was granted not only to the State but to a whole series of individuals, to a considerable number of people (such as the SA, the SS, and so on). Ultimately, everyone in the Nazi State had the power of life and death over his or her neighbors, if only because of the practice of informing, which effectively meant doing away with the people next door, or having them done away with.

So murderous power and sovereign power are unleashed throughout the entire social body. They were also unleashed by the fact that war was explicitly defined as a political objective—and not simply as a basic political objective or as a means, but as a sort of ultimate and decisive phase in all political processes—politics had to lead to war, and war had to be the final decisive phase that would complete everything. The objective of the Nazi regime was therefore not really the destruction of other races. The destruction of other races was one aspect of the project, the other being to expose its own race to the absolute and universal threat of death. Risking one's life, being exposed to total destruction, was one of the principles inscribed in the basic duties of the obedient Nazi, and it was one of the essential objectives of Nazism's policies. It had to reach the point at which the entire population was exposed to death. Exposing the entire population to universal death was the only way it could truly constitute itself as a superior race and bring about its definitive regeneration once other races had been either exterminated or enslaved forever.

We have, then, in Nazi society something that is really quite extraordinary: this is a society which has generalized biopower in an absolute sense, but which has also generalized the sovereign right to kill. The two mechanisms—the classic, archaic mechanism that gave the State the right of life and death over its citizens, and the new mechanism organized around discipline and regulation, or in other words, the new mechanism of biopower—coincide exactly. We can therefore say this: the Nazi State makes the field of the life it manages, protects, guarantees, and cultivates in biological terms absolutely coextensive with the sovereign right to kill anyone, meaning not only other people, but also its own people. There was, in Nazism, a coincidence between a generalized biopower and a dictatorship that was at once absolute and retransmitted throughout the entire social body by this fantastic extension of the right to kill and of exposure to death. We have an absolutely racist State, an absolutely murderous State, and an absolutely suicidal State. A racist State, a murderous State, and a suicidal State. The three were necessarily superimposed, and the result was of course both the "final solution" (or the attempt to eliminate, by eliminating the Jews, all the other races of which the Jews were both the symbol and the manifestation) of the years 1942–1943, and then Telegram 71, in which, in April 1945, Hitler gave the order to destroy the German people's own living conditions.[5]

The final solution for the other races, and the absolute suicide of the [German] race. That is where this mechanism inscribed in the workings of the modern State leads. Of course, Nazism alone took the play between the sovereign right to kill and the mechanisms of biopower to this paroxysmal point. But this play is in fact inscribed in the workings of all States. In all modern States, in all capitalist States? Perhaps not. But I do think that—but this would be a whole new argument—the socialist State, socialism, is as marked by racism as the workings of the modern State, of the capitalist State. In addition to the State racism that developed in the conditions I have been telling you about, a social-racism also came into being, and it did not wait for the formation of socialist States before making its appearance. Socialism was a racism from the outset, even in the nineteenth century. No matter whether it is Fourier at the beginning of the century[6] or the anarchists at the end of it, you will always find a racist component in socialism.

I find this very difficult to talk about. To speak in such terms is to make enormous claims. To prove the point would really take a whole series of lectures (and I would like to do them). But at least let me just say this: in general terms, it seems to me—and here, I am speculating somewhat—that to the extent that it does not, in the first instance, raise the economic or juridical problems of types of property ownership or modes of production—or to the extent that the problem of the mechanics of power or the mechanisms of power is not posed or analyzed—[socialism therefore] inevitably reaffected or reinvested the very power-mechanisms constituted by the capitalist State or the industrial State. One thing at least is certain: Socialism has made no critique of the theme of biopower, which developed at the end of the eighteenth century and throughout the nineteenth; it has in fact taken it up, developed, reimplanted, and modified it in certain respects, but it has certainly not reexamined its basis or its modes of working. Ultimately, the idea that the essential function of society or the State, or whatever it is that must replace the State, is to take control of life, to manage it, to compensate for its aleatory nature, to explore and reduce biological accidents and possibilities...it seems to me that socialism takes this over wholesale. And the result is that we immediately find ourselves in a socialist State which must exercise the right to kill or the right to eliminate, or the right to disqualify. And so, quite naturally, we find that racism—not a truly ethnic racism, but racism of the evolutionist kind, biological racism—is fully operational in the way socialist States (of the Soviet Union type) deal with the mentally ill, criminals, political adversaries, and so on. So much for the State.

The other thing I find interesting, and which has caused me problems for a long time, is that, once again, it is not simply at the level of the socialist State that we find this racism at work; we also find it in the various forms of socialist analysis, or of the socialist project throughout the nineteenth century, and it seems to me that it relates to this: whenever a socialism insists, basically, that the transformation of economic conditions is the precondition for the transformation, for the transition from the capitalist State to the socialist State (or in other words, whenever it tries to explain the transformation in terms of economic processes), it does not need, or at least not in the immediate, racism. Whenever, on the other hand, socialism has been forced to stress the problem of struggle, the struggle against the enemy, of the elimination of the enemy within capitalist society itself, and when, therefore, it has had to think about the physical confrontation with the class enemy in capitalist society, racism does raise its head, because it is the only way in which socialist thought, which is after all very much bound up with the themes of biopower, can rationalize the murder of its enemies. When it is simply a matter of eliminating the adversary in economic terms, or of taking away his privileges, there is no need for racism. Once it is a matter of coming to terms with the thought of a one-to-one encounter with the adversary, and with the need to fight him physically, to risk one's own life and to try to kill him, there is a need for racism.

Whenever you have these socialisms, these forms of socialism or these moments of socialism that stress the problem of the struggle, you therefore have racism. The most racist forms of socialism were, therefore, Blanquism of course, and then the Commune, and then anarchism—much more so than social democracy, much more so than the Second International, and much more so than Marxism itself. Socialist racism was liquidated in Europe only at the end of the nineteenth century, and only by the domination of social democracy (and, it has to be said, by the reformism that was bound up with it) on the one hand, and by a number of processes such as the Dreyfus affair in France on the other. Until the Dreyfus affair, all socialists, or at least the vast majority of socialists, were basically racists. And I think that they were racists to the extent that (and I will finish here) they did not reevaluate—or, if you like, accepted as self-evident—the mechanisms of biopower that the development of society and State had been establishing since the eighteenth century. How can one both make a biopower function and exercise the rights of war, the rights of murder and the function of death, without becoming racist? That was the problem, and that, I think, is still the problem.

Notes

1. On the question of disciplinary technology, see *Surveiller et punir*.
2. On all these questions, see *Cours au Collège de France, année 1978–1979: Le Pouvoir psychiatrique*, forthcoming.
3. Foucault comes back to all these disciplines, especially in *Cours au Collège de France 1977–1978: Sécurité, territoire et population* and *1978–1979: Naissance de la biopolitique*, forthcoming.
4. Foucault refers here to the theory elaborated in mid-nineteenth-century France by certain alienists and in particular by B.-A. Morel (*Traité de dégénérescences physiques, intellectuelles et morales de l'espèce humaine* [Paris, 1857], *Traités des maladies mentales* [Paris, 1870]); V. Magnan (*Leçons cliniques sur les maladies mentales* [Paris, 1893]); and M. Legrain and V. Magnan (*Les Dégénérés, état mental et syndrômes épisodiques* [Paris, 1895]). This theory of degeneracy, which is based upon the principle that a so-called hereditary taint can be transmitted, was the kernel of medical knowledge about madness and abnormality in the second half of the nineteenth century. It was quickly adopted by forensic medicine, and it had a considerable effect on eugenicist doctrines and practices, and was not without its influence on a whole literature, a whole criminology, and a whole anthropology.
5. As early as 19 March, Hitler had drawn up plans to destroy Germany's logistic infrastructure and industrial plant. These dispositions were announced in the decrees of 30 March and 7 April. On these decrees, see A. Speer, *Erinnerungen* (Berlin: Proplyäen-Verlag, 1969) (French translation: *Au Coeur du Troisième Reich* [Paris; Fayard, 1971]; English translation by Richard and Clara Winton: *Inside the Third Reich: Memoirs* [London: Weidenfeld and Nicolson, 1970]). Foucault had definitely read J. Fest's book *Hitler* (Frankfurt am Main, Berlin, and Vienna: Verlag Ulstein, 1973) (French translation: *Hitler* [Paris: Gallimard, 1973]; English translation by Richard and Clara Winton, *Hitler* [London: Weidenfeld and Nicolson, 1974]).
6. In this connection, see in particular Charles Fourier, *Théorie des quatre mouvements et des destinées générales* (Leipzig and Lyon, 1808); *Le Nouveau Monde industriel et sociétaire* (Paris, 1829); *La Fausse Industrie morcelée, répugnante, mensongère*, 2 vols. (Paris, 1836).

CHAPTER 3

THE PERPLEXITIES OF
THE RIGHTS OF MAN

Hannah Arendt

The Declaration of the Rights of Man at the end of the eighteenth century was a turning point in history. It meant nothing more nor less than that from then on Man, and not God's command or the customs of history, should be the source of Law. Independent of the privileges which history had bestowed upon certain strata of society or certain nations, the declaration indicated man's emancipation from all tutelage and announced that he had now come of age.

Beyond this, there was another implication of which the framers of the declaration were only half aware. The proclamation of human rights was also meant to be a much-needed protection in the new era where individuals were no longer secure in the estates to which they were born or sure of their equality before God as Christians. In other words, in the new secularized and emancipated society, men were no longer sure of these social and human rights which until then had been outside the political order and guaranteed not by government and constitution, but by social, spiritual, and religious forces. Therefore throughout the nineteenth century, the consensus of opinion was that human rights had to be invoked whenever individuals needed protection against the new sovereignty of the state and the new arbitrariness of society.

Since the Rights of Man were proclaimed to be "inalienable," irreducible to and undeducible from other rights or laws, no authority was invoked for their establishment; Man himself was their source as well as their ultimate goal. No special law, moreover, was deemed necessary to protect them because all laws were supposed to rest upon them. Man appeared as the only sovereign in matters of law as the people was proclaimed the only sovereign in matters of government. The people's sovereignty (different from that of the prince) was not proclaimed by the grace of God but in the name of Man, so that it seemed only natural that the "inalienable" rights of man would find their guarantee and become an inalienable part of the right of the people to sovereign self-government.

In other words, man had hardly appeared as a completely emancipated, completely isolated being who carried his dignity within himself without reference to some larger encompassing order, when he disappeared again into a member of a people. From the beginning the paradox involved in the declaration of inalienable human rights was that it reckoned with an "abstract" human being who seemed to exist nowhere, for even savages lived in some kind of a social order. If a tribal or other "backward" community did not enjoy human rights, it was obviously because as a whole it had not yet reached that stage of civilization, the stage of popular and national sovereignty, but was oppressed by foreign or native despots. The whole question of human rights, therefore, was quickly and inextricably blended with the question of national emancipation; only the emancipated sovereignty of the people, of one's own people, seemed to be able to insure them. As mankind, since the French Revolution, was conceived in the image of a family of nations, it gradually became self-evident that the people, and not the individual, was the image of man.

The full implication of this identification of the rights of man with the rights of peoples in the European nation-state system came to light only when a growing number of people and peoples suddenly appeared whose elementary rights were as little safeguarded by the ordinary functioning of nation-states in the middle of Europe as they would have been in the heart of Africa. The Rights of Man, after all, had been defined as "inalienable" because they were supposed to be independent of all governments; but it turned out that the moment human beings lacked their own government and had to fall back upon their minimum rights, no authority was left to protect them and no institution was willing to guarantee them. Or when, as in the case of the minorities, an international body arrogated to itself a nongovernmental authority, its failure was apparent even before its measures were fully realized; not only were the governments more or less openly opposed to this encroachment on their sovereignty, but the concerned nationalities themselves did not recognize a nonnational guarantee, mistrusted everything which was not clear-cut support of their "national" (as opposed to their mere "linguistic, religious, and ethnic") rights, and preferred either, like the Germans or Hungarians, to turn to the protection of the "national" mother country, or, like the Jews, to some kind of interterritorial solidarity.[1]

The stateless people were as convinced as the minorities that loss of national rights was identical with loss of human rights, that the former inevitably entailed the latter. The more they were excluded from right in any form, the more they tended to look for a reintegration into a national, into their own national community. The Russian refugees were only the first to insist on their nationality and to defend themselves furiously against attempts to lump them together with other stateless people. Since then, not a single group of refugees or Displaced Persons has failed to develop a fierce, violent group consciousness and to clamor for rights as—and only as—Poles or Jews or Germans, etc.

Even worse was that all societies formed for the protection of the Rights of Man, all attempts to arrive at a new bill of human rights were sponsored by marginal figures—by a few international jurists without political experience or professional philanthropists supported by the uncertain sentiments of professional idealists. The groups they formed, the declarations they issued, showed an uncanny similarity in language and composition to that of societies for the prevention of cruelty to animals. No statesman, no political figure of any importance could possibly take them seriously; and none of the liberal or radical parties in Europe thought it necessary to incorporate into their program a new declaration of human rights. Neither before nor after the second World War have the victims themselves ever invoked these fundamental rights, which were so evidently denied them, in their many attempts to find a way out of the barbed-wire labyrinth into which events had driven them. On the contrary, the victims shared the disdain and indifference of the powers that be for any attempt of the marginal societies to enforce human rights in any elementary or general sense.

The failure of all responsible persons to meet the calamity of an ever-growing body of people forced to live outside the scope of all tangible law with the proclamation of a new bill of rights was certainly not due to ill will. Never before had the Rights of Man, solemnly proclaimed by the French and the American revolutions as the new fundament for civilized societies, been a practical political issue. During the nineteenth century, these rights had been invoked in a rather perfunctory way, to defend individuals against the increasing power of the state and to mitigate the new social insecurity caused by the industrial revolution. Then the meaning of human rights acquired a new connotation: they became the standard slogan of the protectors of the under-privileged, a kind of additional law, a right of exception necessary for those who had nothing better to fall back upon.

The reason why the concept of human rights was treated as a sort of step-child by nineteenth-century political thought and why no liberal or radical party in the twentieth century, even when an urgent need for enforcement of human rights arose, saw fit to include them in its program seems obvious: civil rights—that is the varying rights of citizens in different countries—were supposed to embody and spell out in the form of tangible laws the eternal Rights of Man, which by themselves were supposed to be independent of citizenship and nationality. All human beings were citizens of some kind of political community; if the laws of their country did not live up to the demands of the Rights of Man, they were expected to change them, by legislation in democratic countries or through revolutionary action in despotisms.

The Rights of Man, supposedly inalienable, proved to be unenforceable—even in countries whose constitutions were based upon them—whenever people appeared who were no longer citizens of any sovereign state. To this fact, disturbing enough in itself, one must add the confusion created by the many recent attempts to frame a new bill of human rights, which have demonstrated that no one seems able to define with any assurance what these general human rights, as distinguished from the rights of citizens, really are. Although everyone seems to agree that the plight of these people consists precisely in their loss of the Rights of Man, no one seems to know which rights they lost when they lost these human rights.

The first loss which the rightless suffered was the loss of their homes, and this meant the loss of the entire social texture into which they were born and in which they established for themselves a distinct place in the world. This calamity is far from unprecedented; in the long memory of history, forced migrations of individuals or whole groups of people for political or economic reasons look like everyday occurrences. What is unprecedented is not the loss of a home but the impossibility of finding a new one. Suddenly, there was no place on earth where migrants could go without the severest restrictions, no country where they would be assimilated, no territory where they could found a new community of their own. This, moreover, had next to nothing to do with any material problem of overpopulation; it was a problem not of space but of political organization. Nobody had been aware that mankind, for so long a time considered under the image of a family of nations, had reached the stage where whoever was thrown out of one of these tightly organized closed communities found himself thrown out of the family of nations altogether.[2]

The second loss which the rightless suffered was the loss of government protection, and this did not imply just the loss of legal status in their own, but in all countries. Treaties of reciprocity and international agreements have woven a web around the earth that makes it possible for the citizen of every country to take his legal status with him no matter where he goes (so that, for instance, a German citizen under the Nazi regime might not be able to enter a mixed marriage abroad because of the Nuremberg laws). Yet, whoever is no longer caught in it finds himself out of legality altogether (thus during the last war stateless people were invariably in a worse position than enemy aliens who were still indirectly protected by their governments through international agreements).

By itself the loss of government protection is no more unprecedented than the loss of a home. Civilized countries did offer the right of asylum to those who, for political reasons, had been persecuted by their governments, and this practice, though never officially incorporated into any constitution, has functioned well enough throughout the nineteenth and even in our century. The trouble arose when it appeared that the new categories of persecuted were far too numerous to be handled by an unofficial practice destined for exceptional cases. Moreover, the majority could hardly qualify for the right of asylum, which implicitly presupposed political or religious convictions which were not outlawed in the country of refuge. The new refugees were persecuted not because of what they had done or thought, but because of what they unchangeably were—born into the wrong kind of race or the wrong kind of class or drafted by the wrong kind of government (as in the case of the Spanish Republican Army).[3]

The more the number of rightless people increased, the greater became the temptation to pay less attention to the deeds of the persecuting governments than to the status of the persecuted. And the first glaring fact was that these people, though persecuted under some political pretext, were no longer, as the persecuted had been throughout history, a liability and an image of shame for the persecutors; that they were not considered and hardly pretended to be active enemies (the few thousand Soviet citizens who voluntarily left Soviet Russia after the second World War and found asylum in democratic countries did more damage to the prestige of the Soviet Union than millions of refugees in the twenties who belonged to the wrong class), but that they were and appeared to be nothing but human beings whose very innocence— from every point of view, and especially that of the persecuting government— was their greatest misfortune. Innocence, in the sense of complete lack of responsibility, was the mark of their rightlessness as it was the seal of their loss of political status.

Only in appearance therefore do the needs for a reinforcement of human rights touch upon the fate of the authentic political refugee. Political refugees, of necessity few in number, still enjoy the right to asylum in many countries, and this right acts, in an informal way, as a genuine substitute for national law.

One of the surprising aspects of our experience with stateless people who benefit legally from committing a crime has been the fact that it seems to be easier to deprive a completely innocent person of legality than someone who has committed an offense. Anatole France's famous quip, "If I am accused of stealing the towers of Notre Dame, I can only flee the country," has assumed a horrible reality. Jurists are so used to thinking of law in terms of punishment, which indeed always deprives us of certain rights, that they may find it even more difficult than the layman to recognize that the deprivation of legality, *i.e.*, of *all* rights, no longer has a connection with specific crimes.

This situation illustrates the many perplexities inherent in the concept of human rights. No matter how they have once been defined (life, liberty, and the pursuit of happiness, according to the American formula, or as equality before the law, liberty, protection of property, and national sovereignty, according to the French); no matter how one may attempt to improve an ambiguous formulation like the pursuit of happiness, or an antiquated one like unqualified right to property; the real situation of those whom the twentieth century has driven outside the pale of the law shows that these are rights of citizens whose loss does not entail absolute rightlessness. The soldier during the war is deprived of his right to life, the criminal of his right to freedom, all citizens during an emergency of their right to the pursuit of happiness, but nobody would ever claim that in any of these instances a loss of human rights has taken place. These rights, on the other hand, can be granted (though hardly enjoyed) even under conditions of fundamental rightlessness.

The calamity of the rightless is not that they are deprived of life, liberty, and the pursuit of happiness, or of equality before the law and freedom of opinion—formulas which were designed to solve problems *within* given communities—but that they no longer belong to any community whatsoever.

Their plight is not that they are not equal before the law, but that no law exists for them; not that they are oppressed but that nobody wants even to oppress them. Only in the last stage of a rather lengthy process is their right to live threatened; only if they remain perfectly "superfluous," if nobody can be found to "claim" them, may their lives be in danger. Even the Nazis started their extermination of Jews by first depriving them of all legal status (the status of second-class citizenship) and cutting them off from the world of the living by herding them into ghettos and concentration camps; and before they set the gas chambers into motion they had carefully tested the ground and found out to their satisfaction that no country would claim these people. The point is that a condition of complete rightlessness was created before the right to live was challenged.

The same is true even to an ironical extent with regard to the right of freedom which is sometimes considered to be the very essence of human rights. There is no question that those outside the pale of the law may have more freedom of movement than a lawfully imprisoned criminal or that they enjoy more freedom of opinion in the internment camps of democratic countries than they would in any ordinary despotism, not to mention in a totalitarian country.[4] But neither physical safety—being fed by some state or private welfare agency—nor freedom of opinion changes in the least their fundamental situation of rightlessness. The prolongation of their lives is due to charity and not to right, for no law exists which could force the nations to feed them; their freedom of movement, if they have it at all, gives them no right to residence which even the jailed criminal enjoys as a matter of course; and their freedom of opinion is a fool's freedom, for nothing they think matters anyhow.

These last points are crucial. The fundamental deprivation of human rights is manifested first and above all in the deprivation of a place in the world which makes opinions significant and actions effective. Something much more fundamental than freedom and justice, which are rights of citizens, is at stake when belonging to the community into which one is born is no longer a matter of course and not belonging no longer a matter of choice, or when one is placed in a situation where, unless he commits a crime, his treatment by others does not depend on what he does or does not do. This extremity, and nothing else, is the situation of people deprived of human rights. They are deprived, not of the right to freedom, but of the right to action; not of the right to think whatever they please, but of the right to opinion. Privileges in some cases, injustices in most, blessings and doom are meted out to them according to accident and without any relation whatsoever to what they do, did, or may do.

We became aware of the existence of a right to have rights (and that means to live in a framework where one is judged by one's actions and opinions) and a right to belong to some kind of organized community, only when millions of people emerged who had lost and could not regain these rights because of the new global political situation. The trouble is that this calamity arose not from any lack of civilization, backwardness, or mere tyranny, but, on the contrary, that it could not be repaired, because there was no longer any "uncivilized" spot on earth, because whether we like it or not we have really started to live in One World. Only with a completely organized humanity could the loss of home and political status become identical with expulsion from humanity altogether.

Before this, what we must call a "human right" today would have been thought of as a general characteristic of the human condition which no tyrant could take away. Its loss entails the loss of the relevance of speech (and man, since Aristotle, has been defined as a being commanding the power of speech and thought), and the loss of all human relationship (and man, again since Aristotle, has been thought of as the "political animal," that is one who by definition lives in a community), the loss, in other words, of some of the most essential characteristics of human life. This was to a certain extent the plight of slaves, whom Aristotle therefore did not count among human beings. Slavery's fundamental offense against human rights was not that it took liberty away (which can happen in many other situations), but that it excluded a certain category of people even from the possibility of fighting for freedom—a fight possible under tyranny, and even under the desperate conditions of modern terror (but not under any conditions of concentration-camp life). Slavery's crime against humanity did not begin when one people defeated and enslaved its enemies (though of course this was bad enough), but when slavery became an institution in which some men were "born" free and others slave, when it was forgotten that it was man who had deprived his fellow-men of freedom, and when the sanction for the crime was attributed to nature. Yet in the light of recent events it is possible to say that even slaves still belonged to some sort of human community; their labor was needed, used, and exploited, and this kept them within the pale of humanity. To be a slave was after all to have a distinctive character, a place in society—more than the abstract nakedness of being human and nothing but human. Not the loss of specific rights, then, but the loss of a community willing and able to guarantee any rights whatsoever, has been the calamity which has befallen ever-increasing numbers of people. Man, it turns out, can lose all so-called Rights of Man without losing his essential quality as man, his human dignity. Only the loss of a polity itself expels him from humanity.

The right that corresponds to this loss and that was never even mentioned among the human rights cannot be expressed in the categories of the eighteenth century because they presume that rights spring immediately from the "nature" of man—whereby it makes relatively little difference whether this nature is visualized in terms of the natural law or in terms of a being created in the image of God, whether it concerns "natural" rights or divine commands. The decisive factor is that these rights and the human dignity they bestow should remain valid and real even if only a single human being existed on earth; they are independent of human plurality and should remain valid even if a human being is expelled from the human community.

When the Rights of Man were proclaimed for the first time, they were regarded as being independent of history and the privileges which history had accorded certain strata of society. The new independence constituted the newly discovered dignity of man. From the beginning, this new dignity was of a rather ambiguous nature. Historical rights were replaced by natural rights, "nature" took the place of history, and it was tacitly assumed that nature was less alien than history to the essence of man. The very language of the Declaration of Independence as well as of the *Déclaration des Droits de l'Homme*—"inalienable," "given with birth," "self-evident truths"—implies the belief in a kind of human "nature" which would be subject to the same laws of growth as that of the individual and from which rights and laws could be deduced. Today we are perhaps better qualified to judge exactly what this human "nature" amounts to; in any event it has shown us potentialities that were neither recognized nor even suspected by Western philosophy and religion, which for more than three thousand years have defined and redefined this "nature." But it is not only the, as it were, human aspect of nature that has become questionable to us. Ever since man learned to master it to such an extent that the destruction of all organic life on earth with man-made instruments has become conceivable and technically possible, he has been alienated from nature. Ever since a deeper knowledge of natural processes instilled serious doubts about the existence of natural laws at all, nature itself has assumed a sinister aspect.

How should one be, able to deduce laws and rights from a universe which apparently knows neither the one nor the other category?

Man of the twentieth century has become just as emancipated from nature as eighteenth-century man was from history. History and nature have become equally alien to us, namely, in the sense that the essence of man can no longer be comprehended in terms of either category. On the other hand, humanity, which for the eighteenth century, in Kantian terminology, was no more than a regulative idea, has today become an inescapable fact. This new situation, in which "humanity" has in effect assumed the role formerly ascribed to nature or history, would mean in this context that the right to have rights, or the right of every individual to belong to humanity, should be guaranteed by humanity itself. It is by no means certain whether this is possible. For, contrary to the best-intentioned humanitarian attempts to obtain new declarations of human rights from international organizations, it should be understood that this idea transcends the present sphere of international law which still operates in terms of reciprocal agreements and treaties between sovereign states; and, for the time being, a sphere that is above the nations does not exist. Furthermore, this dilemma would by no means be eliminated by the establishment of a "world government." Such a world government is indeed within the realm of possibility, but one may suspect that in reality it might differ considerably from the version promoted by idealistic-minded organizations. The crimes against human rights, which have become a specialty of totalitarian regimes, can always be justified by the pretext that right is equivalent to being good or useful for the whole in distinction to its parts. (Hitler's motto that "Right is what is good for the German people" is only the vulgarized form of a conception of law which can be found everywhere and which in practice will remain ineffectual only so long as older traditions that are still effective in the constitutions prevent this.) A conception of law which identifies what is right with the notion of what is good for—for the individual, or the family, or the people, or the largest number—becomes inevitable once the absolute and transcendent measurements of religion or the law of nature have lost their authority. And this predicament is by no means solved if the unit to which the "good for" applies is as large as mankind itself. For it is quite conceivable, and even within the realm of practical political possibilities, that one fine day a highly organized and mechanized humanity will conclude quite democratically—namely by majority decision—that for humanity as a whole it would be better to liquidate certain parts thereof. Here, in the problems of factual reality, we are confronted with one of the oldest perplexities of political philosophy, which could remain undetected only so long as a stable Christian theology provided the framework for all political and philosophical problems, but which long ago caused Plato to say: "Not man, but a god, must be the measure of all things."

These facts and reflections offer what seems an ironical, bitter, and belated confirmation of the famous arguments with which Edmund Burke opposed the French Revolution's Declaration of the Rights of Man. They appear to buttress his assertion that human rights were an "abstraction," that it was much wiser to rely on an "entailed inheritance" of rights which one transmits to one's children like life itself, and to claim one's rights to be the "rights of an Englishman" rather than the inalienable rights of man.[5] According to Burke, the rights which we enjoy spring "from within the nation," so that neither natural law, nor divine command, nor any concept of mankind such as Robespierre's "human race," "the sovereign of the earth," are needed as a source of law.[6]

The pragmatic soundness of Burke's concept seems to be beyond doubt in the light of our manifold experiences. Not only did loss of national rights in all instances entail the loss of human rights; the restoration of human rights, as the recent example of the State of Israel proves, has been achieved so far only through the restoration or the establishment of national rights. The conception of human rights, based upon the assumed existence of a human being as such, broke down at the very moment when those who professed to believe in it were for the first time confronted with people who had indeed lost all other qualities and specific relationships—except that they were still human. The world found nothing sacred in the abstract nakedness of being human. And in view of objective political conditions, it is hard to say how the concepts of man upon which human rights are based—that he is created in the image of God (in the American formula), or that he is the representative of mankind, or that he harbors within himself the sacred demands of natural law (in the French formula)—could have helped to find a solution to the problem.

The survivors of the extermination camps, the inmates of concentration and internment camps, and even the comparatively happy stateless people could see without Burke's arguments that the abstract nakedness of being nothing but human was their greatest danger. Because of it they were regarded as savages and, afraid that they might end by being considered beasts, they insisted on their nationality, the last sign of their former citizenship, as their only remaining and recognized tie with humanity. Their distrust of natural, their preference for national rights comes precisely from their realization that natural rights are granted even to savages. Burke had already feared that natural "inalienable" rights would confirm only the "right of the naked savage,"[7] and therefore reduce civilized nations to the status of savagery. Because only savages have nothing more to fall back upon than the minimum fact of their human origin, people cling to their nationality all the more desperately when they have lost the rights and protection that such nationality once gave them. Only their past with its "entailed inheritance" seems to attest to the fact that they still belong to the civilized world.

If a human being loses his political status, he should, according to the implications of the inborn and inalienable rights of man, come under exactly the situation for which the declarations of such general rights provided. Actually the opposite is the case. It seems that a man who is nothing but a man has lost the very qualities which make it possible for other people to treat him as a fellow-man. This is one of the reasons why it is far more difficult to destroy the legal personality of a criminal, that is of a man who has taken upon himself the responsibility for an act whose consequences now determine his fate, than of a man who has been disallowed all common human responsibilities.

Burke's arguments therefore gain an added significance if we look only at the general human condition of those who have been forced out of all political communities. Regardless of treatment, independent of liberties or oppression, justice or injustice, they have lost all those parts of the world and all those aspects of human existence which are the result of our common labor, the outcome of the human artifice. If the tragedy of savage tribes is that they inhabit an unchanged nature which they cannot master, yet upon whose abundance or frugality they depend for their livelihood, that they live and die without leaving any trace, without having contributed anything to a common world, then these rightless people are indeed thrown back into a peculiar state of nature. Certainly they are not barbarians; some of them, indeed, belong to the most educated strata of their respective countries; nevertheless, in a world that has almost liquidated savagery, they appear as the first signs of a possible regression from civilization.

The more highly developed a civilization, the more accomplished the world it has produced, the more at home men feel within the human artifice—the more they will resent everything they have not produced, everything that is merely and mysteriously given them. The human being who has lost his place in a community, his political status in the struggle of his time, and the legal personality which makes his actions and part of his destiny a consistent whole, is left with those qualities which usually can become articulate only in the sphere of private life and must remain unqualified, mere existence in all matters of public concern. This mere existence, that is, all that which is mysteriously given us by birth and which includes the shape of our bodies and the talents of our minds, can be adequately dealt with only by the unpredictable hazards of friendship and sympathy, or by the great and incalculable grace of love, which says with Augustine, "*Volo ut sis* (I want you to be)," without being able to give any particular reason for such supreme and unsurpassable affirmation.

Since the Greeks, we have known that highly developed political life breeds a deep-rooted suspicion of this private sphere, a deep resentment against the disturbing miracle contained in the fact that each of us is made as he is—single, unique, unchangeable. This whole sphere of the merely given, relegated to private life in civilized society, is a permanent threat to the public sphere, because the public sphere is as consistently based on the law of equality as the private sphere is based on the law of universal difference and differentiation. Equality, in contrast to all that is involved in mere existence, is not given us, but is the result of human organization insofar as it is guided by the principle of justice. We are not born equal; we become equal as members of a group on the strength of our decision to guarantee ourselves mutually equal rights.

Our political life rests on the assumption that we can produce equality through organization, because man can act in and change and build a common world, together with his equals and only with his equals. The dark background of mere givenness, the background formed by our unchangeable and unique nature, breaks into the political scene as the alien which in its all too obvious difference reminds us of the limitations of human activity—which are identical with the limitations of human equality. The reason why highly developed political communities, such as the ancient city-states or modern nation-states, so often insist on ethnic homogeneity is that they hope to eliminate as far as possible those natural and always present differences and differentiations which by themselves arouse dumb hatred, mistrust, and discrimination because they indicate all too clearly those spheres where men cannot act and change at will, *i.e.*, the limitations of the human artifice. The "alien" is a frightening symbol of the fact of difference as such, of individuality as such, and indicates those realms in which man cannot change and cannot act and in which, therefore, he has a distinct tendency to destroy. If a Negro in a white community is considered a Negro and nothing else, he loses along with his right to equality that freedom of action which is specifically human; all his deeds are now explained as "necessary" consequences of some "Negro" qualities; he has become some specimen of an animal species, called man. Much the same thing happens to those who have lost all distinctive political qualities and have become human beings and nothing else. No doubt, wherever public life and its law of equality are completely victorious, wherever a civilization succeeds in eliminating or reducing to a minimum the dark background of difference, it will end in complete petrifaction and be punished, so to speak, for having forgotten that man is only the master, not the creator of the world.

The great danger arising from the existence of people forced to live outside the common world is that they are thrown back, in the midst of civilization, on their natural givenness, on their mere differentiation. They lack that tremendous equalizing of differences which comes from being citizens of some commonwealth and yet, since they are no longer allowed to partake in the human artifice, they begin to belong to the human race in much the same way as animals belong to a specific animal species. The paradox involved in the loss of human rights is that such loss coincides with the instant when a person becomes a human being in general—without a profession, without a citizenship, without an opinion, without a deed by which to identify and specify himself—*and* different in general, representing nothing but his own absolutely unique individuality which, deprived of expression within and action upon a common world, loses all significance.

The danger in the existence of such people is twofold: first and more obviously, their ever-increasing numbers threaten our political life, our human artifice, the world which is the result of our common and co-ordinated effort in much the same, perhaps even more terrifying, way as the wild elements of nature once threatened the existence of man-made cities and countrysides. Deadly danger to any civilization is no longer likely to come from without. Nature has been mastered and no barbarians threaten to destroy what they cannot understand, as the Mongolians threatened Europe for centuries. Even the emergence of totalitarian governments is a phenomenon within, not outside, our civilization. The danger is that a global, universally interrelated civilization may produce barbarians from its own midst by forcing millions of people into conditions which, despite all appearances, are the conditions of savages.[8]

Notes

1. Pathetic instances of this exclusive confidence in national rights were the consent, before the second World War, of nearly 75 per cent of the German minority in the Italian Tyrol to leave their homes and resettle in Germany, the voluntary repatriation of a German island in Slovenia which had been there since the fourteenth century or, immediately after the close of the war, the unanimous rejection by Jewish refugees in an Italian DP camp of an offer of mass naturalization by the Italian government. In the face of the experience of European peoples between the two wars, it would be a serious mistake to interpret this behavior simply as another example of fanatic nationalist sentiment; these people no longer felt sure of their elementary rights if these were not protected by a government to which they belonged by birth. See Eugene M. Kulisher, *op. cit.* [Editors' Note: Eugene M. Kulisher, *The Displacement of Population in Europe* (Montreal: Inland Press Limited, 1943)]

2. The few chances for reintegration open to the new migrants were mostly based on their nationality: Spanish refugees, for instance, were welcomed to a certain extent in Mexico. The United States, in the early twenties, adopted a quota system according to which each nationality already represented in the country received, so to speak, the right to receive a number of former countrymen proportionate to its numerical part in the total population.

3. How dangerous it can be to be innocent from the point of view of the persecuting government, became very clear when, during the last war, the American government offered asylum to all those German refugees who were threatened by the extradition paragraph in the German-French Armistice. The condition was, of course, that the applicant could prove that he had done something against the Nazi regime. The proportion of refugees from Germany who were able to fulfill this condition was very small, and they, strangely enough, were not the people who were most in danger.

4. Even under the conditions of totalitarian terror, concentration camps sometimes have been the only place where certain remnants of freedom of thought and discussion still existed. See David Rousset, *Les Jours de Notre Mort*, Paris, 1947, *passim*, for freedom of discussion in Buchenwald, and Anton Ciliga, *The Russian Enigma*, London, 1940, p. 200, about "isles of liberty," "the freedom of mind" that reigned in some of the Soviet places of detention.

5. Edmund Burke, *Reflections on the Revolution in France*, 1790, edited by E. J. Payne, Everyman's Library.

6. Robespierre, *Speeches*, 1927. Speech of April 24, 1793.

7. Introduction by Payne to Burke, *op. cit.*

8. This modern expulsion from humanity has much more radical consequences than the ancient and medieval custom of outlawry. Outlawry, certainly the "most fearful fate

which primitive law could inflict," placing the life of the outlawed person at the mercy of anyone he met, disappeared with the establishment of an effective system of law enforcement and was finally replaced by extradition treaties between the nations. It had been primarily a substitute for a police force, designed to compel criminals to surrender.

The early Middle Ages seem to have been quite conscious of the danger involved in "civil death." Excommunication in the late Roman Empire meant ecclesiastical death but left a person who had lost his membership in the church full freedom in all other respects. Ecclesiastical and civil death became identical only in the Merovingian era, and there excommunication "in general practice [was] limited to temporary withdrawal or suspension of the rights of membership which might be regained." See the articles "Outlawry" and "Excommunication" in the *Encyclopedia of Social Sciences.* Also the article "Friedlosigkeit" in the *Schweizer Lexikon.*

CHAPTER 4

SELECTIONS FROM *THE* *HUMAN CONDITION*

Hannah Arendt

Prologue

In 1957, an earth-born object made by man was launched into the universe, where for some weeks it circled the earth according to the same laws of gravitation that swing and keep in motion the celestial bodies—the sun, the moon, and the stars. To be sure, the man-made satellite was no moon or star, no heavenly body which could follow its circling path for a time span that to us mortals, bound by earthly time, lasts from eternity to eternity. Yet, for a time it managed to stay in the skies; it dwelt and moved in the proximity of the heavenly bodies as though it had been admitted tentatively to their sublime company.

This event, second in importance to no other, not even to the splitting of the atom, would have been greeted with unmitigated joy if it had not been for the uncomfortable military and political circumstances attending it. But, curiously enough, this joy was not triumphal; it was not pride or awe at the tremendousness of human power and mastery which filled the hearts of men, who now, when they looked up from the earth toward the skies, could behold there a thing of their own making. The immediate reaction, expressed on the spur of the moment, was relief about the first "step toward escape from men's imprisonment to the earth." And this strange statement, far from being the accidental slip of some American reporter, unwittingly echoed the extraordinary line which, more than twenty years ago, had been carved on the funeral obelisk for one of Russia's great scientists: "Mankind will not remain bound to the earth forever."

Such feelings have been commonplace for some time. They show that men everywhere are by no means slow to catch up and adjust to scientific discoveries and technical developments, but that, on the contrary, they have outsped them by decades. Here, as in other respects, science has realized and affirmed what men anticipated in dreams that were neither wild nor idle. What is new is only that one of this country's most respectable newspapers finally brought to its front page what up to then had been buried in the highly non-respectable literature of science fiction (to which, unfortunately, nobody yet has paid the attention it deserves as a vehicle of mass sentiments and mass desires). The banality of the statement should not make us overlook how extraordinary in fact it was; for although Christians have spoken of the earth as a vale of tears and philosophers have looked upon their body as a prison of mind or soul, nobody in the history of mankind has ever conceived of the earth as a prison for men's bodies or shown such eagerness to go literally from here to the moon. Should the emancipation and secularization of the modern age, which began with a turning-away, not necessarily from God, but from a god who was the Father of men in heaven, end with an even more fateful repudiation of an Earth who was the Mother of all living creatures under the sky?

The earth is the very quintessence of the human condition, and earthly nature, for all we know, may be unique in the universe in providing human beings with a habitat in which they can move and breathe without effort and without artifice. The human artifice of the world separates human existence from all mere animal environment, but life itself is outside this artificial world, and through life man remains related to all other living organisms. For some time now, a great many scientific endeavors have been directed toward making life also "artificial," toward cutting the last tie through which even man belongs among the children of nature. It is the same desire to escape from imprisonment to the earth that is manifest in the attempt to create life in the test tube, in the desire to mix "frozen germ plasm from people of demonstrated ability under the microscope to produce superior human beings" and "to alter [their] size, shape and function"; and the wish to escape the human condition, I suspect, also underlies the hope to extend man's life-span far beyond the hundred-year limit.

This future man, whom the scientists tell us they will produce in no more than a hundred years, seems to be possessed by a rebellion against human existence as it has been given, a free gift from nowhere (secularly speaking), which he wishes to exchange, as it were, for something he has made himself.

There is no reason to doubt our abilities to accomplish such an exchange, just as there is no reason to doubt our present ability to destroy all organic life on earth. The question is only whether we wish to use our new scientific and technical knowledge in this direction, and this question cannot be decided by scientific means; it is a political question of the first order and therefore can hardly be left to the decision of professional scientists or professional politicians.

While such possibilities still may lie in a distant future, the first boomerang effects of science's great triumphs have made themselves felt in a crisis within the natural sciences themselves. The trouble concerns the fact that the "truths" of the modern scientific world view, though they can be demonstrated in mathematical formulas and proved technologically, will no longer lend themselves to normal expression in speech and thought. The moment these "truths" are spoken of conceptually and coherently, the resulting statements will be "not perhaps as meaningless as a 'triangular circle,' but much more so than a 'winged lion'" (Erwin Schrödinger). We do not yet know whether this situation is final. But it could be that we, who are earth-bound creatures and have begun to act as though we were dwellers of the universe, will forever be unable to understand, that is, to think and speak about the things which nevertheless we are able to do. In this case, it would be as though our brain, which constitutes the physical, material condition of our thoughts, were unable to follow what we do, so that from now on we would indeed need artificial machines to do our thinking and speaking. If it should turn out to be true that knowledge (in the modern sense of know-how) and thought have parted company for good, then we would indeed become the helpless slaves, not so much of our machines as of our know-how, thoughtless creatures at the mercy of every gadget which is technically possible, no matter how murderous it is.

However, even apart from these last and yet uncertain consequences, the situation created by the sciences is of great political significance. Wherever the relevance of speech is at stake, matters become political by definition, for speech is what makes man a political being. If we would follow the advice, so frequently urged upon us, to adjust our cultural attitudes to the present status of scientific achievement, we would in all earnest adopt a way of life in which speech is no longer meaningful. For the sciences today have been forced to adopt a "language" of mathematical symbols which, though it was originally meant only as an abbreviation for spoken statements, now contains statements that in no way can be translated back into speech. The reason why it may be wise to distrust the political judgment of scientists *qua* scientists is not primarily their lack of "character"—that they did not refuse to develop atomic weapons—or their naïveté—that they did not understand that once these weapons were developed they would be the last to be consulted about their use—but precisely the fact that they move in a world where speech has lost its power. And whatever men do or know or experience can make sense only to the extent that it can be spoken about. There may be truths beyond speech, and they may be of great relevance to man in the singular, that is, to man in so far as he is not a political being, whatever else he may be. Men in the plural, that is, men in so far as they live and move and act in this world, can experience meaningfulness only because they can talk with and make sense to each other and to themselves.

Closer at hand and perhaps equally decisive is another no less threatening event. This is the advent of automation, which in a few decades probably will empty the factories and liberate mankind from its oldest and most natural burden, the burden of laboring and the bondage to necessity. Here, too, a fundamental aspect of the human condition is at stake, but the rebellion against it, the wish to be liberated from labor's "toil and trouble," is not modern but as old as recorded history. Freedom from labor itself is not new; it once belonged among the most firmly established privileges of the few. In this instance, it seems as though scientific progress and technical developments had been only taken advantage of to achieve something about which all former ages dreamed but which none had been able to realize.

However, this is so only in appearance. The modern age has carried with it a theoretical glorification of labor and has resulted in a factual transformation of the whole of society into a laboring society. The fulfilment of the wish, therefore, like the fulfilment of wishes in fairy tales, comes at a moment when it can only be self-defeating. It is a society of laborers which is about to be liberated from the fetters of labor, and this society does no longer know of those other higher and more meaningful activities for the sake of which this freedom would deserve to be won. Within this society, which is egalitarian because this is labor's way of making men live together, there is no class left, no aristocracy of either a political or spiritual nature from which a restoration of the other capacities of man could start anew. Even presidents, kings, and prime ministers think of their offices in terms of a job necessary for the life of society, and among the intellectuals, only solitary individuals are left who consider what they are doing in terms of work and not in terms of making a living. What we are confronted with is the prospect of a society of laborers without labor, that is, without the only activity left to them. Surely, nothing could be worse.

To these preoccupations and perplexities, this book does not offer an answer. Such answers are given every day, and they are matters of practical politics, subject to the agreement of many; they can never lie in theoretical considerations or the opinion of one person, as though we dealt here with problems for which only one solution is possible. What I propose in the following is a reconsideration of the human condition from the vantage point of our newest experiences and our most recent fears. This, obviously, is a matter of thought, and thoughtlessness—the heedless recklessness or hopeless confusion or complacent repetition of "truths" which have become trivial and empty—seems to me among, the outstanding characteristics of our time. What I propose, therefore, is very simple: it is nothing more than to think what we are doing.

"What we are doing" is indeed the central theme of this book. It deals only with the most elementary articulations of the human condition, with those activities that traditionally, as well as according to current opinion, are within the range of every human being. For this and other reasons, the highest and perhaps purest activity of which men are capable, the activity of thinking, is left out of these present considerations. Systematically, therefore, the book is limited to a discussion of labor, work, and action, which forms its three central chapters. Historically, I deal in a last chapter with the modern age, and throughout the book with the various constellations within the hierarchy of activities as we know them from Western history.

However, the modern age is not the same as the modern world. Scientifically, the modern age which began in the seventeenth century came to an end at the beginning of the twentieth century; politically, the modern world, in which we live today, was born with the first atomic explosions. I do not discuss this modern world, against whose background this book was written. I confine myself, on the one hand, to an analysis of those general human capacities which grow out of the human condition and are permanent, that is, which cannot be irretrievably lost so long as the human condition itself is not changed. The purpose of the historical analysis, on the other hand, is to trace back modern world alienation, its twofold flight from the earth into the universe and from the world into the self, to its origins, in order to arrive at an understanding of the nature of society as it had developed and presented itself at the very moment when it was overcome by the advent of a new and yet unknown age.

I. *Vita Activa* and the Human Condition

With the term *vita activa*, I propose to designate three fundamental human activities: labor, work, and action. They are fundamental because each corresponds to one of the basic conditions under which life on earth has been given to man.

Labor is the activity which corresponds to the biological process of the human body, whose spontaneous growth, metabolism, and eventual decay are bound to the vital necessities produced and fed into the life process by labor. The human condition of labor is life itself.

Work is the activity which corresponds to the unnaturalness of human existence, which is not imbedded in, and whose mortality is not compensated by, the species' ever-recurring life cycle. Work provides an "artificial" world of things, distinctly different from all natural surroundings. Within its borders each individual life is housed, while this world itself is meant to outlast and transcend them all. The human condition of work is worldliness.

Action, the only activity that goes on directly between men without the intermediary of things or matter, corresponds to the human condition of plurality, to the fact that men, not Man, live on the earth and inhabit the world. While all aspects of the human condition are somehow related to politics, this plurality is specifically *the* condition—not only the *conditio sine qua non*, but the *conditio per quam*—of all political life. Thus the language of the Romans, perhaps the most political people we have known, used the words "to live" and "to be among men" (*inter homines esse*) or "to die" and "to cease to be among men" (*inter homines esse desinere*) as synonyms. But in its most elementary form, the human condition of action is implicit even in Genesis ("Male and female created He *them*"), if we understand that this story of man's creation is distinguished in principle from the one according to which God originally created Man (*adam*), "him" and not "them," so that the multitude of human beings becomes the result of multiplication.[1] Action would be an unnecessary luxury, a capricious interference with general laws of behavior, if men were endlessly reproducible repetitions of the same model, whose nature or essence was the same for all and as predictable as the nature or essence of any other thing. Plurality is the condition of human action because we are all the same, that is, human, in such a way that nobody is ever the same as anyone else who ever lived, lives or will live.

All three activities and their corresponding conditions are intimately connected with the most general condition of human existence: birth and death, natality and mortality. Labor assures not only individual survival, but the life of the species. Work and its product, the human artifact, bestow a measure of permanence and durability upon the futility of mortal life and the fleeting character of human time. Action, in so far as it engages in founding and preserving political bodies, creates the condition for remembrance, that is, for history. Labor and work, as well as action, are also rooted in natality in so far as they have the task to provide and preserve the world for, to foresee and reckon with, the constant influx of newcomers who are born into the world as strangers. However, of the three, action has the closest connection with the human condition of natality; the new beginning inherent in birth can make itself felt in the world only because the newcomer possesses the capacity of beginning something anew, that is, of acting. In this sense of initiative, an element of action, and therefore of natality, is inherent in all human activities. Moreover, since action is the political activity par excellence, natality, and not mortality, may be the central category of political, as distinguished from metaphysical, thought.

The human condition comprehends more than the conditions under which life has been given to man. Men are conditioned beings because everything they come in contact with turns immediately into a condition of their existence. The world in which the *vita activa* spends itself consists of things produced by human activities; but the things that owe their existence exclusively to men nevertheless constantly condition their human makers. In addition to the conditions under which life is given to man on earth, and partly out of them, men constantly create their own, self-made conditions, which, their human origin and their variability notwithstanding, possess the same conditioning power as natural things. Whatever touches or enters into a sustained relationship with human life immediately assumes the character of a condition of human existence. This is why men, no matter what they do, are always conditioned beings. Whatever enters the human world of its own accord or is drawn into it by human effort becomes part of the human condition. The impact of the world's reality upon human existence is felt and received as a conditioning force. The objectivity of the world—its object- or thing-character—and the human condition supplement each other; because human existence is conditioned existence, it would be impossible without things, and things would be a heap of unrelated articles, a non-world, if they were not the conditioners of human existence.

To avoid misunderstanding: the human condition is not the same as human nature, and the sum total of human activities and capabilities which correspond to the human condition does not constitute anything like human nature. For neither those we discuss here nor those we leave out, like thought and reason, and not even the most meticulous enumeration of them all, constitute essential characteristics of human existence in the sense that without them this existence would no longer be human. The most radical change in the human condition we can imagine would be an emigration of men from the earth to some other planet. Such an event, no longer totally impossible, would imply that man would have to live under man-made conditions, radically different from those the earth offers him. Neither labor nor work nor action nor, indeed, thought as we know it would then make sense any longer. Yet even these hypothetical wanderers from the earth would still be human; but the only statement we could make regarding their "nature" is that they still are conditioned beings, even though their condition is now self-made to a considerable extent.

The problem of human nature, the Augustinian *quaestio mihi factus sum* ("a question have I become for myself"), seems unanswerable in both its individual psychological sense and its general philosophical sense. It is highly unlikely that we, who can know, determine, and define the natural essences of all things surrounding us, which we are not, should ever be able to do the same for ourselves—this would be like jumping over our own shadows. Moreover, nothing entitles us to assume that man has a nature or essence in the same sense as other things. In other words, if we have a nature or essence, then surely only a god could know and define it, and the first prerequisite would be that he be able to speak about a "who" as though it were a "what."[2] The perplexity is that the modes of human cognition applicable to things with "natural" qualities, including ourselves to the limited extent that we are specimens of the most highly developed species of organic life, fail us when we raise the question: And *who* are we? This is why attempts to define human nature almost invariably end with some construction of a deity, that is, with the god of the philosophers, who, since Plato, has revealed himself upon closer inspection to be a kind of Platonic idea of man. Of course, to demask such philosophic concepts of the divine as conceptualizations of human capabilities and qualities is not a demonstration of, not even an argument for, the non-existence of God; but the fact that attempts to define the nature of man lead so easily into an idea which definitely strikes us as "superhuman" and therefore is identified with the divine may cast suspicion upon the very concept of "human nature."

On the other hand, the conditions of human existence—life itself, natality and mortality, worldliness, plurality, and the earth—can never "explain" what we are or answer the question of who we are for the simple reason that they never condition us absolutely. This has always been the opinion of philosophy, in distinction from the sciences—anthropology, psychology, biology, etc.—which also concern themselves with man. But today we may almost say that we have demonstrated even scientifically that, though we live now, and probably always will, under the earth's conditions, we are not mere earthbound creatures. Modern natural science owes its great triumphs to having looked upon and treated earth-bound nature from a truly universal viewpoint, that is, from an Archimedean standpoint taken, wilfully and explicitly, outside the earth.

2. The Term *Vita Activa*

The term *vita activa* is loaded and overloaded with tradition. It is as old as (but not older than) our tradition of political thought. And this tradition, far from comprehending and conceptualizing all the political experiences of Western mankind, grew out of a specific historical constellation: the trial of Socrates and the conflict between the philosopher and the *polis*. It eliminated many experiences of an earlier past that were irrelevant to its immediate political purposes and proceeded until its end, in the work of Karl Marx, in a highly selective manner. The term itself, in medieval philosophy the standard translation of the Aristotelian *bios politikos*, already occurs in Augustine, where, as *vita negotiosa* or *actuosa*, it still reflects its original meaning: a life devoted to public-political matters.[3]

Aristotle distinguished three ways of life (*bioi*) which men might choose in freedom, that is, in full independence of the necessities of life and the relationships they originated. This prerequisite of freedom ruled out all ways of life chiefly devoted to keeping one's self alive—not only labor, which was the way of life of the slave, who was coerced by the necessity to stay alive and by the rule of his master, but also the working life of the free craftsman and the acquisitive life of the merchant. In short, it excluded everybody who involuntarily or voluntarily, for his whole life or temporarily, had lost the free disposition of his movements and activities.[4] The remaining three ways of life have in common that they were concerned with the "beautiful," that is, with things neither necessary nor merely useful: the life of enjoying bodily pleasures in which the beautiful, as it is given, is consumed; the life devoted to the matters of the *polis*, in which excellence produces beautiful deeds; and the life of the philosopher devoted to inquiry into, and contemplation of, things eternal, whose everlasting beauty can neither be brought about through the producing interference of man nor be changed through his consumption of them.[5]

The chief difference between the Aristotelian and the later medieval use of the term is that the *bios politikos* denoted explicitly only the realm of human affairs, stressing the action, *praxis*, needed to establish and sustain it. Neither labor nor work was considered to possess sufficient dignity to constitute a *bios* at all, an autonomous and authentically human way of life; since they served and produced what was necessary and useful, they could not be free, independent of human needs and wants.[6] That the political way of life escaped this verdict is due to the Greek understanding of *polis* life, which to them denoted a very special and freely chosen form of political organization and by no means just any form of action necessary to keep men together in an orderly fashion. Not that the Greeks or Aristotle were ignorant of the fact that human life always demands some form of political organization and that ruling over subjects might constitute a distinct way of life; but the despot's way of life, because it was "merely" a necessity, could not be considered free and had no relationship with the *bios politikos*.[7]

With the disappearance of the ancient city-state—Augustine seems to have been the last to know at least what it once meant to be a citizen—the term *vita activa* lost its specifically political meaning and denoted all kinds of active engagement in the things of this world. To be sure, it does not follow that work and labor had risen in the hierarchy of human activities and were now equal in dignity with a life devoted to politics.[8] It was, rather, the other way round: action was now also reckoned among the necessities of earthly life, so that contemplation (the *bios theōrētikos*, translated into the *vita contemplativa*) was left as the only truly free way of life.[9]

However, the enormous superiority of contemplation over activity of any kind, action not excluded, is not Christian in origin. We find it in Plato's political philosophy, where the whole utopian reorganization of *polis* life is not only directed by the superior insight of the philosopher but has no aim other than to make possible the philosopher's way of life. Aristotle's very articulation of the different ways of life, in whose order the life of pleasure plays a minor role, is clearly guided by the ideal of contemplation (*theōria*). To the ancient freedom from the necessities of life and from compulsion by others, the philosophers added freedom and surcease from political activity (*skholē*),[10] so that the later Christian claim to be free from entanglement in worldly affairs, from all the business of this world, was preceded by and originated in the philosophic *apolitia* of late antiquity. What had been demanded only by the few was now considered to be a right of all.

The term *vita activa*, comprehending all human activities and defined from the viewpoint of the absolute quiet of contemplation, therefore corresponds more closely to the Greek *askholia* ("un-quiet"), with which Aristotle designated all activity, than to the Greek *bios politikos*. As early as Aristotle the distinction between quiet and unquiet, between an almost breathless abstention from external physical movement and activity of every kind, is more decisive than the distinction between the political and the theoretical way of life, because it can eventually be found within each of the three ways of life. It is like the distinction between war and peace: just as war takes place for the sake of peace, thus every kind of activity, even the processes of mere thought, must culminate in the absolute quiet of contemplation.[11] Every movement, the movements of body and soul as well as of speech and reasoning, must cease before truth. Truth, be it the ancient truth of Being or the Christian truth of the living God, can reveal itself only in complete human stillness.[12]

Traditionally and up to the beginning of the modern age, the term *vita activa* never lost its negative connotation of "un-quiet," *nec-otium, a-skholia*. As such it remained intimately related to the even more fundamental Greek distinction between things that are by themselves whatever they are and things which owe their existence to man, between things that are *physei* and things that are *nomō*. The primacy of contemplation over activity rests on the conviction that no work of human hands can equal in beauty and truth the physical *kosmos*, which swings in itself in changeless eternity without any interference or assistance from outside, from man or god. This eternity discloses itself to mortal eyes only when all human movements and activities are at perfect rest. Compared with this attitude of quiet, all distinctions and articulations within the *vita activa* disappear. Seen from the viewpoint of contemplation, it does not matter what disturbs the necessary quiet, as long as it is disturbed.

Traditionally, therefore, the term *vita activa* receives its meaning from the *vita contemplativa;* its very restricted dignity is bestowed upon it because it serves the needs and wants of contemplation in a living body.[13] Christianity, with its belief in a hereafter whose joys announce themselves in the delights of contemplation,[14] conferred a religious sanction upon the abasement of the *vita activa* to its derivative, secondary position; but the determination of the order itself coincided with the very discovery of contemplation (*theōria*) as a human faculty, distinctly different from thought and reasoning, which occurred in the Socratic school and from then on has ruled metaphysical and political thought throughout our tradition.[15] It seems unnecessary to my present purpose to discuss the reasons for this tradition. Obviously they are deeper than the historical occasion which gave rise to the conflict between the *polis* and the philosopher and thereby, almost incidentally, also led to the discovery of contemplation as the philosopher's way of life. They must lie in an altogether different aspect of the human condition, whose diversity is not exhausted in the various articulations of the *vita activa* and, we may suspect, would not be exhausted even if thought and the movement of reasoning were included in it.

If, therefore, the use of the term *vita activa*, as I propose it here, is in manifest contradiction to the tradition, it is because I doubt not the validity of the experience underlying the distinction but rather the hierarchical order inherent in it from its inception. This does not mean that I wish to contest or even to discuss, for that matter, the traditional concept of truth as revelation and therefore something essentially given to man, or that I prefer the modern age's pragmatic assertion that man can know only what he makes himself. My contention is simply that the enormous weight of contemplation in the traditional hierarchy has blurred the distinctions and articulations within the *vita activa* itself and that, appearances notwithstanding, this condition has not been changed essentially by the modern break with the tradition and the eventual reversal of its hierarchical order in Marx and Nietzsche. It lies in the very nature of the famous "turning upside down" of philosophic systems or currently accepted values, that is, in the nature of the operation itself, that the conceptual framework is left more or less intact.

The modern reversal shares with the traditional hierarchy the assumption that the same central human preoccupation must prevail in all activities of men, since without one comprehensive principle no order could be established. This assumption is not a matter of course, and my use of the term *vita activa* presupposes that the concern underlying all its activities is not the same as and is neither superior nor inferior to the central concern of the *vita contemplativa*.

3. Eternity versus Immortality

That the various modes of active engagement in the things of this world, on one side, and pure thought culminating in contemplation, on the other, might correspond to two altogether different central human concerns has in one way or another been manifest ever since "the men of thought and the men of action began to take different paths,"[16] that is, since the rise of political thought in the Socratic school. However, when the philosophers discovered— and it is probable, though unprovable, that this discovery was made by Socrates himself—that the political realm did not as a matter of course provide for all of man's higher activities, they assumed at once, not that they had found something different in addition to what was already known, but that they had found a higher principle to replace the principle that ruled the *polis*. The shortest, albeit somewhat superficial, way to indicate these two different and to an extent even conflicting principles is to recall the distinction between immortality and eternity.

Immortality means endurance in time, deathless life on this earth and in this world as it was given, according to Greek understanding, to nature and the Olympian gods. Against this background of nature's ever-recurring life and the gods' deathless and ageless lives stood mortal men, the only mortals in an immortal but not eternal universe, confronted with the immortal lives of their gods but not under the rule of an eternal God. If we trust Herodotus, the difference between the two seems to have been striking to Greek self-understanding prior to the conceptual articulation of the philosophers, and therefore prior to the specifically Greek experiences of the eternal which underlie this articulation. Herodotus, discussing Asiatic forms of worship and beliefs in an invisible God, mentions explicitly that compared with this transcendent God (as we would say today) who is beyond time and life and the universe, the Greek gods are *anthrōpophyeis*, have the same nature, not simply the same shape, as man.[17] The Greeks' concern with immortality grew out of their experience of an immortal nature and immortal gods which together surrounded the individual lives of mortal men. Imbedded in a cosmos where everything was immortal, mortality became the hallmark of human existence. Men are "the mortals," the only mortal things in existence, because unlike animals they do not exist only as members of a species whose immortal life is guaranteed through procreation.[18] The mortality of men lies in the fact that individual life, with a recognizable life-story from birth to death, rises out of biological life. This individual life is distinguished from all other things by the rectilinear course of its movement, which, so to speak, cuts through the circular movement of biological life. This is mortality: to move along a rectilinear line in a universe where everything, if it moves at all, moves in a cyclical order.

The task and potential greatness of mortals lie in their ability to produce things—works and deeds and words[19]—which would deserve to be and, at least to a degree, are at home in everlastingness, so that through them mortals could find their place in a cosmos where everything is immortal except themselves. By their capacity for the immortal deed, by their ability to leave non-perishable traces behind, men, their individual mortality notwithstanding, attain an immortality of their own and prove themselves to be of a "divine" nature. The distinction between man and animal runs right through the human species itself: only the best (*aristoi*), who constantly prove themselves to be the best (*aristeuein*, a verb for which there is no equivalent in any other language) and who "prefer immortal fame to mortal things," are really human; the others, content with whatever pleasures nature will yield them, live and die like animals. This was still the opinion of Heraclitus,[20] an opinion whose equivalent one will find in hardly any philosopher after Socrates.

In our context it is of no great importance whether Socrates himself or Plato discovered the eternal as the true center of strictly metaphysical thought. It weighs heavily in favor of Socrates that he alone among the great thinkers—unique in this as in many other respects—never cared to write down his thoughts; for it is obvious that, no matter how concerned a thinker may be with eternity, the moment he sits down to write his thoughts he ceases to be concerned primarily with eternity and shifts his attention to leaving some trace of them. He has entered the *vita activa* and chosen its way of permanence and potential immortality. One thing is certain: it is only in Plato that concern with the eternal and the life of the philosopher are seen as inherently contradictory and in conflict with the striving for immortality, the way of life of the citizen, the *bios politikos*.

The philosopher's experience of the eternal, which to Plato was *arrhēton* ("unspeakable"), and to Aristotle *aneu logon* ("without word"), and which later was conceptualized in the paradoxical *nunc stans* ("the standing now"), can occur only outside the realm of human affairs and outside the plurality of men, as we know from the Cave parable in Plato's *Republic*, where the philosopher, having liberated himself from the fetters that bound him to his fellow men, leaves the cave in perfect "singularity," as it were, neither accompanied nor followed by others. Politically speaking, if to die is the same as "to cease to be among men," experience of the eternal is a kind of death, and the only thing that separates it from real death is that it is not final because no living creature can endure it for any length of time. And this is precisely what separates the *vita contemplativa* from the *vita activa* in medieval thought.[21] Yet it is decisive that the experience of the eternal, in contradistinction to that of the immortal, has no correspondence with and cannot be transformed into any activity whatsoever, since even the activity of thought, which goes on within one's self by means of words, is obviously not only inadequate to render it but would interrupt and ruin the experience itself.

Theōria, or "contemplation," is the word given to the experience of the eternal, as distinguished from all other attitudes, which at most may pertain to immortality. It may be that the philosophers' discovery of the eternal was helped by their very justified doubt of the chances of the *polis* for immortality or even permanence, and it may be that the shock of this discovery was so overwhelming that they could not but look down upon all striving for immortality as vanity and vainglory, certainly placing themselves thereby into open opposition to the ancient city-state and the religion which inspired it. However, the eventual victory of the concern with eternity over all kinds of aspirations toward immortality is not due to philosophic thought. The fall of the Roman Empire plainly demonstrated that no work of mortal hands can be immortal, and it was accompanied by the rise of the Christian gospel of an everlasting individual life to its position as the exclusive religion of Western mankind. Both together made any striving for an earthly immortality futile and unnecessary. And they succeeded so well in making the *vita activa* and the *bios politikos* the handmaidens of contemplation that not even the rise of the secular in the modern age and the concomitant reversal of the traditional hierarchy between action and contemplation sufficed to save from oblivion the striving for immortality which originally had been the spring and center of the *vita activa*.

4. Man: A Social or a Political Animal

The *vita activa*, human life in so far as it is actively engaged in doing something, is always rooted in a world of men and of man-made things which it never leaves or altogether transcends. Things and men form the environment for each of man's activities, which would be pointless without such location; yet this environment, the world into which we are born, would not exist without the human activity which produced it, as in the case of fabricated things; which takes care of it, as in the case of cultivated land; or which established it through organization, as in the case of the body politic. No human life, not even the life of the hermit in nature's wilderness, is possible without a world which directly or indirectly testifies to the presence of other human beings.

All human activities are conditioned by the fact that men live together, but it is only action that cannot even be imagined outside the society of men. The activity of labor does not need the presence of others, though a being laboring in complete solitude would not be human but an *animal laborans* in the word's most literal significance. Man working and fabricating and building a world inhabited only by himself would still be a fabricator, though not *homo faber*: he would have lost his specifically human quality and, rather, be a god—not, to be sure, the Creator, but a *divine* demiurge as Plato described him in one of his myths. Action alone is the exclusive prerogative of man; neither a beast nor a god is capable of it,[22] and only action is entirely dependent upon the constant presence of others.

This special relationship between action and being together seems fully to justify the early translation of Aristotle's *zōon politikon* by *animal socialis*, already found in Seneca, which then became the standard translation through Thomas Aquinas: *homo est naturaliter politicus, id est, socialis* ("man is by nature political, that is, social").[23] More than any elaborate theory, this unconscious substitution of the social for the political betrays the extent to which the original Greek understanding of politics had been lost. For this, it is significant but not decisive that the word "social" is Roman in origin and has no equivalent in Greek language or thought. Yet the Latin usage of the word *societas* also originally had a clear, though limited, political meaning; it indicated an alliance between people for a specific purpose, as when men organize in order to rule others or to commit a crime.[24] It is only with the later concept of a *societas generis humani*, a "society of man-kind,"[25] that the term "social" begins to acquire the general meaning of a fundamental human condition. It is not that Plato or Aristotle was ignorant of, or unconcerned with, the fact that man cannot live outside the company of men, but they did not count this condition among the specifically human characteristics; on the contrary, it was something human life had in common with animal life, and for this reason alone it could not be fundamentally human. The natural, merely social companionship of the human species was considered to be a limitation imposed upon us by the needs of biological life, which are the same for the human animal as for other forms of animal life.

According to Greek thought, the human capacity for political organization is not only different from but stands in direct opposition to that natural association whose center is the home (*oikia*) and the family. The rise of the city-state meant that man received "besides his private life a sort of second life, his *bios politikos*. Now every citizen belongs to two orders of existence; and there is a sharp distinction in his life between what is his own (*idion*) and what is communal (*koinon*)."[26] It was not just an opinion or theory of Aristotle but a simple historical fact that the foundation of the *polis* was preceded by the destruction of all organized units resting on kinship, such as the *phratria* and the *phylē*.[27] Of all the activities necessary and present in human communities, only two were deemed to be political and to constitute what Aristotle called the *bios politikos*, namely, action (*praxis*) and speech (*lexis*), out of which rises the realm of human affairs (*ta tōn anthrōpōn pragmata*, as Plato used to call it) from which everything merely necessary or useful is strictly excluded.

However, while certainly only the foundation of the city-state enabled men to spend their whole lives in the political realm, in action and speech, the conviction that these two human capacities belonged together and are the highest of all seems to have preceded the *polis* and was already present in pre-Socratic thought. The stature of the Homeric Achilles can be understood only if one sees him as "the doer of great deeds and the speaker of great words."[28] In distinction from modern understanding, such words were not considered to be great because they expressed great thoughts; on the contrary, as we know from the last lines of *Antigone*, it may be the capacity for "great words" (*megaloi logoi*) with which to reply to striking blows that will eventually teach thought in old age.[29] Thought was secondary to speech, but speech and action were considered to be coeval and coequal, of the same rank and the same kind; and this originally meant not only that most political action, in so far as it remains outside the sphere of violence, is indeed transacted in words, but more fundamentally that finding the right words at the right moment, quite apart from the information or communication they may convey, is action. Only sheer violence is mute, and for this reason violence alone can never be great. Even when, relatively late in antiquity, the arts of war and speech (*rhetoric*) emerged as the two principal political subjects of education, the development was still inspired by this older pre-*polis* experience and tradition and remained subject to it.

In the experience of the *polis*, which not without justification has been called the most talkative of all bodies politic, and even more in the political philosophy which sprang from it, action and speech separated and became more and more independent activities. The emphasis shifted from action to speech, and to speech as a means of persuasion rather than the specifically human way of answering, talking back and measuring up to whatever happened or was done.[30] To be political, to live in a *polis*, meant that everything was decided through words and persuasion and not through force and violence. In Greek self-understanding, to force people by violence, to command rather than persuade, were prepolitical ways to deal with people characteristic of life outside the *polis*, of home and family life, where the household head ruled with uncontested, despotic powers, or of life in the barbarian empires of Asia, whose despotism was frequently likened to the organization of the household.

Aristotle's definition of man as *zōon politikon* was not only unrelated and even opposed to the natural association experienced in household life; it can be fully understood only if one adds his second famous definition of man as a *zōon logon ekhon* ("a living being capable of speech"). The Latin translation of this term into *animal rationale* rests on no less fundamental a misunderstanding than the term "social animal." Aristotle meant neither to define man in general nor to indicate man's highest capacity, which to him was not *logos*, that is, not speech or reason, but *nous*, the capacity of contemplation, whose chief characteristic is that its content cannot be rendered in speech.[31] In his two most famous definitions, Aristotle only formulated the current opinion of the *polis* about man and the political way of life, and according to this opinion, everybody outside the *polis*—slaves and barbarians—was *aneu logou*, deprived, of course, not of the faculty of speech, but of a way of life in which speech and only speech made sense and where the central concern of all citizens was to talk with each other.

The profound misunderstanding expressed in the Latin translation of "political" as "social" is perhaps nowhere clearer than in a discussion in which Thomas Aquinas compares the nature of household rule with political rule: the head of the household, he finds, has some similarity to the head of the kingdom, but, he adds, his power is not so "perfect" as that of the king.[32] Not only in Greece and the *polis* but throughout the whole of occidental antiquity, it would indeed have been self-evident that even the power of the tyrant was less great, less "perfect" than the power with which the *paterfamilias*, the *dominus*, ruled over his household of slaves and family. And this was not because the power of the city's ruler was matched and checked by the combined powers of household heads, but because absolute, uncontested rule and a political realm properly-speaking were mutually exclusive.[33]

5. The *Polis* and the Household

Although misunderstanding and equating the political and social realms is as old as the translation of Greek terms into Latin and their adaption to Roman-Christian thought, it has become even more confusing in modern usage and modern understanding of society. The distinction between a private and a public sphere of life corresponds to the household and the political realms, which have existed as distinct, separate entities at least since the rise of the ancient city-state; but the emergence of the social realm, which is neither private nor public, strictly speaking, is a relatively new phenomenon whose origin coincided with the emergence of the modern age and which found its political form in the nation-state.

What concerns us in this context is the extraordinary difficulty with which we, because of this development, understand the decisive division between the public and private realms, between the sphere of the *polis* and the sphere of household and family, and, finally, between activities related to a common world and those related to the maintenance of life, a division upon which all ancient political thought rested as self-evident and axiomatic. In our understanding, the dividing line is entirely blurred, because we see the body of peoples and political communities in the image of a family whose everyday affairs have to be taken care of by a gigantic, nation-wide administration of housekeeping. The scientific thought that corresponds to this development is no longer political science but "national economy" or "social economy" or *Volkswirtschaft*, all of which indicate a kind of "collective housekeeping";[34]

the collective of families economically organized into the facsimile of one super-human family is what we call "society," and its political form of organization is called "nation."[35] We therefore find it difficult to realize that according to ancient thought on these matters, the very term "political economy" would have been a contradiction in terms: whatever was "economic," related to the life of the individual and the survival of the species, was a non-political, household affair by definition.[36]

Historically, it is very likely that the rise of the city-state and the public realm occurred at the expense of the private realm of family and household.[37] Yet the old sanctity of the hearth, though much less pronounced in classical Greece than in ancient Rome, was never entirely lost. What prevented the *polis* from violating the private lives of its citizens and made it hold sacred the boundaries surrounding each property was not respect for private property as we understand it, but the fact that without owning a house a man could not participate in the affairs of the world because he had no location in it which was properly his own.[38] Even Plato, whose political plans foresaw the abolition of private property and an extension of the public sphere to the point of annihilating private life altogether, still speaks with great reverence of Zeus Herkeios, the protector of border lines, and calls the *horoi*, the boundaries between one estate and another, divine, without seeing any contradiction.[39]

The distinctive trait of the household sphere was that in it men lived together because they were driven by their wants and needs. The driving force was life itself—the penates, the household gods, were, according to Plutarch, "the gods who make us live and nourish our body"[40]—which, for its individual maintenance and its survival as the life of the species needs the company of others. That individual maintenance should be the task of the man and species survival the task of the woman was obvious, and both of these natural functions, the labor of man to provide nourishment and the labor of the woman in giving birth, were subject to the same urgency of life. Natural community in the household therefore was born of necessity, and necessity ruled over all activities performed in it.

The realm of the *polis*, on the contrary, was the sphere of freedom, and if there was a relationship between these two spheres, it was a matter of course that the mastering of the necessities of life in the household was the condition for freedom of the *polis*. Under no circumstances could politics be only a means to protect society—a society of the faithful, as in the Middle Ages, or a society of property-owners, as in Locke, or a society relentlessly engaged in a process of acquisition, as in Hobbes, or a society of producers, as in Marx, or a society of jobholders, as in our own society, or a society of laborers, as in socialist and communist countries. In all these cases, it is the freedom (and in some instances so-called freedom) of society which requires and justifies the restraint of political authority. Freedom is located in the realm of the social, and force or violence becomes the monopoly of government.

What all Greek philosophers, no matter how opposed to *polis* life, took for granted is that freedom is exclusively located in the political realm, that necessity is primarily a prepolitical phenomenon, characteristic of the private household organization, and that force and violence are justified in this sphere because they are the only means to master necessity—for instance, by ruling over slaves—and to become free. Because all human beings are subject to necessity, they are entitled to violence toward others; violence is the prepolitical act of liberating oneself from the necessity of life for the freedom of the world. This freedom is the essential condition of what the Greeks called felicity, *eudaimonia*, which was an objective status depending first of all upon wealth and health. To be poor or to be in ill health meant to be subject to physical necessity, and to be a slave meant to be subject, in addition, to man-made violence. This twofold and doubled "unhappiness" of slavery is quite independent of the actual subjective well-being of the slave. Thus, a poor free man preferred the insecurity of a daily-changing labor market to regular assured work, which, because it restricted his freedom to do as he pleased every day, was already felt to be servitude (*douleia*), and even harsh, painful labor was preferred to the easy life of many household slaves.[41]

The prepolitical force, however, with which the head of the household ruled over the family and its slaves and which was felt to be necessary because man is a "social" before he is a "political animal," has nothing in common with the chaotic "state of nature" from whose violence, according to seventeenth-century political thought, men could escape only by establishing a government that, through a monopoly of power and of violence, would abolish the "war of all against all" by "keeping them all in awe."[42] On the contrary, the whole concept of rule and being ruled, of government and power in the sense in which we understand them as well as the regulated order attending them, was felt to be prepolitical and to belong in the private rather than the public sphere.

The *polis* was distinguished from the household in that it knew only "equals," whereas the household was the center of the strictest inequality. To be free meant both not to be subject to the necessity of life or to the command of another *and* not to be in command oneself. It meant neither to rule nor to be ruled.[43] Thus within the realm of the household, freedom did not exist, for the household head, its ruler, was considered to be free only in so far as he had the power to leave the household and enter the political realm, where all were equals. To be sure, this equality of the political realm has very little in common with our concept of equality: it meant to live among and to have to deal only with one's peers, and it presupposed the existence of "unequals" who, as a matter of fact, were always the majority of the population in a city-state.[44] Equality, therefore, far from being connected with justice, as in modern times, was the very essence of freedom: to be free meant to be free from the inequality present in rulership and to move in a sphere where neither rule nor being ruled existed.

However, the possibility of describing the profound difference between the modern and the ancient understanding of politics in terms of a clear-cut opposition ends here. In the modern world, the social and the political realms are much less distinct. That politics is nothing but a function of society, that action, speech, and thought are primarily superstructures upon social interest, is not a discovery of Karl Marx but on the contrary is among the axiomatic assumptions Marx accepted uncritically from the political economists of the modern age. This functionalization makes it impossible to perceive any serious gulf between the two realms; and this is not a matter of a theory or an ideology, since with the rise of society, that is, the rise of the "household" (*oikia*) or of economic activities to the public realm, housekeeping and all matters pertaining formerly to the private sphere of the family have become a "collective" concern.[45] In the modern world, the two realms indeed constantly flow into each other like waves in the never-resting stream of the life process itself.

The disappearance of the gulf that the ancients had to cross daily to transcend the narrow realm of the household and "rise" into the realm of politics is an essentially modern phenomenon. Such a gulf between the private and the public still existed somehow in the Middle Ages, though it had lost much of its significance and changed its location entirely. It has been rightly remarked that after the downfall of the Roman Empire, it was the Catholic Church that offered men a substitute for the citizenship which had formerly been the prerogative of municipal government.[46] The medieval tension between the darkness of everyday life and the grandiose splendor attending everything sacred, with the concomitant rise from the secular to the religious,

corresponds in many respects to the rise from the private to the public in antiquity. The difference is of course very marked, for no matter how "worldly"
the Church became, it was always essentially an otherworldly concern which
kept the community of believers together. While one can equate the public
with the religious only with some difficulty, the secular realm under the rule
of feudalism was indeed in its entirety what the private realm had been in
antiquity. Its hallmark was the absorption of all activities into the household
sphere, where they had only private significance, and consequently the very
absence of a public realm.[47]

It is characteristic of this growth of the private realm, and incidentally of
the difference between the ancient household head and the feudal lord, that
the feudal lord could render justice within the limits of his rule, whereas the
ancient household head, while he might exert a milder or harsher rule, knew
neither of laws nor justice outside the political realm.[48] The bringing of all human activities into the private realm and the modeling of all human relationships upon the example of the household reached far into the specifically
medieval professional organizations in the cities themselves, the guilds, con-
fréries, and compagnons, and even into the early business companies, where
"the original joint household would seem to be indicated by the very word
'company' (companis) . . . [and] such phrases as 'men who eat one bread,' 'men
who have one bread and one wine.'"[49] The medieval concept of the "common
good," far from indicating the existence of a political realm, recognizes only
that private individuals have interests in common, material and spiritual, and
that they can retain their privacy and attend to their own business only if one
of them takes it upon himself to look out for this common interest. What distinguishes this essentially Christian attitude toward politics from the modern
reality is not so much the recognition of a "common good" as the exclusivity
of the private sphere and the absence of that curiously hybrid realm where
private interests assume public significance that we call "society."

It is therefore not surprising that medieval political thought, concerned
exclusively with the secular realm, remained unaware of the gulf between the
sheltered life in the household and the merciless exposure of the polis and,
consequently, of the virtue of courage as one of the most elemental political
attitudes. What remains surprising is that the only postclassical political the-
orist who, in an extraordinary effort to restore its old dignity to politics, perceived the gulf and understood something of the courage needed to cross it
was Machiavelli, who described it in the rise "of the Condottiere from low

condition to high rank," from privacy to princedom, that is, from circumstances common to all men to the shining glory of great deeds.[50]

To leave the household, originally in order to embark upon some adventure and glorious enterprise and later simply to devote one's life to the affairs of the city, demanded courage because only in the household was one primarily concerned with one's own life and survival. Whoever entered the political realm had first to be ready to risk his life, and too great a love for life obstructed freedom, was a sure sign of slavishness.[51] Courage therefore became the political virtue par excellence, and only those men who possessed it could be admitted to a fellowship that was political in content and purpose and thereby transcended the mere togetherness imposed on all—slaves, barbarians, and Greeks alike—through the urgencies of life.[52] The "good life," as Aristotle called the life of the citizen, therefore was not merely better, more carefree or nobler than ordinary life, but of an altogether different quality. It was "good" to the extent that by having mastered the necessities of sheer life, by being freed from labor and work, and by overcoming the innate urge of all living creatures for their own survival, it was no longer bound to the biological life process.

At the root of Greek political consciousness we find an unequaled clarity and articulateness in drawing this distinction. No activity that served only the purpose of making a living, of sustaining only the life process, was permitted to enter the political realm, and this at the grave risk of abandoning trade and manufacture to the industriousness of slaves and foreigners, so that Athens indeed became the "pensionopolis" with a "proletariat of consumers" which Max Weber so vividly described.[53] The true character of this *polis* is still quite manifest in Plato's and Aristotle's political philosophies, even if the borderline between household and *polis* is occasionally blurred, especially in Plato who, probably following Socrates, began to draw his examples and illustrations for the *polis* from everyday experiences in private life, but also in Aristotle when he, following Plato, tentatively assumed that at least the historical origin of the *polis* must be connected with the necessities of life and that only its content or inherent aim (*telos*) transcends life in the "good life."

These aspects of the teachings of the Socratic school, which soon were to become axiomatic to the point of banality, were then the newest and most revolutionary of all and sprang not from actual experience in political life but from the desire to be freed from its burden, a desire which in their own understanding the philosophers could justify only by demonstrating that even this freest of all ways of life was still connected with and subject to necessity. But the background of actual political experience, at least in Plato and Aristotle, remained so strong that the distinction between the spheres of household and political life was never doubted. Without mastering the necessities of life in the household, neither life nor the "good life" is possible, but politics is never for the sake of life. As far as the members of the *polis* are concerned, household life exists for the sake of the "good life" in the *polis*.

* * *

45. The Victory of the *Animal Laborans*

The victory of the *animal laborans* would never have been complete had not the process of secularization, the modern loss of faith inevitably arising from Cartesian doubt, deprived individual life of its immortality, or at least of the certainty of immortality. Individual life again became mortal, as mortal as it had been in antiquity, and the world was even less stable, less permanent, and hence less to be relied upon than it had been during the Christian era. Modern man, when he lost the certainty of a world to come, was thrown back upon himself and not upon this world; far from believing that the world might be potentially immortal, he was not even sure that it was real. And in so far as he was to assume that it was real in the uncritical and apparently unbothered optimism of a steadily progressing science, he had removed himself from the earth to a much more distant point than any Christian otherworldliness had ever removed him. Whatever the word "secular" is meant to signify in current usage, historically it cannot possibly be equated with worldliness; modern man at any rate did not gain this world when he lost the other world, and he did not gain life, strictly speaking, either; he was thrust back upon it, thrown into the closed inwardness of introspection, where the highest he could experience were the empty processes of reckoning of the mind, its play with itself. The only contents left were appetites and desires, the senseless urges of his body which he mistook for passion and which he deemed to be "unreasonable" because he found he could not "reason," that is, not reckon with them. The only thing that could now be potentially immortal, as immortal as the body politic in antiquity and as individual life during the Middle Ages, was life itself, that is, the possibly everlasting life process of the species mankind.

We saw before that in the rise of society it was ultimately the life of the species which asserted itself. Theoretically, the turning point from the earlier modern age's insistence on the "egoistic" life of the individual to its later emphasis on "social" life and "socialized man" (Marx) came when Marx transformed the cruder notion of classical economy—that all men, in so far as they act at all, act for reasons of self-interest—into forces of interest which inform, move, and direct the classes of society, and through their conflicts direct society as a whole. Socialized mankind is that state of society where only one interest rules, and the subject of this interest is either classes or mankind, but neither man nor men. The point is that now even the last trace of action in what men were doing, the motive implied in self-interest, disappeared. What was left was a "natural force," the force of the life process itself, to which all men and all human activities were equally submitted ("the thought process itself is a natural process")[54] and whose only aim, if it had an aim at all, was survival of the animal species man. None of the higher capacities of man was any longer necessary to connect individual life with the life of the species; individual life became part of the life process, and to labor, to assure the continuity of one's own life and the life of his family, was all that was needed. What was not needed, not necessitated by life's metabolism with nature, was either superfluous or could be justified only in terms of a peculiarity of human as distinguished from other animal life—so that Milton was considered to have written his *Paradise Lost* for the same reasons and out of similar urges that compel the silkworm to produce silk.

If we compare the modern world with that of the past, the loss of human experience involved in this development is extraordinarily striking. It is not only and not even primarily contemplation which has become an entirely meaningless experience. Thought itself, when it became "reckoning with consequences," became a function of the brain, with the result that electronic instruments are found to fulfil these functions much better than we ever could. Action was soon and still is almost exclusively understood in terms of making and fabricating, only that making, because of its worldliness and inherent indifference to life, was now regarded as but another form of laboring, a more complicated but not a more mysterious function of the life process.

Meanwhile, we have proved ingenious enough to find ways to ease the toil and trouble of living to the point where an elimination of laboring from the range of human activities can no longer be regarded as utopian. For even now, laboring is too lofty, too ambitious a word for what we are doing, or think we are doing, in the world we have come to live in. The last stage of the laboring society, the society of jobholders, demands of its members a sheer automatic functioning, as though individual life had actually been submerged in the over-all life process of the species and the only active decision still required of the individual were to let go, so to speak, to abandon his individuality, the still individually sensed pain and trouble of living, and acquiesce in a dazed, "tranquilized," functional type of behavior. The trouble with modern theories of behaviorism is not that they are wrong but that they could become true, that they actually are the best possible conceptualization of certain obvious trends in modern society. It is quite conceivable that the modern age—which began with such an unprecedented and promising outburst of human activity—may end in the deadliest, most sterile passivity history has ever known.

But there are other more serious danger signs that man may be willing and, indeed, is on the point of developing into that animal species from which, since Darwin, he imagines he has come. If, in concluding, we return once more to the discovery of the Archimedean point and apply it, as Kafka warned us not to do, to man himself and to what he is doing on this earth, it at once becomes manifest that all his activities, watched from a sufficiently removed vantage point in the universe, would appear not as activities of any kind but as processes, so that, as a scientist recently put it, modern motorization would appear like a process of biological mutation in which human bodies gradually begin to be covered by shells of steel. For the watcher from the universe, this mutation would be no more or less mysterious than the mutation which now goes on before our eyes in those small living organisms which we fought with antibiotics and which mysteriously have developed new strains to resist us. How deep-rooted this usage of the Archimedean point against ourselves is can be seen in the very metaphors which dominate scientific thought today. The reason why scientists can tell us about the "life" in the atom—where apparently every particle is "free" to behave as it wants and the laws ruling these movements are the same statistical laws which, according to the social scientists, rule human behavior and make the multitude behave as it must, no matter how "free" the individual particle may appear to be in its choices—the reason, in other words, why the behavior of the infinitely small particle is not only similar in pattern to the planetary system as it appears to us but resembles the life and behavior patterns in human society is, of course, that we look and live in this society as though we were as far removed from our own human existence as we are from the infinitely small and the immensely large which, even if they could be perceived by the finest instruments, are too far away from us to be experienced.

Needless to say, this does not mean that modern man has lost his capacities or is on the point of losing them. No matter what sociology, psychology, and anthropology will tell us about the "social animal," men persist in making, fabricating, and building, although these faculties are more and more restricted to the abilities of the artist, so that the concomitant experiences of worldliness escape more and more the range of ordinary human experience.[55]

Similarly, the capacity for action, at least in the sense of the releasing of processes, is still with us, although it has become the exclusive prerogative of the scientists, who have enlarged the realm of human affairs to the point of extinguishing the time-honored protective dividing line between nature and the human world. In view of such achievements, performed for centuries in the unseen quiet of the laboratories, it seems only proper that their deeds should eventually have turned out to have greater news value, to be of greater political significance, than the administrative and diplomatic doings of most so-called statesmen. It certainly is not without irony that those whom public opinion has persistently held to be the least practical and the least political members of society should have turned out to be the only ones left who still know how to act and how to act in concert. For their early organizations, which they founded in the seventeenth century for the conquest of nature and in which they developed their own moral standards and their own code of honor, have not only survived all vicissitudes of the modern age, but they have become one of the most potent power-generating groups in all history. But the action of the scientists, since it acts into nature from the standpoint of the universe and not into the web of human relationships, lacks the revelatory character of action as well as the ability to produce stories and become historical, which together form the very source from which meaningfulness springs into and illuminates human existence. In this existentially most important aspect, action, too, has become an experience for the privileged few, and these few who still know what it means to act may well be even fewer than the artists, their experience even rarer than the genuine experience of and love for the world.

Thought, finally—which we, following the premodern as well as the modern tradition, omitted from our reconsideration of the *vita activa*—is still possible, and no doubt actual, wherever men live under the conditions of political freedom. Unfortunately, and contrary to what is currently assumed about the proverbial ivory-tower independence of thinkers, no other human capacity is so vulnerable, and it is in fact far easier to act under conditions of tyranny than it is to think. As a living experience, thought has always been assumed, perhaps wrongly, to be known only to the few. It may not be presumptuous to believe that these few have not become fewer in our time. This may be irrelevant, or of restricted relevance, for the future of the world; it is not irrelevant for the future of man. For if no other test but the experience of being active, no other measure but the extent of sheer activity were to be applied to the various activities within the *vita activa*, it might well be that thinking as such would surpass them all. Whoever has any experience in this matter will know how right Cato was when he said: *Numquam se plus agere quam nihil cum ageret, numquam minus solum esse quam cum solus esset*— "Never is he more active than when he does nothing, never is he less alone than when he is by himself."

Notes

1. In the analysis of postclassical political thought, it is often quite illuminating to find out which of the two biblical versions of the creation story is cited. Thus it is highly characteristic of the difference between the teaching of Jesus of Nazareth and of Paul that Jesus, discussing the relationship between man and wife, refers to Genesis 1:27: "Have ye not read, that he which made *them* at the beginning made them male and female" (Matt. 19:4), whereas Paul on a similar occasion insists that the woman was created "of the man" and hence "for the man," even though he then somewhat attenuates the dependence: "neither is the man without the woman, neither the woman without the man" (I Cor. 11:8–12). The difference indicates much more than a different attitude to the role of woman. For Jesus, faith was closely related to action; for Paul, faith was primarily related to salvation. Especially interesting in this respect is Augustine (*De civitate Dei* xii. 21), who not only ignores Genesis 1:27 altogether but sees the difference between man and animal in that man was created *unum ac singulum*, whereas all animals were ordered "to come into being several at once" (*plura simul iussit exsistere*). To Augustine, the creation story offers a welcome opportunity to stress the species character of animal life as distinguished from the singularity of human existence.

2. Augustine, who is usually credited with having been the first to raise the so-called anthropological question in philosophy, knew this quite well. He distinguishes between the questions of "Who am I?" and "What am I?" the first being directed by man at himself ("And I directed myself at myself and said to me: You, who are you? And I answered: A man"—*tu, quis es?* [*Confessiones* x. 6]) and the second being addressed to God ("What then am I, my God? What is my nature?"—*Quid ergo sum, Deus meus? Quae natura*

sum? [x. 17]). For in the "great mystery," the *grande profundum*, which man is (iv. 14), there is "something of man [*aliquid hominis*] which the spirit of man which is in him itself knoweth not. But Thou, Lord, who has made him [*fecisti eum*] knowest everything of him [*eius omnia*]" (x. 5). Thus, the most familiar of these phrases which I quoted in the text, the *quaestio mihi factus sum*, is a question raised in the presence of God, "in whose eyes I have become a question for myself" (x. 33). In brief, the answer to the question "Who am I?" is simply: "You are a man—whatever that may be"; and the answer to the question "What am I?" can be given only by God who made man. The question about the nature of man is no less a theological question than the question about the nature of God; both can be settled only within the framework of a divinely revealed answer.

3. See Augustine *De civitate Dei* xix. 2, 19.

4. William L. Westermann ("Between Slavery and Freedom," *American Historical Review*, Vol. L [1945]) holds that the "statement of Aristotle . . . that craftsmen live in a condition of limited slavery meant that the artisan, when he made a work contract, disposed of two of the four elements of his free status [viz., of freedom of economic activity and right of unrestricted movement], but by his own volition and for a temporary period"; evidence quoted by Westermann shows that freedom was then understood to consist of "status, personal inviolability, freedom of economic activity, right of unrestricted movement," and slavery consequently "was the lack of these four attributes." Aristotle, in his enumeration of "ways of life" in the *Nicomachean Ethics* (i. 5) and the *Eudemian Ethics* (1215a35 ff.), does not even mention a craftsman's way of life; to him it is obvious that a *banausos* is not free (cf. *Politics* 1337b5). He mentions, however, "the life of money-making" and rejects it because it too is "undertaken under compulsion" (*Nic. Eth.* 1096a5). That the criterion is freedom is stressed in the *Eudemian Ethics*: he enumerates only those lives that are chosen *ep' exousian*.

5. For the opposition of the beautiful to the necessary and the useful see *Politics* 1333a30 ff., 1332b32.

6. For the opposition of the free to the necessary and the useful see *ibid.* 1332b2.

7. See *ibid.* 1277b8 for the distinction between despotic rule and politics. For the argument that the life of the despot is not equal to the life of a free man because the former is concerned with "necessary things," see *ibid.* 1325a24.

8. On the widespread opinion that the modern estimate of labor is Christian in origin, see §44.

9. See Aquinas *Summa theologica* ii. 2. 179, esp. art. 2, where the *vita activa* arises out of the *necessitas vitae praesentis*, and *Expositio in Psalmos* 45.3, where the body politic is assigned the task of finding all that is necessary for life: *in civitate oportet invenire omnia necessaria ad vitam*.

10. The Greek word *skholē*, like the Latin *otium*, means primarily freedom from political activity and not simply leisure time, although both words are also used to indicate freedom from labor and life's necessities. In any event, they always indicate a condition free from worries and cares. An excellent description of the everyday life of an ordinary Athenian citizen, who enjoys full freedom from labor and work, can be found in

Fustel de Coulanges, *The Ancient City* (Anchor ed.; 1956), pp. 334–36; it will convince everybody how time-consuming political activity was under the conditions of the city-state. One can easily guess how full of worry this ordinary political life was if one remembers that Athenian law did not permit remaining neutral and punished those who did not want to take sides in factional strife with loss of citizenship.

11. See Aristotle *Politics* 1333a30–33. Aquinas defines contemplation as *quies ab exterioribus motibus* (*Summa theologica* ii. 2. 179. 1).

12. Aquinas stresses the stillness of the soul and recommends the *vita activa* because it exhausts and therefore "quietens interior passions" and prepares for contemplation (*Summa theologica* ii. 2.182. 3).

13. Aquinas is quite explicit on the connection between the *vita activa* and the wants and needs of the human body which men and animals have in common (*Summa theologica* ii. 2. 182. 1).

14. Augustine speaks of the "burden" (*sarcina*) of active life imposed by the duty of charity, which would be unbearable without the "sweetness" (*suavitas*) and the "delight of truth" given in contemplation (*De civitate Dei* xix. 19).

15. The time-honored resentment of the philosopher against the human condition of having a body is not identical with the ancient contempt for the necessities of life; to be subject to necessity was only one aspect of bodily existence, and the body, once freed of this necessity, was capable of that pure appearance the Greeks called beauty. The philosophers since Plato added to the resentment of being forced by bodily wants the resentment of movement of any kind. It is because the philosopher lives in complete quiet that it is only his body which, according to Plato, inhabits the city. Here lies also the origin of the early reproach of busy-bodiness (*polypragmosynē*) leveled against those who spent their lives in politics.

16. See F. M. Cornford, "Plato's Commonwealth," in *Unwritten Philosophy* (1950), p. 54: "The death of Pericles and the Peloponnesian War mark the moment when the men of thought and the men of action began to take different paths, destined to diverge more and more widely till the Stoic sage ceased to be a citizen of his own country and became a citizen of the universe."

17. Herodotus (i. 131), after reporting that the Persians have "no images of the gods, no temples nor altars, but consider these doings to be foolish," goes on to explain that this shows that they "do not believe, as the Greeks do, that the gods are *anthrōpophyeis*, of human nature," or, we may add, that gods and men have the same nature. See also Pindar *Carmina Nemaea* vi.

18. See Ps. Aristotle *Economics* 1343b24: Nature guarantees to the species their being forever through recurrence (*periodos*), but cannot guarantee such being forever to the individual. The same thought, "For living things, life is being," appears in *On the Soul* 415b13.

19. The Greek language does not distinguish between "works" and "deeds," but calls both *erga* if they are durable enough to last and great enough to be remembered. It is only when the philosophers, or rather the Sophists, began to draw their "endless distinctions" and to distinguish between making and acting (*poiein* and *prattein*) that the nouns *poiēmata* and *pragmata* received wider currency (see Plato's *Charmides* 163).

Homer does not yet know the word *pragmata*, which in Plato (*ta tōn anthrōpōn pragmata*) is best rendered by "human affairs" and has the connotations of trouble and futility. In Herodotus *pragmata* can have the same connotation (cf., for instance, i. 155).

20. Heraclitus, frag. B29 (Diels, *Fragmente der Vorsokratiker* [4th ed.; 1922]).

21. *In vita activa fixi permanere possumus; in contemplativa autem intenta mente manere nullo modo valemus* (Aquinas *Summa theologica* ii. 2. 181. 4).

22. It seems quite striking that the Homeric gods act only with respect to men, ruling them from afar or interfering in their affairs. Conflicts and strife between the gods also seem to arise chiefly from their part in human affairs or their conflicting partiality with respect to mortals. What then appears is a story in which men and gods act together, but the scene is set by the mortals, even when the decision is arrived at in the assembly of gods on Olympus. I think such a "co-operation" is indicated in the Homeric *erg' andrōn te theōn te* (*Odyssey* i. 338): the bard sings the deeds of gods and men, not stories of the gods and stories of men. Similarly, Hesiod's *Theogony* deals not with the deeds of gods but with the genesis of the world (116); it therefore tells how things came into being through begetting and giving birth (constantly recurring). The singer, servant of the Muses, sings "the glorious deeds of men of old and the blessed gods" (97 ff.), but nowhere, as far as I can see, the glorious deeds of the gods.

23. The quotation is from the Index Rerum to the Taurinian edition of Aquinas (1922). The word "politicus" does not occur in the text, but the Index summarizes Thomas' meaning correctly, as can be seen from *Summa theologica* i. 96. 4; ii. 2. 109. 3.

24. *Societas regni* in Livius, *societas sceleris* in Cornelius Nepos. Such an alliance could also be concluded for business purposes, and Aquinas still holds that a "true *societas*" between businessmen exists only "where the investor himself shares in the risk," that is, where the partnership is truly an alliance (see W. J. Ashley, *An Introduction to English Economic History and Theory* [1931], p. 419).

25. I use here and in the following the word "man-kind" to designate the human species, as distinguished from "mankind," which indicates the sum total of human beings.

26. Werner Jaeger, *Paideia* (1945), III, 111.

27. Although Fustel de Coulanges' chief thesis, according to the Introduction to *The Ancient City* (Anchor ed.; 1956), consists of demonstrating that "the same religion" formed the ancient family organization and the ancient city-state, he brings numerous references to the fact that the regime of the *gens* based on the religion of the family and the regime of the city "were in reality two antagonistic forms of government. . . . Either the city could not last, or it must in the course of time break up the family" (p. 252). The reason for the contradiction in this great book seems to me to be in Coulanges' attempt to treat Rome and the Greek city-states together; for his evidence and categories he relies chiefly on Roman institutional and political sentiment, although he recognizes that the Vesta cult "became weakened in Greece at a very early date . . . but it never became enfeebled at Rome" (p. 146). Not only was the gulf between household and city much deeper in Greece than in Rome, but only in Greece was the Olympian religion, the religion of Homer and the city-state, separate from and superior to the older religion of family and household. While Vesta, the goddess of the hearth, became the protectress

of a "city hearth" and part of the official, political cult after the unification and second foundation of Rome, her Greek colleague, Hestia, is mentioned for the first time by Hesiod, the only Greek poet who, in conscious opposition to Homer, praises the life of the hearth and the household; in the official religion of the *polis*, she had to cede her place in the assembly of the twelve Olympian gods to Dionysos (see Mommsen, *Römische Geschichte* [5th ed.], Book I, ch. 12, and Robert Graves, *The Greek Myths* [1955], 27. k).

28. The passage occurs in Phoenix' speech, *Iliad* ix. 443. It clearly refers to education for war and *agora*, the public meeting, in which men can distinguish themselves. The literal translation is: "[your father] charged me to teach you all this, to be a speaker of words and a doer of deeds" (*mythōn te rhētēr' emenai prēktēra te ergōn*).

29. The literal translation of the last lines of *Antigone* (1350–54) is as follows: "But great words, counteracting [or paying back] the great blows of the overproud, teach understanding in old age." The content of these lines is so puzzling to modern understanding that one rarely finds a translator who dares to give the bare sense. An exception is Hölderlin's translation: "Grosse Blicke aber, / Grosse Streiche der hohen Schultern / Vergeltend, / Sie haben im Alter gelehrt, zu denken." An anecdote, reported by Plutarch, may illustrate the connection between acting and speaking on a much lower level. A man once approached Demosthenes and related how terribly he had been beaten. "But you," said Demosthenes, "suffered nothing of what you tell me." Whereupon the other raised his voice and cried out: "I suffered nothing?" "Now," said Demosthenes, "I hear the voice of somebody who was injured and who suffered" (*Lives*, "Demosthenes"). A last remnant of this ancient connection of speech and thought, from which our notion of expressing thought through words is absent, may be found in the current Ciceronian phrase of *ratio et oratio*.

30. It is characteristic for this development that every politician was called a "rhetor" and that rhetoric, the art of public speaking, as distinguished from dialectic, the art of philosophic speech, is defined by Aristotle as the art of persuasion (see *Rhetoric* 1354a12 ff., 1355b26 ff.). (The distinction itself is derived from Plato, *Gorgias* 448.) It is in this sense that we must understand the Greek opinion of the decline of Thebes, which was ascribed to Theban neglect of rhetoric in favor of military exercise (see Jacob Burckhardt, *Griechische Kulturgeschichte*, ed. Kroener, III, 190).

31. *Nicomachean Ethics* 1142a25 and 1178a6 ff.

32. Aquinas *op. cit.* ii. 2. 50. 3.

33. The terms *dominus* and *paterfamilias* therefore were synonymous, like the terms *servus* and *familiaris: Dominum patrem familiae appellaverunt; servos . . . familiares* (Seneca *Epistolae* 47. 12). The old Roman liberty of the citizen disappeared when the Roman emperors adopted the title *dominus*, "ce nom, qu'Auguste et que Tibère encore, repoussaient comme une malédiction et une injure" (H. Wallon, *Histoire de l'esclavage dans l'antiquité* [1847], III, 21).

34. According to Gunnar Myrdal (*The Political Element in the Development of Economic Theory* [1953], p. xl), the "idea of Social Economy or collective housekeeping (*Volkswirtschaft*)" is one of the "three main foci" around which "the political speculation which has permeated economics from the very beginning is found to be crystallized."

35. This is not to deny that the nation-state and its society grew out of the medieval kingdom and feudalism, in whose framework the family and household unit have an importance unequalled in classical antiquity. The difference, however, is marked. Within the feudal framework, families and households were mutually almost independent, so that the royal household, representing a given territorial region and ruling the feudal lords as *primus inter pares*, did not pretend, like an absolute ruler, to be the head of one family. The medieval "nation" was a conglomeration of families; its members did not think of themselves as members of one family comprehending the whole nation.

36. The distinction is very clear in the first paragraphs of the Ps. Aristotelian *Economics*, because it opposes the despotic one-man rule (*mon-archia*) of the household organization to the altogether different organization of the *polis*.

37. In Athens, one may see the turning point in Solon's legislation. Coulanges rightly sees in the Athenian law that made it a filial duty to support parents the proof of the loss of paternal power (*op. cit.*, pp. 315–16). However, paternal power was limited only if it conflicted with the interest of the city and never for the sake of the individual family member. Thus the sale of children and the exposure of infants lasted throughout antiquity (see R. H. Barrow, *Slavery in the Roman Empire* [1928], p. 8: "Other rights in the *patria potestas* had become obsolete; but the right of exposure remained unforbidden till A.D. 374").

38. It is interesting for this distinction that there were Greek cities where citizens were obliged by law to share their harvest and consume it in common, whereas each of them had the absolute uncontested property of his soil. See Coulanges (*op. cit.*, p. 61), who calls this law "a singular contradiction"; it is no contradiction, because these two types of property had nothing in common in ancient understanding.

39. See *Laws* 842.

40. Quoted from Coulanges, *op. cit.*, p. 96; the reference to Plutarch is *Quaestiones Romanae* 51. It seems strange that Coulanges' one-sided emphasis on the underworld deities in Greek and Roman religion should have overlooked that these gods were not mere gods of the dead and the cult not merely a "death cult," but that this early earth-bound religion served life and death as two aspects of the same process. Life rises out of the earth and returns to it; birth and death are but two different stages of the same biological life over which the subterranean gods hold sway.

41. The discussion between Socrates and Eutherus in Xenophon's *Memorabilia* (ii. 8) is quite interesting: Eutherus is forced by necessity to labor with his body and is sure that his body will not be able to stand this kind of life for very long and also that in his old age he will be destitute. Still, he thinks that to labor is better than to beg. Whereupon Socrates proposes that he look for somebody "who is better off and needs an assistant." Eutherus replies that he could not bear servitude (*douleia*).

42. The reference is to Hobbes, *Leviathan*, Part I, ch. 13.

43. The most famous and the most beautiful reference is the discussion of the different forms of government in Herodotus (iii. 80–83), where Otanes, the defender of Greek equality (*isonomiē*), states that he "wishes neither to rule nor to be ruled." But it is the same spirit in which Aristotle states that the life of a free man is better than that of a

despot, denying freedom to the despot as a matter of course (*Politics* 1325a24). According to Coulanges, all Greek and Latin words which express some rulership over others, such as *rex, pater, anax, basileus*, refer originally to household relationships and were names the slaves gave to their master (*op. cit.*, pp. 89 ff., 228).

44. The proportion varied and is certainly exaggerated in Xenophon's report from Sparta, where among four thousand people in the market place, a foreigner counted no more than sixty citizens (*Hellenica* iii. 35).

45. See Myrdal, *op. cit.*: "The notion that society, like the head of a family, keeps house for its members, is deeply rooted in economic terminology. . . . In German *Volkswirtschaftslehre* suggests . . . that there is a collective subject of economic activity . . . with a common purpose and common values. In English, . . . 'theory of wealth' or 'theory of welfare' express similar ideas" (p. 140). "What is meant by a social economy whose function is social housekeeping? In the first place, it implies or suggests an analogy between the individual who runs his own or his family household and society. Adam Smith and James Mill elaborated this analogy explicitly. After J. S. Mill's criticism, and with the wider recognition of the distinction between practical and theoretical political economy, the analogy was generally less emphasized" (p. 143). The fact that the analogy was no longer used may also be due to a development in which society devoured the family unit until it became a full-fledged substitute for it.

46. R. H. Barrow, *The Romans* (1953), p. 194.

47. The characteristics which E. Levasseur (*Histoire des classes ouvrières et le de l'industrie en France avant 1789* [1900]) finds for the feudal organization of labor are true for the whole of feudal communities: "Chacun vivait chez soi et vivait de soi-même, le noble sur sa seigneurie, le vilain sur sa culture, le citadin dans sa ville" (p. 229).

48. The fair treatment of slaves which Plato recommends in the *Laws* (777) has little to do with justice and is not recommended "out of regard for the [slaves], but more out of respect to ourselves." For the coexistence of two laws, the political law of justice and the household law of rule, see Wallon, *op. cit.*, II, 200: "La loi, pendant bien longtemps, donc . . . s'abstenait de pénétrer dans la famille, où elle reconnaissait l'empire d'une autre loi." Ancient, especially Roman, jurisdiction with respect to household matters, treatment of slaves, family relationships, etc., was essentially designed to restrain the otherwise unrestricted power of the household head; that there could be a rule of justice within the entirely "private" society of the slaves themselves was unthinkable—they were by definition outside the realm of the law and subject to the rule of their master. Only the master himself, in so far as he was also a citizen, was subject to the rules of laws, which for the sake of the city eventually even curtailed his powers in the household.

49. W. J. Ashley, *op. cit.*, p. 415.

50. This "rise" from one realm or rank to a higher is a recurrent theme in Machiavelli (see esp. *Prince*, ch. 6 about Hiero of Syracuse and ch. 7; and *Discourses*, Book II, ch. 13).

51. "By Solon's time slavery had come to be looked on as worse than death" (Robert Schlaifer, "Greek Theories of Slavery from Homer to Aristotle," *Harvard Studies in Classical Philology* [1936], XLVII). Since then, *philopsychia* ("love of life") and cowardice became identified with slavishness. Thus, Plato could believe he had demonstrated the natural

slavishness of slaves by the fact that they had not preferred death to enslavement (*Republic* 386A). A late echo of this might still be found in Seneca's answer to the complaints of slaves: "Is freedom so close at hand, yet is there any one a slave?" (*Ep.* 77. 14) or in his *vita si moriendi virtus abest, servitus est*—"life is slavery without the virtue which knows how to die" (77. 13). To understand the ancient attitude toward slavery, it is not immaterial to remember that the majority of slaves were defeated enemies and that generally only a small percentage were born slaves. And while under the Roman Republic slaves were, on the whole, drawn from outside the limits of Roman rule, Greek slaves usually were of the same nationality as their masters; they had proved their slavish nature by not committing suicide, and since courage was the political virtue par excellence, they had thereby shown their "natural" unworthiness, their unfitness to be citizens. The attitude toward slaves changed in the Roman Empire, not only because of the influence of Stoicism but because a much greater portion of the slave population were slaves by birth. But even in Rome, *labos* is considered to be closely connected with unglorious death by Vergil (*Aeneis* vi).

52. That the free man distinguishes himself from the slave through courage seems to have been the theme of a poem by the Cretan poet Hybrias: "My riches are spear and sword and the beautiful shield. . . . But those who do not dare to bear spear and sword and the beautiful shield that protects the body fall all down unto their knees with awe and address me as Lord and great King" (quoted from Eduard Meyer, *Die Sklaverei im Altertum* [1898], p. 22).

53. Max Weber, "Agrarverhältnisse im Altertum," *Gesammelte Aufsätze zur Sozial- und Wirtschaftsgeschichte* (1924), p. 147.

54. In a letter Marx wrote to Kugelmann in July, 1868.

55. This inherent worldliness of the artist is of course not changed if a "non-objective art" replaces the representation of things; to mistake this "non-objectivity" for subjectivity, where the artist feels called upon to "express himself," his subjective feelings, is the mark of charlatans, not of artists. The artist, whether painter or sculptor or poet or musician, produces worldly objects, and his reification has nothing in common with the highly questionable and, at any rate, wholly unartistic practice of expression. Expressionist art, but not abstract art, is a contradiction in terms.

CHAPTER 5

INTRODUCTION TO *HOMO SACER*

SOVEREIGN POWER AND BARE LIFE

Giorgio Agamben

The Greeks had no single term to express what we mean by the word "life." They used two terms that, although traceable to a common etymological root, are semantically and morphologically distinct: *zoē*, which expressed the simple fact of living common to all living beings (animals, men, or gods), and *bios*, which indicated the form or way of living proper to an individual or a group. When Plato mentions three kinds of life in the *Philebus*, and when Aristotle distinguishes the contemplative life of the philosopher (*bios theōrētikos*) from the life of pleasure (*bios apolaustikos*) and the political life (*bios politikos*) in the *Nichomachean Ethics*, neither philosopher would ever have used the term *zoē* (which in Greek, significantly enough, lacks a plural). This follows from the simple fact that what was at issue for both thinkers was not at all simple natural life but rather a qualified life, a particular way of life. Concerning God, Aristotle can certainly speak of a *zoē aristē kai aidios*, a more noble and eternal life (*Metaphysics*, 1072b, 28), but only insofar as he means to underline the significant truth that even God is a living being (similarly, Aristotle uses the term *zoē* in the same context—and in a way that is just as meaningful—to define the act of thinking). But to speak of a *zoē politikē* of the citizens of Athens would have made no sense. Not that the classical world had no familiarity with the idea that natural life, simple *zoē* as such, could be a good in itself. In a passage of the *Politics*, after noting that the end of the city is life according to the good, Aristotle expresses his awareness of that idea with the most perfect lucidity:

> This [life according to the good] is the greatest end both in common for all men and for each man separately. But men also come together and maintain

the political community in view of simple living, because there is probably some kind of good in the mere fact of living itself [*kata to zēn auto monon*]. If there is no great difficulty as to the way of life [*kata ton bion*], clearly most men will tolerate much suffering and hold on to life [*zoē*] as if it were a kind of serenity [*euēmeria*, beautiful day] and a natural sweetness. (1278b, 23–31)

In the classical world, however, simple natural life is excluded from the *polis* in the strict sense, and remains confined—as merely reproductive life—to the sphere of the *oikos*, "home" (*Politics*, 1252a, 26–35). At the beginning of the *Politics*, Aristotle takes the greatest care to distinguish the *oiko-nomos* (the head of an estate) and the *despotēs* (the head of the family), both of whom are concerned with the reproduction and the subsistence of life, from the politician, and he scorns those who think the difference between the two is one of quantity and not of kind. And when Aristotle defined the end of the perfect community in a passage that was to become canonical for the political tradition of the West (1252b, 30), he did so precisely by opposing the simple fact of living (*to zēn*) to politically qualified life (*to eu zēn*): *ginomenē men oun tou zēn heneken, ousa de tou eu zēn*, "born with regard to life, but existing essentially with regard to the good life" (in the Latin translation of William of Moerbeke, which both Aquinas and Marsilius of Padua had before them: *facta quidem igitur vivendi gratia, existens autem gratia bene vivendi*).

It is true that in a famous passage of the same work, Aristotle defines man as a *politikon zōon* (*Politics*, 1253a, 4). But here (aside from the fact that in Attic Greek the verb *bionai* is practically never used in the present tense), "political" is not an attribute of the living being as such, but rather a specific difference that determines the genus *zōon*. (Only a little later, after all, human politics is distinguished from that of other living beings in that it is founded, through a supplement of politicity [*policità*] tied to language, on a community not simply of the pleasant and the painful but of the good and the evil and of the just and the unjust.)

Michel Foucault refers to this very definition when, at the end of the first volume of *The History of Sexuality*, he summarizes the process by which, at the threshold of the modern era, natural life begins to be included in the mechanisms and calculations of State power, and politics turns into *biopolitics*. "For millennia," he writes, "man remained what he was for Aristotle: a living animal with the additional capacity for political existence; modern man is an animal whose politics calls his existence as a living being into question" (*La volonté*, p. 188).

According to Foucault, a society's "threshold of biological modernity" is situated at the point at which the species and the individual as a simple living body become what is at stake in a society's political strategies. After 1977, the courses at the Collège de France start to focus on the passage from the "territorial State" to the "State of population" and on the resulting increase in importance of the nation's health and biological life as a problem of sovereign power, which is then gradually transformed into a "government of men" (*Dits et écrits*, 3: 719). "What follows is a kind of bestialization of man achieved through the most sophisticated political techniques. For the first time in history, the possibilities of the social sciences are made known, and at once it becomes possible both to protect life and to authorize a holocaust." In particular, the development and triumph of capitalism would not have been possible, from this perspective, without the disciplinary control achieved by the new bio-power, which, through a series of appropriate technologies, so to speak created the "docile bodies" that it needed.

Almost twenty years before *The History of Sexuality*, Hannah Arendt had already analyzed the process that brings *homo laborans*—and, with it, biological life as such—gradually to occupy the very center of the political scene of modernity. In *The Human Condition*, Arendt attributes the transformation and decadence of the political realm in modern societies to this very primacy of natural life over political action. That Foucault was able to begin his study of biopolitics with no reference to Arendt's work (which remains, even today, practically without continuation) bears witness to the difficulties and resistances that thinking had to encounter in this area. And it is most likely these very difficulties that account for the curious fact that Arendt establishes no connection between her research in *The Human Condition* and the penetrating analyses she had previously devoted to totalitarian power (in which a biopolitical perspective is altogether lacking), and that Foucault, in just as striking a fashion, never dwelt on the exemplary places of modern biopolitics: the concentration camp and the structure of the great totalitarian states of the twentieth century.

Foucault's death kept him from showing how he would have developed the concept and study of biopolitics. In any case, however, the entry of *zoē* into the sphere of the *polis*—the politicization of bare life as such—constitutes the decisive event of modernity and signals a radical transformation of the political-philosophical categories of classical thought. It is even likely that if politics today seems to be passing through a lasting eclipse, this is because politics has failed to reckon with this foundational event of modernity. The "enigmas" (Furet, *L'Allemagne nazi*, p. 7) that our century has proposed to historical reason and that remain with us (Nazism is only the most disquieting among them) will be solved only on the terrain—biopolitics—on which they were formed. Only within a biopolitical horizon will it be possible to decide whether the categories whose opposition founded modern politics (right/left, private/public, absolutism/democracy, etc.)—and which have been steadily dissolving, to the point of entering today into a real zone of indistinction—will have to be abandoned or will, instead, eventually regain the meaning they lost in that very horizon. And only a reflection that, taking up Foucault's and Benjamin's suggestion, thematically interrogates the link between bare life and politics, a link that secretly governs the modern ideologies seemingly most distant from one another, will be able to bring the political out of its concealment and, at the same time, return thought to its practical calling.

One of the most persistent features of Foucault's work is its decisive abandonment of the traditional approach to the problem of power, which is based on juridico-institutional models (the definition of sovereignty, the theory of the State), in favor of an unprejudiced analysis of the concrete ways in which power penetrates subjects' very bodies and forms of life. As shown by a seminar held in 1982 at the University of Vermont, in his final years Foucault seemed to orient this analysis according to two distinct directives for research: on the one hand, the study of the *political techniques* (such as the science of the police) with which the State assumes and integrates the care of the natural life of individuals into its very center; on the other hand, the examination of the *technologies of the self* by which processes of subjectivization bring the individual to bind himself to his own identity and consciousness and, at the same time, to an external power. Clearly these two lines (which carry on two tendencies present in Foucault's work from the very beginning) intersect in many points and refer back to a common center. In one of his last writings, Foucault argues that the modern Western state has integrated techniques of subjective individualization with procedures of objective totalization to an unprecedented degree, and he speaks of a real "political 'double bind,' constituted by individualization and the simultaneous totalization of structures of modern power" (*Dits et écrits*, 4: 229–32).

Yet the point at which these two faces of power converge remains strangely unclear in Foucault's work, so much so that it has even been claimed that Foucault would have consistently refused to elaborate a unitary theory of power. If Foucault contests the traditional approach to the problem of power, which is exclusively based on juridical models ("What legitimates power?") or on institutional models ("What is the State?"), and if he calls for a "liberation from the theoretical privilege of sovereignty" in order to construct an analytic of power that would not take law as its model and code, then where, in the body of power, is the zone of indistinction (or, at least, the point of intersection) at which techniques of individualization and totalizing procedures converge? And, more generally, is there a unitary center in which the political "double bind" finds its *raison d'être?* That there is a subjective aspect in the genesis of power was already implicit in the concept of *servitude volontaire* in Étienne de La Boétie. But what is the point at which the voluntary servitude of individuals comes into contact with objective power? Can one be content, in such a delicate area, with psychological explanations such as the suggestive notion of a parallelism between external and internal neuroses? Confronted with phenomena such as the power of the society of the spectacle that is everywhere transforming the political realm today, is it legitimate or even possible to hold subjective technologies and political techniques apart?

Although the existence of such a line of thinking seems to be logically implicit in Foucault's work, it remains a blind spot to the eye of the researcher, or rather something like a vanishing point that the different perspectival lines of Foucault's inquiry (and, more generally, of the entire Western reflection on power) converge toward without reaching.

The present inquiry concerns precisely this hidden point of intersection between the juridico-institutional and the biopolitical models of power. What this work has had to record among its likely conclusions is precisely that the two analyses cannot be separated, and that the inclusion of bare life in the political realm constitutes the original—if concealed—nucleus of sovereign power. *It can even be said that the production of a biopolitical body is the original activity of sovereign power.* In this sense, biopolitics is at least as old as the sovereign exception. Placing biological life at the center of its calculations, the modern State therefore does nothing other than bring to light the secret tie uniting power and bare life, thereby reaffirming the bond (derived from a tenacious correspondence between the modern and the archaic which one encounters in the most diverse spheres) between modern power and the most immemorial of the *arcana imperii*.

If this is true, it will be necessary to reconsider the sense of the Aristotelian definition of the *polis* as the opposition between life (*zēn*) and good life (*eu zēn*). The opposition is, in fact, at the same time an implication of the first in the second, of bare life in politically qualified life. What remains to be interrogated in the Aristotelian definition is not merely—as has been assumed until now—the sense, the modes, and the possible articulations of the "good life" as the *telos* of the political. We must instead ask why Western politics first constitutes itself through an exclusion (which is simultaneously an inclusion) of bare life. What is the relation between politics and life, if life presents itself as what is included by means of an exclusion?

The structure of the exception delineated in the first part of this book appears from this perspective to be consubstantial with Western politics. In Foucault's statement according to which man was, for Aristotle, a "living animal with the additional capacity for political existence," it is therefore precisely the meaning of this "additional capacity" that must be understood as problematic. The peculiar phrase "born with regard to life, but existing essentially with regard to the good life" can be read not only as an implication of being born (*ginomenē*) in being (*ousa*), but also as an inclusive exclusion (an *exceptio*) of *zoē* in the *polis*, almost as if politics were the place in which life had to transform itself into good life and in which what had to be politicized were always already bare life. In Western politics, bare life has the peculiar privilege of being that whose exclusion founds the city of men.

It is not by chance, then, that a passage of the *Politics* situates the proper place of the *polis* in the transition from voice to language. The link between bare life and politics is the same link that the metaphysical definition of man as "the living being who has language" seeks in the relation between *phonē* and *logos*:

> Among living beings, only man has language. The voice is the sign of pain and pleasure, and this is why it belongs to other living beings (since their nature has developed to the point of having the sensations of pain and pleasure and of signifying the two). But language is for manifesting the fitting and the unfitting and the just and the unjust. To have the sensation of the good and the bad and of the just and the unjust is what is proper to men as opposed to other living beings, and the community of these things makes dwelling and the city. (1253a, 10–18)

The question "In what way does the living being have language?" corresponds exactly to the question "In what way does bare life dwell in the *polis?*" The living being has *logos* by taking away and conserving its own voice in it, even as it dwells in the *polis* by letting its own bare life be excluded, as an exception, within it. Politics therefore appears as the truly fundamental structure of Western metaphysics insofar as it occupies the threshold on which the relation between the living being and the *logos* is realized. In the "politicization" of bare life—the metaphysical task *par excellence*—the humanity of living man is decided. In assuming this task, modernity does nothing other than declare its own faithfulness to the essential structure of the metaphysical tradition. The fundamental categorial pair of Western politics is not that of friend/enemy but that of bare life/political existence, *zoē/bios*, exclusion/inclusion. There is politics because man is the living being who, in language, separates and opposes himself to his own bare life and, at the same time, maintains himself in relation to that bare life in an inclusive exclusion.

The protagonist of this book is bare life, that is, the life of *homo sacer* (sacred man), who *may be killed and yet not sacrificed*, and whose essential function in modern politics we intend to assert. An obscure figure of archaic Roman law, in which human life is included in the juridical order [*ordinamento*][1] solely in the form of its exclusion (that is, of its capacity to be killed), has thus offered the key by which not only the sacred texts of sovereignty but also the very codes of political power will unveil their mysteries. At the same time, however, this ancient meaning of the term *sacer* presents us with the enigma of a figure of the sacred that, before or beyond the religious, constitutes the first paradigm of the political realm of the West. The Foucauldian thesis will then have to be corrected or, at least, completed, in the sense that what characterizes modern politics is not so much the inclusion of *zoē* in the *polis*—which is, in itself, absolutely ancient—nor simply the fact that life as such becomes a principal object of the projections and calculations of State power. Instead the decisive fact is that, together with the process by which the exception everywhere becomes the rule, the realm of bare life—which is originally situated at the margins of the political order—gradually begins to coincide with the political realm, and exclusion and inclusion, outside and inside, *bios* and *zoē*, right and fact, enter into a zone of irreducible indistinction. At once excluding bare life from and capturing it within the political order, the state of exception actually constituted, in its very separateness, the hidden foundation on which the entire political system rested. When its borders begin to be blurred, the bare life that dwelt there frees itself in the city and becomes both subject and object of the conflicts of the political order, the one place for both the organization of State power and emancipation from it. Everything happens as if, along with the disciplinary process by which State power makes man as a living being into its own specific object, another process is set in motion that in large measure corresponds to the birth of modern democracy, in which man as a living being presents himself no longer as an *object* but as the *subject* of political power. These processes—which in many ways oppose and (at least apparently) bitterly conflict with each other—nevertheless converge insofar as both concern the bare life of the citizen, the new biopolitical body of humanity.

If anything characterizes modern democracy as opposed to classical democracy, then, it is that modern democracy presents itself from the beginning as a vindication and liberation of *zoē*, and that it is constantly trying to transform its own bare life into a way of life and to find, so to speak, the *bios* of *zoē*. Hence, too, modern democracy's specific aporia: it wants to put the freedom and happiness of men into play in the very place—"bare life"—that marked their subjection. Behind the long, strife-ridden process that leads to the recognition of rights and formal liberties stands once again the body of the sacred man with his double sovereign, his life that cannot be sacrificed yet may, nevertheless, be killed. To become conscious of this aporia is not to belittle the conquests and accomplishments of democracy. It is, rather, to try to understand once and for all why democracy, at the very moment in which it seemed to have finally triumphed over its adversaries and reached its greatest height, proved itself incapable of saving *zoē*, to whose happiness it had dedicated all its efforts, from unprecedented ruin. Modern democracy's decadence and gradual convergence with totalitarian states in post-democratic spectacular societies (which begins to become evident with Alexis de Tocqueville and finds its final sanction in the analyses of Guy Debord) may well be rooted in this aporia, which marks the beginning of modern democracy and forces it into complicity with its most implacable enemy. Today politics knows no value (and, consequently, no nonvalue) other than life, and until the contradictions that this fact implies are dissolved, Nazism and fascism—which transformed the decision on bare life into the supreme political principle—will remain stubbornly with us. According to the testimony of Robert Antelme, in fact, what the camps taught those who lived there was precisely that "calling into question the quality of man provokes an almost biological assertion of belonging to the human race" (*L'éspèce humaine*, p. 11).

The idea of an inner solidarity between democracy and totalitarianism (which here we must, with every caution, advance) is obviously not (like Leo Strauss's thesis concerning the secret convergence of the final goals of liberalism and communism) a historiographical claim, which would authorize the liquidation and leveling of the enormous differences that characterize their history and their rivalry. Yet this idea must nevertheless be strongly maintained on a historico-philosophical level, since it alone will allow us to orient ourselves in relation to the new realities and unforeseen convergences of the end of the millennium. This idea alone will make it possible to clear the way for the new politics, which remains largely to be invented.

In contrasting the "beautiful day" (*euēmeria*) of simple life with the "great difficulty" of political *bios* in the passage cited above, Aristotle may well have given the most beautiful formulation to the aporia that lies at the foundation of Western politics. The 24 centuries that have since gone by have brought only provisional and ineffective solutions. In carrying out the metaphysical task that has led it more and more to assume the form of a biopolitics, Western politics has not succeeded in constructing the link between *zoē* and *bios*, between voice and language, that would have healed the fracture. Bare life remains included in politics in the form of the exception, that is, as something that is included solely through an exclusion. How is it possible to "politicize" the "natural sweetness" of *zoē*? And first of all, does *zoē* really need to be politicized, or is politics not already contained in *zoē* as its most precious center? The biopolitics of both modern totalitarianism and the society of mass hedonism and consumerism certainly constitute answers to these questions. Nevertheless, until a completely new politics—that is, a politics no longer founded on the *exceptio* of bare life—is at hand, every theory and every praxis will remain imprisoned and immobile, and the "beautiful day" of life will be given citizenship only either through blood and death or in the perfect senselessness to which the society of the spectacle condemns it.

Carl Schmitt's definition of sovereignty ("Sovereign is he who decides on the state of exception") became a commonplace even before there was any understanding that what was at issue in it was nothing less than the limit concept of the doctrine of law and the State, in which sovereignty borders (since every limit concept is always the limit between two concepts) on the sphere of life and becomes indistinguishable from it. As long as the form of the State constituted the fundamental horizon of all communal life and the political, religious, juridical, and economic doctrines that sustained this form were still strong, this "most extreme sphere" could not truly come to light. The problem of sovereignty was reduced to the question of who within the political order was invested with certain powers, and the very threshold of the political order itself was never called into question. Today, now that the great State structures have entered into a process of dissolution and the emergency has, as Walter Benjamin foresaw, become the rule, the time is ripe to place the problem of the originary structure and limits of the form of the State in a new perspective. The weakness of anarchist and Marxian critiques of the State was precisely to have not caught sight of this structure and thus to have quickly left the *arcanum imperii* aside, as if it had no substance outside of the simulacra and the ideologies invoked to justify it. But one ends up identifying with an enemy whose structure one does not understand, and the theory of the State (and in particular of the state of exception, which is to say, of the dictatorship of the proletariat as the transitional phase leading to the stateless society) is the reef on which the revolutions of our century have been shipwrecked.

This book, which was originally conceived as a response to the bloody mystification of a new planetary order, therefore had to reckon with problems—first of all that of the sacredness of life—which the author had not, in the beginning, foreseen. In the course of the undertaking, however, it became clear that one cannot, in such an area, accept as a guarantee any of the notions that the social sciences (from jurisprudence to anthropology) thought they had defined or presupposed as evident, and that many of these notions demanded—in the urgency of catastrophe—to be revised without reserve.

Note

1. "Order" renders the Italian *ordinamento*, which carries the sense not only of order but of political and juridical rule, regulation, and system. The word *ordinamento* is also the Italian translation of Carl Schmitt's *Ordnung*. Where the author refers to *ordinamento* as *Ordnung*, the English word used is the one chosen by Schmitt's translators, "ordering."—Trans.

References

Antelme, Robert. *L'espèce humaine*. Paris: Gallimard, 1994. (*The Human Race*. Trans. Jeffrey Haight and Annie Mahler. Malboro, Vt.: Malboro Press, 1992.)

Foucault, Michel. *Dits et écrits*. Vols. 3–4. Paris: Gallimard, 1994.

———. *La volonté de savoir*. Paris: Gallimard, 1976. (*History of Sexuality, Volume 1: An Introduction*. Trans. Robert Hurley. New York: Random House, 1978.)

Furet, François, ed. *L'Allemagne nazi et le génocide juif*. Paris: Seuil, 1985. (*Unanswered Questions: Nazi Germany and the Genocide of the Jews*. New York: Schocken, 1989.)

CHAPTER 6

THE POLITICIZATION OF LIFE

Giorgio Agamben

1.1

In the last years of his life, while he was working on the history of sexuality and unmasking the deployments of power at work within it, Michel Foucault began to direct his inquiries with increasing insistence toward the study of what he defined as *biopolitics*, that is, the growing inclusion of man's natural life in the mechanisms and calculations of power. At the end of the first volume of *The History of Sexuality*, Foucault, as we have seen, summarizes the process by which life, at the beginning of the modern age, comes to be what is at stake in politics: "For millennia, man remained what he was for Aristotle: a living animal with the additional capacity for political existence; modern man is an animal whose politics calls his existence as a living being into question." Until the very end, however, Foucault continued to investigate the "processes of subjectivization" that, in the passage from the ancient to the modern world, bring the individual to objectify his own self, constituting himself as a subject and, at the same time, binding himself to a power of external control. Despite what one might have legitimately expected, Foucault never brought his insights to bear on what could well have appeared to be the exemplary place of modern biopolitics: the politics of the great totalitarian states of the twentieth century. The inquiry that began with a reconstruction of the *grand enfermement* in hospitals and prisons did not end with an analysis of the concentration camp.

If, on the other hand, the pertinent studies that Hannah Arendt dedicated to the structure of totalitarian states in the postwar period have a limit, it is precisely the absence of any biopolitical perspective. Arendt very clearly discerns the link between totalitarian rule and the particular condition of life that is the camp: "The supreme goal of all totalitarian states," she writes, in a plan for research on the concentration camps, which, unfortunately, was not carried through, "is not only the freely admitted, long-ranging ambition to global rule, but also the never admitted and immediately realized attempt at total domination. The concentration camps are the laboratories in the experiment of total domination, for human nature being what it is, this goal can be achieved only under the extreme circumstances of human made hell" (*Essays*, p. 240). Yet what escapes Arendt is that the process is in a certain sense the inverse of what she takes it to be, and that precisely the radical transformation of politics into the realm of bare life (that is, into a camp) legitimated and necessitated total domination. Only because politics in our age had been entirely transformed into biopolitics was it possible for politics to be constituted as totalitarian politics to a degree hitherto unknown.

The fact that the two thinkers who may well have reflected most deeply on the political problem of our age were unable to link together their own insights is certainly an index of the difficulty of this problem. The concept of "bare life" or "sacred life" is the focal lens through which we shall try to make their points of view converge. In the notion of bare life the interlacing of politics and life has become so tight that it cannot easily be analyzed. Until we become aware of the political nature of bare life and its modern avatars (biological life, sexuality, etc.), we will not succeed in clarifying the opacity at their center. Conversely, once modern politics enters into an intimate symbiosis with bare life, it loses the intelligibility that still seems to us to characterize the juridico-political foundation of classical politics.

1.2

Karl Löwith was the first to define the fundamental character of totalitarian states as a "politicization of life" and, at the same time, to note the curious contiguity between democracy and totalitarianism:

> Since the emancipation of the third estate, the formation of bourgeois democracy and its transformation into mass industrial democracy, the neutralization of politically relevant differences and postponement of a decision about them has developed to the point of turning into its opposite: a total politicization

[*totale Politisierung*] of everything, even of seemingly neutral domains of life. Thus in Marxist Russia there emerged a worker-state that was "more intensively state-oriented than any absolute monarchy"; in fascist Italy, a corporate state normatively regulating not only national work, but also "after-work" [*Dopolavoro*] and all spiritual life; and, in National Socialist Germany, a wholly integrated state, which, by means of racial laws and so forth, politicizes even the life that had until then been private. (*Der okkasionelle Dezionismus*, p. 33)

The contiguity between mass democracy and totalitarian states, nevertheless, does not have the form of a sudden transformation (as Löwith, here following in Schmitt's footsteps, seems to maintain); before impetuously coming to light in our century, the river of biopolitics that gave *homo sacer* his life runs its course in a hidden but continuous fashion. It is almost as if, starting from a certain point, every decisive political event were double-sided: the spaces, the liberties, and the rights won by individuals in their conflicts with central powers always simultaneously prepared a tacit but increasing inscription of individuals' lives within the state order, thus offering a new and more dreadful foundation for the very sovereign power from which they wanted to liberate themselves. "The 'right' to life," writes Foucault, explaining the importance assumed by sex as a political issue, "to one's body, to health, to happiness, to the satisfaction of needs and, beyond all the oppressions or 'alienation,' the 'right' to rediscover what one is and all that one can be, this 'right'—which the classical juridical system was utterly incapable of comprehending—was the political response to all these new procedures of power" (*La volonté*, p. 191). The fact is that one and the same affirmation of bare life leads, in bourgeois democracy, to a primacy of the private over the public and of individual liberties over collective obligations and yet becomes, in totalitarian states, the decisive political criterion and the exemplary realm of sovereign decisions. And only because biological life and its needs had become the *politically* decisive fact is it possible to understand the otherwise incomprehensible rapidity with which twentieth-century parliamentary democracies were able to turn into totalitarian states and with which this century's totalitarian states were able to be converted, almost without interruption, into parliamentary democracies. In both cases, these transformations were produced in a context in which for quite some time politics had already turned into biopolitics, and in which the only real question to be decided was which form of organization would be best suited to the task of assuring the care, control, and use of bare life. Once their fundamental referent becomes bare life, traditional political distinctions (such as those between Right and Left, liberalism and totalitarianism, private and public) lose their clarity and intelligibility and enter into a zone of indistinction. The ex-communist ruling classes' unexpected fall into the most extreme racism (as in the Serbian program of "ethnic cleansing") and the rebirth of new forms of fascism in Europe also have their roots here.

Along with the emergence of biopolitics, we can observe a displacement and gradual expansion beyond the limits of the decision on bare life, in the state of exception, in which sovereignty consisted. If there is a line in every modern state marking the point at which the decision on life becomes a decision on death, and biopolitics can turn into thanatopolitics, this line no longer appears today as a stable border dividing two clearly distinct zones. This line is now in motion and gradually moving into areas other than that of political life, areas in which the sovereign is entering into an ever more intimate symbiosis not only with the jurist but also with the doctor, the scientist, the expert, and the priest. In the pages that follow, we shall try to show that certain events that are fundamental for the political history of modernity (such as the declaration of rights), as well as others that seem instead to represent an incomprehensible intrusion of biologico-scientific principles into the political order (such as National Socialist eugenics and its elimination of "life that is unworthy of being lived," or the contemporary debate on the normative determination of death criteria), acquire their true sense only if they are brought back to the common biopolitical (or thanatopolitical) context to which they belong. From this perspective, the camp—as the pure, absolute, and impassable biopolitical space (insofar as it is founded solely on the state of exception)—will appear as the hidden paradigm of the political space of modernity, whose metamorphoses and disguises we will have to learn to recognize.

1.3

The first recording of bare life as the new political subject is already implicit in the document that is generally placed at the foundation of modern democracy: the 1679 writ of *habeas corpus*. Whatever the origin of this formula, used as early as the eighteenth century to assure the physical presence of a person before a court of justice, it is significant that at its center is neither the old subject of feudal relations and liberties nor the future *citoyen*, but rather a pure and simple *corpus*. When John the Landless conceded Magna Carta to his subjects in 1215, he turned his attention to the "archbishops, bishops, abbots, counts, barons, viscounts, provosts, officials and bailiffs," to the "cities, towns, villages," and, more generally, to the "free men of our kingdom," so that they might enjoy "their ancient liberties and free customs" as well as the ones he now specifically recognized. Article 29, whose task was to guarantee the physical freedom of the subjects, reads: "No free man [*homo liber*] may be arrested, imprisoned, dispossessed of his goods, or placed outside the law [*utlagetur*] or molested in any way; we will not place our hands on him nor will have others place their hands on him [*nec super eum ibimis, nec super eum mittimusi*], except after a legal judgment by his peers according to the law of the realm." Analogously, an ancient writ that preceded the *habeas corpus* and was understood to assure the presence of the accused in a trial bears the title *de homine replegiando* (or *repigliando*).

Consider instead the formula of the writ that the act of 1679 generalizes and makes into law: *Praecipimus tibi quod Corpus X, in custodia vestra detentum, ut dicitur, una cum causa captionis et detentionis, quodcumque nomine idem X censeatur in eadem, habeas coram nobis, apud Westminster, ad subjiciendum*, "We command that you have before us to show, at Westminster, that body X, by whatsoever name he may be called therein, which is held in your custody, as it is said, as well as the cause of the arrest and the detention." Nothing allows one to measure the difference between ancient and medieval freedom and the freedom at the basis of modern democracy better than this formula. It is not the free man and his statutes and prerogatives, nor even simply *homo*, but rather *corpus* that is the new subject of politics. And democracy is born precisely as the assertion and presentation of this "body": *habeas corpus ad subjiciendum*, "you will have to have a body to show."

The fact that, of all the various jurisdictional regulations concerned with the protection of individual freedom, it was *habeas corpus* that assumed the form of law and thus became inseparable from the history of Western democracy is surely due to mere circumstance. It is just as certain, however, that nascent European democracy thereby placed at the center of its battle against absolutism not *bios*, the qualified life of the citizen, but *zoē*—the bare, anonymous life that is as such taken into the sovereign ban ("the body of being taken . . . ," as one still reads in one modern formulation of the writ, "by whatsoever name he may be called therein").

What comes to light in order to be exposed *apud Westminster* is, once again, the body of *homo sacer*, which is to say, bare life. This is modern democracy's strength and, at the same time, its inner contradiction: modern democracy does not abolish sacred life but rather shatters it and disseminates it into every individual body, making it into what is at stake in political conflict. And the root of modern democracy's secret biopolitical calling lies here: he who will appear later as the bearer of rights and, according to a curious oxymoron, as the new sovereign subject (*subiectus superaneus*, in other words, what is below and, at the same time, most elevated) can only be constituted as such through the repetition of the sovereign exception and the isolation of *corpus*, bare life, in himself. If it is true that law needs a body in order to be in force, and if one can speak, in this sense, of "law's desire to have a body," democracy responds to this desire by compelling law to assume the care of this body. This ambiguous (or polar) character of democracy appears even more clearly in the *habeas corpus* if one considers the fact that the same legal procedure that was originally intended to assure the presence of the accused at the trial and, therefore, to keep the accused from avoiding judgment, turns—in its new and definitive form—into grounds for the sheriff to detain and exhibit the body of the accused. *Corpus is a two-faced being, the bearer both of subjection to sovereign power and of individual liberties.*

This new centrality of the "body" in the sphere of politico-juridical terminology thus coincides with the more general process by which *corpus* is given such a privileged position in the philosophy and science of the Baroque age, from Descartes to Newton, from Leibniz to Spinoza. And yet in political reflection *corpus* always maintains a close tie to bare life, even when it becomes the central metaphor of the political community, as in *Leviathan* or *The Social Contract*. Hobbes's use of the term is particularly instructive in this regard. If it is true that in *De homine* he distinguishes man's natural body from his political body (*homo enim non modo corpus naturale est, sed etiam civitatis, id est, ut ita loquar, corporis politici pars*, "Man is not only a natural body, but also a body of the city, that is, of the so-called political part" [*De homine*, p. 1]), in the *De cive* it is precisely the body's capacity to be killed that founds both the natural equality of men and the necessity of the "Commonwealth":

> If we look at adult men and consider the fragility of the unity of the human body (whose ruin marks the end of every strength, vigor, and force) and the ease with which the weakest man can kill the strongest man, there is no reason for someone to trust in his strength and think himself superior to others by nature. Those who can do the same things to each other are equals. And those

who can do the supreme thing—that is, kill—are by nature equal among themselves. (*De cive*, p. 93)

The great metaphor of the Leviathan, whose body is formed out of all the
bodies of individuals, must be read in this light. The absolute capacity of the
subjects' bodies to be killed forms the new political body of the West.

References

Hobbes, Thomas. *De cive: The Latin Version*. Ed. Howard Warrender. Oxford: Claren-
don Press, 1983.
———. *De homine*. In Thomas Hobbes, *Opera philosophica quae latine scripsit omnia
in unum corpus*, ed. William Molesworth, vol. 2. London: Apud J. Bonn, 1983.
Löwith, Karl. *Der okkasionelle Dezionismus von Carl Schmitt*. In Karl Löwith,
Sämtliche Schriften, ed. Klaus Stichweh and Marc B. de Launay, vol. 8. Stuttgart:
Metzler, 1984.

CHAPTER 7

BIOPOLITICS AND THE
RIGHTS OF MAN

Giorgio Agamben

2.1

Hannah Arendt entitled the fifth chapter of her book on imperialism, which is dedicated to the problem of refugees, "The Decline of the Nation-State and the End of the Rights of Man." Linking together the fates of the rights of man and of the nation-state, her striking formulation seems to imply the idea of an intimate and necessary connection between the two, though the author herself leaves the question open. The paradox from which Arendt departs is that the very figure who should have embodied the rights of man par excellence—the refugee—signals instead the concept's radical crisis. "The conception of human rights," she states, "based upon the assumed existence of a human being as such, broke down at the very moment when those who professed to believe in it were for the first time confronted with people who had indeed lost all other qualities and specific relationships—except that they were still human" (*Origins*, p. 299). In the system of the nation-state, the so-called sacred and inalienable rights of man show themselves to lack every protection and reality at the moment in which they can no longer take the form of rights belonging to citizens of a state. If one considers the matter, this is in fact implicit in the ambiguity of the very title of the French Declaration of the Rights of Man and Citizen, of 1789. In the phrase *La déclaration des droits de l'homme et du citoyen*, it is not clear whether the two terms *homme* and *citoyen* name two autonomous beings or instead form a unitary system in which the first is always already included in the second. And if the latter is the case, the kind of relation that exists between *homme* and *citoyen* still remains unclear. From this perspective, Burke's *boutade* according to which he preferred his "Rights of an Englishman" to the inalienable rights of man acquires an unsuspected profundity.

Arendt does no more than offer a few, essential hints concerning the link between the rights of man and the nation-state, and her suggestion has therefore not been followed up. In the period after the Second World War, both the instrumental emphasis on the rights of man and the rapid growth of declarations and agreements on the part of international organizations have ultimately made any authentic understanding of the historical significance of the phenomenon almost impossible. Yet it is time to stop regarding declarations of rights as proclamations of eternal, metajuridical values binding the legislator (in fact, without much success) to respect eternal ethical principles, and to begin to consider them according to their real historical function in the modern nation-state. Declarations of rights represent the originary figure of the inscription of natural life in the juridico-political order of the nation-state. The same bare life that in the *ancien régime* was politically neutral and belonged to God as creaturely life and in the classical world was (at least apparently) clearly distinguished as *zoē* from political life (*bios*) now fully enters into the structure of the state and even becomes the earthly foundation of the state's legitimacy and sovereignty.

A simple examination of the text of the Declaration of 1789 shows that it is precisely bare natural life—which is to say, the pure fact of birth—that appears here as the source and bearer of rights. "Men," the first article declares, "are born and remain free and equal in rights" (from this perspective, the strictest formulation of all is to be found in La Fayette's project elaborated in July 1789: "Every man is born with inalienable and indefeasible rights"). At the same time, however, the very natural life that, inaugurating the biopolitics of modernity, is placed at the foundation of the order vanishes into the figure of the citizen, in whom rights are "preserved" (according to the second article: "The goal of every political association is the preservation of the natural and indefeasible rights of man"). And the Declaration can attribute sovereignty to the "nation" (according to the third article: "The principle of all sovereignty resides essentially in the nation") precisely because it has already inscribed this element of birth in the very heart of the political community. The nation—the term derives etymologically from *nascere* (to be born)—thus closes the open circle of man's birth.

2.2

Declarations of rights must therefore be viewed as the place in which the passage from divinely authorized royal sovereignty to national sovereignty is accomplished. This passage assures the *exceptio* of life in the new state order that will succeed the collapse of the *ancien régime*. The fact that in this process the "subject" is, as has been noted, transformed into a "citizen" means that birth—which is to say, bare natural life as such—here for the first time becomes (thanks to a transformation whose biopolitical consequences we are only beginning to discern today) the immediate bearer of sovereignty. The principle of nativity and the principle of sovereignty, which were separated in the *ancien régime* (where birth marked only the emergence of a *sujet*, a subject), are now irrevocably united in the body of the "sovereign subject" so that the foundation of the new nation-state may be constituted. It is not possible to understand the "national" and biopolitical development and vocation of the modern state in the nineteenth and twentieth centuries if one forgets that what lies at its basis is not man as a free and conscious political subject but, above all, man's bare life, the simple birth that as such is, in the passage from subject to citizen, invested with the principle of sovereignty. The fiction implicit here is that *birth* immediately becomes *nation* such that there can be no interval of separation [*scarto*] between the two terms. Rights are attributed to man (or originate in him) solely to the extent that man is the immediately vanishing ground (who must never come to light as such) of the citizen.

Only if we understand this essential historical function of the doctrine of rights can we grasp the development and metamorphosis of declarations of rights in our century. When the hidden difference [*scarto*] between birth and nation entered into a lasting crisis following the devastation of Europe's geopolitical order after the First World War, what appeared was Nazism and fascism, that is, two properly biopolitical movements that made of natural life the exemplary place of the sovereign decision. We are used to condensing the essence of National Socialist ideology into the syntagm "blood and soil" (*Blut und Boden*). When Alfred Rosenberg wanted to express his party's vision of the world, it is precisely to this hendiadys that he turned. "The National Socialist vision of the world," he writes, "springs from the conviction that soil and blood constitute what is essential about Germanness, and that it is therefore in reference to these two givens that a cultural and state politics must be directed" (*Blut und Ehre*, p. 242). Yet it has too often been forgotten that this formula, which is so highly determined politically, has, in truth, an innocuous juridical origin. The formula is nothing other than the concise expression of the two criteria that, already in Roman law, served to identify citizenship (that is, the primary inscription of life in the state order): *ius soli* (birth in a certain territory) and *ius sanguinis* (birth from citizen parents). In the *ancien régime*, these two traditional juridical criteria had no essential meaning, since they expressed only a relation of subjugation. Yet with the French Revolution they acquire a new and decisive importance. Citizenship now does not simply identify a generic subjugation to royal authority or a determinate system of laws, nor does it simply embody (as Chalier maintained when he suggested to the convention on September 23, 1792, that the title of citizen be substituted for the traditional title *monsieur* or *sieur* in every public act) the new egalitarian principle; citizenship names the new status of life as origin and ground of sovereignty and, therefore, literally identifies—to cite Jean-Denis Lanjuinais's words to the convention—*les membres du souverain*, "the members of the sovereign." Hence the centrality (and the ambiguity) of the notion of "citizenship" in modern political thought, which compels Rousseau to say, "No author in France . . . has understood the true meaning of the term 'citizen.'" Hence too, however, the rapid growth in the course of the French Revolution of regulatory provisions specifying which *man* was a *citizen* and which one not, and articulating and gradually restricting the area of the *ius soli* and the *ius sanguinis*. Until this time, the questions "What is French? What is German?" had constituted not a political problem but only one theme among others discussed in philosophical anthropologies. Caught in a constant work of redefinition, these questions now begin to become essentially political, to the point that, with National Socialism, the answer to the question "Who and what is German?" (and also, therefore, "Who and what is not German?") coincides immediately with the highest political task. Fascism and Nazism are, above all, redefinitions of the relations between man and citizen, and become fully intelligible only when situated—no matter how paradoxical it may seem—in the biopolitical context inaugurated by national sovereignty and declarations of rights.

Only this tie between the rights of man and the new biopolitical determination of sovereignty makes it possible to understand the striking fact, which has often been noted by historians of the French Revolution, that at the very moment in which native rights were declared to be inalienable and indefeasible, the rights of man in general were divided into active rights and passive rights. In his *Préliminaires de la constitution*, Sieyès already clearly stated:

Natural and civil rights are those rights *for* whose preservation society is formed, and political rights are those rights *by* which society is formed. For the sake of clarity, it would be best to call the first ones passive rights, and the second ones active rights. . . . All inhabitants of a country must enjoy the rights of passive citizens . . . all are not active citizens. Women, at least in the present state, children, foreigners, and also those who would not at all contribute to the public establishment must have no active influence on public matters. (*Écrits politiques*, pp. 189–206)

And after defining the *membres du souverain*, the passage of Lanjuinais cited above continues with these words: "Thus children, the insane, minors, women, those condemned to a punishment either restricting personal freedom or bringing disgrace [*punition afflictive ou inflammante*] . . . will not be citizens" (quoted in Sewell, "Le citoyen," p. 105).

Instead of viewing these distinctions as a simple restriction of the democratic and egalitarian principle, in flagrant contradiction to the spirit and letter of the declarations, we ought first to grasp their coherent biopolitical meaning. One of the essential characteristics of modern biopolitics (which will continue to increase in our century) is its constant need to redefine the threshold in life that distinguishes and separates what is inside from what is outside. Once it crosses over the walls of the *oikos* and penetrates more and more deeply into the city, the foundation of sovereignty—nonpolitical life—is immediately transformed into a line that must be constantly redrawn. Once *zoē* is politicized by declarations of rights, the distinctions and thresholds that make it possible to isolate a sacred life must be newly defined. And when natural life is wholly included in the *polis*—and this much has, by now, already happened—these thresholds pass, as we will see, beyond the dark boundaries separating life from death in order to identify a new living dead man, a new sacred man.

2.3

If refugees (whose number has continued to grow in our century, to the point of including a significant part of humanity today) represent such a disquieting element in the order of the modern nation-state, this is above all because by breaking the continuity between man and citizen, *nativity* and *nationality*, they put the originary fiction of modern sovereignty in crisis. Bringing to light the difference between birth and nation, the refugee causes the secret presupposition of the political domain—bare life—to appear for an instant within that domain. In this sense, the refugee is truly "the man of rights," as Arendt suggests, the first and only real appearance of rights outside the fiction of the citizen that always covers them over. Yet this is precisely what makes the figure of the refugee so hard to define politically.

Since the First World War, the birth-nation link has no longer been capable of performing its legitimating function inside the nation-state, and the two terms have begun to show themselves to be irreparably loosened from each other. From this perspective, the immense increase of refugees and stateless persons in Europe (in a short span of time 1,500,000 White Russians, 700,000 Armenians, 500,000 Bulgarians, 1,000,000 Greeks, and hundreds of thousands of Germans, Hungarians, and Rumanians were displaced from their countries) is one of the two most significant phenomena. The other is the contemporaneous institution by many European states of juridical measures allowing for the mass denaturalization and denationalization of large portions of their own populations. The first introduction of such rules into the juridical order took place in France in 1915 with respect to naturalized citizens of "enemy" origin; in 1922, Belgium followed the French example and revoked the naturalization of citizens who had committed "antinational" acts during the war; in 1926, the fascist regime issued an analogous law with respect to citizens who had shown themselves to be "unworthy of Italian citizenship"; in 1933, it was Austria's turn; and so it continued until the Nuremberg laws on "citizenship in the Reich" and the "protection of German blood and honor" brought this process to the most extreme point of its development, introducing the principle according to which citizenship was something of which one had to prove oneself worthy and which could therefore always be called into question. And one of the few rules to which the Nazis constantly adhered during the course of the "Final Solution" was that Jews could be sent to the extermination camps only after they had been fully denationalized (stripped even of the residual citizenship left to them after the Nuremberg laws).

These two phenomena—which are, after all, absolutely correlative—show that the birth-nation link, on which the declaration of 1789 had founded national sovereignty, had already lost its mechanical force and power of self-regulation by the time of the First World War. On the one hand, the nation-states become greatly concerned with natural life, discriminating within it between a so-to-speak authentic life and a life lacking every political value.

(Nazi racism and eugenics are only comprehensible if they are brought back to this context.) On the other hand, the very rights of man that once made sense as the presupposition of the rights of the citizen are now progressively separated from and used outside the context of citizenship, for the sake of the supposed representation and protection of a bare life that is more and more driven to the margins of the nation-states, ultimately to be recodified into a new national identity. The contradictory character of these processes is certainly one of the reasons for the failure of the attempts of the various committees and organizations by which states, the League of Nations, and, later, the United Nations confronted the problem of refugees and the protection of human rights, from the Bureau Nansen (1922) to the contemporary High Commission for Refugees (1951), whose actions, according to statute, are to have not a political but rather a "solely humanitarian and social" mission. What is essential is that, every time refugees represent not individual cases but—as happens more and more often today—a mass phenomenon, both these organizations and individual states prove themselves, despite their solemn invocations of the "sacred and inalienable" rights of man, absolutely incapable of resolving the problem and even of confronting it adequately.

2.4

The separation between humanitarianism and politics that we are experiencing today is the extreme phase of the separation of the rights of man from the rights of the citizen. In the final analysis, however, humanitarian organizations—which today are more and more supported by international commissions—can only grasp human life in the figure of bare or sacred life, and therefore, despite themselves, maintain a secret solidarity with the very powers they ought to fight. It takes only a glance at the recent publicity campaigns to gather funds for refugees from Rwanda to realize that here human life is exclusively considered (and there are certainly good reasons for this) as sacred life—which is to say, as life that can be killed but not sacrificed—and that only as such is it made into the object of aid and protection. The "imploring eyes" of the Rwandan child, whose photograph is shown to obtain money but who "is now becoming more and more difficult to find alive," may well be the most telling contemporary cipher of the bare life that humanitarian organizations, in perfect symmetry with state power, need. A humanitarianism separated from politics cannot fail to reproduce the isolation of sacred life at the basis of sovereignty, and the camp—which is to say, the pure space of exception—is the biopolitical paradigm that it cannot master.

The concept of the refugee (and the figure of life that this concept represents) must be resolutely separated from the concept of the rights of man, and we must seriously consider Arendt's claim that the fates of human rights and the nation-state are bound together such that the decline and crisis of the one necessarily implies the end of the other. The refugee must be considered for what he is: nothing less than a limit concept that radically calls into question the fundamental categories of the nation-state, from the birth-nation to the man-citizen link, and that thereby makes it possible to clear the way for a long-overdue renewal of categories in the service of a politics in which bare life is no longer separated and excepted, either in the state order or in the figure of human rights.

The pamphlet *Make More of an Effort, Frenchmen, if You Want to Be Republicans*, read by the libertine Dolmancé in the Marquis de Sade's *Philosophy in the Boudoir*, is the first and perhaps most radical biopolitical manifesto of modernity. At the very moment in which the revolution makes birth—which is to say, bare life—into the foundation of sovereignty and rights, Sade stages (in his entire work, and in particular in *120 Days of Sodom*) the *theatrum politicum* as a theater of bare life, in which the very physiological life of bodies appears, through sexuality, as the pure political element. But the political meaning of Sade's work is nowhere as explicit as it is in this pamphlet, in which the *maisons* in which every citizen can publicly summon any other citizen in order to compel him to satisfy his own needs emerge as the political realm par excellence. Not only philosophy (Lefort, *Écrire*, pp. 100–101) but also and above all politics is sifted through the boudoir. Indeed, in Dolmancé's project, the boudoir fully takes the place of the *cité*, in a dimension in which the public and the private, political existence and bare life change places.

The growing importance of sadomasochism in modernity has its root in this exchange. Sadomasochism is precisely the technique of sexuality by which the bare life of a sexual partner is brought to light. Not only does Sade consciously invoke the analogy with sovereign power ("there is no man," he writes, "who does not want to be a despot when he has an erection"), but we also find here the symmetry between *homo sacer* and sovereign, in the complicity that ties the masochist to the sadist, the victim to the executioner.

Sade's modernity does not consist in his having foreseen the unpolitical primacy of sexuality in our unpolitical age. On the contrary, Sade is as contemporary as he is because of his incomparable presentation of the absolutely political (that is, "biopolitical") meaning of sexuality and physiological life itself. Like the concentration camps of our century, the totalitarian character of the organization of life in Silling's castle—with its meticulous regulations that do not spare any aspect of physiological life (not even the digestive function, which is obsessively codified and publicized)—has its root in the fact that what is proposed here for the first time is a normal and collective (and hence political) organization of human life founded solely on bare life.

References

Arendt, Hannah. *The Origins of Totalitarianism.* New York: Harcourt Brace Jovanovich, 1979.

Lefort, Claude. *Écrire à l'épreuve du politique.* Paris: Calmann-Levy, 1994.

Sewell, W. H. "Le citoyen/La citoyenne: Activity, Passivity, and the Revolutionary Concept of Citizenship." In *The French Revolution and the Creation of Modern Political Culture,* ed. Lucas Colin. Oxford: Pergamon, 1988.

Sieyès, Emmanuel-Joseph. *Écrits politiques.* Paris: Éditions des Archives contemporains, 1985.

CHAPTER 8

NECROPOLITICS

Achille Mbembe

TRANSLATED BY LIBBY MEINTJES

> Wa syo' lukasa pebwe
> Umwime wa pita
> [He left his footprint on the stone
> He himself passed on]
> Lamba proverb, Zambia

This essay assumes that the ultimate expression of sovereignty resides, to a large degree, in the power and the capacity to dictate who may live and who must die.[1] Hence, to kill or to allow to live constitute the limits of sovereignty, its fundamental attributes. To exercise sovereignty is to exercise control over mortality and to define life as the deployment and manifestation of power.

One could summarize in the above terms what Michel Foucault meant by *biopower*: that domain of life over which power has taken control.[2] But under what practical conditions is the right to kill, to allow to live, or to expose to death exercised? Who is the subject of this right? What does the implementation of such a right tell us about the person who is thus put to death and about the relation of enmity that sets that person against his or her murderer? Is the notion of biopower sufficient to account for the contemporary ways in which the political, under the guise of war, of resistance, or of the fight against terror, makes the murder of the enemy its primary and absolute objective? War, after all, is as much a means of achieving sovereignty as a way of exercising the right to kill. Imagining politics as a form of war, we must ask: What place is given to life, death, and the human body (in particular the wounded or slain body)? How are they inscribed in the order of power?

Politics, the Work of Death, and the "Becoming Subject"

In order to answer these questions, this essay draws on the concept of biopower and explores its relation to notions of sovereignty (*imperium*) and the state of exception.[3] Such an analysis raises a number of empirical and philosophical questions I would like to examine briefly. As is well known, the concept of the state of exception has been often discussed in relation to Nazism, totalitarianism, and the concentration/extermination camps. The death camps in particular have been interpreted variously as the central metaphor for sovereign and destructive violence and as the ultimate sign of the absolute power of the negative. Says Hannah Arendt: "There are no parallels to the life in the concentration camps. Its horror can never be fully embraced by the imagination for the very reason that it stands outside of life and death."[4] Because its inhabitants are divested of political status and reduced to bare life, the camp is, for Giorgio Agamben, "the place in which the most absolute *conditio inhumana* ever to appear on Earth was realized."[5] In the political-juridical structure of the camp, he adds, the state of exception ceases to be a temporal suspension of the state of law. According to Agamben, it acquires a permanent spatial arrangement that remains continually outside the normal state of law.

The aim of this essay is not to debate the singularity of the extermination of the Jews or to hold it up by way of example.[6] I start from the idea that modernity was at the origin of multiple concepts of sovereignty—and therefore of the biopolitical. Disregarding this multiplicity, late-modern political criticism has unfortunately privileged normative theories of democracy and has made the concept of reason one of the most important elements of both the project of modernity and of the topos of sovereignty.[7] From this perspective, the ultimate expression of sovereignty is the production of general norms by a body (the demos) made up of free and equal men and women. These men and women are posited as full subjects capable of self-understanding, self-consciousness, and self-representation. Politics, therefore, is defined as twofold: a project of autonomy and the achieving of agreement among a collectivity through communication and recognition. This, we are told, is what differentiates it from war.[8]

In other words, it is on the basis of a distinction between reason and unreason (passion, fantasy) that late-modern criticism has been able to articulate a certain idea of the political, the community, the subject—or, more fundamentally, of what the good life is all about, how to achieve it, and, in the process, to become a fully moral agent. Within this paradigm, reason is the truth of the subject and politics is the exercise of reason in the public sphere. The exercise of reason is tantamount to the exercise of freedom, a key element for individual autonomy. The romance of sovereignty, in this case, rests on the belief that the subject is the master and the controlling author of his or her own meaning. Sovereignty is therefore defined as a twofold process of *self-institution* and *self-limitation* (fixing one's own limits for oneself). The exercise of sovereignty, in turn, consists in society's capacity for self-creation through recourse to institutions inspired by specific social and imaginary significations.[9]

This strongly normative reading of the politics of sovereignty has been the object of numerous critiques, which I will not rehearse here.[10] My concern is those figures of sovereignty whose central project is not the struggle for autonomy but *the generalized instrumentalization of human existence and the material destruction of human bodies and populations.* Such figures of sovereignty are far from a piece of prodigious insanity or an expression of a rupture between the impulses and interests of the body and those of the mind. Indeed, they, like the death camps, are what constitute the *nomos* of the political space in which we still live. Furthermore, contemporary experiences of human destruction suggest that it is possible to develop a reading of politics, sovereignty, and the subject different from the one we inherited from the philosophical discourse of modernity. Instead of considering reason as the truth of the subject, we can look to other foundational categories that are less abstract and more tactile, such as life and death.

Significant for such a project is Hegel's discussion of the relation between death and the "becoming subject." Hegel's account of death centers on a bipartite concept of negativity. First, the human negates nature (a negation exteriorized in the human's effort to reduce nature to his or her own needs); and second, he or she transforms the negated element through work and struggle. In transforming nature, the human being creates a world; but in the process, he or she also is exposed to his or her own negativity. Within the Hegelian paradigm, human death is essentially voluntary. It is the result of risks consciously assumed by the subject. According to Hegel, in these risks the "animal" that constitutes the human subject's natural being is defeated.

In other words, the human being truly *becomes a subject*—that is, separated from the animal—in the struggle and the work through which he or she confronts death (understood as the violence of negativity). It is through this confrontation with death that he or she is cast into the incessant movement of history. Becoming subject therefore supposes upholding the work of death. To uphold the work of death is precisely how Hegel defines the life of the Spirit. The life of the Spirit, he says, is not that life which is frightened of death, and spares itself destruction, but that life which assumes death and lives with it. Spirit attains its truth only by finding itself in absolute dismemberment.[11] Politics is therefore death that lives a human life. Such, too, is the definition of absolute knowledge and sovereignty: risking the entirety of one's life.

Georges Bataille also offers critical insights into how death structures the idea of sovereignty, the political, and the subject. Bataille displaces Hegel's conception of the linkages between death, sovereignty, and the subject in at least three ways. First, he interprets death and sovereignty as the paroxysm of exchange and superabundance—or, to use his own terminology: *excess*. For Bataille, life is defective only when death has taken it hostage. Life itself exists only in bursts and in exchange with death.[12] He argues that death is the putrefaction of life, the stench that is at once the source and the repulsive condition of life. Therefore, although it destroys what was to be, obliterates what was supposed to continue being, and reduces to nothing the individual who takes it, death does not come down to the pure annihilation of being. Rather, it is essentially self-consciousness; moreover, it is the most luxurious form of life, that is, of effusion and exuberance: a power of proliferation. Even more radically, Bataille withdraws death from the horizon of meaning. This is in contrast to Hegel, for whom nothing is definitively lost in death; indeed, death is seen as holding great signification as a means to truth.

Second, Bataille firmly anchors death in the realm of *absolute expenditure* (the other characteristic of sovereignty), whereas Hegel tries to keep death within the economy of absolute knowledge and meaning. Life beyond utility, says Bataille, is the domain of sovereignty. This being the case, death is therefore the point at which destruction, suppression, and sacrifice constitute so irreversible and radical an expenditure—an expenditure without reserve—that they can no longer be determined as negativity. Death is therefore the very principle of excess—an *anti-economy*. Hence the metaphor of luxury and of *the luxurious character of death*.

Third, Bataille establishes a correlation among death, sovereignty, and sexuality. Sexuality is inextricably linked to violence and to the dissolution of the boundaries of the body and self by way of orgiastic and excremental impulses. As such, sexuality concerns two major forms of polarized human impulses—excretion and appropriation—as well as the regime of the taboos surrounding them.[13] The truth of sex and its deadly attributes reside in the experience of loss of the boundaries separating reality, events, and fantasized objects.

For Bataille, sovereignty therefore has many forms. But ultimately it is the refusal to accept the limits that the fear of death would have the subject respect. The sovereign world, Bataille argues, "is the world in which the limit of death is done away with. Death is present in it, its presence defines that world of violence, but while death is present it is always there only to be negated, never for anything but that. The sovereign," he concludes, "is he who is, as if death were not. . . . He has no more regard for the limits of identity than he does for limits of death, or rather these limits are the same; he is the transgression of all such limits." Since the natural domain of prohibitions includes death, among others (e.g., sexuality, filth, excrement), sovereignty requires "the strength to violate the prohibition against killing, although it's true this will be under the conditions that customs define." And contrary to subordination that is always rooted in necessity and the alleged need to avoid death, sovereignty definitely calls for the risk of death.[14]

By treating sovereignty as the violation of prohibitions, Bataille reopens the question of the limits of the political. Politics, in this case, is not the forward dialectical movement of reason. Politics can only be traced as a spiral transgression, as that difference that disorients the very idea of the limit. More specifically, politics is the difference put into play by the violation of a taboo.[15]

Biopower and the Relation of Enmity

Having presented a reading of politics as the work of death, I turn now to sovereignty, expressed predominantly as the right to kill. For the purpose of my argument, I relate Foucault's notion of biopower to two other concepts: the state of exception and the state of siege.[16] I examine those trajectories by which the state of exception and the relation of enmity have become the normative basis of the right to kill. In such instances, power (and not necessarily state power) continuously refers and appeals to exception, emergency, and a fictionalized notion of the enemy. It also labors to produce that same exception, emergency, and fictionalized enemy. In other words, the question is: What is the relationship between politics and death in those systems that can function only in a state of emergency?

In Foucault's formulation of it, biopower appears to function through dividing people into those who must live and those who must die. Operating on the basis of a split between the living and the dead, such a power defines itself in relation to a biological field—which it takes control of and vests itself in. This control presupposes the distribution of human species into groups, the subdivision of the population into subgroups, and the establishment of a biological caesura between the ones and the others. This is what Foucault labels with the (at first sight familiar) term *racism*.[17]

That *race* (or for that matter *racism*) figures so prominently in the calculus of biopower is entirely justifiable. After all, more so than class-thinking (the ideology that defines history as an economic struggle of classes), race has been the ever present shadow in Western political thought and practice, especially when it comes to imagining the inhumanity of, or rule over, foreign peoples. Referring to both this ever-presence and the phantomlike world of race in general, Arendt locates their roots in the shattering experience of otherness and suggests that the politics of race is ultimately linked to the politics of death.[18] Indeed, in Foucault's terms, racism is above all a technology aimed at permitting the exercise of biopower, "that old sovereign right of death."[19] In the economy of biopower, the function of racism is to regulate the distribution of death and to make possible the murderous functions of the state. It is, he says, "the condition for the acceptability of putting to death."[20]

Foucault states clearly that the sovereign right to kill (*droit de glaive*) and the mechanisms of biopower are inscribed in the way all modern states function;[21] indeed, they can be seen as constitutive elements of state power in modernity. According to Foucault, the Nazi state was the most complete example of a state exercising the right to kill. This state, he claims, made the management, protection, and cultivation of life coextensive with the sovereign right to kill. By biological extrapolation on the theme of the political enemy, in organizing the war against its adversaries and, at the same time, exposing its own citizens to war, the Nazi state is seen as having opened the way for a formidable consolidation of the right to kill, which culminated in the project of the "final solution." In doing so, it became the archetype of a power formation that combined the characteristics of the racist state, the murderous state, and the suicidal state.

It has been argued that the complete conflation of war and politics (and racism, homicide, and suicide), until they are indistinguishable from one another, is unique to the Nazi state. The perception of the existence of the Other as an attempt on my life, as a mortal threat or absolute danger whose biophysical elimination would strengthen my potential to life and security—this, I suggest, is one of the many imaginaries of sovereignty characteristic of both early and late modernity itself. Recognition of this perception to a large extent underpins most traditional critiques of modernity, whether they are dealing with nihilism and its proclamation of the will for power as the essence of the being; with reification understood as the *becoming-object* of the human being; or the subordination of everything to impersonal logic and to the reign of calculability and instrumental rationality.[22] Indeed, from an anthropological perspective, what these critiques implicitly contest is a definition of politics as the warlike relation par excellence. They also challenge the idea that, of necessity, the calculus of life passes through the death of the Other; or that sovereignty consists of the will and the capacity to kill in order to live.

Taking a historical perspective, a number of analysts have argued that the material premises of Nazi extermination are to be found in colonial imperialism on the one hand and, on the other, in the serialization of technical mechanisms for putting people to death—mechanisms developed between the Industrial Revolution and the First World War. According to Enzo Traverso, the gas chambers and the ovens were the culmination of a long process of dehumanizing and industrializing death, one of the original features of which was to integrate instrumental rationality with the productive and administrative rationality of the modern Western world (the factory, the bureaucracy, the prison, the army). Having become mechanized, serialized execution was transformed into a purely technical, impersonal, silent, and rapid procedure. This development was aided in part by racist stereotypes and the flourishing of a class-based racism that, in translating the social conflicts of the industrial world in racial terms, ended up comparing the working classes and "stateless people" of the industrial world to the "savages" of the colonial world.[23]

In reality, the links between modernity and terror spring from multiple sources. Some are to be found in the political practices of the ancien régime. From this perspective, the tension between the public's passion for blood and notions of justice and revenge is critical. Foucault shows in *Discipline and Punish* how the execution of the would-be regicide Damiens went on for hours, much to the satisfaction of the crowd.[24] Well known is the long procession of the condemned through the streets prior to execution, the parade of body parts—a ritual that became a standard feature of popular violence—and the final display of a severed head mounted on a pike. In France, the advent of the guillotine marks a new phase in the "democratization" of the means of disposing of the enemies of the state. Indeed, this form of execution that had once been the prerogative of the nobility is extended to all citizens. In a context in which decapitation is viewed as less demeaning than hanging, innovations in the technologies of murder aim not only at "civilizing" the ways of killing. They also aim at disposing of a large number of victims in a relatively short span of time. At the same time, a new cultural sensibility emerges in which killing the enemy of the state is an extension of play. More intimate, lurid, and leisurely forms of cruelty appear.

But nowhere is the conflation of reason and terror so manifest as during the French Revolution.[25] During the French Revolution, terror is construed as an almost necessary part of politics. An absolute transparency is claimed to exist between the state and the people. As a political category, "the people" is gradually displaced from concrete reality to rhetorical figure. As David Bates has shown, the theorists of terror believe it possible to distinguish between authentic expressions of sovereignty and the actions of the enemy. They also believe it possible to distinguish between the "error" of the citizen and the "crime" of the counterrevolutionary in the political sphere. Terror thus becomes a way of marking aberration in the body politic, and politics is read both as the mobile force of reason and as the errant attempt at creating a space where "error" would be reduced, truth enhanced, and the enemy disposed of.[26]

Finally, terror is not linked solely to the utopian belief in the unfettered power of human reason. It is also clearly related to various narratives of mastery and emancipation, most of which are underpinned by Enlightenment understandings of truth and error, the "real" and the symbolic. Marx, for example, conflates labor (the endless cycle of production and consumption required for the maintenance of human life) with work (the creation of lasting artifacts that add to the world of things). Labor is viewed as the vehicle for the historical self-creation of humankind. The historical self-creation of humankind is itself a life-and-death conflict, that is, a conflict over what paths should lead to the truth of history: the overcoming of capitalism and the commodity form and the contradictions associated with both. According to Marx, with the advent of communism and the abolition of exchange relations, things will appear as they really are; the "real" will present itself as it actually is, and the distinction between subject and object or being and consciousness will be transcended.[27] But by making human emancipation dependent upon the abolition of commodity production, Marx blurs the all-important divisions among the man-made realm of freedom, the nature-determined realm of necessity, and the contingent in history.

The commitment to the abolition of commodity production and the dream of direct and unmediated access to the "real" make these processes—the fulfillment of the so-called logic of history and the fabrication of humankind—almost necessarily violent processes. As shown by Stephen Louw, the central tenets of classical Marxism leave no choice but to "try to introduce communism by administrative fiat, which, in practice, means that social relations must be decommodified forcefully."[28] Historically, these attempts have taken such forms as labor militarization, the collapse of the distinction between state and society, and revolutionary terror.[29] It may be argued that they aimed at the eradication of the basic human condition of plurality. Indeed, the overcoming of class divisions, the withering away of the state, the flowering of a truly general will, presuppose a view of human plurality as the chief obstacle to the eventual realization of a predetermined telos of history. In other words, the subject of Marxian modernity is, fundamentally, a subject who is intent on proving his or her sovereignty through the staging of a fight to the death. Just as with Hegel, the narrative of mastery and emancipation here is clearly linked to a narrative of truth and death. Terror and killing become the means of realizing the already known telos of history.

Any historical account of the rise of modern terror needs to address slavery, which could be considered one of the first instances of biopolitical experimentation. In many respects, the very structure of the plantation system and its aftermath manifests the emblematic and paradoxical figure of the state of exception.[30] This figure is paradoxical here for two reasons. First, in the context of the plantation, the humanity of the slave appears as the perfect figure of a shadow. Indeed, the slave condition results from a triple loss: loss of a "home," loss of rights over his or her body, and loss of political status. This triple loss is identical with absolute domination, natal alienation, and social death (expulsion from humanity altogether). To be sure, as a political-juridical structure, the plantation is a space where the slave belongs to a master. It is not a community if only because by definition, a community implies the exercise of the power of speech and thought. As Paul Gilroy says, "The extreme patterns of communication defined by the institution of plantation slavery dictate that we recognize the anti-discursive and extralinguistic ramifications of power at work in shaping communicative acts. There may, after all, be no reciprocity on the plantation outside of the possibilities of rebellion and suicide, flight and silent mourning, and there is certainly no grammatical unity of speech to mediate communicative reason. In many respects, the plantation inhabitants live non-synchronously."[31] As an instrument of labor, the slave has a price. As a property, he or she has a value. His or her labor is needed and used. The slave is therefore kept alive but in a *state of injury*, in a phantomlike world of horrors and intense cruelty and profanity. The violent tenor of the slave's life is manifested through the overseer's disposition to behave in a cruel and intemperate manner and in the spectacle of pain inflicted on the slave's body.[32] Violence, here, becomes an element in manners,[33] like whipping or taking of the slave's life itself: an act of caprice and pure destruction aimed at instilling terror.[34] Slave life, in many ways, is a form of death-in-life. As Susan Buck-Morss has suggested, the slave condition produces a contradiction between freedom of property and freedom of person. An unequal relationship is established along with the inequality of the power over life. This power over the life of another takes the form of commerce: a person's humanity is dissolved to the point where it becomes possible to say that the slave's life is possessed by the master.[35] Because the slave's life is like a "thing," possessed by another person, the slave existence appears as a perfect figure of a shadow.

In spite of the terror and the symbolic sealing off of the slave, he or she maintains alternative perspectives toward time, work, and self. This is the second paradoxical element of the plantation world as a manifestation of the state of exception. Treated as if he or she no longer existed except as a mere tool and instrument of production, the slave nevertheless is able to draw almost any object, instrument, language, or gesture into a performance and then stylize it. Breaking with uprootedness and the pure world of things of which he or she is but a fragment, the slave is able to demonstrate the protean capabilities of the human bond through music and the very body that was supposedly possessed by another.[36]

If the relations between life and death, the politics of cruelty, and the symbolics of profanity are blurred in the plantation system, it is notably in the colony and under the apartheid regime that there comes into being a peculiar terror formation I will now turn to.[37] The most original feature of this terror formation is its concatenation of biopower, the state of exception, and the state of siege. Crucial to this concatenation is, once again, race.[38] In fact, in most instances, the selection of races, the prohibition of mixed marriages, forced sterilization, even the extermination of vanquished peoples are to find their first testing ground in the colonial world. Here we see the first syntheses between massacre and bureaucracy, that incarnation of Western rationality.[39] Arendt develops the thesis that there is a link between national-socialism and traditional imperialism. According to her, the colonial conquest revealed a potential for violence previously unknown. What one witnesses in World War II is the extension to the "civilized" peoples of Europe of the methods previously reserved for the "savages."

That the technologies which ended up producing Nazism should have originated in the plantation or in the colony or that, on the contrary—Foucault's thesis—Nazism and Stalinism did no more than amplify a series of mechanisms that already existed in Western European social and political formations (subjugation of the body, health regulations, social Darwinism, eugenics, medico-legal theories on heredity, degeneration, and race) is, in the end, irrelevant. A fact remains, though: in modern philosophical thought and European political practice and imaginary, the colony represents the site where sovereignty consists fundamentally in the exercise of a power outside the law (*ab legibus solutus*) and where "peace" is more likely to take on the face of a "war without end."

Indeed, such a view corresponds to Carl Schmitt's definition of sovereignty at the beginning of the twentieth century, namely, the power to decide on the state of exception. To properly assess the efficacy of the colony as a formation of terror, we need to take a detour into the European imaginary itself as it relates to the critical issue of the domestication of war and the creation of a European juridical order (*Jus publicum Europaeum*). At the basis of this order were two key principles. The first postulated the juridical equality of all states. This equality was notably applied to *the right to wage war* (the taking of life). The right to war meant two things. On the one hand, to kill or to conclude peace was recognized as one of the preeminent functions of any state. It went hand in hand with the recognition of the fact that no state could make claims to rule outside of its borders. But conversely, the state could recognize no authority above it within its own borders. On the other hand, the state, for its part, undertook to "civilize" the ways of killing and to attribute rational objectives to the very act of killing.

The second principle related to the territorialization of the sovereign state, that is, to the determination of its frontiers within the context of a newly imposed global order. In this context, the *Jus publicum* rapidly assumed the form of a distinction between, on the one hand, those parts of the globe available for colonial appropriation and, on the other, Europe itself (where the *Jus publicum* was to hold sway).[40] This distinction, as we will see, is crucial in terms of assessing the efficacy of the colony as a terror formation. Under *Jus publicum*, a legitimate war is, to a large extent, a war conducted by one state against another or, more precisely, a war between "civilized" states. The centrality of the state in the calculus of war derives from the fact that the state is the model of political unity, a principle of rational organization, the embodiment of the idea of the universal, and a moral sign.

In the same context, colonies are similar to the frontiers. They are inhabited by "savages." The colonies are not organized in a state form and have not created a human world. Their armies do not form a distinct entity, and their wars are not wars between regular armies. They do not imply the mobilization of sovereign subjects (citizens) who respect each other as enemies. They do not establish a distinction between combatants and noncombatants, or again between an "enemy" and a "criminal."[41] It is thus impossible to conclude peace with them. In sum, colonies are zones in which war and disorder, internal and external figures of the political, stand side by side or alternate with each other. As such, the colonies are the location par excellence where the controls and guarantees of judicial order can be suspended—the zone where the violence of the state of exception is deemed to operate in the service of "civilization."

That colonies might be ruled over in absolute lawlessness stems from the racial denial of any common bond between the conqueror and the native. In the eyes of the conqueror, *savage life* is just another form of *animal life*, a horrifying experience, something alien beyond imagination or comprehension. In fact, according to Arendt, what makes the savages different from other human beings is less the color of their skin than the fear that they behave like a part of nature, that they treat nature as their undisputed master. Nature thus remains, in all its majesty, an overwhelming reality compared to which they appear to be phantoms, unreal and ghostlike. The savages are, as it were, "natural" human beings who lack the specifically human character, the specifically human reality, "so that when European men massacred them they somehow were not aware that they had committed murder."[42]

For all the above reasons, the sovereign right to kill is not subject to any rule in the colonies. In the colonies, the sovereign might kill at any time or in any manner. Colonial warfare is not subject to legal and institutional rules. It is not a legally codified activity. Instead, colonial terror constantly intertwines with colonially generated fantasies of wilderness and death and fictions to create the effect of the real.[43] Peace is not necessarily the natural outcome of a colonial war. In fact, the distinction between war and peace does not avail. Colonial wars are conceived of as the expression of an absolute hostility that sets the conqueror against an absolute enemy.[44] All manifestations of war and hostility that had been marginalized by a European legal imaginary find a place to reemerge in the colonies. Here, the fiction of a distinction between "the ends of war" and the "means of war" collapses; so does the fiction that war functions as a rule-governed contest, as opposed to pure slaughter without risk or instrumental justification. It becomes futile, therefore, to attempt to resolve one of the intractable paradoxes of war well captured by Alexandre Kojève in his reinterpretation of Hegel's *Phenomenology of the Spirit*: its simultaneous idealism and apparent inhumanity.[45]

Necropower and Late Modern Colonial Occupation

It might be thought that the ideas developed above relate to a distant past. In the past, indeed, imperial wars did have the objective of destroying local powers, installing troops, and instituting new models of military control over civil populations. A group of local auxiliaries could assist in the management of conquered territories annexed to the empire. Within the empire, the vanquished populations were given a status that enshrined their despoilment. In these configurations, violence constituted the original form of the right, and exception provided the structure of sovereignty. Each stage of imperialism also involved certain key technologies (the gunboat, quinine, steamship lines, submarine telegraph cables, and colonial railroads).[46]

Colonial occupation itself was a matter of seizing, delimiting, and asserting control over a physical geographical area—of writing on the ground a new set of social and spatial relations. The writing of new spatial relations (territorialization) was, ultimately, tantamount to the production of boundaries and hierarchies, zones and enclaves; the subversion of existing property arrangements; the classification of people according to different categories; resource extraction; and, finally, the manufacturing of a large reservoir of cultural imaginaries. These imaginaries gave meaning to the enactment of differential rights to differing categories of people for different purposes within the same

space; in brief, the exercise of sovereignty. Space was therefore the raw material of sovereignty and the violence it carried with it. Sovereignty meant
occupation, and occupation meant relegating the colonized into a third zone
between subjecthood and objecthood.

Such was the case of the apartheid regime in South Africa. Here, the *township* was the structural form and the *homelands* became the reserves (rural
bases) whereby the flow of migrant labor could be regulated and African urbanization held in check.[47] As Belinda Bozzoli has shown, the township in
particular was a place where "severe oppression and poverty were experienced
on a racial and class basis."[48] A sociopolitical, cultural, and economic formation, the township was a peculiar spatial institution scientifically planned for
the purposes of control.[49] The functioning of the homelands and townships
entailed severe restrictions on production for the market by blacks in white
areas, the terminating of land ownership by blacks except in reserved areas,
the illegalization of black residence on white farms (except as servants in the
employ of whites), the control of urban influx, and later, the denial of citizenship to Africans.[50]

Frantz Fanon describes the spatialization of colonial occupation in vivid
terms. For him, colonial occupation entails first and foremost a division of
space into compartments. It involves the setting of boundaries and internal
frontiers epitomized by barracks and police stations; it is regulated by the
language of pure force, immediate presence, and frequent and direct action;
and it is premised on the principle of reciprocal exclusivity.[51] But more important, it is the very way in which necropower operates: "The town belonging to
the colonized people . . . is a place of ill fame, peopled by men of evil repute.
They are born there, it matters little where or how; they die there, it matters
not where, nor how. It is a world without spaciousness; men live there on top
of each other. The native town is a hungry town, starved of bread, of meat, of
shoes, of coal, of light. The native town is a crouching village, a town on its
knees."[52] In this case, sovereignty means the capacity to define who matters
and who does not, who is *disposable* and who is not.

Late-modern colonial occupation differs in many ways from early-modern
occupation, particularly in its combining of the disciplinary, the biopolitical,
and the necropolitical. The most accomplished form of necropower is the contemporary colonial occupation of Palestine.

Here, the colonial state derives its fundamental claim of sovereignty and
legitimacy from the authority of its own particular narrative of history and

identity. This narrative is itself underpinned by the idea that the state has a divine right to exist; the narrative competes with another for the same sacred space. Because the two narratives are incompatible and the two populations are inextricably intertwined, any demarcation of the territory on the basis of pure identity is quasi-impossible. Violence and sovereignty, in this case, claim a divine foundation: peoplehood itself is forged by the worship of one deity, and national identity is imagined as an identity against the Other, other deities.[53] History, geography, cartography, and archaeology are supposed to back these claims, thereby closely binding identity and topography. As a consequence, colonial violence and occupation are profoundly underwritten by the sacred terror of truth and exclusivity (mass expulsions, resettlement of "stateless" people in refugee camps, settlement of new colonies). Lying beneath the terror of the sacred is the constant excavation of missing bones; the permanent remembrance of a torn body hewn in a thousand pieces and never self-same; the limits, or better, the impossibility of representing for oneself an "original crime," an unspeakable death: the terror of the Holocaust.[54]

To return to Fanon's spatial reading of colonial occupation, the late-modern colonial occupation in Gaza and the West Bank presents three major characteristics in relation to the working of the specific terror formation I have called necropower. First is the dynamics of territorial fragmentation, the sealing off and expansion of settlements. The objective of this process is twofold: to render any movement impossible and to implement separation along the model of the apartheid state. The occupied territories are therefore divided into a web of intricate internal borders and various isolated cells. According to Eyal Weizman, by departing from a planar division of a territory and embracing a principle of creation of three-dimensional boundaries across sovereign bulks, this dispersal and segmentation clearly redefines the relationship between sovereignty and space.[55]

For Weizman, these actions constitute "the politics of verticality." The resultant form of sovereignty might be called "vertical sovereignty." Under a regime of vertical sovereignty, colonial occupation operates through schemes of over- and underpasses, a separation of the airspace from the ground. The ground itself is divided between its crust and the subterrain. Colonial occupation is also dictated by the very nature of the terrain and its topographical variations (hilltops and valleys, mountains and bodies of water). Thus, high ground offers strategic assets not found in the valleys (effectiveness of sight, self-protection, panoptic fortification that generates gazes to many different ends). Says Weizman: "Settlements could be seen as urban optical devices for surveillance and the exercise of power." Under conditions of late-modern colonial occupation, surveillance is both inward- and outward-oriented, the eye acting as weapon and vice versa. Instead of the conclusive division between two nations across a boundary line, "the organization of the West Bank's particular terrain has created multiple separations, provisional boundaries, which relate to each other through surveillance and control," according to Weizman. Under these circumstances, colonial occupation is not only akin to control, surveillance, and separation, it is also tantamount to seclusion. It is a *splintering occupation*, along the lines of the splintering urbanism characteristic of late modernity (suburban enclaves or gated communities).[56]

From an infrastructural point of view, a splintering form of colonial occupation is characterized by a network of fast bypass roads, bridges, and tunnels that weave over and under one another in an attempt at maintaining the Fanonian "principle of reciprocal exclusivity." According to Weizman, "the bypass roads attempt to separate Israeli traffic networks from Palestinian ones, preferably without allowing them ever to cross. They therefore emphasize the overlapping of two separate geographies that inhabit the same landscape. At points where the networks do cross, a makeshift separation is created. Most often, small dust roads are dug out to allow Palestinians to cross under the fast, wide highways on which Israeli vans and military vehicles rush between settlements."[57]

Under conditions of vertical sovereignty and splintering colonial occupation, communities are separated across a y-axis. This leads to a proliferation of the sites of violence. The battlegrounds are not located solely at the surface of the earth. The underground as well as the airspace are transformed into conflict zones. There is no continuity between the ground and the sky. Even the boundaries in airspace are divided between lower and upper layers. Everywhere, the symbolics of the *top* (who is on top) is reiterated. Occupation of the skies therefore acquires a critical importance, since most of the policing is done from the air. Various other technologies are mobilized to this effect: sensors aboard unmanned air vehicles (UAVs), aerial reconnaissance jets, early warning Hawkeye planes, assault helicopters, an Earth-observation satellite, techniques of "hologrammatization." Killing becomes precisely targeted.

Such precision is combined with the tactics of medieval siege warfare adapted to the networked sprawl of urban refugee camps. An orchestrated and systematic sabotage of the enemy's societal and urban infrastructure network complements the appropriation of land, water, and airspace resources. Critical to these techniques of disabling the enemy is *bulldozing*: demolishing houses and cities; uprooting olive trees; riddling water tanks with bullets; bombing and jamming electronic communications; digging up roads; destroying electricity transformers; tearing up airport runways; disabling television and radio transmitters; smashing computers; ransacking cultural and politico-bureaucratic symbols of the proto-Palestinian state; looting medical equipment. In other words, *infrastructural warfare*.[58] While the Apache helicopter gunship is used to police the air and to kill from overhead, the armored bulldozer (the Caterpillar D-9) is used on the ground as a weapon of war and intimidation. In contrast to early-modern colonial occupation, these two weapons establish the superiority of high-tech tools of late-modern terror.[59]

As the Palestinian case illustrates, late-modern colonial occupation is a concatenation of multiple powers: disciplinary, biopolitical, and necropolitical. The combination of the three allocates to the colonial power an absolute domination over the inhabitants of the occupied territory. The *state of siege* is itself a military institution. It allows a modality of killing that does not distinguish between the external and the internal enemy. Entire populations are the target of the sovereign. The besieged villages and towns are sealed off and cut off from the world. Daily life is militarized. Freedom is given to local military commanders to use their discretion as to when and whom to shoot. Movement between the territorial cells requires formal permits. Local civil institutions are systematically destroyed. The besieged population is deprived of their means of income. Invisible killing is added to outright executions.

War Machines and Heteronomy

After having examined the workings of necropower under the conditions of late-modern colonial occupation, I would like to turn now to contemporary wars. Contemporary wars belong to a new moment and can hardly be understood through earlier theories of "contractual violence" or typologies of "just" and "unjust" wars or even Carl von Clausewitz's instrumentalism.[60] According to Zygmunt Bauman, wars of the globalization era do not include the conquest, acquisition, and takeover of a territory among their objectives. Ideally, they are hit-and-run affairs.

The growing gap between high-tech and low-tech means of war has never been as evident as in the Gulf War and the Kosovo campaign. In both cases, the doctrine of "overwhelming or decisive force" was implemented to its full effect thanks to a military-technological revolution that has multiplied the capacity for destruction in unprecedented ways.[61] Air war as it relates to altitude, ordnance, visibility, and intelligence is here a case in point. During the Gulf War, the combined use of smart bombs and bombs coated with depleted uranium (DU), high-tech stand-off weapons, electronic sensors, laser-guided missiles, cluster and asphyxiation bombs, stealth capabilities, unmanned aerial vehicles, and cyber-intelligence quickly crippled the enemy's capabilities.

In Kosovo, the "degrading" of Serbian capabilities took the form of an infrastructural war that targeted and destroyed bridges, railroads, highways, communications networks, oil storage depots, heating plants, power stations, and water treatment facilities. As can be surmised, the execution of such a military strategy, especially when combined with the imposition of sanctions, results in shutting down the enemy's life-support system. The enduring damage to civilian life is particularly telling. For example, the destruction of the Pancevo petrochemical complex in the outskirts of Belgrade during the Kosovo campaign "left the vicinity so toxic with vinyl chloride, ammonia, mercury, naphtha and dioxin that pregnant women were directed to seek abortions, and all local women were advised to avoid pregnancy for two years."[62]

Wars of the globalization era therefore aim to force the enemy into submission regardless of the immediate consequences, side effects, and "collateral damage" of the military actions. In this sense, contemporary wars are more reminiscent of the warfare strategy of the nomads than of the sedentary nations or the "conquer-and-annex" territorial wars of modernity. In Bauman's words: "They rest their superiority over the settled population on the speed of their own movement; their own ability to descend from nowhere without notice and vanish again without warning, their ability to travel light and not to bother with the kind of belongings which confine the mobility and the maneuvering potential of the sedentary people."[63]

This new moment is one of global mobility. An important feature of the age of global mobility is that military operations and the exercise of the right to kill are no longer the sole monopoly of states, and the "regular army" is no longer the unique modality of carrying out these functions. The claim to ultimate or final authority in a particular political space is not easily made. Instead, a patchwork of overlapping and incomplete rights to rule emerges, inextricably superimposed and tangled, in which different de facto juridical instances are geographically interwoven and plural allegiances, asymmetrical suzerainties, and enclaves abound.[64] In this heteronymous organization of territorial rights and claims, it makes little sense to insist on distinctions between "internal" and "external" political realms, separated by clearly demarcated boundaries.

Let's take Africa as an example. Here, the political economy of statehood dramatically changed over the last quarter of the twentieth century. Many African states can no longer claim a monopoly on violence and on the means of coercion within their territory. Nor can they claim a monopoly on territorial boundaries. Coercion itself has become a market commodity. Military manpower is bought and sold on a market in which the identity of suppliers and purchasers means almost nothing. Urban militias, private armies, armies of regional lords, private security firms, and state armies all claim the right to exercise violence or to kill. Neighboring states or rebel movements lease armies to poor states. Nonstate deployers of violence supply two critical coercive resources: labor and minerals. Increasingly, the vast majority of armies are composed of citizen soldiers, child soldiers, mercenaries, and privateers.[65]

Alongside armies have therefore emerged what, following Deleuze and Guattari, we could refer to as *war machines*.[66] War machines are made up of segments of armed men that split up or merge with one another depending on the tasks to be carried out and the circumstances. Polymorphous and diffuse organizations, war machines are characterized by their capacity for metamorphosis. Their relation to space is mobile. Sometimes, they enjoy complex links with state forms (from autonomy to incorporation). The state may, of its own doing, transform itself into a war machine. It may moreover appropriate to itself an existing war machine or help to create one. War machines function by borrowing from regular armies while incorporating new elements well adapted to the principle of segmentation and deterritorialization. Regular armies, in turn, may readily appropriate some of the characteristics of war machines.

A war machine combines a plurality of functions. It has the features of a political organization and a mercantile company. It operates through capture and depredations and can even coin its own money. In order to fuel the extraction and export of natural resources located in the territory they control, war machines forge direct connections with transnational networks. War machines emerged in Africa during the last quarter of the twentieth century in direct relation to the erosion of the postcolonial state's capacity to build the economic underpinnings of political authority and order. This capacity involves raising revenue and commanding and regulating access to natural resources within a well-defined territory. In the mid-1970s, as the state's ability to maintain this capacity began to erode, there emerged a clear-cut link between monetary instability and spatial fragmentation. In the 1980s, the brutal experience of money suddenly losing its value became more commonplace, with various countries undergoing cycles of hyperinflation (which included such stunts as the sudden replacement of a currency). During the last decades of the twentieth century, monetary circulation has influenced state and society in at least two different ways.

First, we have seen a general drying-up of liquidities and their gradual concentration along certain channels, access to which has been subject to increasingly draconian conditions. As a result, the number of individuals endowed with the material means to control dependents through the creation of debts has abruptly decreased. Historically, capturing and fixing dependents through the mechanism of debt has always been a central aspect of both the production of people and the constitution of the political bond.[67] Such bonds were crucial in determining the value of persons and gauging their value and utility. When their value and utility were not proven, they could be disposed of as slaves, pawns, or clients.

Second, the controlled inflow and the fixing of movements of money around zones in which specific resources are extracted has made possible the formation of *enclave economies* and has shifted the old calculus between people and things. The concentration of activities connected with the extraction of valuable resources around these enclaves has, in return, turned the enclaves into privileged spaces of war and death. War itself is fed by increased sales of the products extracted.[68] New linkages have therefore emerged between war making, war machines, and resource extraction.[69] War machines are implicated in the constitution of highly transnational local or regional economies. In most places, the collapse of formal political institutions under the strain of violence tends to lead to the formation of militia economies. War machines (in this case militias or rebel movements) rapidly become highly organized mechanisms of predation, taxing the territories and the population they occupy and drawing on a range of transnational networks and diasporas that provide both material and financial support.

Correlated to the new geography of resource extraction is the emergence of an unprecedented form of governmentality that consists in the *manage-*

ment of the multitudes. The extraction and looting of natural resources by war machines goes hand in hand with brutal attempts to immobilize and spatially fix whole categories of people or, paradoxically, to unleash them, to force them to scatter over broad areas no longer contained by the boundaries of a territorial state. As a political category, populations are then disaggregated into rebels, child soldiers, victims or refugees, or civilians incapacitated by mutilation or simply massacred on the model of ancient sacrifices, while the "survivors," after a horrific exodus, are confined in camps and zones of exception.[70]

This form of governmentality is different from the colonial *commandement.*[71] The techniques of policing and discipline and the choice between obedience and simulation that characterized the colonial and postcolonial potentate are gradually being replaced by an alternative that is more tragic because more extreme. Technologies of destruction have become more tactile, more anatomical and sensorial, in a context in which the choice is between life and death.[72] If power still depends on tight control over bodies (or on concentrating them in camps), the new technologies of destruction are less concerned with inscribing bodies within disciplinary apparatuses as inscribing them, when the time comes, within the order of the maximal economy now represented by the "massacre." In turn, the generalization of insecurity has deepened the societal distinction between those who bear weapons and those who do not (*loi de repartition des armes*). Increasingly, war is no longer waged between armies of two sovereign states. It is waged by armed groups acting behind the mask of the state against armed groups that have no state but control very distinct territories; both sides having as their main targets civilian populations that are unarmed or organized into militias. In cases where armed dissidents have not completely taken over state power, they have provoked territorial partitions and succeeded in controlling entire regions that they administer on the model of fiefdoms, especially where there are mineral deposits.[73]

The ways of killing do not themselves vary much. In the case of massacres in particular, lifeless bodies are quickly reduced to the status of simple skeletons. Their morphology henceforth inscribes them in the register of undifferentiated generality: simple relics of an unburied pain, empty, meaningless corporealities, strange deposits plunged into cruel stupor. In the case of the Rwandan genocide—in which a number of skeletons were at least preserved in a visible state, if not exhumed—what is striking is the tension between the petrification of the bones and their strange coolness on one hand, and on the other, their stubborn will to mean, to signify something.

In these impassive bits of bone, there seems to be no *ataraxia*: nothing but the illusory rejection of a death that has already occurred. In other cases, in which physical amputation replaces immediate death, cutting off limbs opens the way to the deployment of techniques of incision, ablation, and excision that also have bones as their target. The traces of this demiurgic surgery persist for a long time, in the form of human shapes that are alive, to be sure, but whose bodily integrity has been replaced by pieces, fragments, folds, even immense wounds that are difficult to close. Their function is to keep before the eyes of the victim—and of the people around him or her—the morbid spectacle of severing.

Of Motion and Metal

Let us return to the example of Palestine where two apparently irreconcilable logics are confronting each other: the *logic of martyrdom* and the *logic of survival*. In examining these two logics, I would like to reflect on the twin issues of death and terror on the one hand and terror and freedom on the other.

In the confrontation between these two logics, terror is not on one side and death on the other. Terror and death are at the heart of each. As Elias Canetti reminds us, the survivor is the one who, having stood in the path of death, knowing of many deaths and standing in the midst of the fallen, is still alive. Or, more precisely, the survivor is the one who has taken on a whole pack of enemies and managed not only to escape alive, but to kill his or her attackers. This is why, to a large extent, the lowest form of survival is killing. Canetti points out that in the logic of survival, "each man is the enemy of every other." Even more radically, in the logic of survival one's horror at the sight of death turns into satisfaction that it is someone else who is dead. It is the death of the other, his or her physical presence as a corpse, that makes the survivor feel unique. And each enemy killed makes the survivor feel more secure.[74]

The logic of martyrdom proceeds along different lines. It is epitomized by the figure of the "suicide bomber," which itself raises a number of questions. What intrinsic difference is there between killing with a missile helicopter or a tank and killing with one's own body? Does the distinction between the arms used to inflict death prevent the establishment of a system of general exchange between the manner of killing and the manner of dying?

The "suicide bomber" wears no ordinary soldier's uniform and displays no weapon. The candidate for martyrdom chases his or her targets; the enemy is a prey for whom a trap is set. Significant in this respect is the location of the ambush laid: the bus stop, the café, the discotheque, the marketplace, the checkpoint, the road—in sum, the spaces of everyday life.

The trapping of the body is added to the ambush location. The candidate for martyrdom transforms his or her body into a mask that hides the soon-to-be-detonated weapon. Unlike the tank or the missile that is clearly visible, the weapon carried in the shape of the body is invisible. Thus concealed, it forms part of the body. It is so intimately part of the body that at the time of detonation it annihilates the body of its bearer, who carries with it the bodies of others when it does not reduce them to pieces. The body does not simply conceal a weapon. The body is transformed into a weapon, not in a metaphorical sense but in the truly ballistic sense.

In this instance, my death goes hand in hand with the death of the Other. Homicide and suicide are accomplished in the same act. And to a large extent, resistance and self-destruction are synonymous. To deal out death is therefore to reduce the other and oneself to the status of pieces of inert flesh, scattered everywhere, and assembled with difficulty before the burial. In this case, war is the war of body on body (*guerre au corps-à-corps*). To kill, one has to come as close as possible to the body of the enemy. To detonate the bomb necessitates resolving the question of distance, through the work of proximity and concealment.

How are we to interpret this manner of spilling blood in which death is not simply that which is *my own*, but always goes hand in hand with the death of the other?[75] How does it differ from death inflicted by a tank or a missile, in a context in which the cost of my survival is calculated in terms of my capacity and readiness to kill someone else? In the logic of "martyrdom," the will to die is fused with the willingness to take the enemy with you, that is, with closing the door on the possibility of life for everyone. This logic seems contrary to another one, which consists in wishing to impose death on others while preserving one's own life. Canetti describes this moment of survival as a moment of power. In such a case, triumph develops precisely from the possibility of being there when the others (in this case the enemy) are no longer there.

Such is the logic of heroism as classically understood: to execute others while holding one's own death at a distance.

In the logic of martyrdom, a new semiosis of killing emerges. It is not necessarily based on a relationship between form and matter. As I have already indicated, the body here becomes the very uniform of the martyr. But the body as such is not only an object to protect against danger and death. The body in itself has neither power nor value. The power and value of the body result from a process of abstraction based on the desire for eternity. In that sense, the martyr, having established a moment of supremacy in which the subject overcomes his own mortality, can be seen as laboring under the sign of the future. In other words, in death the future is collapsed into the present.

In its desire for eternity, the besieged body passes through two stages. First, it is transformed into a mere thing, malleable matter. Second, the manner in which it is put to death—suicide—affords it its ultimate signification. The matter of the body, or again the matter which is the body, is invested with properties that cannot be deduced from its character as a thing, but from a transcendental *nomos* outside it. The besieged body becomes a piece of metal whose function is, through sacrifice, to bring eternal life into being. The body duplicates itself and, in death, literally and metaphorically escapes the state of siege and occupation.

Let me explore, in conclusion, the relation between terror, freedom, and sacrifice. Martin Heidegger argues that the human's "being toward death" is the decisive condition of all true human freedom.[76] In other words, one is free to live one's own life only because one is free to die one's own death. Whereas Heidegger grants an existential status to being-toward-death and considers it an event of freedom, Bataille suggests that "sacrifice in reality reveals nothing." It is not simply the absolute manifestation of negativity. It is also a comedy. For Bataille, death reveals the human subject's animal side, which he refers to moreover as the subject's "natural being." "For man to reveal himself in the end, he has to die, but he will have to do so while alive—by looking at himself ceasing to exist," he adds. In other words, the human subject has to be fully alive at the very moment of dying, to be aware of his or her death, to live with the impression of actually dying. Death itself must become awareness of the self at the very time that it does away with the conscious being. "In a sense, this is what happens (what at least is on the point of taking place, or what takes place in an elusive, fugitive manner), by means of a subterfuge in the sacrifice. In the sacrifice, the sacrificed identifies himself with the animal on the point of death. Thus he dies seeing himself die, and even, in some sense, through his own will, at one with the weapon of sacrifice. But this is play!" And for Bataille, play is more or less the means by which the human subject "voluntarily tricks himself."[77]

How does the notion of play and trickery relate to the "suicide bomber"? There is no doubt that in the case of the suicide bomber the sacrifice consists of the spectacular putting to death of the self, of becoming his or her own victim (self-sacrifice). The self-sacrificed proceeds to take power over his or her death and to approach it head-on. This power may be derived from the belief that the destruction of one's own body does not affect the continuity of the being. The idea is that the being exists outside us. The self-sacrifice consists, here, in the removal of a twofold prohibition: that of self-immolation (suicide) and that of murder. Unlike primitive sacrifices, however, there is no animal to serve as a substitute victim. Death here achieves the character of a transgression. But unlike crucifixion, it has no expiatory dimension. It is not related to the Hegelian paradigms of prestige or recognition. Indeed, a dead person cannot recognize his or her killer, who is also dead. Does this imply that death occurs here as pure annihilation and nothingness, excess and scandal?

Whether read from the perspective of slavery or of colonial occupation, death and freedom are irrevocably interwoven. As we have seen, terror is a defining feature of both slave and late-modern colonial regimes. Both regimes are also specific instances and experiences of unfreedom. To live under late modern occupation is to experience a permanent condition of "being in pain": fortified structures, military posts, and roadblocks everywhere; buildings that bring back painful memories of humiliation, interrogations, and beatings; curfews that imprison hundreds of thousands in their cramped homes every night from dusk to daybreak; soldiers patrolling the unlit streets, frightened by their own shadows; children blinded by rubber bullets; parents shamed and beaten in front of their families; soldiers urinating on fences, shooting at the rooftop water tanks just for fun, chanting loud offensive slogans, pounding on fragile tin doors to frighten the children, confiscating papers, or dumping garbage in the middle of a residential neighborhood; border guards kicking over a vegetable stand or closing borders at whim; bones broken; shootings and fatalities—a certain kind of madness.[78]

In such circumstances, the discipline of life and the necessities of hardship (trial by death) are marked by excess. What connects terror, death, and freedom is an *ecstatic* notion of temporality and politics. The future, here, can be authentically anticipated, but not in the present. The present itself is but a moment of vision—vision of the freedom not yet come. Death in the present is the mediator of redemption. Far from being an encounter with a limit, boundary, or barrier, it is experienced as "a release from terror and bondage."[79] As Gilroy notes, this preference for death over continued servitude is a commentary on the nature of freedom itself (or the lack thereof). If this lack is the very nature of what it means for the slave or the colonized to exist, the same lack is also precisely the way in which he or she takes account of his or her mortality. Referring to the practice of individual or mass suicide by slaves cornered by the slave catchers, Gilroy suggests that death, in this case, can be represented as agency. For death is precisely that from and over which I have power. But it is also that space where freedom and negation operate.

Conclusion

In this essay I have argued that contemporary forms of subjugation of life to the power of death (necropolitics) profoundly reconfigure the relations among resistance, sacrifice, and terror. I have demonstrated that the notion of biopower is insufficient to account for contemporary forms of subjugation of life to the power of death. Moreover I have put forward the notion of necropolitics and necropower to account for the various ways in which, in our contemporary world, weapons are deployed in the interest of maximum destruction of persons and the creation of *death-worlds*, new and unique forms of social existence in which vast populations are subjected to conditions of life conferring upon them the status of *living dead*. The essay has also outlined some of the repressed topographies of cruelty (the plantation and the colony in particular) and has suggested that under conditions of necropower, the lines between resistance and suicide, sacrifice and redemption, martyrdom and freedom are blurred.

Notes

This essay is the result of sustained conversations with Arjun Appadurai, Carol Breckenridge, and Françoise Vergès. Excerpts were presented at seminars and workshops in Evanston, Chicago, New York, New Haven, and Johannesburg. Useful criticisms were provided by Paul Gilroy, Dilip Parameshwar Gaonkar, Beth Povinelli, Ben Lee, Charles

Taylor, Crawford Young, Abdoumaliq Simone, Luc Sindjoun, Souleymane Bachir Diagne, Carlos Forment, Ato Quayson, Ulrike Kistner, David Theo Goldberg, and Deborah Posel. Additional comments and insights as well as critical support and encouragement were offered by Rehana Ebr-Vally and Sarah Nuttall. The essay is dedicated to my late friend Tshikala Kayembe Biaya.

1. The essay distances itself from traditional accounts of sovereignty found in the discipline of political science and the subdiscipline of international relations. For the most part, these accounts locate sovereignty within the boundaries of the nation-state, within institutions empowered by the state, or within supranational institutions and networks. See, for example, *Sovereignty at the Millennium*, special issue, *Political Studies* 47 (1999). My own approach builds on Michel Foucault's critique of the notion of sovereignty and its relation to war and biopower in *Il faut défendre la société: Cours au Collège de France, 1975–1976* (Paris: Seuil, 1997), 37–55, 75–100, 125–48, 213–44. See also Giorgio Agamben, *Homo sacer. Le pouvoir souverain et la vie nue* (Paris: Seuil, 1997), 23–80.

2. Foucault, *Il faut défendre la société*, 213–34.

3. On the state of exception, see Carl Schmitt, *La dictature*, trans. Mira Köller and Dominique Séglard (Paris: Seuil, 2000), 210–28, 235–36, 250–51, 255–56; *La notion de politique. Théorie du partisan*, trans. Marie-Louise Steinhauser (Paris: Flammarion, 1992).

4. Hannah Arendt, *The Origins of Totalitarianism* (New York: Harvest, 1966), 444.

5. Giorgio Agamben, *Moyens sans fins. Notes sur la politique* (Paris: Payot & Rivages, 1995), 50–51.

6. On these debates, see Saul Friedlander, ed., *Probing the Limits of Representation: Nazism and the "Final Solution"* (Cambridge: Harvard University Press, 1992); and, more recently, Bertrand Ogilvie, "Comparer l'incomparable," *Multitudes*, no. 7 (2001): 130–66.

7. See James Bohman and William Rehg, eds., *Deliberative Democracy: Essays on Reason and Politics* (Cambridge: MIT Press, 1997); Jürgen Habermas, *Between Facts and Norms* (Cambridge: MIT Press, 1996).

8. James Schmidt, ed., *What Is Enlightenment? Eighteenth-Century Answers and Twentieth-Century Questions* (Berkeley: University of California Press, 1996).

9. Cornelius Castoriadis, *L'institution imaginaire de la société* (Paris: Seuil, 1975) and *Figures du pensable* (Paris: Seuil, 1999).

10. See, in particular, Paul Gilroy, *The Black Atlantic: Modernity and Double Consciousness* (Cambridge: Harvard University Press, 1993), especially chap. 2.

11. G. W. F. Hegel, *Phénoménologie de l'esprit*, trans. J. P. Lefebvre (Paris: Aubier, 1991). See also the critique by Alexandre Kojève, *Introduction à la lecture de Hegel* (Paris: Gallimard, 1947), especially Appendix II, "L'idée de la mort dans la philosophie de Hegel"; and Georges Bataille, *Oeuvres complètes XII* (Paris: Gallimard, 1988), especially "Hegel, la mort et le sacrifice," 326–48, and "Hegel, l'homme et l'histoire," 349–69.

12. See Jean Baudrillard, "Death in Bataille," in *Bataille: A Critical Reader*, ed. Fred Botting and Scott Wilson (Oxford: Blackwell, 1998), especially 139–41.

13. Georges Bataille, *Visions of Excess: Selected Writings, 1927–1939*, trans. A. Stoekl (Minneapolis: University of Minnesota Press, 1985), 94–95.

14. Fred Botting and Scott Wilson, eds., *The Bataille Reader* (Oxford: Blackwell, 1997), 318–19. See also Georges Bataille, *The Accursed Share: An Essay on General Economy*, vol. 1, *Consumption*, trans. Robert Hurley (New York: Zone, 1988), and *Erotism: Death & Sensuality*, trans. Mary Dalwood (San Francisco: City Lights, 1986).

15. Bataille, *Accursed Share*, vol. 2, *The History of Eroticism*; vol. 3, *Sovereignty*.

16. On the state of siege, see Schmitt, *La dictature*, chap. 6.

17. See Foucault, *Il faut défendre la société*, 57–74.

18. "Race is, politically speaking, not the beginning of humanity but its end . . . , not the natural birth of man but his unnatural death." Arendt, *Origins of Totalitarianism*, 157.

19. Foucault, *Il faut défendre la société*, 214.

20. Foucault, *Il faut défendre la société*, 228.

21. Foucault, *Il faut défendre la société*, 227–32.

22. See Jürgen Habermas, *The Philosophical Discourse of Modernity: Twelve Lectures*, trans. Frederick G. Lawrence (Cambridge: MIT Press, 1987), especially chaps. 3, 5, 6.

23. Enzo Traverso, *La violence nazie: Une généalogie européenne* (Paris: La Fabrique Editions, 2002).

24. Michel Foucault, *Discipline and Punish: The Birth of the Prison* (New York: Pantheon, 1977).

25. See Robert Wokler, "Contextualizing Hegel's Phenomenology of the French Revolution and the Terror," *Political Theory* 26 (1998): 33–55.

26. David W. Bates, *Enlightenment Aberrations: Error and Revolution in France* (Ithaca, N.Y.: Cornell University Press, 2002), chap. 6.

27. Karl Marx, *Capital: A Critique of Political Economy*, vol. 3 (London: Lawrence & Wishart, 1984), 817. See also *Capital*, vol. 1, trans. Ben Fowkes (Harmondsworth, England: Penguin, 1986), 172.

28. Stephen Louw, "In the Shadow of the Pharaohs: The Militarization of Labour Debate and Classical Marxist Theory," *Economy and Society* (29) 2000: 240.

29. On labor militarization and the transition to communism, see Nikolai Bukharin, *The Politics and Economics of the Transition Period*, trans. Oliver Field (London: Routledge & Kegan Paul, 1979); and Leon Trotsky, *Terrorism and Communism: A Reply to Karl Kautsky* (Ann Arbor: University of Michigan Press, 1961). On the collapse of the distinction between state and society, see Karl Marx, *The Civil War in France* (Moscow: Progress, 1972); and Vladimir Il'ich Lenin, *Selected Works in Three Volumes*, vol. 2 (Moscow: Progress, 1977). For a critique of "revolutionary terror," see Maurice Merleau-Ponty, *Humanism and Terror: An Essay on the Communist Problem*, trans. John O'Neill (Boston: Beacon, 1969). For a more recent example of "revolutionary terror," see Steve J. Stern, ed., *Shining and Other Paths: War and Society in Peru, 1980–1995* (Durham, N.C.: Duke University Press, 1998).

30. See Saidiya V. Hartman, *Scenes of Subjection: Terror, Slavery, and Self-Making in Nineteenth-Century America* (Oxford: Oxford University Press, 1997); and Manuel

Moreno Fraginals, *The Sugarmill: The Socioeconomic Complex of Sugar in Cuba, 1760–1860* (New York: Monthly Review Press, 1976).

31. Gilroy, *Black Atlantic*, 57.

32. See Frederick Douglass, *Narrative of the Life of Frederick Douglass, an American Slave*, ed. Houston A. Baker (New York: Penguin, 1986).

33. The term *manners* is used here to denote the links between *social grace* and *social control*. According to Norbert Elias, manners embody what is "considered socially acceptable behavior," the "precepts on conduct," and the framework for "conviviality." *The History of Manners*, vol. 1, *The Civilizing Process*, trans. Edmund Jephcott (New York: Pantheon, 1978), chap. 2.

34. "The louder she screamed, the harder he whipped; and where the blood ran faster, there he whipped longest," says Douglass in his narration of the whipping of his aunt by Mr. Plummer. "He would whip her to make her scream, and whip her to make her hush; and not until overcome by fatigue, would he cease to swing the blood-clotted cowskin. . . . It was a most terrible spectacle." Douglass, *Narrative of the Life*, 51. On the random killing of slaves, see 67–68.

35. Susan Buck-Morss, "Hegel and Haiti," *Critical Inquiry* 26 (2000): 821–66.

36. Roger D. Abrahams, *Singing the Master: The Emergence of African American Culture in the Plantation South* (New York: Pantheon, 1992).

37. In what follows I am mindful of the fact that colonial forms of sovereignty were always fragmented. They were complex, "less concerned with legitimizing their own presence and more excessively violent than their European forms." As importantly, "European states never aimed at governing the colonial territories with the same uniformity and intensity as was applied to their own populations." T. B. Hansen and Finn Stepputat, "Sovereign Bodies: Citizens, Migrants and States in the Post-colonial World" (paper, 2002).

38. In *The Racial State* (Maiden, Mass: Blackwell, 2002), David Theo Goldberg argues that from the nineteenth century on, there are at least two historically competing traditions of racial rationalization: naturism (based on an inferiority claim) and historicism (based on the claim of the historical "immaturity"—and therefore "educabuility"—of the natives). In a private communication (23 August 2002), he argues that these two traditions played out differently when it came to issues of sovereignty, states of exception, and forms of necropower. In his view, necropower can take multiple forms: the terror of actual death; or a more "benevolent" form—the result of which is the destruction of a culture in order to "save the people" from themselves.

39. Arendt, *Origins of Totalitarianism*, 185–221.

40. Etienne Balibar, "Prolégomènes à la souveraineté: La frontière, l'Etat, le peuple," *Les temps modernes* 610 (2000): 54–55.

41. Eugene Victor Walter, *Terror and Resistance: A Study of Political Violence with Case Studies of Some Primitive African Communities* (Oxford: Oxford University Press, 1969).

42. Arendt, *Origins of Totalitarianism*, 192.

43. For a powerful rendition of this process, see Michael Taussig, *Shamanism, Colonialism,*

and the Wild Man: A Study in Terror and Healing (Chicago: University of Chicago Press, 1987).

44. On the "enemy," see *L'ennemi*, special issue, *Raisons politiques*, no. 5 (2002).

45. Kojève, *Introduction à la lecture de Hegel*.

46. See Daniel R. Headrick, *The Tools of Empire: Technology and European Imperialism in the Nineteenth Century* (New York: Oxford University Press, 1981).

47. On the township, see G. G. Maasdorp and A. S. B. Humphreys, eds., *From Shantytown to Township: An Economic Study of African Poverty and Rehousing in a South African City* (Cape Town: Juta, 1975).

48. Belinda Bozzoli, "Why Were the 1980s 'Millenarian'? Style, Repertoire, Space and Authority in South Africa's Black Cities," *Journal of Historical Sociology* 13 (2000): 79.

49. Bozzoli, "Why Were the 1980s 'Millenarian'?"

50. See Herman Giliomee, ed., *Up against the Fences: Poverty, Passes and Privileges in South Africa* (Cape Town: David Philip, 1985); Francis Wilson, *Migrant Labour in South Africa* (Johannesburg: Christian Institute of Southern Africa, 1972).

51. Frantz Fanon, *The Wretched of the Earth*, trans. C. Farrington (New York: Grove Weidenfeld, 1991), 39.

52. Fanon, *Wretched of the Earth*, 37–39.

53. See Regina M. Schwartz, *The Curse of Cain: The Violent Legacy of Monotheism* (Chicago: University of Chicago Press, 1997).

54. See Lydia Flem, *L'Art et la mémoire des camps: Représenter exterminer*, ed. Jean-Luc Nancy (Paris: Seuil, 2001).

55. See Eyal Weizman, "The Politics of Verticality," *openDemocracy* (Web publication at www.openDemocracy.net), 25 April 2002.

56. See Stephen Graham and Simon Marvin, *Splintering Urbanism: Networked Infrastructures, Technological Mobility and the Urban Condition* (London: Routledge, 2001).

57. Weizman, "Politics of Verticality."

58. See Stephen Graham, " 'Clean Territory': Urbicide in the West Bank," *openDemocracy* (Web publication at www.openDemocracy.net), 7 August 2002.

59. Compare with the panoply of new bombs the United States deployed during the Gulf War and the war in Kosovo, most aimed at raining down graphite crystals to disable comprehensively electrical power and distribution stations. Michael Ignatieff, *Virtual War* (New York: Metropolitan Books, 2000).

60. See Michael Walzer, *Just and Unjust Wars: A Moral Argument with Historical Illustrations* (New York: Basic Books, 1977).

61. Benjamin Ederington and Michael J. Mazarr, eds., *Turning Point: The Gulf War and U.S. Military Strategy* (Boulder, Colo.: Westview, 1994).

62. Thomas W. Smith, "The New Law of War: Legitimizing Hi-Tech and Infrastructural Violence," *International Studies Quarterly* 46 (2002): 367. On Iraq, see G. L. Simons, *The Scourging of Iraq: Sanctions, Law and Natural Justice*, 2d ed. (New York: St. Martin's, 1998); see also A. Shehabaldin and W. M. Laughlin Jr., "Economic Sanctions against Iraq: Human and Economic Costs," *International Journal of Human Rights* 3, no. 4 (2000): 1–18.

63. Zygmunt Bauman, "Wars of the Globalization Era," *European Journal of Social Theory* 4, no. 1 (2001): 15. "Remote as they are from their 'targets,' scurrying over those they hit too fast to witness the devastation they cause and the blood they spill, the pilots-turned-computer-operators hardly ever have a chance of looking their victims in the face and to survey the human misery they have sowed," adds Bauman. "Military professionals of our time see no corpses and no wounds. They may sleep well; no pangs of conscience will keep them awake" (27). See also "Penser la guerre aujourd'hui," *Cahiers de la Villa Gillet* no. 16 (2002): 75–152.

64. Achille Mbembe, "At the Edge of the World: Boundaries, Territoriality, and Sovereignty in Africa," *Public Culture* 12 (2000): 259–84.

65. In international law, "privateers" are defined as "vessels belonging to private owners, and sailing under a commission of war empowering the person to whom it is granted to carry on all forms of hostility which are permissible at sea by the usages of war." I use the term here to mean armed formations acting independently of any politically organized society, in the pursuit of private interests, whether under the mask of the state or not. See Janice Thomson, *Mercenaries, Pirates, and Sovereigns* (Princeton, N.J.: Princeton University Press, 1997).

66. Gilles Deleuze and Felix Guattari, *Capitalisme et schizophrénie* (Paris: Editions de minuit, 1980), 434–527.

67. Joseph C. Miller, *Way of Death: Merchant Capitalism and the Angolan Slave Trade, 1730–1830* (Madison: University of Wisconsin Press, 1988), especially chaps. 2 and 4.

68. See Jakkie Cilliers and Christian Dietrich, eds., *Angola's War Economy: The Role of Oil and Diamonds* (Pretoria: Institute for Security Studies, 2000).

69. See, for example, "Rapport du Groupe d'experts sur l'exploitation illégale des ressources naturelles et autres richesses de la République démocratique du Congo," United Nations Report No. 2/2001/357, submitted by the Secretary-General to the Security Council, 12 April 2001. See also Richard Snyder, "Does Lootable Wealth Breed Disorder? States, Regimes, and the Political Economy of Extraction" (paper).

70. See Loren B. Landau, "The Humanitarian Hangover: Transnationalization of Governmental Practice in Tanzania's Refugee-Populated Areas," *Refugee Survey Quarterly* 21, no. 1 (2002): 260–99, especially 281–87.

71. On the *commandement*, see Achille Mbembe, *On the Postcolony* (Berkeley: University of California Press, 2001), chaps. 1–3.

72. See Leisel Talley, Paul B. Spiegel, and Mona Girgis, "An Investigation of Increasing Mortality among Congolese Refugees in Lugufu Camp, Tanzania, May–June 1999," *Journal of Refugee Studies* 14, no. 4 (2001): 412–27.

73. See Tony Hodges, *Angola: From Afro-Stalinism to Petro-Diamond Capitalism* (Oxford: James Currey, 2001), chap. 7; Stephen Ellis, *The Mask of Anarchy: The Destruction of Liberia and the Religious Dimension of an African Civil War* (London: Hurst & Company, 1999).

74. See Elias Canetti, *Crowds and Power*, trans. C. Stewart (New York: Farrar Straus Giroux, 1984), 227–80.

75. Martin Heidegger, *Etre et temps* (Paris: Gallimard, 1986), 289–322.

76. Heidegger, *Etre et temps.*

77. Bataille, *Oeuvres complètes,* 336.

78. For what precedes, see Amira Hass, *Drinking the Sea at Gaza: Days and Nights in a Land under Siege* (New York: Henry Holt, 1996).

79. Gilroy, *Black Atlantic,* 63.

CHAPTER 9

NECRO-ECONOMICS ADAM SMITH AND DEATH IN THE LIFE OF THE UNIVERSAL

Warren Montag

Louis Althusser began *Reading Capital* with the statement, 'We have all certainly read and are all reading [Marx's] *Capital.*' While Althusser is undoubtedly addressing here his seminar, the focus of which was precisely Marx's *Capital*, the sentence that follows elevates the act of reading this particular text to the status of the universal: the entire world has read and is reading *Capital*. Marx has been read for 'nearly a century' not only *by* 'us' (that is, all of us) but *for* us and *to* us even, and especially when we are not aware of it. And this paradox—that of our having read a text without knowing it—is made possible by the fact that *Capital*, Marx's theoretical work, is not limited to or contained by a book or set of books: 'we have been able to read it every day transparently in the dramas and dreams of our history, in its debates and conflicts.'[1] It is thus written in the history of the 'workers movement' and therefore in the words and acts of its leaders and its partisans, as well as its adversaries, whose works represent both a commentary on and a continuation of Marx's text. Althusser insists, however, that the very universalization of *Capital*, the text, which undoubtedly occurs simultaneously with the universalization of the capital which is the object it seeks to analyse, renders a reading of Marx's words, 'to the letter', all the more urgent.

To take Althusser's position seriously today, forty years since he articulated it to his seminar, is to recognize that coextensive with, but distinct from, the theoretical imperative that requires us to read Marx 'to the letter' is the correlative necessity to read Adam Smith. For if the last forty years have shown us anything it is that we all have read and are still reading Smith, that he is read for us and to us far more than was ever the case with Marx and that his words shape our dreams and destinies especially when we cite them without knowing it, taking his words as our own. Smith is then the universal element within which our theory and practice takes shape, within which what lives on in Marx's thought has its existence. This universality does not derive from the force of argument or empirical proof; the universality of Smith, a universality once contested and now reasserted, is immanent in a certain global balance of forces. Smith is the very idea of this now more or less stable balance of forces, the idea it has of itself.

How, then, is it possible to read Smith or to make sure that the Smith we read is not himself already a reading, Smith read for us rather than by us? Perhaps the best way, or even the only way, to begin to read him is to examine a reader in the act of reading Smith. I propose, then, to take as my starting point a reader who neither admits that he is reading Smith nor in his reading is particularly faithful to the text or texts he reads, but whose reading, by virtue of its singular force, opens a certain space for thought, making it possible to read Smith in a new way.

The Virtue of Greed

I will begin by following Hegel's reading of Smith, not where he explicitly refers to Smith in the discussion of the 'system of needs' in the *Philosophy of Right*, but in the *Phenomenology of Spirit* at the point where reason understands that its essence cannot exist in observation alone but only in its own actualization. Hegel argues that reason's actualization of itself necessarily takes the form of a community (*Gemeinschaft*), the universal community, not as an ideal or in a formal, juridical sense, but as a reality produced by concrete individuals. He is careful to note, however, that the universal is produced by individuals who not only do not labour with the aim of producing the universal community, but who, on the contrary, seek only to satisfy their own needs, even at the expense of others. It is at this precise point that Hegel invokes Smith, specifically Smith's concept of the market, as the concrete form of the universal:

> The *labor* of the individual for his own needs is just as much a satisfaction of the needs of others as of his own, and the satisfaction of his own needs he obtains only through the labor of others. As the individual in his *individual* work already unconsciously performs a universal work, so he again also produces

the universal as his conscious object; the whole becomes, as *a* whole, his own work, for which he sacrifices himself and precisely in doing so receives back from it his own self.[2]

The reference to Smith here is clear. As he argues in the *Wealth of Nations*, an individual in 'a civilized society . . . stands at all times in need of the cooperation and assistance of great multitudes'. And, despite the apparent qualification introduced by the phrase 'in a civilized society', Smith a few lines later posits cooperation as the necessary condition of human existence per se, going so far as to ascribe it to the natural condition of the species. The individual member of 'almost every other race of animals' is 'entirely independent and in its natural state has occasion for the assistance of no other living creature', while the human individual remains dependent and has for mere survival 'almost constant occasion for the help of his brethren'.[3] Read from Hegel's perspective, then, society or community is not simply necessary for humanity's development and progress, it is necessary from the point of view of human life itself. The species cannot reproduce or survive in the absence of cooperation. The life of the individual, for Hegel, depends upon the 'life of a people' (*dem Leben eines Volks*) which furnishes 'the universal sustaining medium' necessary to human life. It is thus only the 'power of the whole people' (*die Macht des ganzen Volks*) that confers upon the individual sufficient power to exist. In the universal there is life: in the particular only death.[4] The term 'people' should be understood here as a biological entity, the concrete form of the universal that arises in the course of the natural history of humanity and the irreducible foundation of life, human life, itself.

Yet if the cooperation necessary to the sustaining of life itself characterizes the life and power of a people, this cooperation itself must be explained, and it was precisely in explaining this cooperation that seventeenth- and eighteenth-century European philosophy divided into two opposing camps. Smith alludes to this division as he develops his analysis of the optimal form of cooperation. In particular, he is compelled to confront the argument that there exists in the human individual a social instinct as powerful as self-interest that drives individuals to assist others in the satisfaction of their needs with the same urgency that impels them to satisfy their own. Here, Smith's discussion of Hutcheson's moral philosophy in *The Theory of Moral Sentiments* is particularly interesting. Because Hutcheson, following Shaftesbury and Butler, postulates the existence of what Smith calls an 'instinctive good-will',[5] he is led to devalue those actions which originate from other motives, especially self-interested motives, so that, regardless of the effects of such actions, their self-interested origins deprive such actions of any consideration of benevolence. The latter becomes, in effect, the principle in relation to which even the mere attempt to secure one's survival—that is, the principle of self-preservation—is subject to moral condemnation. Significantly, Smith sees Mandeville, otherwise his predecessor in so many ways, as tending merely to invert the philosophy of benevolence. The 'fellow-feeling' or benevolent inclination that ought to reign over our sentiments is redefined as a base, nearly animalistic passion that the most hardened criminal feels, given that its involuntary, instinctual character can no more be described as virtuous than the supposedly selfish passions of greed and lust.

Further, greed ought to be judged by its effects rather than by its motives, and the effects of the mass of individuals acting at the behest of the passion of greed are far superior to the effects of self-denial and benevolence. Therefore lust and greed, if not virtuous in themselves, lead to the production not only of a prosperous world but a world which can be regarded as virtuous in so far as it will relieve the sufferings of the poor more effectively and to a far greater degree than any system of charity based on self-denial or asceticism. For Smith, the problem is that Mandeville refers to all self-interested actions as vices (even if 'private vices are public benefits'), a reduction that prevents him from distinguishing between the rational and laudable self-interest of a merchant seeking to maximize the return on his investment and the vicious behaviour of a common thief seeking to convey my property into his own possession. Smith does not regard the 'popular ascetic doctrines'[6] to which Mandeville's system, as he read it, constituted a response as a serious threat to the prosperity of society. The social passions that he groups together under the label of benevolence are not even common enough to interfere with the degree of self-interest necessary to progress. The cooperation that constitutes the necessarily universal existence of human individuals derives from each seeking his own betterment at the expense of others. Precisely because individuals believe that their actions will lead to their advantage, they act in such a way that will produce the very universality that they appear to deny. For Smith, this 'veil of ignorance' that prevents individuals from knowing the benevolent consequences of their self-interested actions is necessary to the design of the whole.[7] As Seneca put it in De Providentia, a crucial text for Smith, the problem of evil in a world governed by providence is a problem of knowledge: 'What seem to be evils are not actually such.[8] Thus, individuals are governed by self-interest that they may better serve their fellows by producing and exchanging as much as they possibly can. In the famous passage in *The Theory of Moral Sentiments*, Smith remarks of 'the rich' that

> in spite of their natural selfishness and rapacity, though they mean only their own conveniency, though the sole end which they propose from the labors of all the thousands whom they employ, be the gratification of their own vain and insatiable desires, they divide with the poor the produce of all their improvements. They are led by an invisible hand to make nearly the same distribution of the necessaries of life, which would have been made had the earth been divided into equal portions among all its inhabitants, and thus, without intending it, without knowing it, advance the interests of the society and afford means to the multiplication of the species.[9]

It is here, in relation to a passage that certainly furnished one of the major reference points for Hegel's reading of Smith in the *Phenomenology*, that the precise effects of Hegel's reading become clear. First, in Smith's work, the discrepancy between the intentions and knowledge of individual actors and their actions on the one hand and the consequences of these actions on the other is, as we have seen, a necessary and permanent feature of society. It is in fact, as Smith himself clearly says in the lines following the passage from the *Theory of Moral Sentiments* cited above, the providential design of a society that is itself part of a universal Providence, neither a secular theodicy nor an economic theology but a continuation in the human world of the Providence that governs all things. Interestingly, Hegel, who does not reject providential thinking (even if by historicizing it he ends up positing an end that can only be perpetually deferred), cannot allow the dislocation between consciousness and action, between intention and consequence, to become functions of a stable system, the very principles of a social equilibrium. Instead, this dislocation marks the site of a contradiction that propels Smith's system beyond itself, namely into the becoming conscious of universality, in which consciousness begins to undertake the work of its own rational actualization, not merely discovering and observing a world but making it. By rejecting the theodicy proper to Smith's theory, Hegel allows us to see the essential role of the concept of theodicy, understood both as a natural and as a human system for Smith. For this concept alone will allow us to understand the emergence of another notion that otherwise would appear absent in Smith's works, that of life itself.

From Biopolitics to Necropolitics

The importance of life as a political concept has been underscored in recent years, beginning with Foucault's reflections on biopower, and continuing with such thinkers as Giorgio Agamben and Achille Mbembe. Of course, one might immediately object to the inclusion of Smith in the discussion invoked above. For this line of thought has defined itself as political, concerned with life in so far as it constitutes the object of sovereignty and government. Further, it might be argued that even if we can agree with Hegel that a certain concept of life is present in Smith, it is undoubtedly quite different from that imagined by contemporary theories of biopower, life prior to its capture by politics to the extent that human individuals must survive and reproduce in order then to be subjected or governed. Is it, then, life understood in its natural state, prior to its social existence; bodies as they must exist before they are directed, managed or even destroyed? Such a question might appear naive: after all, for the theoreticians named above is not life always already inscribed in the political? Has not Foucault in particular demonstrated the meticulous attention to detail characteristic of a biopolitics that leaves no aspect of life unexamined?

Agamben approaches these problems in *Homo Sacer* by referring to the distinction in Greek between *zoe* and *bios*. The former Agamben calls 'bare life', the life 'common to all living beings (animals, men, or gods)', whereas *bios* represents the form of life available to those who inhabit the polis, a political life specific to humanity by virtue of language. Thus the two senses of life in classical Greek serve not so much to distinguish the human from all other living things as to divide the human into two realms: the *bios*, or realm of the polis in which not simply living but the good life becomes possible, and *zoe*, the realm of the *oikos*, or household, the site of mere survival and procreation, that which is common to humans and all other living things. This distinction is crucial to Agamben's argument: if, for a millennium, bare life remained (and indeed was placed) as an object of reflection outside of the sphere of the political, 'the decisive event of modernity' was 'the entry of zoe into the sphere of the polis—the politicization of bare life as such'. This transformation is nothing less than (and here Agamben cites Foucault) 'a bestialization of man' and (citing Arendt) a 'decadence' of modern societies brought about by the 'primacy of natural life over political action'.[10]

'Bestialization' and 'natural life': these terms, designed certainly to evoke the 'dehumanization' of individuals and groups in the face of genocide, may have another, quite different, function as well. The isolation of the human realm of the polis, the place of rational debate and deliberation, from the sub-human realm of the *oikos*, the site of production and reproduction, has the effect of separating what we would now call the realm of the political from the realm of the economic. Thus, the horrors of the modern world are those of a biopolitics in the service of sovereignty (to follow Agamben's modification of Foucault's historicism), defined as the power to decide the state of exception. It would appear, then, that the *oikos* is a stand-in for the economic which marks it as a prepolitical backdrop that is simultaneously 'natural' and there-fore outside of the sphere of human action (and, increasingly, that which must be allowed to exist free of human interference, like a delicate and exotic eco-system) and 'bestial', a degraded realm in which what is specifically human disappears and the human becomes indistinguishable from the animal. We may well ask whether the bracketing of the economic in the current analyses of sovereign power does not constitute simultaneously the return of a repressed humanism (with its transcendence of mere nature and its hierarchization of life into the human, the subhuman and inevitably the superhuman—so that those who degrade humans to the level of beasts are themselves beasts, with all that such a definition entails) and the placing out of bounds (and Arendt was absolutely explicit about this) the economic, a movement which renders unthinkable any relation between the economic and the political. This disso-ciation is often marked, as if producing a kind of surplus, by a denunciation of Marx, who has come to represent both the theoretical error of positing any sort of relation between the economic and the political and the horror of the reduction of the human to the animal said to have characterized the peculiar form of totalitarianism for which Marx was responsible.

Thus, Achille Mbembe, in his essay 'Necropolitics', takes Marx (who, ac-cording to his argument, belongs to the tradition of terror which culminates in colonial genocide and the Nazi state) to task for 'conflating' the mere 'la-bour' necessary 'for the maintenance of human life' and 'work', which tran-scends the 'endless cycle of production and consumption' through 'the *creation* [emphasis added] of lasting artifacts that add to the world of things'. On the one side mere work, necessary to bare life, its products destined for immediate consumption in order for life to continue; and on the other a creative, genuinely human activity undertaken freely outside of any necessity, natural or historical, and whose creations 'last' by virtue of their transcending the animal realm of bare life to which they precisely contribute nothing. Mbembe argues that the conflation of labour and work thus defined is determined by the fact Marx 'blurs the all-important divisions among the man-made realm of freedom, the nature determined realm of necessity, and the contingent in history.[11] Marx's failure to distinguish between the realm of freedom and the natural realm of necessity within human existence, which therefore remains suspended between the man-made freedom of the polis and the 'nature determined realm of necessity' that characterizes the *oikos*, his refusal to differentiate between the political and the economic, has had devastating consequences for humanity. Because the economy, according to Mbembe, lies outside the effective sphere of human action, revolutions inspired by Marxism must try unsuccessfully to force unwilling populations to submit to their attempt to dominate the sphere of economic relations, which is in fact part of the natural realm of necessity. Their very failure to impose man-made designs on nature results in their resorting to an act of will, namely terror, a fight to the death, to bring about the telos that their faith has instructed them surely awaits. But the critique of Marxism (which is otherwise perfectly banal and drawn from the ideological repertoire of Cold War liberalism) is important here only in so far as Marxism, for Mbembe, is one possible variant of the evolution of biopolitics into necropolitics, 'politics as the work of death', and sovereignty as consisting primarily of the right to kill. The figure of the modern Homo Sacer as understood by Agamben is found in its purest state in the Nazi death camps; Mbembe shows that the populations of European colonies had long been regarded as bare life whose destruction could not be thought of as murder.

I would argue that this line of thought, which moves from biopolitics to necropolitics and which poses Homo Sacer as a central figure of modern politics, is both provocative and productive. There is no question, however, of accepting or rejecting it as if the work of the late Foucault, Agamben and Mbembe constituted a unified body of propositions, and this heterogeneity is not simply the consequence of the different emphases and interests of the three authors named above. Instead, I want to ask a question, or set of questions, that is simultaneously posed and held in abeyance in this theoretical constellation. It is held in abeyance in so far as these theoreticians insist on a dualism of life, the separation internal to humanity of human and animal functions, the separation of the polis and the *oikos*, the political and the economic, the man-made realm of freedom and the natural realm of necessity. If we can speak of a necropolitics, can we, and indeed must we, also, simultaneously, in one and the same gesture, speak of a necro-economics? Mbembe has implicitly contested Foucault's description of biopolitics as the inverse of the operation of sovereignty; while the latter brings death or permits life (*faire mourir et laisser vivre*), biopower operates by making live and letting die (*faire vivre et laisser mourir*).[12] Following Agamben in insisting on the coexistence of sovereign power and biopower, Mbembe assigns modern politics a far more active relation to death, which indeed becomes its primary objective. The question of necro-economics compels us to return to the notion of 'letting die' or of 'exposing to death' and not simply death in battle. This should not be taken as an alternative to necropolitics as understood by Mbembe but, again as its complement, as if the two were one and the same process understood in different ways. To think this possibility, however, requires us to abandon the perspective of any dualism, a difficult task indeed, when we have been assured that the only alternatives to dualism are conflation, blurring and indistinction.

To proceed I will resume my reading of Hegel reading Smith, pausing only to note that this Hegel is far from and opposed to the Hegel invoked by Mbembe (which is, in fact, Hegel read by Kojève and therefore—as Althusser remarked[13]—an existentialist Hegel in which the confrontation between consciousnesses takes place in the solitude of a state of nature). For Hegel, Smith's rejection of any pre-social human existence, his declaring as necessary to mere life cooperation and therefore not simply the labour of dissociated individuals perhaps exchanging after the fact, but a certain minimal form of society and therefore politics, renders him a thinker of the immanence of the universal in human life by virtue of the necessarily collective labour which makes human life possible. He is therefore for Hegel the thinker of universality not in a juridical or moral sense but in so far as it is realized in the production of life. The question we must now pose—for, despite the ritual denunciation of Hegel that one finds in so much theory today, it is not Hegel (or Marx) whose 'central tenets'[14] govern the world today but Adam Smith's—is whether Hegel's reading of Smith is a tenable one. To put it in another way, is the market, understood globally, if not universally, that natural–human sphere of the production and reproduction of life, the life of a people, the life of people? As I argued earlier, Hegel could make Smith the thinker of the universal and of life only by depriving his system of its providential character, turning the unconsciousness of Smith's producers into a temporary failure of knowledge that could only destabilize and call into question their relation to the world of their making, setting it on the course to that becoming other characteristic of the moments of Spirit's long return to itself. If, to part company with Hegel, we allow Smith to think the global market as a theodicy that is itself part of a larger natural teleology that exceeds the grasp of the human intellect, what is the relation of the market to life (and, correlatively, to death)?

Killing and Letting Die

I will answer this question by returning to the famous passage from *The Theory of Moral Sentiments*, cited earlier, in which Smith sketches out the providential nature of the 'distribution of the necessaries of life':

> [the rich] are led by an invisible hand to make nearly the same distribution of the necessaries of life, which would have been made, had the earth been divided into equal portions among its inhabitants and thus without intending it, without knowing it, advance the interests of the society, and afford means to the multiplication of the species. When Providence divided the earth among a few lordly masters, it neither forgot nor abandoned those who seem to be left out in the partition. These last too enjoy their share of all that it produces. In what constitutes the real happiness of human life, they are in no respect inferior to those who would seem so much above them. In ease of body and peace of mind all the different ranks of life are nearly upon a level, and the beggar, who suns himself by the side of a highway, possess that security which kings are fighting for.[15]

Jacob Viner has examined in some detail the function of the concepts of providence and theodicy in the history of economic thought in the seventeenth and eighteenth centuries, both as a model of a system that cannot fail and whose putative failures are nothing other than a failure of knowledge, and consequently as a justification of inequality, as an only apparent evil necessary to the (all too often invisible) moral function of the whole.[16] While his observations are certainly pertinent to Smith, they do not exhaust the effects of the notion of theodicy on Smith's conception of the market. It also serves to identify the market as a meta-human realm which neither individuals nor collective entities can master or direct. In fact, it is constructed in such a way that evil, originally absent from the whole itself, arises only from human attempts to 'interfere' with the workings of a providential design whose magnitude escapes our knowledge or control. Providence, thus understood, is not a system of absolute determination, but a design or plan accessible to humanity through the exercise of reason and through the rational pursuit of self-interest, which we must choose to follow. Its perfection in no way inhibits individuals or whole societies from turning away from the only true way to reason and justice.

Hence, Smith's own rather pronounced necropolitics, his interest in death, and the infliction of death not only by the state, but by the individual himself at the moment he understands he 'is the just and proper object of the hatred and contempt of his fellow creatures'. For Smith, if society is naturally necessary to the sustaining of human life, 'the dread of death, the great poison to the happiness, but the great restraint upon the injustice of mankind, which while it afflicts and mortifies the individual, guards and protects the society'. Every man 'in the race for wealth, and honors and preferments . . . may run as hard as he can and strain every nerve and muscle, in order to outstrip all his competitors'; if he were, however, to 'jostle or throw down any of them' he would become the object of 'hatred and indignation' and as such liable to punishment. A necessary part, then, of collective production of life, a process driven by self-interest, is an awareness of the ever-present force of justice which takes, or ought to take, life with a machine-like regularity that will immediately attend to the excess of self-interest that leads an individual to step outside the realm of fair competition and engage in theft or fraud to acquire the possessions he desires. In fact, the sociability necessary to human existence is itself only possible through the constant example of the taking of the life of the individual judged guilty. Without this example before them, men 'feel so little for another with whom they have no particular connection in comparison with what they feel for themselves' that, in the absence of a terror of merited punishment, they would, 'like wild beasts, be at all times ready to fly upon him: and a man would enter an assembly of men as he enters a den of lions'. Further, the desire to inflict capital punishment is simultaneously rational and rooted in the human passion for vengeance, a simultaneity which again expresses the working of providence; the production of life both requires and induces the exercise of the right to kill. Thus, 'a man of humanity . . . applauds with ardor, and even with transport, the just retaliation which seems due' to crimes against the lives and properties of others. And if the transport one feels at an execution appears itself ignoble, we must understand that, like the passionate pursuit of self-interest, the instinct of self-preservation, it is the actually existing as opposed to ideal means nature has provided to achieve 'the end which she proposes'. This arrangement of means and ends is the surest sign that the 'oeconomy of nature is in this respect exactly of a piece with what it is upon many other occasions'.[17]

The phrase 'oeconomy of nature', which here marks the junction of the political and the economic, allows us to make the transition from Smith's necropolitics, his founding of life on death, of the production of life on the production of death, to his necro-economics. If societies, by virtue of the oeconomy of nature, must exercise, and not merely possess, the right to kill, the market, understood as the very form of human universality as life, must necessarily, at certain precise moments, 'let die'. In order to approach this question, we may turn to Smith's discussion in the *Wealth of Nations* of the precise means by which the world's rich, led by the invisible hand, distribute to the rest of the earth's inhabitants the 'necessaries of life'. Apart from the small sum that the world's beggars succeed in 'extorting' (Smith's term) from them, this distribution takes the form of the payment of wages. Here, and I refer to Chapter 8 of Part I of the *Wealth of Nations*, we no longer confront a world of autonomous individuals led by self-interest to truck, barter and exchange for their advantage, a theoretical framework which could easily accommodate the labour contract, understood as an exchange between individuals. Instead, Smith explains the antagonism that, in part, determines the rate of wages—that is, the extent of the distributions made by the world's rich—as collective in nature:

> what are the common wages of labor, depends everywhere on the contract made between those parties, whose interests are by no means the same. The workmen desire to get as much as possible, the masters to give as little as possible. The former are disposed to combine in order to raise, the latter in order to lower the wages of labor.[18]

I will leave to the side the fact that the very notion of collective action invoked here poses a series of questions and problems that Smith does not, and perhaps cannot, address given the constraints of his theory. Suffice it to say, though, that the competing 'parties', a term that allows him to move freely between the individual and the collective, function exactly as individuals whose competition and opposition produce, without their knowledge or consent, a 'nearly' equal distribution of life's necessities. Appearances are indeed deceiving: the nature of the market is, of course, such that all the advantage in this contest between workmen and their masters lies with the latter. The workmen cannot quit, nor can they refrain from work in protest over wages for more than a few days. Their ability to maintain themselves, the very subsistence, depends on their earning a wage. The masters, in contrast, have sufficient stock in most cases to 'live a year or two' without employing labour. This advantage allows them 'to force the workmen into compliance with their terms'. And their terms are often not very favourable: Smith's masters 'are always and everywhere in a sort of tacit, but constant and uniform combination, not to raise the wages of labor above their actual rate'. Further, they will 'sometimes enter into particular combinations to sink the wages of labor below this rate'. The market appears, then, to have placed few, if any, limits on the ability of the masters to increase their profit simply by lowering the amount they expend on wages. The limit Smith does in fact set on the lowering of wages is the limit of the market itself: it is none other than the bare life of the workman, whose 'wages must at least be sufficient to maintain him . . . at a rate consistent with common humanity' and even 'somewhat more; otherwise it would be impossible for him to bring up a family and the race of such workmen could not last beyond the first generation'. Such a postulate might seem to condemn the great majority in any society to a life of hard labour for their mere subsistence; in fact, it is the foundation for the only rational means to increase the rate of wages and thus improve their lives. A reduction of wages to the level of bare life paradoxically (dialectically?) allows the fund available for the payment of wages to accumulate to such an extent that the only outcome can be the employment of more hands.

> When in any country the demand for those who live by wages; laborers, journeymen, servants of every kind is continually increasing; when every year furnishes employment for a greater number than had been employed the year before, the workman have no occasion to combine in order to raise their wages.[19]

Yet there exist certain societies, and Smith adduces examples only from the non-European world, where the nature of the 'laws and institutions' does not permit them to acquire greater wealth: societies he deems 'stationary' and incapable of growth, in which the downward limit on wages appears far more variable that the phrase 'consistent with common humanity' would appear to suggest. For in China, as Smith imagines it, not even a high rate of infant mortality such as is consequent to the poverty of the Scottish Highlanders (where, he has heard, perhaps only two out of twenty children survive) will suffice to allocate wages to the degree necessary to maintain the labourer. Instead, even in the face of high infant mortality, the fact that many thousands of families subsist on such scant resources as 'the carcass of a dead dog or cat, for example, though half putrid and stinking', which is 'as welcome to them as the most wholesome food is to people of other countries', means that in order for the labourer to subsist, his children must be destroyed, 'exposed in the street or drowned like puppies in the water'.[20] Here, the rigour of the market as a mechanism that adjusts the proportion of labourers to the fund available for wages by liberally distributing malnutrition to the social ranks whose numbers exceed their ability to obtain subsistence, thereby 'destroying a great part of the children' without any agent 'intending it or knowing it', must be supplemented by direct human agency.

Market Death

The case of famine—and here Smith privileges eighteenth-century Bengal rather than late-seventeenth- and early-eighteenth-century France, where nearly 2 million French citizens perished in the famines of 1694 and 1708/9—is perhaps even more instructive.[21] 'In a country where the funds destined for the maintenance of labor were sensibly decaying' wages would be reduced 'to the most miserable and scanty subsistence of the laborer'.[22] It becomes clear at this point that the term 'subsistence', as denoting the 'rate below which it seems impossible to reduce' wages, has no fixed social or biological limit. A decaying wage fund lowers the demand for labour so far that the subsistence of the individual workman is no longer necessary, given the vast numbers of unemployed prepared to take the place of those fortunate enough to have found employment. The rest

> would either starve or be driven to seek a subsistence either by begging or by the perpetration of the greatest enormities. Want famine and mortality would immediately prevail in that class, and from thence extend themselves to all the superior classes, till the number of inhabitants in the country was

reduced to what could be easily maintained by the revenue and stock which remained in it.[23]

If it appears that a kind of infallible rationality immanent in nature itself restores even by means of mortality an equilibrium between workmen and the wage fund sufficient to guarantee the mere life of the labourer, such a 'calamity', as he calls it, can arise only as the consequence of 'improper regulations' and 'injudicious restraints' imposed by governments on trade. The market, if allowed to work without interference, will always and everywhere prevent what he calls dearth (shortages of food as a result of decline in production) from turning into famine. Smith's theory of famine constitutes one of the most contested and debated sections of the *Wealth of Nations*, cited frequently by Amartya Sen,[24] among others, for its empirical and theoretical failings. While I have no quarrel with those who seek to refute Smith's arguments, a task as important today as it has ever been, my aim here is to understand his discussion of famine, with all its theological overtones, as symptomatic of conflicts that animate his work as a whole.

At first glance, the position that 'famine has never arisen from any other cause but the violence of government attempting, by improper means, to remedy the inconveniences of a dearth', and its corollary that 'the unlimited, unrestrained freedom of the corn trade . . . is the only effectual means preventative of the miseries of a famine',[25] appear so categorical as to be absurd, nothing more than a declaration of faith without any necessary connection to historical reality (Mike Davis's *Late Victorian Holocausts* can be regarded as the definitive empirical refutation of this doctrine). It is here, however, around the very question of famine and therefore of life itself—the point at which Smith can no longer continue to divide and subdivide subsistence so that we are no longer discussing individual lives of workmen and their families (or more specifically children), given that, as Smith has demonstrated, the life of the individual is no longer a reliable or useful unit of analysis, but the life of a population—that the stakes of Smith's position become clear. The subsistence of a population may, and does in specific circumstances, require the death of a significant number of individuals: to be precise it requires that they be allowed to die so that others may live.

In particular, a qualitative distinction between dearth and famine—that is, between shortages that bring malnutrition, disease and a small increase in mortality, and larger, catastrophic increases in mortality causing significant decline in a population over a relatively brief period of time—appears increasingly questionable. Critics have focused on what appears to be no more than a leap of faith, an unquestioning belief in the providential hand of the market: where there exists

> free commerce and communication, the scarcity occasioned by the most unfavourable seasons can never be so great as to produce a famine; and the scantiest crop, if managed with frugality and oeconomy, will maintain, through the year, the same number of people that are commonly fed in a more affluent manner by one of moderate plenty.[26]

This has appeared as little more than a gesture of theoretical/historical denial, an attempt to explain away those famines (far more frequent after than before Smith) in which perfectly unhampered markets did nothing to prevent famine, and on the contrary seem to have exacerbated them. But it is possible to extract from the *Wealth of Nations* a more moderate and defensible position which is, however, no less grounded in an economic theodicy.

Without holding Smith to the argument that markets will maintain the same number of people in years of scarcity as in years of affluence (an argument that poses again all the problems of defining the verb 'maintain', the limit of which, as we have seen, is pushed from subsistence to sub-subsistence), we can nevertheless credit him with the position that the market is a more rational mechanism for managing dearth than any other available alternative, and that if indeed dearth declines into famine, the mortality rate, however great, must necessarily be less than it otherwise would have been. And once again this rationality is not the consequence of the will or knowledge of those individuals who are its bearers, nor does its distribution of food in times of scarcity (whether absolute or relative) depend upon the benevolence of those concerned. On the contrary, it is precisely the grain merchant's seeking the greatest profit he can realize without the slightest intention of allaying the hunger of others that will lead him to carry out that distribution and, more importantly, do so in a way that will protect the hungry from their own improvident and irrational impulses.

Left to their own devices, those threatened with starvation and moved by the pangs of hunger will consume the available food supply 'so fast as must necessarily produce a famine before the end of the season'. Indeed, any misguided attempt on the part of a government to regulate prices in order to increase access to food will inevitably produce such a result. Merchants who raise prices in the face of rising demand are not only right to do so from the point of view of their self-interest ('it is in years of scarcity, when prices are high, that the corn merchant expects to make his principal profit'), but the unintended effect of their profit is the disciplining of the hungry by the market itself, which distributes to them only the meagre portion that their falling wages will procure. Smith addresses the possible objection that merchants will withhold or hoard supplies in order precisely to drive up prices and increase profits, thus actively preventing food from being purchased by those who most need it and thereby contributing to, if not actually causing, famine. The merchant, he tells us, must exactly calibrate price to supply, so that, if he raises his prices without warrant, or holds back his product when no real scarcity exists, he will be ruined by those who undersell him or rush to fill the vacuum. He 'hurts himself much more than he can hurt the particular people whom he may hinder from supplying themselves'. In opposition, 'if he judges right, instead of hurting the great body of people, he renders them a most important service.'[27]

For whatever difficulties the 'inconveniences of a dearth' cause those who are by high prices prevented from consuming as much as they want or need, these inconveniences are not nearly as severe as those they might feel were they allowed to consume as they like. Again, to give Smith his due, the 'inconveniences of dearth' may not be restricted to the pangs of hunger and the effects of malnutrition; nothing excludes a greater than normal mortality rate. His point is merely that the market is the best of all possible forms of supply and that, truth be told, it rations not simply food, but life itself, allowing the greatest possible survival rate in a given circumstance. Nothing in Smith's own argument compels us to follow him in his leap of faith and hold that the market will maintain the same number of people in times of scarcity as in times of plenty. But even if there are those who perish slowly from malnutrition and the disease that accompanies it, or from starvation, but over a longer period of time than one might see in a catastrophic famine in which millions may perish in a few months (as in the case of Bengal in 1770), we will be secure that the rationing by the market of food precisely because it is not the effect of any human design will proceed in the most reasonable manner possible.

Yet, as his numerous critics have shown, the rationality of the market during times of scarcity resides, for Smith, solely in the determination of price. If steep rises in prices are accompanied, as they often are, by falling wages and widescale unemployment, the market no longer rations food to the otherwise avaricious and short-sighted consumer, but precisely places it out of reach, or diverts it elsewhere where the fund of wages is growing and greater profits are to be made. Although Smith does not consider this objection in his discussion of dearth and famine, he offers the elements of a response in the discussion of wages in Chapter 7 discussed earlier. There, where 'the funds destined for the maintenance of the laboring poor are fast decaying', the equilibrium of the market not only can but will by a necessity greater than the market itself be achieved by a 'reduction' of the 'number of inhabitants to what can easily by maintained by the revenue and stock which remained in it'.[28] The instruments of this reduction are 'want and famine', and the form it takes mortality. And thus Smith can say with Seneca that 'what is evil only appears as such'. Death establishes the conditions of life; death as by an invisible hand restores the market to what it must be to support life. Smith, perhaps understandably, drew back from the conclusion that any form of famine relief—not simply an attempt to lower prices, but perhaps even more importantly any attempt at a mass distribution of food by the state, drawing from public granaries without cost to the penniless (as was the case in eighteenth-century China, which avoided famines not only on the scale of Bengal but even on the scale of early-eighteenth-century France)—could only dissuade merchants from engaging in so precarious a trade. Such efforts would lead to a decrease in the production and supply of food and not only postpone but aggravate the inevitable day of reckoning.

Thus, we seem to have arrived at a reading of Smith more Hegelian than that of Hegel himself; Smith postulates an equilibrium or harmony productive of life that is paradoxically created and maintained by the power of the negative, of death; that the allowing of death is necessary to the production of the life of the universal. Smith's economics is a necro-economics. The market reduces and rations life; it not only allows death, it demands that death be allowed by the sovereign power, as well as by those who suffer it. In other words it demands and requires that the latter allow themselves to die. From this we must conclude that underneath the appearance of a system whose intricate harmony might be appreciated as a kind of austere and awful beauty, a self-regulating system, not the ideal perhaps, but the best of all possible systems, is the demand that some must allow themselves to die. This of course raises the possibility that those so called upon will refuse this demand—that is, that they will refuse to allow themselves to die. It is at this point that the state, which might appear to have no other relation to the market than one of a contemplative acquiescence, is called into action; those who refuse to allow themselves to die must be compelled by force to do so. This force, then, while external to the market, is necessary to its existence and function. This, to borrow a phrase from Carl Schmitt, is the moment of decision which makes possible the very systemacity of the market system.

Let us begin not with the extreme cases of dearth or famine, but merely with the case of a reduction in the workmen's wages (and therefore a reduction in their subsistence forced on them by their masters). As Smith notes, a reduction in wages can be of such magnitude that it is 'severely felt' by wage earners, whose ability to purchase 'provisions' is significantly compromised. In the face of the masters seeking to increase their profit in this particular manner, the workmen may 'yield, as they sometimes do, without resistance'.[29] In fact, their unwillingness to resist even a severe reduction in their level of subsistence may derive from their acute awareness of the competition for work characteristic of a specific market. Their lack of resistance may also be determined by a recognition of the natural advantage of the masters discussed earlier, that is, their ability to outlast the workmen thanks to the stock they possess.

Yet market forces alone, for reasons Smith treats only elliptically, are 'frequently' insufficient to prevent the resistance of workmen. They often respond to a wage reduction by 'a defensive combination' which is 'always abundantly heard of . . . they have always recourse to the loudest clamor and sometimes to the most shocking violence and outrage'. Smith explains such behaviour with disarming honesty: 'They are desperate and act with the folly and extravagance of desperate men who must either starve, or frighten their master into an immediate compliance with their demands'.[30]

In such a situation, when market forces alone do not protect the masters from the indignation of those faced with starvation (which, as recent theoreticians have reminded us, does not automatically or immediately lead to death), the civil magistrate must intervene by rigorously enforcing the laws against the combination of workmen. The threat of 'punishment or ruin' will thereby break their resistance and allow the market to protect them as it will. Smith, so willing elsewhere to pass judgement on laws that he finds inefficient or unjust, is strangely silent on the matter of anti-combination laws that form an unalterable backdrop to the struggles he describes. They seem unjust, in that they prohibit only the combination of workmen, but the injustice, from the point of view of Smith's system, is only apparent; in reality, they free the market to reward the workmen to the greatest extent possible while protecting them from the effects of their own avarice and short-sightedness.

The case of grain merchants, 'dealers in corn', whose product, unlike that of pin makers, is necessary to the mere survival of a population, is one to which Smith devotes a great deal of attention. The peculiarities of the trade mean that the corn merchant not only 'deserves the full protection of the law' but in fact requires it. Their role as provisioners of the nation exposes them 'to popular odium.... In years of scarcity, the inferior ranks of the people impute their distress to the corn merchant who becomes the object of their hatred and indignation'. The rationing of grain, which the merchant's search for profits effects, is represented in the popular imagination as 'engrossing and forestalling' (that is, as hoarding and price speculation), a representation which, Smith argues, 'may be compared to the popular terrors and suspicions of witchcraft', the victims of which were 'not more innocent of the misfortunes imputed to them'.[31] The 'imaginary crime' imputed to corn merchants, however comparable to that of the unfortunates accused of witchcraft, is far more severely punished. Such punishment may take the form of a government moved by 'popular odium' and the threat of disorder to order the merchants to sell their stock at lower prices than the market would otherwise permit. The effect of such an improvident act is to allow the inferior ranks of society the immediate gratification they demand, while in fact exposing them to the famine that their immoderate consumption of all available grain will in a short time bring about. It is as if the bodies of the poor undergo such transformations in times of shortfall that they are able to consume far more food than they can during times of plenty.

Yet far more menacing is the danger that the merchant will be 'utterly ruined and ... his magazines plundered and destroyed' by mobs driven by 'hatred and indignation'.[32] The inferior ranks of society do not, and indeed cannot be expected to, understand that their distress, even their destitution and slow starvation, are necessary and that with the market's rationing of food must inevitably follow a rationing of life itself, an allowing of some to die, so that others, a majority perhaps, may live. The mob, faced not with absolute scarcity—that is, with the demonstrated absence of food at any price—but with a relative scarcity in which enough food exists to feed an entire population, though which, by virtue of price, lies beyond their means, may refuse mortality or even slow starvation and simply seize the stores themselves. It is here that the sovereign power must intervene, not necessarily to kill those who refuse to die, but to ensure, through the use of force, that they will be exposed to death and compelled to accept the rationing of life by the market.

Thus alongside the figure of Homo Sacer, the one who may be killed with impunity, is another figure, one whose death is no doubt less spectacular than the first and is the object of no memorial or commemoration; he who with impunity may be allowed to die, slowly or quickly, in the name of the rationality and equilibrium of the market.

Notes

1. Louis Althusser and Étienne Balibar, *Reading Capital*, New Left Books, London, 1970, p. 13.
2. G.W.F. Hegel, *The Phenomenology of Spirit*, trans. A.V. Miller, Oxford University Press, Oxford, 1977, p. 213.
3. Adam Smith, *An Inquiry into the Nature and Causes of the Wealth of Nations*, 2 vols., Liberty Fund, Indianapolis, 1981, vol. 1, pp. 26, 25.
4. Hegel, *Phenomenology*, p. 213.
5. Adam Smith, *The Theory of Moral Sentiments*, Liberty Fund, Indianapolis, 1986, p. 301.
6. Ibid., p. 313.
7. See the commentary of Michel Foucault, *Naissance de la Biopolitique: Cours aux Collège de France, 1978–1979*, Gallimard, Paris, 2005, pp. 282–90.
8. Seneca, *The Stoic Philosophy of Seneca: Essays and Letters,* Norton, New York, 1958, p. 32.
9. Smith, *Theory of Moral Sentiments*, pp. 184–5.
10. Giorgio Agamben, *Homo Sacer: Sovereign Power and Bare Life*, Stanford University Press, Stanford, 1998, pp. 3–4.
11. Achille Mbembe, 'Necropolitics', *Public Culture*, vol. 15, no. 1, 2003, pp. 19–20.
12. Michel Foucault, *The History of Sexuality: An Introduction*, Vintage, New York, 1978, p. 136.
13. Louis Althusser, 'L'homme, cette nuit', in *Écrits philosophiques et politiques*, vol. 1, pp. 239–42.
14. Mbembe, 'Necropolitics', p. 20.
15. Smith, *Theory of Moral Sentiments*, pp. 184–5.
16. Jacob Viner, *The Role of Providence in the Social Order*, American Philosophical Society, Philadelphia, 1972.
17. Smith, *Theory of Moral Sentiments*, pp. 84, 83, 86, 90, 77.
18. Smith, *Wealth of Nations*, p. 83.
19. Ibid., pp. 83–6.
20. Ibid., p. 90.
21. For a discussion of the French famines, see Cormac Ó Gráda, 'Markets and Famine in

Pre-industrial Europe', *Journal of Interdisciplinary History*, vol. 36, no. 2, Autumn 2005, pp. 143–6.

22. Smith, *Wealth of Nations*, pp. 90–91.

23. Ibid., p. 91.

24. Amartya Sen, *Poverty and Famine: An Essay on Entitlement and Deprivation*, Oxford University Press, Oxford, 1981.

25. Smith, *Wealth of Nations*, pp. 526–7.

26. Ibid., p. 526.

27. Ibid., pp. 527, 533.

28. Ibid., p. 91.

29. Ibid., p. 84.

30. Ibid., p. 84, 85.

31. Ibid., pp. 527, 534.

32. Ibid., p. 527.

CHAPTER 10

BIOPOLITICAL PRODUCTION

Michael Hardt and Antonio Negri

> The "police" appears as an administration heading the state,
> together with the judiciary, the army, and the exchequer. True.
> Yet in fact, it embraces everything else. Turquet says so: "It
> branches out into all of the people's conditions, everything they
> do or undertake. Its field comprises the judiciary, finance, and
> the army." The *police* includes everything.
>   Michel Foucault

From the juridical perspective we have been able to glimpse some of the elements of the ideal genesis of Empire, but from that perspective alone it would be difficult if not impossible to understand how the imperial machine is actually set in motion. Juridical concepts and juridical systems always refer to something other than themselves. Through the evolution and exercise of right, they point toward the material condition that defines their purchase on social reality. Our analysis must now descend to the level of that materiality and investigate there the material transformation of the paradigm of rule. We need to discover the means and forces of the production of social reality along with the subjectivities that animate it.

Biopower in the Society of Control

In many respects, the work of Michel Foucault has prepared the terrain for such an investigation of the material functioning of imperial rule. First of all, Foucault's work allows us to recognize a historical, epochal passage in social forms from *disciplinary society* to the *society of control*.[1] Disciplinary society is that society in which social command is constructed through a diffuse network of *dispositifs* or apparatuses that produce and regulate customs, habits, and productive practices. Putting this society to work and ensuring obedience to its rule and its mechanisms of inclusion and/or exclusion are accomplished through disciplinary institutions (the prison, the factory, the asylum, the hospital, the university, the school, and so forth) that structure the social terrain and present logics adequate to the "reason" of discipline. Disciplinary power rules in effect by structuring the parameters and limits of thought and practice, sanctioning and prescribing normal and/or deviant behaviors. Foucault generally refers to the ancien régime and the classical age of French civilization to illustrate the emergence of disciplinarity, but more generally we could say that the entire first phase of capitalist accumulation (in Europe and elsewhere) was conducted under this paradigm of power. We should understand the society of control, in contrast, as that society (which develops at the far edge of modernity and opens toward the postmodern) in which mechanisms of command become ever more "democratic," ever more immanent to the social field, distributed throughout the brains and bodies of the citizens. The behaviors of social integration and exclusion proper to rule are thus increasingly interiorized within the subjects themselves. Power is now exercised through machines that directly organize the brains (in communication systems, information networks, etc.) and bodies (in welfare systems, monitored activities, etc.) toward a state of autonomous alienation from the sense of life and the desire for creativity. The society of control might thus be characterized by an intensification and generalization of the normalizing apparatuses of disciplinarity that internally animate our common and daily practices, but in contrast to discipline, this control extends well outside the structured sites of social institutions through flexible and fluctuating networks.

Second, Foucault's work allows us to recognize the *biopolitical* nature of the new paradigm of power.[2] Biopower is a form of power that regulates social life from its interior, following it, interpreting it, absorbing it, and rearticulating it. Power can achieve an effective command over the entire life of the population only when it becomes an integral, vital function that every individual embraces and reactivates of his or her own accord. As Foucault says, "Life has now become . . . an object of power."[3] The highest function of this power is to invest life through and through, and its primary task is to administer life. Biopower thus refers to a situation in which what is directly at stake in power is the production and reproduction of life itself.

These two lines of Foucault's work dovetail with each other in the sense that only the society of control is able to adopt the biopolitical context as its *exclusive* terrain of reference. In the passage from disciplinary society to the society of control, a new paradigm of power is realized which is defined by the technologies that recognize society as the realm of biopower. In disciplinary society the effects of biopolitical technologies were still partial in the sense that disciplining developed according to relatively closed, geometrical, and quantitative logics. Disciplinarity fixed individuals within institutions but did not succeed in consuming them completely in the rhythm of productive practices and productive socialization; it did not reach the point of permeating entirely the consciousnesses and bodies of individuals, the point of treating and organizing them in the totality of their activities. In disciplinary society, then, the relationship between power and the individual remained a static one: the disciplinary invasion of power corresponded to the resistance of the individual. By contrast, when power becomes entirely biopolitical, the whole social body is comprised by power's machine and developed in its virtuality. This relationship is open, qualitative, and affective. Society, subsumed within a power that reaches down to the ganglia of the social structure and its processes of development, reacts like a single body. Power is thus expressed as a control that extends throughout the depths of the consciousnesses and bodies of the population—and at the same time across the entirety of social relations.[4]

In this passage from disciplinary society to the society of control, then, one could say that the increasingly intense relationship of mutual implication of all social forces that capitalism has pursued throughout its development has now been fully realized. Marx recognized something similar in what he called the passage from the formal subsumption to the real subsumption of labor under capital,[5] and later the Frankfurt School philosophers analyzed a closely related passage of the subsumption of culture (and social relations) under the totalitarian figure of the state, or really within the perverse dialectic of Enlightenment.[6] The passage we are referring to, however, is fundamentally different in that instead of focusing on the unidimensionality of the process described by Marx and reformulated and extended by the Frankfurt School, the Foucauldian passage deals fundamentally with the paradox of plurality and multiplicity—and Deleuze and Guattari develop this perspective even more clearly.[7] The analysis of the real subsumption, when this is understood as investing not only the economic or only the cultural dimension of society but rather the social *bios* itself, and when it is attentive to the modalities of disciplinarity and/or control, disrupts the linear and totalitarian figure of capitalist development. Civil society is absorbed in the state, but the consequence of this is an explosion of the elements that were previously coordinated and mediated in civil society. Resistances are no longer marginal but active in the center of a society that opens up in networks; the individual points are singularized in a thousand plateaus. What Foucault constructed implicitly (and Deleuze and Guattari made explicit) is therefore the paradox of a power that, while it unifies and envelops within itself every element of social life (thus losing its capacity effectively to mediate different social forces), at that very moment reveals a new context, a new milieu of maximum plurality and uncontainable singularization—a milieu of the event.[8]

These conceptions of the society of control and biopower both describe central aspects of the concept of Empire. The concept of Empire is the framework in which the new omniversality of subjects has to be understood, and it is the end to which the new paradigm of power is leading. Here a veritable chasm opens up between the various old theoretical frameworks of international law (in either its contractual and/or U.N. form) and the new reality of imperial law. All the intermediary elements of the process have in fact fallen aside, so that the legitimacy of the international order can no longer be constructed through mediations but must rather be grasped immediately in all its diversity. We have already acknowledged this fact from the juridical perspective. We saw, in effect, that when the new notion of right emerges in the context of globalization and presents itself as capable of treating the universal, planetary sphere as a single, systemic set, it must assume an immediate prerequisite (acting in a state of exception) and an adequate, plastic, and constitutive technology (the techniques of the police).

Even though the state of exception and police technologies constitute the solid nucleus and the central element of the new imperial right, however, this new regime has nothing to do with the juridical arts of dictatorship or totalitarianism that in other times and with such great fanfare were so thoroughly described by many (in fact too many!) authors.[9] On the contrary, the rule of law continues to play a central role in the context of the contemporary passage: right remains effective and (precisely by means of the state of exception and police techniques) becomes procedure. This is a radical transformation that reveals the unmediated relationship between power and subjectivities, and hence demonstrates both the impossibility of "prior" mediations and the uncontainable temporal variability of the event.[10] Throughout the unbounded global spaces, to the depths of the biopolitical world, and confronting an unforeseeable temporality—these are the determinations on which the new supranational right must be defined. Here is where the concept of Empire must struggle to establish itself, where it must prove its effectiveness, and hence where the machine must be set in motion.

From this point of view, the biopolitical context of the new paradigm is completely central to our analysis. This is what presents power with an alternative, not only between obedience and disobedience, or between formal political participation and refusal, but also along the entire range of life and death, wealth and poverty, production and social reproduction, and so forth. Given the great difficulties the new notion of right has in representing this dimension of the power of Empire, and given its inability to touch biopower concretely in all its material aspects, imperial right can at best only partially represent the underlying design of the new constitution of world order, and cannot really grasp the motor that sets it in motion. Our analysis must focus its attention rather on the *productive* dimension of biopower.[11]

The Production of Life

The question of production in relation to biopower and the society of control, however, reveals a real weakness of the work of the authors from whom we have borrowed these notions. We should clarify, then, the "vital" or biopolitical dimensions of Foucault's work in relation to the dynamics of production. Foucault argued in several works in the mid-1970s that one cannot understand the passage from the "sovereign" state of the ancien régime to the modern "disciplinary" state without taking into account how the biopolitical context was progressively put at the service of capitalist accumulation: "The control of society over individuals is not conducted only through consciousness or ideology, but also in the body and with the body. For capitalist society biopolitics is what is most important, the biological, the somatic, the corporeal."[12]

One of the central objectives of his research strategy in this period was to go beyond the versions of historical materialism, including several variants of Marxist theory, that considered the problem of power and social reproduction on a superstructural level separate from the real, base level of production. Foucault thus attempted to bring the problem of social reproduction and all the elements of the so-called superstructure back to within the material, fundamental structure and define this terrain not only in economic terms but also in cultural, corporeal, and subjective ones. We can thus understand how Foucault's conception of the social whole was perfected and realized when in a subsequent phase of his work he uncovered the emerging outlines of the society of control as a figure of power active throughout the entire biopolitics of society. It does not seem, however, that Foucault—even when he powerfully grasped the biopolitical horizon of society and defined it as a field of immanence—ever succeeded in pulling his thought away from that structuralist epistemology that guided his research from the beginning. By structuralist epistemology here we mean the reinvention of a functionalist analysis in the realm of the human sciences, a method that effectively sacrifices the dynamic of the system, the creative temporality of its movements, and the ontological substance of cultural and social reproduction.[13] In fact, if at this point we were to ask Foucault who or what drives the system, or rather, who is the "bios," his response would be ineffable, or nothing at all. What Foucault fails to grasp finally are the real dynamics of production in biopolitical society.[14]

By contrast, Deleuze and Guattari present us with a properly poststructuralist understanding of biopower that renews materialist thought and grounds itself solidly in the question of the production of social being. Their work demystifies structuralism and all the philosophical, sociological, and political conceptions that make the fixity of the epistemological frame an ineluctable point of reference. They focus our attention clearly on the ontological substance of social production. Machines produce. The constant functioning of social machines in their various apparatuses and assemblages produces the world along with the subjects and objects that constitute it. Deleuze and Guattari, however, seem to be able to conceive positively only the tendencies toward continuous movement and absolute flows, and thus in their thought, too, the creative elements and the radical ontology of the production of the social remain insubstantial and impotent. Deleuze and Guattari discover the productivity of social reproduction (creative production, production of values, social relations, affects, becomings), but manage to articulate it only superficially and ephemerally, as a chaotic, indeterminate horizon marked by the ungraspable event.[15]

We can better grasp the relationship between social production and biopower in the work of a group of contemporary Italian Marxist authors who recognize the biopolitical dimension in terms of the new nature of productive labor and its living development in society, using terms such as "mass intellectuality," "immaterial labor," and the Marxian concept of "general intellect."[16]

These analyses set off from two coordinated research projects. The first consists in the analysis of the recent transformations of productive labor and its tendency to become increasingly immaterial. The central role previously occupied by the labor power of mass factory workers in the production of surplus value is today increasingly filled by intellectual, immaterial, and communicative labor power. It is thus necessary to develop a new political theory of value that can pose the problem of this new capitalist accumulation of value at the center of the mechanism of exploitation (and thus, perhaps, at the center of potential revolt). The second, and consequent, research project developed by this school consists in the analysis of the immediately social and communicative dimension of living labor in contemporary capitalist society, and thus poses insistently the problem of the new figures of subjectivity, in both their exploitation and their revolutionary potential. The immediately social dimension of the exploitation of living immaterial labor immerses labor in all the relational elements that define the social but also at the same time activate the critical elements that develop the potential of insubordination and revolt through the entire set of laboring practices. After a new theory of value, then, a new theory of subjectivity must be formulated that operates primarily through knowledge, communication, and language.

These analyses have thus reestablished the importance of production within the biopolitical process of the social constitution, but they have also in certain respects isolated it—by grasping it in a pure form, refining it on the ideal plane. They have acted as if discovering the new forms of productive forces—immaterial labor, massified intellectual labor, the labor of "general intellect"—were enough to grasp concretely the dynamic and creative relationship between material production and social reproduction. When they reinsert production into the biopolitical context, they present it almost exclusively on the horizon of language and communication. One of the most serious shortcomings has thus been the tendency among these authors to treat the new laboring practices in biopolitical society *only* in their intellectual and incorporeal aspects. The productivity of bodies and the value of affect, however, are absolutely central in this context. We will elaborate the three primary aspects of immaterial labor in the contemporary economy: the communicative labor of industrial production that has newly become linked in informational networks, the interactive labor of symbolic analysis and problem solving, and the labor of the production and manipulation of affects (see Section 3.4). This third aspect, with its focus on the productivity of the corporeal, the somatic, is an extremely important element in the contemporary networks of biopolitical production. The work of this school and its analysis of general intellect, then, certainly marks a step forward, but its conceptual framework remains too pure, almost angelic. In the final analysis, these new conceptions too only scratch the surface of the productive dynamic of the new theoretical framework of biopower.[17]

Our task, then, is to build on these partially successful attempts to recognize the potential of biopolitical production. Precisely by bringing together coherently the different defining characteristics of the biopolitical context that we have described up to this point, and leading them back to the ontology of production, we will be able to identify the new figure of the collective biopolitical body, which may nonetheless remain as contradictory as it is paradoxical. This body becomes structure not by negating the originary productive force that animates it but by recognizing it; it becomes language (both scientific language and social language) because it is a multitude of singular and determinate bodies that seek relation. It is thus both production and reproduction, structure and superstructure, because it is life in the fullest sense and politics in the proper sense. Our analysis has to descend into the jungle of productive and conflictual determinations that the collective biopolitical body offers us.[18] The context of our analysis thus has to be the very unfolding of life itself, the process of the constitution of the world, of history. The analysis must be proposed not through ideal forms but within the dense complex of experience.

Corporations and Communication

In asking ourselves how the political and sovereign elements of the imperial machine come to be constituted, we find that there is no need to limit our analysis to or even focus it on the established supranational regulatory institutions. The U.N. organizations, along with the great multi- and transnational finance and trade agencies (the IMF, the World Bank, the GATT, and so forth), all become relevant in the perspective of the supranational juridical constitution only when they are considered within the dynamic of the biopolitical production of world order. The function they had in the old international order, we should emphasize, is not what now gives legitimacy to these organizations. What legitimates them now is rather their newly possible function in the symbology of the imperial order. Outside of the new framework, these institutions are ineffectual. At best, the old institutional framework contributes to the formation and education of the administrative personnel of the imperial machine, the "dressage" of a new imperial élite.

The huge transnational corporations construct the fundamental connective fabric of the biopolitical world in certain important respects. Capital has indeed always been organized with a view toward the entire global sphere, but only in the second half of the twentieth century did multinational and transnational industrial and financial corporations really begin to structure global territories biopolitically. Some claim that these corporations have merely come to occupy the place that was held by the various national colonialist and imperialist systems in earlier phases of capitalist development, from nineteenth-century European imperialism to the Fordist phase of development in the twentieth century.[19] This is in part true, but that place itself has been substantially transformed by the new reality of capitalism. The activities of corporations are no longer defined by the imposition of abstract command and the organization of simple theft and unequal exchange. Rather, they directly structure and articulate territories and populations. They tend to make nation-states merely instruments to record the flows of the commodities, monies, and populations that they set in motion. The transnational corporations directly distribute labor power over various markets, functionally allocate resources, and organize hierarchically the various sectors of world production. The complex apparatus that selects investments and directs financial and monetary maneuvers determines the new geography of the world market, or really the new biopolitical structuring of the world.[20]

The most complete figure of this world is presented from the monetary perspective. From here we can see a horizon of values and a machine of distribution, a mechanism of accumulation and a means of circulation, a power and a language. There is nothing, no "naked life," no external standpoint, that can be posed outside this field permeated by money; nothing escapes money. Production and reproduction are dressed in monetary clothing. In fact, on the global stage, every biopolitical figure appears dressed in monetary garb. "Accumulate, accumulate! This is Moses and the Prophets!"[21]

The great industrial and financial powers thus produce not only commodities but also subjectivities. They produce agentic subjectivities within the biopolitical context: they produce needs, social relations, bodies, and minds—which is to say, they produce producers.[22] In the biopolitical sphere, life is made to work for production and production is made to work for life. It is a great hive in which the queen bee continuously oversees production and re-production. The deeper the analysis goes, the more it finds at increasing levels of intensity the interlinking assemblages of interactive relationships.[23]

One site where we should locate the biopolitical production of order is in the immaterial nexuses of the production of language, communication, and the symbolic that are developed by the communications industries.[24] The development of communications networks has an organic relationship to the emergence of the new world order—it is, in other words, effect and cause, product and producer. Communication not only expresses but also organizes the movement of globalization. It organizes the movement by multiplying and structuring interconnections through networks. It expresses the movement and controls the sense and direction of the imaginary that runs throughout these communicative connections; in other words, the imaginary is guided and channeled within the communicative machine. What the theories of power of modernity were forced to consider transcendent, that is, external to productive and social relations, is here formed inside, immanent to the productive and social relations. Mediation is absorbed within the productive machine. The political synthesis of social space is fixed in the space of communication. This is why communications industries have assumed such a central position. They not only organize production on a new scale and impose a new structure adequate to global space, but also make its justification immanent. Power, as it produces, organizes; as it organizes, it speaks and expresses itself as authority. Language, as it communicates, produces commodities but moreover creates subjectivities, puts them in relation, and orders them. The communications industries integrate the imaginary and the symbolic within the biopolitical fabric, not merely putting them at the service of power but actually integrating them into its very functioning.[25]

At this point we can begin to address the question of the *legitimation* of the new world order. Its legitimation is not born of the previously existing international accords nor of the functioning of the first, embryonic supranational organizations, which were themselves created through treaties based on international law. The legitimation of the imperial machine is born at least in part of the communications industries, that is, of the transformation of the new mode of production into a machine. It is a subject that produces its own image of authority. This is a form of legitimation that rests on nothing outside itself and is reproposed ceaselessly by developing its own languages of self-validation.

One further consequence should be treated on the basis of these premises. If communication is one of the hegemonic sectors of production and acts over the entire biopolitical field, then we must consider communication and the biopolitical context coexistent. This takes us well beyond the old terrain as Jürgen Habermas described it, for example. In fact, when Habermas developed the concept of communicative action, demonstrating so powerfully its productive form and the ontological consequences deriving from that, he still relied on a standpoint outside these effects of globalization, a standpoint of life and truth that could oppose the informational colonization of being.[26] The imperial machine, however, demonstrates that this external standpoint no longer exists. On the contrary, communicative production and the construction of imperial legitimation march hand in hand and can no longer be separated. The machine is self-validating, autopoietic—that is, systemic. It constructs social fabrics that evacuate or render ineffective any contradiction; it creates situations in which, before coercively neutralizing difference, seem to absorb it in an insignificant play of self-generating and self-regulating equilibria. As we have argued elsewhere, any juridical theory that addresses the conditions of postmodernity has to take into account this specifically communicative definition of social production.[27] The imperial machine lives by producing a context of equilibria and/or reducing complexities, pretending to put forward a project of universal citizenship and toward this end intensifying the effectiveness of its intervention over every element of the communicative relationship, all the while dissolving identity and history in a completely postmodernist fashion.[28] Contrary to the way many postmodernist accounts would have it, however, the imperial machine, far from eliminating master narratives, actually produces and reproduces them (ideological master narratives in particular) in order to validate and celebrate its own power.[29] In this coincidence of production through language, the linguistic production of reality, and the language of self-validation resides a fundamental key to understanding the effectiveness, validity, and legitimation of imperial right.

Intervention

This new framework of legitimacy includes new forms and new articulations of *the exercise of legitimate force*. During its formation, the new power must demonstrate the effectiveness of its force at the same time that the bases of its legitimation are being constructed. In fact, the legitimacy of the new power is in part based directly on the effectiveness of its use of force.

The way the effectiveness of the new power is demonstrated has nothing to do with the old international order that is slowly dying away; nor has it much use for the instruments the old order left behind. The deployments of the imperial machine are defined by a whole series of new characteristics, such as the unbounded terrain of its activities, the singularization and symbolic localization of its actions, and the connection of repressive action to all the aspects of the biopolitical structure of society. For lack of a better term we continue to call these "interventions." This is merely a terminological and not a conceptual deficiency, for these are not really interventions into independent juridical territories but rather actions within a unified world by the ruling structure of production and communication. In effect, intervention has been internalized and universalized. In the previous section we referred to both the structural means of intervention that involve the deployments of monetary mechanisms and financial maneuvers over the transnational field of interdependent productive regimes and interventions in the field of communication and their effects on the legitimation of the system. Here we want to investigate the new forms of intervention that involve the exercise of physical force on the part of the imperial machine over its global territories. The enemies that Empire opposes today may present more of an ideological threat than a military challenge, but nonetheless the power of Empire exercised through force and all the deployments that guarantee its effectiveness are already very advanced technologically and solidly consolidated politically.[30]

The arsenal of legitimate force for imperial intervention is indeed already vast, and should include not only military intervention but also other forms such as moral intervention and juridical intervention. In fact, the Empire's powers of intervention might be best understood as beginning not directly with its weapons of lethal force but rather with its moral instruments. What we are calling moral intervention is practiced today by a variety of bodies, including the news media and religious organizations, but the most important may be some of the so-called non-governmental organizations (NGOs), which, precisely because they are not run directly by governments, are assumed to act on the basis of ethical or moral imperatives. The term refers to a wide variety of groups, but we are referring here principally to the global, regional, and local organizations that are dedicated to relief work and the protection of human rights, such as Amnesty International, Oxfam, and

Médecins sans Frontières. Such humanitarian NGOs are in effect (even if this runs counter to the intentions of the participants) some of the most powerful pacific weapons of the new world order—the charitable campaigns and the mendicant orders of Empire. These NGOs conduct "just wars" without arms, without violence, without borders. Like the Dominicans in the late medieval period and the Jesuits at the dawn of modernity, these groups strive to identify universal needs and defend human rights. Through their language and their action they first define the enemy as privation (in the hope of preventing serious damage) and then recognize the enemy as sin.

It is hard not to be reminded here of how in Christian moral theology evil is first posed as privation of the good and then sin is defined as culpable negation of the good. Within this logical framework it is not strange but rather all too natural that in their attempts to respond to privation, these NGOs are led to denounce publicly the sinners (or rather the Enemy in properly inquisitional terms); nor is it strange that they leave to the "secular wing" the task of actually addressing the problems. In this way, moral intervention has become a frontline force of imperial intervention. In effect, this intervention prefigures the state of exception from below, and does so without borders, armed with some of the most effective means of communication and oriented toward the symbolic production of the Enemy. These NGOs are completely immersed in the biopolitical context of the constitution of Empire; they anticipate the power of its pacifying and productive intervention of justice. It should thus come as no surprise that honest juridical theorists of the old international school (such as Richard Falk) should be drawn in by the fascination of these NGOs.[31] The NGOs' demonstration of the new order as a peaceful biopolitical context seems to have blinded these theorists to the brutal effects that moral intervention produces as a prefiguration of world order.[32]

Moral intervention often serves as the first act that prepares the stage for military intervention. In such cases, military deployment is presented as an internationally sanctioned police action. Today military intervention is progressively less a product of decisions that arise out of the old international order or even U.N. structures. More often it is dictated unilaterally by the United States, which charges itself with the primary task and then subsequently asks its allies to set in motion a process of armed containment and/or repression of the current enemy of Empire. These enemies are most often called terrorist, a crude conceptual and terminological reduction that is rooted in a police mentality.

The relationship between prevention and repression is particularly clear in the case of intervention in ethnic conflicts. The conflicts among ethnic groups and the consequent reenforcement of new and/or resurrected ethnic identities effectively disrupt the old aggregations based on national political lines. These conflicts make the fabric of global relations more fluid and, by affirming new identities and new localities, present a more malleable material for control. In such cases repression can be articulated through preventive action that constructs new relationships (which will eventually be consolidated in peace but only after new wars) and new territorial and political formations that are functional (or rather more functional, better adaptable) to the constitution of Empire.[33] A second example of repression prepared through preventive action is the campaigns against corporative business groups or "mafias," particularly those involved in the drug trade. The actual repression of these groups may not be as important as criminalizing their activities and managing social alarm at their very existence in order to facilitate their control. Even though controlling "ethnic terrorists" and "drug mafias" may represent the center of the wide spectrum of police control on the part of the imperial power, this activity is nonetheless normal, that is, systemic. The "just war" is effectively supported by the "moral police," just as the validity of imperial right and its legitimate functioning is supported by the necessary and continuous exercise of police power.

It is clear that international or supranational courts are constrained to follow this lead. Armies and police anticipate the courts and preconstitute the rules of justice that the courts must then apply. The intensity of the moral principles to which the construction of the new world order is entrusted cannot change the fact that this is really an inversion of the conventional order of constitutional logic. The active parties supporting the imperial constitution are confident that when the construction of Empire is sufficiently advanced, the courts will be able to assume their leading role in the definition of justice. For now, however, although international courts do not have much power, public displays of their activities are still very important. Eventually a new judicial function must be formed that is adequate to the constitution of Empire. Courts will have to be transformed gradually from an organ that simply decrees sentences against the vanquished to a judicial body or system of bodies that dictate and sanction the interrelation among the moral order, the exercise of police action, and the mechanism legitimating imperial sovereignty.[34]

This kind of continual intervention, then, which is both moral and military, is really the logical form of the exercise of force that follows from a paradigm of legitimation based on a state of permanent exception and police action. Interventions are always exceptional even though they arise continually; they take the form of police actions because they are aimed at maintaining an internal order. In this way intervention is an effective mechanism that through police deployments contributes directly to the construction of the moral, normative, and institutional order of Empire.

Royal Prerogatives

What were traditionally called the royal prerogatives of sovereignty seem in effect to be repeated and even substantially renewed in the construction of Empire. If we were to remain within the conceptual framework of classic domestic and international law, we might be tempted to say that a supranational quasi-state is being formed. That does not seem to us, however, an accurate characterization of the situation. When the royal prerogatives of modern sovereignty reappear in Empire, they take on a completely different form. For example, the sovereign function of deploying military forces was carried out by the modern nation-states and is now conducted by Empire, but, as we have seen, the justification for such deployments now rests on a state of permanent exception, and the deployments themselves take the form of police actions. Other royal prerogatives such as carrying out justice and imposing taxes also have the same kind of liminal existence. We have already discussed the marginal position of judicial authority in the constitutive process of Empire, and one could also argue that imposing taxes occupies a marginal position in that it is increasingly linked to specific and local urgencies. In effect, one might say that the sovereignty of Empire itself is realized at the margins, where borders are flexible and identities are hybrid and fluid. It would be difficult to say which is more important to Empire, the center or the margins. In fact, center and margin seem continually to be shifting positions, fleeing any determinate locations. We could even say that the process itself is virtual and that its power resides in the power of the virtual.

One could nonetheless object at this point that even while being virtual and acting at the margins, the process of constructing imperial sovereignty is in many respects very real! We certainly do not mean to deny that fact. Our claim, rather, is that we are dealing here with a special kind of sovereignty—a discontinuous form of sovereignty that should be considered liminal or marginal insofar as it acts "in the final instance," a sovereignty that locates its only point of reference in the definitive absoluteness of the power that it can exercise. Empire thus appears in the form of a very high tech machine: it is virtual, built to control the marginal event, and organized to dominate and when necessary intervene in the breakdowns of the system (in line with the most advanced technologies of robotic production). The virtuality and discontinuity of imperial sovereignty, however, do not minimize the effectiveness of its force; on the contrary, those very characteristics serve to reinforce its apparatus, demonstrating its effectiveness in the contemporary historical context and its legitimate force to resolve world problems in the final instance.

We are now in the position to address the question whether, on the basis of these new biopolitical premises, the figure and the life of Empire can today be grasped in terms of a juridical model. We have already seen that this juridical model cannot be constituted by the existing structures of international law, even when understood in terms of the most advanced developments of the United Nations and the other great international organizations. Their elaborations of an international order could at the most be recognized as a process of transition toward the new imperial power. The constitution of Empire is being formed neither on the basis of any contractual or treaty-based mechanism nor through any federative source. The source of imperial normativity is born of a new machine, a new economic-industrial-communicative machine—in short, a globalized biopolitical machine. It thus seems clear that we must look at something other than what has up until now constituted the bases of international order, something that does not rely on the form of right that, in the most diverse traditions, was grounded in the modern system of sovereign nation-states. The impossibility, however, of grasping the genesis of Empire and its virtual figure with any of the old instruments of juridical theory, which were deployed in the realist, institutionalist, positivist, or natural right frameworks, should not force us to accept a cynical framework of pure force or some such Machiavellian position. In the genesis of Empire there is indeed a rationality at work that can be recognized not so much in terms of the juridical tradition but more clearly in the often hidden history of industrial management and the political uses of technology. (We should not forget here too that proceeding along these lines will reveal the fabric of class struggle and its institutional effects, but we will treat that issue in the next section.) This is a rationality that situates us at the heart of biopolitics and biopolitical technologies.

If we wanted to take up again Max Weber's famous three-part formula of the forms of legitimation of power, the qualitative leap that Empire introduces into the definition would consist in the unforeseeable mixture of (1) elements typical of traditional power, (2) an extension of bureaucratic power that is adapted physiologically to the biopolitical context, and (3) a rationality defined by the "event" and by "charisma" that rises up as a power of the singularization of the whole and of the effectiveness of imperial interventions.[35] The logic that characterizes this neo-Weberian perspective would be functional rather than mathematical, and rhizomatic and undulatory rather than inductive or deductive. It would deal with the management of linguistic sequences as sets of machinic sequences of denotation and at the same time of creative, colloquial, and irreducible innovation.

The fundamental object that the imperial relations of power interpret is the productive force of the system, the new biopolitical economic and institutional system. The imperial order is formed not only on the basis of its powers of accumulation and global extension, but also on the basis of its capacity to develop itself more deeply, to be reborn, and to extend itself throughout the biopolitical latticework of world society. The absoluteness of imperial power is the complementary term to its complete immanence to the ontological machine of production and reproduction, and thus to the biopolitical context. Perhaps, finally, this cannot be represented by a juridical order, but it nonetheless is an order, an order defined by its virtuality, its dynamism, and its functional inconclusiveness. The fundamental norm of legitimation will thus be established in the depths of the machine, at the heart of social production. Social production and juridical legitimation should not be conceived as primary and secondary forces nor as elements of the base and superstructure, but should be understood rather in a state of absolute parallelism and intermixture, coextensive throughout biopolitical society. In Empire and its regime of biopower, economic production and political constitution tend increasingly to coincide.

Notes

1. The passage from disciplinary society to the society of control is not articulated explicitly by Foucault but remains implicit in his work. We follow the excellent commentaries of Gilles Deleuze in this interpretation. See Gilles Deleuze, *Foucault* (Paris: Minuit, 1986); and "Post-scriptum sur les sociétés de contrôle," in *Pourparlers* (Paris: Minuit, 1990). See also Michael Hardt, "The Withering of Civil Society," *Social Text*, no. 45 (Winter 1995), 27–44.

2. See primarily Michel Foucault, *The History of Sexuality*, trans. Robert Hurley (New York: Vintage, 1978), 1:135–145. For other treatments of the concept of biopolitics in Foucault's opus, see "The Politics of Health in the Eighteenth Century," in *Power/Knowledge*, ed. Colin Gordon (New York: Pantheon, 1980), pp. 166–182; "La naissance de la médecine sociale," in *Dits et écrits* (Paris: Gallimard, 1994), 3:207–228, particularly p. 210; and "Naissance de la biopolitique," in *Dits et écrits*, 3:818–825. For examples of work by other authors following Foucault's notion of biopolitics, see Hubert Dreyfus and Paul Rabinow, eds., *Michel Foucault: Beyond Structuralism and Hermeneutics* (Chicago: University of Chicago Press, 1992), pp. 133–142; and Jacques Donzelot, *The Policing of Families*, trans. Robert Hurley (New York: Pantheon, 1979).

3. Michel Foucault, "Les mailles du pouvoir," in *Dits et écrits* (Paris: Gallimard, 1994), 4:182–201; quotation p. 194.

4. Many thinkers have followed Foucault along these lines and successfully problematized the welfare state. See primarily Jacques Donzelot, *L'invention du social* (Paris: Fayard, 1984); and François Ewald, *L'état providence* (Paris: Seuil, 1986).

5. See Karl Marx, "Results of the Immediate Process of Production," trans. Rodney Livingstone, published as the appendix to *Capital*, trans. Ben Fowkes (New York: Vintage, 1976), 1:948–1084. See also Antonio Negri, *Marx beyond Marx*, trans. Harry Cleaver, Michael Ryan, and Maurizio Viano (New York: Autonomedia, 1991).

6. See Max Horkheimer and Theodor Adorno, *The Dialectic of Enlightenment*, trans. John Cumming (New York: Herder and Herder, 1972).

7. See Gilles Deleuze and Félix Guattari, *A Thousand Plateaus*, trans. Brian Massumi (Minneapolis: University of Minnesota Press, 1987).

8. See, for example, Peter Dews, *Logics of Disintegration: Poststructuralist Thought and the Claims of Critical Theory* (London: Verso, 1987), chaps. 6 and 7. When one adopts this definition of power and the crises that traverse it, Foucault's discourse (and even more so that of Deleuze and Guattari) presents a powerful theoretical framework for critiquing the welfare state. For analyses that are more or less in line with this discourse, see Claus Offe, *Disorganized Capitalism: Contemporary Transformations of Work and Politics* (Cambridge, Mass.: MIT Press, 1985); Antonio Negri, *Revolution Retrieved: Selected Writings* (London: Red Notes, 1988); and the essays by Antonio Negri included in Michael Hardt and Antonio Negri, *Labor of Dionysus* (Minneapolis: University of Minnesota Press, 1994).

9. The notions of "totalitarianism" that were constructed during the period of the cold war proved to be useful instruments for propaganda but completely inadequate analytical tools, leading most often to pernicious inquisitional methods and damaging moral arguments. The numerous shelves of our libraries that are filled with analyses of totalitarianism should today be regarded only with shame and could be thrown away with no hesitation. For a brief sample of the literature on totalitarianism from the most coherent to the most absurd, see Hannah Arendt, *The Origins of Totalitarianism* (New York: Harcourt, Brace, 1951); and Jeanne Kirkpatrick, *Dictatorships and Double Standards* (New York: Simon and Schuster, 1982). We will return to the concept of totalitarianism in more detail in Section 2.2.

10. We are referring here to the thematics of *Mobilmachtung* that were developed in the Germanic world primarily in the 1920s and 1930s, more or less from Ernst Jünger to Carl Schmitt. In French culture, too, such positions emerged in the 1930s, and the polemics around them have still not died down. The figure of Georges Bataille is at the center of this discussion. Along different lines, on "general mobilization" as a paradigm of the constitution of collective labor power in Fordist capitalism, see Jean Paul de Gaudemar, *La mobilisation générale* (Paris: Maspero, 1978).

11. One could trace a very interesting line of discussions that effectively develop the Foucauldian interpretation of biopower from Jacques Derrida's reading of Walter Benjamin's "Critique of Violence" ("Force of Law," in Drucilla Cornell, Michel Rosenfeld, and David Gray Carlson, eds., *Deconstruction and the Possibility of Justice* [New York: Routledge, 1992], pp. 3–67) to Giorgio Agamben's more recent and more stimulating contribution, *Homo sacer: il potere sovrano e la nuda vita* (Turin: Einaudi, 1995). It seems fundamental to us, however, that all of these discussions be brought back to the question of the productive dimensions of "bios," identifying in other words the materialist dimension of the concept beyond any conception that is purely naturalistic (life as "zoe") or simply anthropological (as Agamben in particular has a tendency to do, making the concept in effect indifferent).

12. Michel Foucault, "La naissance de la médecine sociale," in *Dits et écrits* (Paris: Gallimard, 1994), 3:210.

13. See Henri Lefebvre, *L'ideologie structuraliste* (Paris: Anthropos, 1971); Gilles Deleuze, "A quoi reconnait-on le structuralisme?" in François Châtelet, ed., *Histoire de la philosophie*, vol. 8 (Paris: Hachette, 1972), pp. 299–335; and Fredric Jameson, *The Prison-House of Language* (Princeton: Princeton University Press, 1972).

14. When Deleuze formulates his methodological differences with Foucault in a private letter written in 1977, the primary point of disagreement comes down precisely to just such a question of production. Deleuze prefers the term "desire" to Foucault's "pleasure," he explains, because desire grasps the real and active dynamic of the production of social reality whereas pleasure is merely inert and reactive: "Pleasure interrupts the positivity of desire and the constitution of its plane of immanence." See Gilles Deleuze, "Désir et plaisir," *Magazine Littéraire*, no. 325 (October 1994), 59–65; quotation p. 64.

15. Félix Guattari has perhaps developed the extreme consequences of this type of social critique, while carefully avoiding falling into the anti-"grand narrative" style of postmodernist argument, in his *Chaosmosis*, trans. Paul Bains and Julian Pefanis (Sydney: Power Publications, 1995). From a metaphysical point of view, among the followers of Nietzsche, we find roughly analogous positions expressed in Massimo Cacciari, *DRAN: méridiens de la décision dans la pensée contemporaine* (Paris: L'Éclat, 1991).

16. In English, see primarily the essays in Paolo Virno and Michael Hardt, eds., *Radical Thought in Italy* (Minneapolis: University of Minnesota Press, 1996). See also Christian Marazzi, *Il posto dei calzini: la svolta linguistica dell'economia e i suoi effetti nella politica* (Bellinzona: Edizioni Casagrande); and numerous issues of the French journal *Futur antérieur*, particularly nos. 10 (1992) and 35–36 (1996). For an analysis that appropriates

central elements of this project but ultimately fails to capture its power, see André Gorz, *Misère du présent, richesse du possible* (Paris: Galilée, 1997).

17. The framework on which this line of inquiry is built is both its great wealth and its real limitation. The analysis must in effect be carried beyond the constraints of the "worker-ist" (*operaista*) analysis of capitalist development and the state-form. One of its limita-tions, for example, is highlighted by Gayatri Spivak, *In Other Worlds: Essays in Cultural Politics* (New York: Routledge, 1988), p. 162, who insists on the fact that the conception of value in this line of Marxist analysis may function in the dominant countries (including in the context of certain streams of feminist theory) but completely misses the mark in the context of the subordinated regions of the globe. Spivak's questioning is certainly extremely important for the problematic we are developing in this study. In fact, from a methodological point of view, we would say that the most profound and solid problem-atic complex that has yet been elaborated for the critique of biopolitics is found in femi-nist theory, particularly Marxist and socialist feminist theories that focus on women's work, affective labor, and the production of biopower. This presents the framework per-haps best suited to renew the methodology of the European "workerist" schools.

18. The theories of the "turbulence" of the international order, and even more of the new world order, which we cited earlier (see primarily the work of J. G. Ruggie), generally avoid in their explanation of the causes of this turbulence any reference to the contra-dictory character of capitalist relations. Social turbulence is considered merely a conse-quence of the international dynamics among state actors in such a way that turbulence can be normalized within the strict disciplinary limits of international relations. Social and class struggles are effectively hidden by the method of analysis itself. From this perspective, then, the "productive bios" cannot really be understood. The same is more or less the case for the authors of the world-systems perspective, who focus primarily on the cycles of the system and systemic crises (see the works of Wallerstein and Arri-ghi cited earlier). Theirs is in effect a world (and a history) without subjectivity. What they miss is the function of the productive bios, or really the fact that capital is not a thing but a social relationship, an antagonistic relationship, one side of which is ani-mated by the productive life of the multitude.

19. Giovanni Arrighi, *The Long Twentieth Century* (London: Verso, 1995), for example, claims such a continuity in the role of capitalist corporations. For an excellent con-trasting view in terms of periodization and methodological approach, see Luciano Ferrari Bravo, "Introduzione: vecchie e nuove questioni nella teoria dell'imperialismo," in Luciano Ferrari Bravo, ed., *Imperialismo e classe operaia multinazionale* (Milan: Feltrinelli, 1975), pp. 7–70.

20. See, from the perspective of political analysis, Paul Kennedy, *Preparing for the Twenty-first Century* (New York: Random House, 1993); and from the perspective of economic topography and socialist critique, David Harvey, *The Condition of Postmodernity* (Oxford: Blackwell, 1989).

21. Marx, *Capital*, 1:742.

22. On this point the bibliography we could cite is seemingly endless. In effect, theories of advertising and consumption have been integrated (just in time) into the theories of

production, to the point where we now have ideologies of "attention" posed as economic value! In any case, for a selection of the numerous works that touch on this field, one would do well to see Susan Strasser, *Satisfaction Guaranteed: The Making of the American Mass Market* (New York: Pantheon, 1989); Gary Cross, *Time and Money: The Making of Consumer Culture* (New York: Routledge, 1993); and, for a more interesting analysis from another perspective, The Project on Disney, *Inside the Mouse* (Durham: Duke University Press, 1995). The production of the producer, however, is not only the production of the consumer. It also involves the production of hierarchies, mechanisms of inclusion and exclusion, and so forth. It involves finally the production of crises. From this point of view, see Jeremy Rifkin, *The End of Work: The Decline of Global Labor Force and the Dawn of the Post-market Era* (New York: Putnam, 1995); and Stanley Aronowitz and William DiFazio, *The Jobless Future* (Minneapolis: University of Minnesota Press, 1994).

23. We are indebted to Deleuze and Guattari and their *A Thousand Plateaus* for the most fully elaborated phenomenological description of this industrial-monetary-world-nature, which constitutes the first level of the world order.

24. See Edward Comor, ed., *The Global Political Economy of Communication* (London: Macmillan, 1994).

25. See Stephen Bradley, ed., *Globalization, Technologies, and Competition: The Fusion of Computers and Telecommunications in the 90s* (Cambridge, Mass.: Harvard Business School Press, 1993); and Simon Serfaty, *The Media and Foreign Policy* (London: Macmillan, 1990).

26. See Jürgen Habermas, *Theory of Communicative Action*, trans. Thomas McCarthy (Boston: Beacon Press, 1984). We discuss this relationship between communication and production in more detail in Section 3.4.

27. See Hardt and Negri, *Labor of Dionysus*, chaps. 6 and 7.

28. Despite the extremism of the authors presented in Martin Albrow and Elizabeth King, eds., *Globalization, Knowledge, and Society* (London: Sage, 1990), and the relative moderation of Bryan S. Turner, *Theories of Modernity and Postmodernity* (London: Sage, 1990), and Mike Featherstone, ed., *Global Culture, Nationalism, Globalization, and Modernity* (London: Sage, 1991), the differences among their various positions are really relatively minor. We should always keep in mind that the image of a "global civil society" is born not only in the minds of certain postmodernist philosophers and among certain followers of Habermas (such as Jean Cohen and Andrew Arato), but also and more importantly in the Lockean tradition of international relations. This latter group includes such important theorists as Richard Falk, David Held, Anthony Giddens, and (in certain respects) Danilo Zolo. On the concept of civil society in the global context, see Michael Walzer, ed., *Toward a Global Civil Society* (Providence: Berghahn Books, 1995).

29. With the iconoclastic irony of Jean Baudrillard's more recent writings such as *The Gulf War Did Not Take Place*, trans. Paul Patton (Bloomington: Indiana University Press, 1995), a certain vein of French postmodernism has gone back to a properly surrealist framework.

30. There is an uninterrupted continuity from the late cold war notions of "democracy enforcing" and "democratic transition" to the imperial theories of "peace enforcing."

We have already highlighted the fact that many moral philosophers supported the Gulf War as a just cause, whereas juridical theorists, following the important lead of Richard Falk, were generally opposed. See, for example, Richard Falk, "Twisting the U.N. Charter to U.S. Ends," in Hamid Mowlana, George Gerbner, and Herbert Schiller, eds., *Triumph of the Image: The Media's War in the Persian Gulf* (Boulder: Westview Press, 1992), pp. 175–190. See also the discussion of the Gulf War in Danilo Zolo, *Cosmopolis: Prospects for World Government*, trans. David McKie (Cambridge: Polity Press, 1997).

31. For a representative example, see Richard Falk, *Positive Prescriptions for the Future*, World Order Studies Program occasional paper no. 20 (Princeton: Center for International Studies, 1991). To see how NGOs are integrated into this more or less Lockean framework of "global constitutionalism," one should refer to the public declarations of Antonio Cassese, president of the United Nations Criminal Court in Amsterdam, in addition to his books, *International Law in a Divided World* (Oxford: Clarendon Press, 1986), and *Human Rights in a Changing World* (Philadelphia: Temple University Press, 1990).

32. Even the proposals to reform the United Nations proceed more or less along these lines. For a good bibliography of such works, see Joseph Preston Baratta, *Strengthening the United Nations: A Bibliography on U.N. Reform and World Federalism* (New York: Greenwood, 1987).

33. This is the line that is promoted in some of the strategic documents published by the U.S. military agencies. According to the present Pentagon doctrine, the project of the enlargement of market democracy should be supported by both adequate microstrategies that are based on (both pragmatic and systemic) zones of application and the continual identification of critical points and fissures in the antagonistic strong cultural blocs that would lead toward their dissolution. In this regard, see the work of Maurice Rounai of the Strategic Institute in Paris. See also the works on U.S. interventionism cited in Section 1.1, note 28.

34. One should refer, once again, to the work of Richard Falk and Antonio Cassese. We should emphasize, in particular, how a "weak" conception of the exercise of judicial functions by the U.N. Court of Justice has gradually, often under the influence of Left political forces, been transformed into a "strong" conception. In other words, there is a passage from the demand that the Court of Justice be invested with the functions of judicial sanction that come under the authority of the U.N. structure to the demand that the court play a direct and active role in the decisions of the U.N. and its organs regarding norms of parity and material justice among states, to the point of carrying out direct intervention in the name of human rights.

35. See Max Weber, *Economy and Society*, trans. Guenther Roth and Claus Wittich (Berkeley: University of California Press, 1968), vol. 1, chap. 3, sec. 2, "The Three Pure Types of Authority," pp. 215–216.

CHAPTER 11

BIOPOLITICS AS EVENT

Michael Hardt and Antonio Negri

> I am painting, I am Nature, I am truth.
> —Gustave Courbet

To grasp how Michel Foucault understands biopower, we have to situate it in the context of the broader theory of power he develops in the period when he begins working with the concept, the second half of the 1970s, in *Discipline and Punish* (1975) and the first volume of *The History of Sexuality* (1976). In these books Foucault's notion of power is always double. He devotes most of his attention to disciplinary regimes, architectures of power, and the applications of power through distributed and capillary networks, a power that does not so much repress as produce subjects. Throughout these books, however, sometimes in what seem like asides or marginal notes, Foucault also constantly theorizes an other to power (or even an other power), for which he seems unable to find an adequate name. Resistance is the term he most often uses, but it does not really capture what he has in mind, since resistance, as it is generally understood, is too dependent on and subordinate to the power it opposes. One might suggest to Foucault the Marxist notion of "counter-power," but that term implies a second power that is homologous to the one it opposes. In our view, the other power that runs through these books is best defined as an alternative production of subjectivity, which not only resists power but also seeks autonomy from it.

This understanding of the doubleness of power helps us approach Foucault's attempts to develop the concept of biopower. Here too Foucault's attention is focused primarily on the power over life—or, really, the power to administer and produce life—that functions through the government of populations, managing their health, reproductive capacities, and so forth. But there is always a minor current that insists on life as resistance, an other power of life that strives toward an alternative existence. The perspective of resistance makes clear the difference between these two powers: the biopower against which we struggle is not comparable in its nature or form to the power of life by which we defend and seek our freedom. To mark this difference between the two "powers of life," we adopt a terminological distinction, suggested by Foucault's writings but not used consistently by him, between biopower and biopolitics, whereby the former could be defined (rather crudely) as the power over life and the latter as the power of life to resist and determine an alternative production of subjectivity.

The major streams of Foucault interpretation, however, do not adequately grasp the dual nature of biopolitics. One stream, which is presented first by François Ewald and later by Roberto Esposito, analyzes the terrain of biopolitics primarily from the standpoint of the normative management of populations. This amounts to an *actuarial* administration of life that generally requires viewing individuals from a statistical perspective, classifying them into large normative sets, which become more coherent the more the micro-systems that compose them are de-subjectivized and made homogeneous. Although this interpretation has the merit of philological fidelity (albeit with a rather narrow perspective on Foucault's opus), it leaves us with merely a "liberal" image of Foucault and biopolitics insofar as it poses against this threatening, all-encompassing power over life no alternative power or effective resistance but only a vague sense of critique and moral indignation.[1]

A second major stream, which centers on the interpretation of Giorgio Agamben (and emerges to some extent from the work of Jacques Derrida and Jean-Luc Nancy), accepts that biopolitics is an ambiguous and conflictive terrain but sees resistance acting only at its most extreme limit, on the margins of a totalitarian form of power, on the brink of impossibility. Here such authors could easily be interpreting the famous lines from Hölderlin's poem "Patmos": "Wo aber Gefahr ist, wächst / Das Rettende auch" (Where there is danger, / The rescue grows as well). This stream of interpretation thus does to a certain extent distinguish biopolitics from biopower but leaves biopolitics powerless and without subjectivity. These authors seek in Foucault a definition of biopolitics that strips it of every possibility of autonomous, creative action, but really they fall back on Heidegger in these points of the analysis to negate any constructive capacity of biopolitical resistance. Agamben transposes biopolitics in a theological-political key, claiming that the only possibility of rupture with biopower resides in "inoperative" activity *(inoperosità)*, a blank refusal that recalls Heidegger's notion of *Gelassenheit,* completely incapable of constructing an alternative.[2]

Finally, we can construct something like a third stream of interpretation of biopolitics, even if it is generally not posed in reference to Foucault and his terminology, that includes authors who understand life with reference to naturalistic and/or transcendental invariables of existence. From this perspective there is a certain autonomy conceded to biopolitical subjectivity, for example, in the invariable logical-linguistic structures proposed by Noam Chomsky or the ontological duration of preindividual and interindividual linguistic and productive relations in authors such as Gilbert Simondon, Bernard Stiegler, and Peter Sloterdijk. But this subjectivity, though posed as resistance to the existing power structures, lacks a dynamic character because it is closed within its invariable, naturalistic framework. The biopolitical resistance of these invariables can never create alternative forms of life.[3]

None of these interpretations captures what for us is most important in Foucault's notion of biopolitics. Our reading not only identifies biopolitics with the localized productive powers of life—that is, the production of affects and languages through social cooperation and the interaction of bodies and desires, the invention of new forms of the relation to the self and others, and so forth—but also affirms biopolitics as the creation of new subjectivities that are presented at once as resistance and de-subjectification. If we remain too closely tied to a philological analysis of Foucault's texts, we might miss this central point: his analyses of biopower are aimed not merely at an empirical description of how power works for and through subjects but also at the potential for the production of alternative subjectivities, thus designating a distinction between qualitatively different forms of power. This point is implicit in Foucault's claim that freedom and resistance are necessary preconditions for the exercise of power. "When one defines the exercise of power as a mode of action upon the actions of others, when one characterizes these actions by the government of men by other men—in the broadest sense of the term—one includes an important element: freedom. Power is exercised only over free subjects, and only insofar as they are free.... At the very heart of the power relationship, and constantly provoking it, are the recalcitrance of the will and the intransigence of freedom.[4] Biopolitics appears in this light as an event or, really, as a tightly woven fabric of events of freedom.

Biopolitics, in contrast to biopower, has the character of an *event* first of all in the sense that the "intransigence of freedom" disrupts the normative system. The biopolitical event comes from the outside insofar as it ruptures the continuity of history and the existing order, but it should be understood not only negatively, as rupture, but also as innovation, which emerges, so to speak, from the inside. Foucault grasps the creative character of the event in his earlier work on linguistics: *la parole* intervenes in and disrupts *la langue* as an event that also extends beyond it as a moment of linguistic invention.[5] For the biopolitical context, though, we need to understand the event on not only the linguistic and epistemological but also the anthropological and ontological terrain, as an act of freedom. In this context the event marked by the innovative disruption of *la parole* beyond *la langue* translates to an intervention in the field of subjectivity, with its accumulation of norms and modes of life, by a force of subjectification, a new production of subjectivity. This irruption of the biopolitical event is the source of innovation and also the criterion of truth. A materialist teleology, that is, a conception of history that emerges from below guided by the desires of those who make it and their search for freedom, connects here, paradoxically, with a Nietzschean idea of eternal return. The singularity of the event, driven by the will to power, demonstrates the truth of the eternal; the event, and the subjectivity that animates it, constructs and gives meaning to history, displacing any notion of history as a linear progression defined by determinate causes. Grasping this relation between the event and truth allows us to cast aside the accusation of relativism that is too often lodged against Foucault's biopolitics. And recognizing biopolitics as an event allows us both to understand life as a fabric woven by constitutive actions and to comprehend time in terms of strategy.

Foucault's notion of the event is at this point easily distinguishable from the one proposed by Alain Badiou. Badiou has done a great service by posing the event as the central question of contemporary philosophy, proposing it as the locus of truth. The event, with its irreducible multiplicity, that is, its "equivocal" nature, subtracts, according to Badiou, the examination of truths from the mere form of judgment. The difference between Badiou and Foucault in this respect is most clearly revealed by looking at where, temporally, each author focuses attention with respect to the event. In Badiou an event—such as Christ's crucifixion and resurrection, the French Revolution, or the Chinese Cultural Revolution, to cite his most frequent examples—acquires value and meaning primarily *after* it takes place. He thus concentrates on the intervention that retrospectively gives meaning to the event and the fidelity and generic procedures that continually refer to it. Foucault, in contrast, emphasizes the production and productivity of the event, which requires a forward- rather than backward-looking gaze. The event is, so to speak, inside existence and the strategies that traverse it. What Badiou's approach to the event fails to grasp, in other words, is the link between freedom and power that Foucault emphasizes from within the event. A retrospective approach to the event in fact does not give us access to the rationality of insurrectional activity, which must strive within the historical processes to create revolutionary events and break from the dominant political subjectivities. Without the internal logic of making events, one can only affirm them from the outside as a matter of faith, repeating the paradox commonly attributed to Tertullian, *credo quia absurdum*, "I believe because it is absurd."[6]

The biopolitical event that poses the production of life as an act of resistance, innovation, and freedom leads us back to the figure of the multitude as political strategy. Consider, to take an example from a very different domain, how Luciano Bolis, an Italian antifascist partisan, poses in his memoir the relation between grains of sand and the resistance of the multitude (in terms reminiscent of Walt Whitman's democratic leaves of grass). Bolis is fully aware that his sacrifice is only a grain of sand in the desert among the sufferings of the multitude engaged in struggle. "I believe, though," he explains, "that it is the duty of the survivors to write the story of those 'grains of sand' because even those who, because of particular circumstances or different sensibilities, were not part of that 'multitude' understand that our Liberation and the set of values on which it stands was paid for in the form of blood, terror, and expectations, and all that stands behind the word 'partisan,' which is still today misunderstood, scorned, and rejected with vacuous complacency."[7] Biopolitics is a partisan relationship between subjectivity and history that is crafted by a multitudinous strategy, formed by events and resistances, and articulated by a discourse that links political decision making to the construction of bodies in struggle. Gilles Deleuze casts the biopolitical production of life, in a similarly partisan way, as "believing in the world" when he laments that we have lost the world or it has been taken from us. "If you believe in the world you precipitate events, however inconspicuous, that elude control, you engender new space-times, however small their surface or volume. . . . Our ability to resist control, or our submission to it, has to be assessed at the level of our every move."[8] Events of resistance have the power not only to escape control but also to create a new world.

As one final example of the biopolitical power of bodies, from still another domain, consider a passage from Meister Eckhart's sermon "Jesus Entered":

> Now pay attention and look! If a human were to remain a virgin forever, he would never bear fruit. If he is to become fruitful, he must necessarily be a wife. "Wife," here, is the noblest name that can be given to the mind, and it is indeed more noble than "virgin." That man should receive God in himself is good, and by this reception he is a virgin. But that God should become fruitful in him is better; for the fruitfulness of a gift is the only gratitude for the gift. The spirit is wife when in gratitude it gives birth in return and bears Jesus back into God's fatherly heart.[9]

Eckhart is trying to focus our attention on the productivity of the biopolitical event, but what baggage comes with it! To read a passage like this, one has to pass it through decades of feminist theory, like so many baths of photographic solvents: starting with Simone de Beauvoir's analysis of how Woman is a patriarchal construct that subordinates women, in large part by tethering them to biological reproductive capacities; then feminist religious scholars who reveal the particularly Christian modes of patriarchy and the persistence of the virgin/whore dichotomy; and finally feminist political theorists who demonstrate how figures of women function in the canon of European political philosophy as markers of chaos and dangerous fecundity that must be excluded from the public realm. As these masculinist and heterosexist layers are stripped away, the image from Eckhart's passage that rises to the surface is a decidedly queer one! Productivity bursts forth as man becomes female, and here Eckhart's mystical visions recall the deliriums of President Schreber, who, as Freud reports, believes he is becoming woman in order to be impregnated by God and bear a new race of humanity. Interestingly, productivity in Eckhart coincides with the moment of gender crossing. (Could Eckhart recognize the same productivity in female masculinity that he finds in male femininity?) The biopolitical event, in fact, is always a queer event, a subversive process of subjectivization that, shattering ruling identities and norms, reveals the link between power and freedom, and thereby inaugurates an alternative production of subjectivity.

The biopolitical event thus breaks with all forms of metaphysical substantialism or conceptualism. Being is made in the event. It is interesting to note the strong resonance of this notion of the biopolitical event with American Pragmatism. "If nature seems highly uniform to us," writes Charles Peirce, "it is only because our powers are adapted to our desires."[10] Pragmatists propose, in effect, a performative analysis of the biopolitical event and demonstrate that the movement of biopolitical powers functions equally in the opposite direction: our desires, in other words, are also adapted to nature. We will return to this point in *De Homine* 1 at the end of Part 2 (and readers should keep in mind that these concluding discussions can also be read separately as one continuous argument).

Notes

1. See François Ewald, *L'État-providence* (Paris: Grasset, 1986); and Roberto Esposito, *Bios: Biopolitics and Philosophy*, trans. Timothy Campbell (Minneapolis: University of Minnesota Press, 2008).

2. See Georgio Agamben, *Homo Sacer: Sovereign Power and Bare Life* (Stanford, CA: Stanford University Press, 1998); and Jean-Luc Nancy, *The Inoperative Community*, trans. Peter Connor, Lisa Garbus, Michael Holland, and Simona Sawhney (Minneapolis: University of Minnesota Press, 1991). Jacques Derrida's early works, such as *Writing and Difference* and *Margins of Philosophy*, although they take an entirely different approach, arrive at similar results. In some respects Derrida's later work attempts to define a political approach in "biopolitical" terms. See in particular *Specters of Marx*, trans. Peggy Kamuf (New York: Routledge, 1994); and *Politics of Friendship*, trans. George Collins (London: Verso, 1997).

3. See, for example, Noam Chomsky and Michel Foucault, *The Chomsky-Foucault Debate* (New York: New Press, 2006).

4. Michel Foucault, "The Subject and Power," in Hubert Dreyfus and Paul Rabinow, *Michel Foucault: Beyond Structuralism and Hermeneutics* (Chicago: University of Chicago Press, 1982), pp. 221–222.

5. On linguistic innovation in Foucault, see Judith Revel, *Foucault* (Paris: Bordas, 2006); and Arnold Davidson, *The Emergence of Sexuality: Historical Epistemology and the Formation of Concepts* (Cambridge, Mass.: Harvard University Press, 2001).

6. The theory of the event runs throughout Badiou's work. For a representative treatment, see Alain Badiou, *Being and Event*, trans. Oliver Feltham (New York: Continuum, 2005), pts. 4 and 5, pp. 173–261. For Badiou's claim that contemporary political movements cannot break from the "dominant political subjectivities" with the current mechanisms of domination, see "Prefazione all'edizione italiana," in Badiou, *Metapolitica* (Naples: Cronopio, 2001), pp. 9–15, esp. pp. 13–14.

7. Luciano Bolis, *Il miogranello di sabbia* (Turin: Einaudi, 1946), p. 4.

244 | Michael Hardt and Antonio Negri

8. Gilles Deleuze, *Negotiations*, trans. Martin Joughin (New York: Columbia University Press, 1995), p. 176.
9. Reiner Schürmann, ed. and commentary, *Meister Eckhart: Mystic and Philosopher* (Bloomington: Indiana University Press, 1978), p. 4.
10. Charles Peirce, *Elements of Logic*, in *Collected Papers of Charles Sanders Peirce*, ed. Charles Hartshorne and Paul Weiss (Cambridge, Mass.: Harvard University Press, 1960), p. 474.

CHAPTER 12

LABOR, ACTION, INTELLECT

Paolo Virno

In our previous seminar I tried to illustrate the mode of being of the multitude, beginning with the dialectic dread-safe haven. Today, I would like to discuss the classical division of human experience into three fundamental spheres: Labor (or poiesis), political Action (or praxis) and Intellect (or life of the mind). The goal here is still the same: to articulate and to investigate in depth the notion of multitude.

As you will recall, "multitude" is a central category of political thought: it is called into question here in order to explain some of the salient features of the post-Ford mode of production. We do so on the condition that we understand "mode of production" to mean not only one particular economic configuration, but also a composite unity of forms of life, a social, anthropological and ethical cluster: "ethical," let us note, and not "moral"; in question here are common practices, usages and customs, not the dimension of the must-be. So then, I would like to maintain that the contemporary multitude has as its background the crisis of the subdivision of human experience into Labor, (political) Action and Intellect. The multitude affirms itself, in high relief, as a mode of being in which there is a juxtaposition, or at least a hybridization, between spheres which, until very recently, even during the Ford era, seemed clearly distinct and separated.

Labor, Action, Intellect: in the style of a tradition which goes back to Aristotle and which has been revisited with particular efficacy and passion by Hannah Arendt (Arendt, *The Human Condition*), this tripartitioning has seemed clear, realistic, nearly unquestionable. It has put down solid roots in the realm of common sense: it is not a question, then, of an undertaking which is only philosophical, but of a widely shared pattern of thought. When I began to get involved in politics, in the Sixties, I considered this subdivision to be something indisputable; it seemed to me as unquestionable as any immediate tactile or visual perception. It was not necessary to have read Aristotle's *Nicomachean Ethics* to know that labor, political action, and intellectual reflection constituted three spheres supported by radically heterogeneous principles and criteria. Obviously, this heterogeneity did not exclude intersection: political reflection could be applied to politics; in turn, political action was often, and willingly, nourished by themes related to the sphere of production, etc. But, as numerous as the intersections were, Labor, Intellect, and Politics remained essentially distinct. For structural reasons.

Labor is the organic exchange with nature, the production of new objects, a repetitive and foreseeable process. The pure intellect has a solitary and inconspicuous character: the meditation of the thinker escapes the notice of others; theoretical reflection mutes the world of appearances. Differently from Labor, political Action comes between social relations, not between natural materials; it has to do with the possible and the unforeseen; it does not obstruct, with ulterior motives, the context in which it operates; rather, it modifies, this very context. Differently from the Intellect, political Action is public, consigned to exteriority, to contingency, to the buzzing of the "many;" it involves, to use the words of Hannah, "the presence of others" (*Human Condition*, Chap. V, "Action"). The concept of political Action can be deduced by opposition with respect to the other two spheres.

So then, this ancient tripartitioning, which was still encysted into the realm of common sense of the generation which made its appearance in the public scene in the Sixties, is exactly what has failed today. That is to say, the boundaries between pure intellectual activity, political action, and labor have dissolved. I will maintain, in particular, that the world of so-called post-Fordist labor has absorbed into itself many of the typical characteristics of political action; and that this fusion between Politics and Labor constitutes a decisive physiognomic trait of the contemporary multitude.

Juxtaposition of Poiesis and Praxis

Contemporary labor has introjected into itself many characteristics which originally marked the experience of politics. *Poiesis* has taken on numerous aspects of *praxis*. This is the first aspect of the most general form of hybridization which I would like to address.

But let us note that even Hannah Arendt insisted on denouncing the collapse of the border between labor and politics—whereby politics does not mean life in some local party headquarters, but the generically human experience of beginning something again, an intimate relationship with contingency and the unforeseen, being in the presence of others. Politics, according to Arendt, has taken to imitating labor. The politics of the twentieth century, in her judgment, has become a sort of fabrication of new objects: the State, the political party, history, etc. So then, I maintain that things have gone in the opposite direction from what Arendt seems to believe: it is not that politics has conformed to labor; it is rather that labor has acquired the traditional features of political action. My reasoning is opposite and symmetrical with respect to that of Arendt. I maintain that it is in the world of contemporary labor that we find the "being in the presence of others," the relationship with the presence of others, the beginning of new processes, and the constitutive familiarity with contingency, the unforeseen and the possible. I maintain that post-Fordist labor, the productive labor of surplus, subordinate labor, brings into play the talents and the qualifications which, according to a secular tradition, had more to do with political action.

Incidentally, this explains, in my opinion, the crisis of politics, the sense of scorn surrounding political praxis today, the disrepute into which action has fallen. In fact, political action now seems, in a disastrous way, like some superfluous duplication of the experience of labor, since the latter experience, even if in a deformed and despotic manner, has subsumed into itself certain structural characteristics of political action. The sphere of politics, in the strictest sense of the word, follows closely the procedures and stylistic elements which define the current state of labor; but let us note: it follows them closely while offering a poorer, cruder and more simplistic version of these procedures and stylistic elements. Politics offers a network of communication and a cognitive content of a more wretched variety than what is carried out in the current productive process. While less complex than labor and yet too similar to it, political action seems, all the same, like something not very desirable at all.

The inclusion of certain structural features of political praxis in contemporary production helps us to understand why the post-Ford multitude might be seen, today, as a *de-politicized* multitude. There is already too much politics in the world of wage labor (*in as much as it is* wage labor) in order for politics as such to continue to, enjoy an autonomous dignity.

On Virtuosity: From Aristotle to Glenn Gould

The subsumption into the labor process of what formerly guaranteed an indisputable physiognomy for public Action can be clarified by means of an ancient, but by no means ineffective, category: *virtuosity*.

Accepting, for now, the normal meaning of the word, by "virtuosity" I mean the special capabilities of a performing artist. A virtuoso, for example, is the pianist who offers us a memorable performance of Schubert; or it is a skilled dancer, or a persuasive orator, or a teacher who is never boring, or a priest who delivers a fascinating sermon. Let us consider carefully what defines the activity of virtuosos, of performing artists. First of all, theirs is *an activity which finds its own fulfillment (that is, its own purpose) in itself*, without objectifying itself into an end product, without settling into a "finished product," or into an object which would survive the performance. Secondly, it is *an activity which requires the presence of others*, which exists only in the presence of an audience.

An activity without an end product: the performance of a pianist or of a dancer does not leave us with a defined object distinguishable from the performance itself, capable of continuing after the performance has ended. An activity which requires the presence of others: the *performance* [Author uses the English word here] makes sense only if it is seen or heard. It is obvious that these two characteristics are inter-related: virtuosos need the presence of an audience precisely because they are not producing an end product, an object which will circulate through the world once the activity has ceased. Lacking a specific extrinsic product, the virtuoso has to rely on witnesses.

The category of virtuosity is discussed in the *Nicomachean Ethics*; it appears here and there in modern political thought, even in the twentieth century; it even holds a small place in Marx's criticism of political economics. In the *Nicomachean Ethics* Aristotle distinguishes labor (or poiesis) from political action (or praxis), utilizing precisely the notion of virtuosity: we have labor when an object is produced, an opus which can be separated from action; we have praxis when the purpose of action is found in action itself. Aristotle writes: "For while making has an end other than itself, action cannot; for good action [understood both as ethical conduct and as political action, Virno adds] itself is its end" (*Nicomachean Ethics*, VI, 1140 b). Implicitly resuming Aristotle's idea, Hannah Arendt compares the performing artists, the virtuosos, to those who are engaged in political action. She writes: "The performing arts [. . .] have indeed a strong affinity with politics. Performing artists—dancers, play-actors, musicians, and the like—need an audience to show their virtuosity, just as acting men need the presence of others before whom they can appear; both need a publicly organized space for their 'work,' and both depend upon others for the performance itself" (Arendt, *Between Past and Future*: 154).

One could say that every political action is *virtuosic*. Every political action, in fact, shares with virtuosity a sense of contingency, the absence of a "finished product," the immediate and unavoidable presence of others. On the one hand, all virtuosity is intrinsically *political*. Think about the case of Glenn Gould (Gould, *The Glenn Gould Reader*, and Schneider, *Glenn Gould Piano Solo*). This great pianist paradoxically, hated the distinctive characteristics of his activity as a performing artist; to put it another way, he detested public exhibition. Throughout his life he fought against the "political dimension" intrinsic to his profession. At a certain point Gould declared that he wanted to abandon the *"active life,"* that is, the act of being exposed to the eyes of others (note: *"active life"* is the traditional name for politics). In order to make his own virtuosity non-political, he sought to bring his activity as a performing artist as close as possible to the idea of labor, in the strictest sense, which leaves behind extrinsic products. This meant closing himself inside a recording studio, passing off the production of records (excellent ones, by the way) as an "end product." In order to avoid the public-political dimension ingrained in virtuosity, he had to pretend that his masterly performances produced a defined object (independent of the performance itself). Where there is an end product, an autonomous product, there is labor, no longer virtuosity, nor, *for that reason*, politics.

Even Marx speaks of pianists, orators, dancers, etc. He speaks of them in some of his most important writings: in his "Results of the Immediate Process of Production," and then, in almost identical terms, in his *Theories of Surplus-value*. Marx analyzes intellectual labor, distinguishing between its two principal types. On one hand, there is immaterial or mental activity which "results in commodities which exist separately from the producer [. . .] books, paintings and all products of art as distinct from the artistic achievement of the practicing artist" (in Appendix to *Capital, Vol. I*, "Results of the Immediate Process of Production": 1048). This is the first type of intellectual labor. On the other hand, Marx writes, we need to consider all those activities in which the "product is not separable from the act of producing" (ibid., 1048)—those activities, that is, which find in themselves their own fulfillment without being objectivized into an end product which might surpass them. This is the same distinction which Aristotle made between material production and political action. The only difference is that Marx in this instance is not concerned with political action; rather, he is analyzing two different representations of labor. To these specifically defined types of poiesis he applies the distinction between activity-with-end-product and activity-without-end-product. The second type of intellectual labor (activities in which "product is not separable from the act of producing,") includes, according to Marx, all those whose labor turns into a virtuosic performance: pianists, butlers, dancers, teachers, orators, medical doctors, priests, etc.

So then, if intellectual labor which produces an end product does not pose any special problems, labor without an end product (virtuosic labor) places Marx in an embarrassing situation. The first type of intellectual labor conforms to the definition of "productive labor." But what about the second type? I remember in passing, that for Marx, productive labor is not subordinate or fatiguing or menial labor, but is precisely and only that kind of labor which produces surplus-value. Of course, even virtuosic performances can, in principle, produce surplus-value: the activity of the dancer, of the pianist, etc., if organized in a capitalistic fashion, can be a source of profit. But Marx is disturbed by the strong resemblance between the activity of the performing artist and the *servile* duties which, thankless and frustrating as they are, do not produce surplus value, and thus return to the realm of non-productive labor. Servile labor is that labor in which no *capital* is invested, but a wage is paid (example: the personal services of a butler). According to Marx, even if the "virtuosist" workers represent, on one hand, a not very significant exception to the quantitative point of view, on the other hand, and this is what counts more, they almost always converge into the realm of servile/non-productive labor. Such convergence is sanctioned precisely by the fact that their activity does not give way to an independent end product: where an autonomous finished product is lacking, for the most part one cannot speak of productive (surplus-value) labor. Marx virtually accepts the equation work-without-end-product = personal services. In conclusion, virtuosic labor, for Marx, is a form of wage labor which is not, at the same time, productive labor (*Theories of Surplus-value*: 410–411).

Let us try to sum things up. Virtuosity is open to two alternatives: either it conceals the structural characteristics of political activity (lack of an end product, being exposed to the presence of others, sense of contingency, etc.), as Aristotle and Hannah Arendt suggest; or, as in Marx, it takes on the features of "wage labor which is not productive labor." This bifurcation decays and falls to pieces when *productive* labor, in its totality, appropriates the special characteristics of the performing artist. In post-Fordism, those who produce surplus-value behave—from the structural point of view, of course—like the pianists, the dancers, etc., and *for this reason*, like the politicians. With reference to contemporary production, Hannah Arendt's observation on the activity of the performing artist and the politician rings clear: in order to work, one needs a "publicly organized space." In post-Fordism, Labor requires a "publicly organized space" and resembles a virtuosic performance (without end product). This publicly organized space is called "cooperation" by Marx. One could say: at a certain level in the development of productive social forces, labor cooperation introjects verbal communication into itself, or, more precisely, a complex of *political actions*.

Do you remember the extremely renowned commentary of Max Weber on politics as profession? (Weber, *Politics as a Vocation*) Weber elaborates on a series of qualities which define the politician: knowing how to place the health of one's own soul in danger; an equal balance between the ethics of convincing and the ethics of responsibility; dedication to one's goal, etc. We should re-read this text with reference to Toyotaism, to labor based upon language, to the productive mobilization of the cognitive faculties. Weber's wisdom speaks to us of the qualities required today for material production.

The Speaker as Performing Artist

Each one of us is, and has always been, a virtuoso, a performing artist, at times mediocre or awkward, but, in any event, a virtuoso. In fact, the fundamental model of virtuosity, the experience which is the base of the concept, is *the activity of the speaker*. This is not the activity of a knowledgeable and erudite locutor, but of *any* locutor. Human verbal language, not being a pure tool or a complex of instrumental signals (these are characteristics which are inherent, if anything, in the languages of non-human animals: one need only think of bees and of the signals which they use for coordinating the procurement of food), has its fulfillment in itself and does not produce (at least not as a rule, not necessarily) an "object" independent of the very act of having been uttered.

Language is "without end product." Every utterance is a virtuosic performance. And this is so, also because, obviously, utterance is connected (directly or indirectly) to the presence of others. Language presupposes and, at the same time, institutes once again the "publicly organized space" which Arendt speaks about. One would need to reread the passages from the *Nicomachean Ethics* on the essential difference between poiesis (production) and praxis (politics) with very close connection to the notion of *parole* in Saussure (Saussure, *Course*) and, above all, to the analyses of Emile Benveniste (Benveniste, *Problems*) on the subject of utterance (where "utterance" is not understood to mean the content of what is uttered, that "which is said," but the interjection of a word as such, the very fact of speaking). In this way one would establish that the differential characteristics of praxis with respect to poiesis coincide absolutely with the differential characteristics of verbal language with respect to motility or even to non-verbal communication.

There is more to the story. The speaker alone—unlike the pianist, the dancer or the actor—can do without a script or a score. The speaker's virtuosity is twofold: not only does it not produce an end product which is distinguishable from performance, but it does not even leave behind an end product which could be actualized by means of performance. In fact, the act of *parole* makes use only of the *potentiality* of language, or better yet, of the generic faculty of language: not of a pre-established text in detail. The virtuosity of the speaker is the prototype and apex of all other forms of virtuosity, precisely because it includes within itself the potential/act relationship, whereas ordinary or derivative virtuosity, instead, presupposes a determined act (as in Bach's *"Goldberg" Variations*, let us say), which can be relived over and over again. But I will return to this point later.

It is enough to say, for now, that contemporary production becomes "virtuosic" (and thus political) precisely because it includes within itself linguistic experience as such. If this is so, the matrix of post-Fordism can be found in the industrial sectors in which there is "production of communication, by means of communication"; hence, in the culture industry.

Culture Industry: Anticipation and Paradigm

Virtuosity becomes labor for the masses with the onset of a culture industry. It is here that the virtuoso begins to punch a time card. Within the sphere of a culture industry, in fact, activity without an end product, that is to say, communicative activity which has itself as an end, is a distinctive, central and necessary element. But, exactly for this reason, it is above all within the culture industry that the structure of wage labor has overlapped with that of political action.

Within the sectors where communication is produced by means of communication, responsibilities and roles are, at the same time, "virtuosic" and "political." In his most important novel, *La vita agra* [*Bitter Life*], a distinguished Italian writer, Luciano Bianciardi, describes the splendors and miseries of the culture industry in Milan during the Fifties. In one remarkable page of this book, he effectively illustrates what distinguishes culture industry from traditional industry and from agriculture. The protagonist of *La vita agra*, having arrived in Milan from Grosseto with the intention of avenging recent job related deaths that took place in his region, ends up becoming involved in the budding culture industry. After a brief time, however, he is fired. The following is a passage which, today, has unmistakable theoretical merit: "[. . .] And they fired me, only on account of the fact that I drag my feet, I move slowly, I look around even when it is not absolutely necessary. In our business, however, we need to lift our feet high off the ground, and bang them down again on the floor noisily, we need to move, hit the pavement, jump up, create dust, possibly a cloud of dust and then hide inside it. It is not like being a peasant or a worker. The peasant moves slowly because the work is so related to the seasons; the peasant cannot sow in July and harvest in February. Workers move quickly, but if they are on the assembly line, because on the line there are measured out periods of production, and if they do not move following that rhythm, they are in trouble [. . .]. But the fact is that the peasant belongs to the realm of primary activities and the worker to the realm of secondary activities. One produces something from nothing; the other transforms one thing into another. There is an easy measuring stick for the worker and for the peasant, one which is quantitative: does the factory produce so many pieces per hour, does the farm yield a profit? In our professions it is different, there are no quantitative measuring sticks. How does one measure the skill of a priest, or of a journalist, or of someone in public relations? *These people neither produce from scratch, nor transform.* They are neither primary nor secondary. Tertiary is what they are and what's more, I would dare say [. . .] even four times removed. They are neither instruments of production, nor drive belts of transmission. They are a lubricant, at the most pure Vaseline. How can one evaluate a priest, a journalist, a public relations person? How can one calculate the amount of faith, of purchasing desire, of likeability that these people have managed to muster up? No, we have no other yardstick in this case than the one which can measure one's capacity to float above water, and to ascend even higher, in short, to become a bishop. In other words, those who choose a tertiary or quaternary profession need *skills and aptitudes of a political kind*. Politics, as everybody knows has for a long time ceased to be the science of good government and has become, instead, the art of conquering and maintaining power. Therefore, the excellence of politicians is not measured according to the good that they manage to do for others, but is based on the swiftness with which they get to the top and on the amount of time they last there. [. . .] In the same way, in the tertiary and quaternary professions, *since there is no visible production of goods to function as a measuring stick*, the criterion will be the same" (Bianciardi, *La vita agra*: 129–32; Virno's italics [note: English translation from the original Italian by the translators]).

In many ways, Bianciardi's analysis is clearly dated, since it presents the functions of the culture industry as a marginal and outlandish exception to the rule. Moreover, it is at best superficial to reduce politics to a pure and simple overthrowing of power. In spite of this, the passage which I have just read shows exceptional intuition. In its own way, this intuition recalls and rehashes Arendt's thesis on the similarity between virtuosos and politicians, as well as Marx's notations about labor which does not have a separate "end product" as its goal. Bianciardi underscores the emerging "political dimension" of labor within the culture industry. But, and this is crucial, he links this dimension to the fact that in the culture industry there is no production of labor independent from activity itself. Where an extrinsic "end product" is lacking, there lies the ground for political action. I should clarify: in the culture industry (as is the case, after all, today in the post-Ford era for industry in general) the finished products which can be sold at the end of the productive process are surely not scarce. The crucial point is, though, that while the material production of objects is delegated to an automated system of machines, the services rendered by living labor, instead, resemble linguistic-virtuosic services more and more.

We should ask ourselves what role the culture industry assumed with relation to overcoming the Ford/Taylor model. I believe that it fine-tuned the paradigm of post-Fordist production on the whole. I believe therefore, that the mode of action of the culture industry became, from a certain point on, exemplary and pervasive. Within the culture industry, even in its archaic incarnation examined by Benjamin and Adorno, one can grasp early signs of a mode of production which later, in the post-Ford era, becomes generalized and elevated to the rank of *canon*.

To clarify, let us return, for a moment, to the critique of the communication industry leveled by the thinkers of the Frankfurt School. In the *Dialectic of Enlightenment* (Adorno and Horckheimer: 120–167) the authors maintain, roughly, that the "factories of the soul" (publishing, cinema, radio, television, etc.) also conform to the Fordist criteria of serialization and parcelization. In those factories, also, the conveyer belt, the dominant symbol of automobile factories, seems to assert itself. Capitalism—this is the thesis—shows that it can mechanize and parcelize even its spiritual production, exactly as it has done with agriculture and the processing of metals. Serialization, insignificance of individual tasks, the econometrics of feelings: these are the recurrent *refrains*. Evidently, this critical approach allowed, in the peculiar case of the culture industry, for the continuation of some elements which resist a complete assimilation to the Fordist organization of the labor process. In the culture industry, that is to say, it was therefore necessary to maintain a certain space that was informal, not programmed, one which was open to the unforeseen spark, to communicative and creative improvisation: not in order to favor human creativity, naturally, but in order to achieve satisfactory levels of corporate productivity. However, for the Frankfurt School, these aspects were nothing but un-influential remnants, remains of the past, waste. What counted was the general Fordization of the culture industry. Now, it seems to me, from our present perspective, that it is not difficult to recognize that these purported remnants (with a certain space granted to the informal, to the unexpected, to the "unplanned") were, after all, loaded with future possibilities.

These were not remnants, but anticipatory omens. The informality of communicative behavior, the competitive interaction typical of a meeting, the abrupt diversion that can enliven a television program (in general, everything which it would have been dysfunctional to rigidify and regulate beyond a certain threshold), has become now, in the post-Ford era, a typical trait of the *entire* realm of social production. This is true not only for our contemporary culture industry, but also for Fiat in Melfi. If Bianciardi was discussing labor organized by a nexus between (virtuosic) activity-without-end-product and political attitudes as a marginal aberration, this has now become the rule. The intermingling of virtuosity, politics and labor has extended everywhere. What is left to question, if anything, is what specific role is carried out *today* by the communication industry, since all industrial sectors are inspired by its model. Has the very thing that once upon a time anticipated the post-Ford turning point become entirely unfolded? In order to answer this question, we should linger a while on the concept of "spectacle" and "society of the spectacle."

Language on the Stage

I believe that the notion of "spectacle," though itself rather vague, provides a useful tool for deciphering some aspects of the post-Ford multitude (which is, in fact, a multitude of virtuosos, of workers who, in order to work, rely on generically "political" skills).

The concept of "spectacle," coined in the Sixties by the Situationists, is a truly theoretical concept, not foreign to the tenet of Marxian argumentation. According to Guy Debord "spectacle" is human communication which has become a commodity. What is delivered through the spectacle is precisely the human ability to communicate, verbal language as such. As we can see, the core of the issue is not a rancorous objection to consumer society (which is always slightly suspect, the risk being, as in the case of Pasolini, that of bemoaning the blessed cohabitation between low levels of consumerism and pellagra). Human communication, as spectacle, is a commodity among others, not outfitted with special qualities or prerogatives. On the other hand, it is a commodity which concerns, from a certain point on, all industrial sectors. This is where the problem lies.

On one hand, spectacle is the specific product of a specific industry, the so-called culture industry, in fact. On the other hand, in the post-Ford era, human communication is also an essential ingredient of productive cooperation in general; thus, it is the reigning productive force, something that goes beyond the domain of its own sphere, pertaining, instead, to the industry as a whole, to poiesis in its totality. In the spectacle we find exhibited, in a separate and fetishized form, the most relevant productive forces of society, those productive forces on which every contemporary work process must draw: linguistic competence, knowledge, imagination, etc. Thus, the spectacle has a *double nature*: a specific product of a particular industry, but also, at the same time, the quintessence of the mode of production in its entirety. Debord writes that the spectacle is "the general gloss on the rationality of the system." (Debord, ibid., Thesis 15) What presents the spectacle, so to speak, are the productive forces themselves of society as they overlap, in ever-greater measure, with linguistic-communicative competencies and with the *general intellect*.

The double nature of the spectacle is reminiscent, in some ways, of the double nature of money. As you know, money is a commodity among others, manufactured by the State Mint, in Rome, endowed of a metallic or paper form. But it also has a second nature: it is an equivalent, a unit of measurement, of all other commodities. Money is particular and universal at the same time; spectacle is particular and universal at the same time. This comparison, though without a doubt an attractive one, is incorrect. Unlike money, which measures the result of a productive process, one which has been concluded, spectacle concerns, instead, the productive process *in fieri*, in its unfolding, in its potential. The spectacle, according to Debord, reveals what women and men *can* do. While money mirrors in itself the value of commodities, thus showing what society has *already* produced, the spectacle exposes in a separate form that which the aggregate of society *can* be and do. If money is the "real abstraction" (to use a classic Marxian expression) which refers back to finished labor, to labor's past, according to Debord the spectacle is, instead, the "real abstraction" which portrays labor in itself, the present tense of labor. If money spearheads exchange, then the spectacle, human communication which has become a commodity, spearheads, if anything, productive communication. We must conclude, then, that the spectacle, which is human communicative capacity turned into commodity, does have a double nature which is different from that of money. But different in what way?

My hypothesis is that the communication industry (or rather, the spectacle, or even yet, the culture industry) is an industry among others, with its specific techniques, its particular procedures, its peculiar profits, etc.; on the other hand, it also plays the role of *industry of the means of production*. Traditionally, the industry of the means of production is the industry that produces machinery and other instruments to be used in the most varied sectors of production. However, in a situation in which the means of production are not reducible to machines but consist of linguistic-cognitive competencies inseparable from living labor, it is legitimate to assume that a conspicuous part of the so-called "means of production" consists of techniques and communicative procedures. Now, where are these techniques and procedures created, if not in the culture industry? The culture industry produces (regenerates, experiments with) communicative procedures, which are then destined to function also as means of production in the more traditional sectors of our contemporary economy. This is the role of the communication industry, once post-Fordism has become fully entrenched: an industry of the means of communication.

Virtuosity in the Workplace

Virtuosity, with its intrinsic political dimension, not only characterizes the culture industry but the totality of contemporary social production. One could say that in the organization of labor in the post-Ford era, activity without an end product, previously a special and problematic case (one need only recall, in this regard, Marx's uncertainties), becomes the prototype of all wage labor. Let me repeat a point I made before: this does not mean that car dashboards are no longer produced but that, for an ever increasing numbers of professional tasks, the fulfillment of an action is internal to the action itself (that is, it does not consist of giving rise to an independent semi-labor).

A situation of this kind is foreshadowed by Marx himself in the *Grundrisse*, when he writes that with the advent of large, automated industry and the intensive and systematic application of the natural sciences to the productive process, labor activity moves "*to the side* of the production process instead of being its chief actor" (*Grundrisse*: 705). This placing of labor activity "to the side" of the immediate process of production indicates, Marx adds, that labor corresponds more and more to "a supervisory and regulatory activity" (ibid., 709). In other words: the tasks of a worker or of a clerk no longer involve the completion of a single particular assignment, but the changing and intensifying of social cooperation. Please allow me to digress. The concept of *social cooperation*, which is so complex and subtle in Marx, can be thought of in two different ways. There is, first of all, an "objective" meaning: each individual does different, specific, things which are put in relation to one another by the engineer or by the factory foreman: cooperation, in this case, transcends individual activity; it has no relevance to the way in which individual workers function. Secondly, however, we must consider also a "subjective" notion of cooperation: it materializes when a conspicuous portion of individual work consists of developing, refining, and intensifying cooperation itself. With post-Fordism the second definition of cooperation prevails. I am going-to try to explain this better by means of a comparison. From the beginning, one resource of capitalistic enterprise has been the so-called "misappropriation of workers' know how." That is to say: when workers found a way to execute their labor with less effort, taking an extra break, etc., the corporate hierarchy took advantage of this minimal victory, knowing it was happening, in order to modify the organization of labor. In my opinion, a significant change takes place when the task of the worker or of the clerk to some extent consists in actually finding, in discovering expedients, "tricks," solutions which ameliorate the organization of labor. In the latter case, workers' knowledge is not used on the sly but it is requested explicitly; that is to say, it becomes one of the stipulated working assignments. The same change takes place, in fact, with regards to cooperation; it is not the same thing if workers are coordinated de facto by the engineer or if they are asked to invent and produce new cooperative procedures. Instead of remaining in the background, the act of cooperating, linguistic integration, comes to the very foreground.

When "subjective" cooperation becomes the primary productive force, labor activities display a marked linguistic-communicative quality, they entail the presence of others. The monological feature of labor dies away: the relationship with others is a driving, basic element, not something accessory. Where labor moves *to the side* of the immediate productive process, instead of being one of its components, productive cooperation is a "publicly organized space." This "publicly organized space"—interjected into the labor process—mobilizes attitudes which are traditionally political. Politics (in the broad sense) becomes productive force, task, "tool box." One could say that the heraldic motto of post-Fordism is, rightfully, "politics above all." After all, what else could the discourse of "total quality" mean, if not a request to surrender to production a taste for action, the capacity to face the possible and the unforeseen, the capacity to communicate something new?

When hired labor involves the desire for action, for a relational capacity, for the presence of others—all things that the preceding generation was trying out within the local party headquarters—we can say that some distinguishing traits of the human animal, above all the possession of a language, are subsumed within capitalistic production. The inclusion of the very *anthropogenesis* in the existing mode of production is an extreme event. Forget the Heideggerian chatter about the "technical era" . . . This event does not assuage, but radicalizes, instead, the antinomies of economic-social capitalistic formation. Nobody is as poor as those who see their own relation to the presence of others, that is to say, their own communicative faculty, their own possession of a language, reduced to wage labor.

Intellect as Score

If the entirety of post-Fordist labor is productive (of surplus-value) labor precisely because it functions in a political-virtuosic manner, then the question to ask is this: what is the *score* which the virtuosos-workers perform? What is the script of their linguistic-communicative *performances*?

The pianist performs a Chopin waltz, the actor is more or less faithful to a preliminary script, the orator has at the least some notes to refer to; all performing artists can count on a score. But when virtuosity applies to the totality of social labor, which one is the proper score? From my perspective, I maintain without too many reservations that the score performed by the multitude in the post-Ford era is the Intellect, intellect as generic human faculty. According to Marx, the score of modern virtuosos is the *general intellect*, the general intellect of society, abstract thought which has become a pillar of social production. We thus go back to a theme (*general intellect*, public intellect, "commonplaces," etc.) which we considered during the first day.

By *general intellect* Marx means science, knowledge in general, the know-how on which social productivity relies by now. The politicization of work (that is, the subsumption into the sphere of labor of what had hitherto belonged to political action) occurs precisely when thought becomes the primary source of the production of wealth. Thought ceases to be an invisible activity and becomes something exterior, "public," as it breaks into the productive process. One could say: only then, only when it has linguistic intellect as its barycenter, can the activity of labor absorb into itself many of the characteristics which had previously belonged to the sphere of political action.

Up to this point we have discussed the juxtaposition between Labor and Politics. Now, however, the third facet of human experience comes into play, Intellect. It is the "score" which is always performed, over and again, by the workers-virtuosos. I believe that the hybridization between the different spheres (pure thought, political life and labor) begins precisely when the Intellect, as principal productive force, becomes public. Only then does labor assume a virtuosic (or communicative) semblance, and, thus, it colors itself with "political" hues.

Marx attributes to thought an exterior character, a public disposition, on two different occasions. Above all, when he makes use of the expression "real abstraction," which is a very beautiful expression also from a philosophical point of view, and then, when he discusses *"general intellect."* Money, for instance, is a real abstraction. Money, in fact, embodies, makes *real*, one of the cardinal principles of human thought: the idea of equivalency. This idea, which is in itself utterly abstract, acquires a concrete existence, even jingles inside a wallet. A thought becoming a *thing*: here is what a real abstraction is. On the other hand, the concept of *general intellect* does nothing but advance, excessively, the notion of real abstraction. With the term *general intellect* Marx indicates the stage in which certain realities (for instance, a coin) no longer have the value and validity of a thought, but rather it is our thoughts, as such, that immediately acquire the value of material facts. If in the case of abstract thought it is the empirical fact (for example, the exchange of equivalencies) which exhibits the sophisticated structure of pure thought, in the case of *general intellect* the relation is overturned: now it is our thoughts which present themselves with the weight and incidence typical of facts. The *general intellect* is the stage at which mental abstractions are immediately, in themselves, real abstractions.

Here, however, is where the problems arise. Or, if you wish, a certain dissatisfaction arises with relation to Marx's formulations. The difficulty derives from the fact that Marx conceives the "general intellect" as a scientific objectified capacity, as a system of machines. Obviously, this aspect of the "general intellect" matters, but it is not everything. We should consider the dimension where the general intellect, instead of being incarnated (or rather, *cast in iron*) into the system of machines, exists as attribute of living labor. The *general intellect* manifests itself today, above all, as the communication, abstraction, self-reflection of living subjects. It seems legitimate to maintain that, according to the very logic of economic development, it is necessary that a part of the *general intellect* not congeal as fixed capital but unfold in communicative interaction, under the guise of epistemic paradigms, dialogical *performances*, linguistic games. In other words, public intellect is one and the same as cooperation, the acting in concert of human labor, the communicative competence of individuals.

In the fifth chapter of the first book of the *Capital*, Marx writes: "The labour process, as we have just presented it in its simple and abstract elements, is purposeful activity aimed at the production of use-values [. . .] We did not, therefore, have to present the worker in his relationship with other workers; it was enough to present man and his labour on one side, nature and its materials on the other" (*Capital*, Volume 1: 290). In this chapter Marx describes the labor process as a natural process of organic renewal between humans and nature, thus in abstract and general terms, without paying attention to historical-social relations. Nonetheless, we should ask whether it is legitimate, while remaining on this very general (almost anthropological) level, to expurgate from the concept of labor the interactive aspect, one's relation with other workers. It is certainly not legitimate as long as the activity of labor has its core in communicative performance. It is impossible, then, to trace the process of labor without presenting, from the beginning, the worker in relation with other workers; or, if we wish to employ again the category of virtuosity, in relation with one's "public."

The concept of cooperation comprises in itself, fully, the communicative capacity of human beings. That is true, above all, where cooperation is truly a specific "product" of the activity of labor, something which is promoted, elaborated, refined by those who cooperate. The *general intellect* demands virtuosic action (that is, in the broad sense, political action), precisely because a consistent portion of this intellect is not channeled in the machine system, but manifests itself in the direct activity of human labor, in its linguistic cooperation.

The intellect, the pure faculty of thought, the simple fact of having-a-language: let us repeat, here lies the "score" which is always and again performed by the post-Fordist virtuosos. (We should notice the difference in approach between today's lecture and that of our previous seminar: what today we are calling the "score" of the virtuoso, the intellect, in our previous meeting was seen as an apotropaic resource, as shelter against the indeterminate hazards of the worldly context. It is important to consider both of these concepts together: the contemporary multitude, with its forms of life and its linguistic games, places itself at the crossroads between these two meanings of "public intellect.") I would like to go back to, and emphasize here, an important point I have made before. While the virtuoso in the strictest sense of the word (the pianist, the dancer, for instance) makes use of a well defined score, that is to say, of an *end product* in its most proper and restricted sense, the post-Fordist virtuosos, "performing" their own linguistic faculties, can not take for granted a determined *end product*. *General intellect* should not necessarily mean the aggregate of the knowledge acquired by the species, but the *faculty* of thinking; potential as such, not its countless particular realizations. The "general intellect" is nothing but the *intellect in general*. Here it is useful to go back to the example of the speaker which we have already examined. With the infinite potential of one's own linguistic faculty as the only "score," a locutor (any locutor) articulates determined acts of speech: so then, the faculty of language is the opposite of a determined script, of an end product with these or those unmistakable characteristics. Virtuosity for the post-Fordist multitude is one and the same as the virtuosity of the speaker: virtuosity without a script, or rather, based on the premise of a script that coincides with pure and simple *dynamis*, with pure and simple potential.

It is useful to add that the relation between "score" and virtuosic performance is regulated by the norms of capitalistic enterprise. Putting to work (and to profit) the most generic communicative and cognitive faculties of the human animal has a historical index, a historically determined form. The *general intellect* manifests itself, today, as a perpetuation of wage labor, as a hierarchical system, as a pillar of the production of surplus-value.

Reason of State and Exit

At this point we can sketch some of the consequences of the hybridization between Labor, (political) Action and Intellect. Consequences which occur both on the level of production and within the public sphere (State, administrative apparatus).

The Intellect becomes public as soon as it links itself to labor; we must observe, however, that once it has been linked to wage labor, its typical publicness is also inhibited and distorted. This publicness is evoked over and over again in its role as productive force; and it is suppressed over and over again in its role as *public sphere* (in the proper sense of the term), as possible root of political Action, as a different constitutional principle.

The *general intellect* is the foundation of a social cooperation broader than that cooperation which is specifically related to labor. Broader and, at the same time, totally heterogeneous. We go back to one of the themes addressed during the first day of our seminar. While the connections of the productive process are based on a technical and hierarchical *division* of tasks, the acting in concert which hinges upon the *general intellect* moves from common participation to "life of the mind," that is, from the preliminary *sharing* of communicative and cognitive abilities. However, cooperation *in excess* of the Intellect, instead of annulling the co-actions of capitalistic production, figures as its most eminent resource. Its heterogeneity has neither voice nor visibility. On the contrary, since the appearance of the Intellect becomes the technical prerequisite of Labor, the acting in concert beyond labor which it brings about is in turn subsumed into the criteria and hierarchies which characterize the regime of the factory.

There are two principal consequences of this paradoxical situation. The first pertains to the nature and form of political power. The peculiar publicness of the Intellect, deprived of its own true expression by that very Labor which at the same time reclaims it as productive power, manifests itself indirectly within the sphere of the State by way of a *hypertrophic growth of the administrative apparatus.* The administration, and no longer the political-parliamentary system, is the heart of "stateness" ["statualità"]: but this is so, in fact, because the administration represents an authoritarian coalescence of the *general intellect,* the point of fusion between knowledge and control, the inverted image of excess cooperation. It is true that people have noticed for years the increasing and determining weight of bureaucracy within the "body politic," the preeminence of the decree with respect to the law: here, however, I would like to indicate a new threshold. In short, we no longer face the well-known processes of rationalization of the State; on the contrary, we must acknowledge the achieved *statization* [*statizzazione*] *of the Intellect* which has occurred. The old expression "reason of State" acquires for the first time a non-metaphorical significance. Hobbes saw the principle of legitimization of absolute power in the *transfer* of the natural right of each single individual to the person of the sovereign; now, on the other hand, we should talk about a *transfer* of the Intellect, or rather, of its immediate and irreducible publicness to the state administration.

The second consequence pertains to the prevailing nature of the post-Fordist regime. Since the "publicly organized space" opened up by the Intellect is constantly reduced to labor cooperation, that is, to a thick net of hierarchical relations, the nullifying function of the "presence of others" in all concrete operations of production takes the form of *personal dependence.* In other words, virtuosic activity shows itself as universal *servile work.* The affinity between a pianist and a waiter, which Marx had foreseen, finds an unexpected confirmation in the epoch in which all wage labor has something in common with the "performing artist." It is just that the very labor which produces the surplus-value is what takes on the appearance of servile labor. When "the product is inseparable from the act of producing," this act calls into question the personhood of the one who performs the work and, above all, the relation of this personhood to that of the one who has commissioned the work or for whom it is being done. Putting to work that which is *common,* that is, the intellect and language, renders the impersonal technical division of tasks fictitious, because such community does not translate into a public sphere (that is to say, into a political community); but is also induces a viscous personalization of subjection.

The crucial question goes like this: is it possible to split that which today is united, that is, the Intellect (the *general intellect*) and (wage) Labor, and to unite that which today is divided, that is, Intellect and political Action? Is it possible to move from the "ancient alliance" of Intellect/Labor to a "new alliance" of Intellect/political Action?

Rescuing political action from its current paralysis is no different from developing the publicness of the Intellect outside the realm of wage Labor, in opposition to it. This matter shows two distinct profiles, between which, however, there exists the strongest complementary bond. On one hand, the *general intellect* asserts itself as an autonomous public sphere only if the juncture that ties it to the production of goods and wage labor is severed. On the other hand, the subversion of capitalistic relations of production can manifest itself, at this point, only with the institution of a *non-state run public sphere*, of a political community that hinges on the *general intellect*. The salient traits of post-Fordist experience (servile virtuosity, exploitation of the very faculty of language, unfailing relation to the "presence of others," etc.) postulate, as a form of conflictual retaliation, nothing less than a radically new form of democracy.

The *non-state run public sphere* is a public sphere which conforms to the way of being of the multitude. It benefits from the "publicness" of language/thought, of the extrinsic, conspicuous, shared character of the Intellect in the guise of a score for the virtuosos. It is a "publicness"—as we have already observed during the first day of our seminar—totally heterogeneous with respect to that which is instituted by state sovereignty, or to quote Hobbes, "by the unity of the body politic." This "publicness," which manifests itself today as an eminent productive resource, can become a constitutional principle, a *public sphere*, in fact.

How is non-servile virtuosity possible? How do we move, hypothetically, from a servile virtuosity to a "republican" virtuosity (understanding "republic of the multitude" to mean a sphere of common affairs which is no longer state-run)? How do we conceive, in principle, of political action based on the *general intellect*? We must tread this terrain carefully. All we can do is to point to the *logical form* of something that is still lacking a solid empirical experience. I am proposing two key-terms: civil disobedience and exit.

"Civil disobedience" represents, perhaps, the fundamental form of political action of the multitude, provided that the multitude is emancipated from the liberal tradition within which it is encapsulated. It is not a matter of ignoring a specific law because it appears incoherent or contradictory to other fundamental norms, for example to the constitutional charter. In such case, in fact, reluctance would signal only a deeper loyalty to state control. Conversely, the radical disobedience which concerns us here casts doubt on the State's actual ability to control. Let us digress for a moment in order to understand this better.

According to Hobbes, with the institution of the "body politic," we force ourselves to obey *before* we even know what we will be ordered to do: "our obligation to civil obedience, by vertue whereof the civill Lawes are valid, is before all civill Lawe" (*De Cive*, Chap. XIV, Section XXI). For this reason we shall not find a particular law which explicitly dictates that people should not revolt. If the unconditional acceptance of the controlling power were not already *presupposed*, the concrete legislative presuppositions (including, obviously, that which states "thou shalt not rebell") would have no validity whatsoever. Hobbes maintains that the initial bond of obedience derives from "Lawes of nature," that is from a common interest in self-preservation and security. Still, he quickly adds that this "natural law," the Super-law which compels people to observe all of the orders of the sovereign, effectively becomes law only when we have left the state of nature, thus when the State has already been instituted. Thus, a real paradox takes shape: the duty to obey is both the cause and the effect of the existence of the State; this duty is supported by the very State which depends upon it for the constitution of its own foundation; it precedes *and* follows, at the same time, the development of a "supreme empire."

So then, the multitude aims precisely at this preliminary form of obedience without content, which is the foundation solely of the gloomy dialectic between acquiescence and "transgression." By breaking a particular law meant for dismantling socialized medicine or for stopping immigration, the multitude goes back to the covert presupposition hidden behind every act of mandating law and taints its ability to remain in force. Radical disobedience also "precedes civil laws," since it is not limited to the breaking of these laws but also calls into question the very foundation of their validity.

And now let us move on to the second key word: exit. The breeding ground of disobedience does not lie exclusively in the social conflicts which express *protest*, but, and above all, in those which express *defection* (as Albert O. Hirschman has explained [Hirschman, *Exit*]: not as *voice* but as *exit*).

Nothing is less passive than the act of fleeing, of exiting. Defection modifies the conditions within which the struggle takes place, rather than presupposing those conditions to be an unalterable horizon; it modifies the context within which a problem has arisen, rather than facing this problem by opting for one or the other of the provided alternatives. In short, *exit* consists of unrestrained invention which alters the rules of the game and throws the adversary completely off balance. While remembering what was discussed on this subject during the first day of our seminar, we need only think of the mass exodus from the regime of the factory, carried out by American workers in the middle of the nineteenth century. By venturing into the "frontier" to colonize inexpensive land, they seized upon the opportunity to reverse their own initial condition. Something similar took place in the late Seventies in Italy, when the young labor-power, challenging all expectations, chose temporary and part-time work over full-time employment in big corporations. Though it lasted only for a brief period, professional mobility functioned as a political resource, giving rise to the eclipse of industrial discipline and allowing for the establishing of a certain degree of self-determination.

Exit, or defection, is the polar opposite of the desperate cry "there is nothing to lose but one's own chains:" on the contrary, exit hinges on a latent kind of wealth, on an exuberance of possibilities, in short, on the principle of the *tertium datur.* But for the contemporary multitude, what is this virtual abundance which presses for the flee-option at the expense of the resistance-option? What is at stake, obviously, is not a spatial "frontier," but the surplus of knowledge, communication, virtuosic acting in concert, all presupposed by the publicness of the *general intellect.* Defection allows for a dramatic, autonomous, and affirmative expression of this surplus; and in this way it impedes the "transfer" of this surplus into the power of state administration, impedes its configuration as productive resource of the capitalistic enterprise.

Disobedience, exit. It is clear, however, that these are only allusions to what the true *political,* and not servile, virtuosity of the multitude could be.

References

Adorno, Theodor W., and Max Horckheimer. *Dialektik den Aufklärung* (1947), *Dialectic of Enlightenment,* translated by John Gumming. New York: Herder and Herder, 1972.

Arendt, Hannah. *Between Past and Future: Eight Exercises in Political Thought.* New York: Viking Press, 1968.

Arendt, Hannah. *The Human Condition*. Chicago: The University of Chicago Press, 1958.

Aristotle. *Nicomachean Ethics* in *The Basic Works of Aristotle*, edited by Richard McKeon. New York: Random House, 1941.

Benveniste, Emile. "L'appareil fennel de l'énunciation" in *Problèmes de linguistique générale* (1970), *Problems in General Linquistics*, translated by Mart Elizabeth Meek. Coral Gables, Florida: University of Miami Press, 1997.

Bianciardi, Luciano. *La vita agra*. Milano: Rizzoli, 1962.

Debord, Guy. *La société du spectacle* (1967). Society of the Spectacle, translated by Donald Nicholson-Smith. New York: Zone Books, 1994.

Gould, Glenn. *The Glenn Gould Reader*, edited by Tim Page. New York: Knopf, 1984.

Hirschman, Albert O. *Exit, Voice and Loyalty*. Cambridge, Massachusetts: Harvard University Press, 1970.

Hobbes, Thomas. *De Cive* (1642), edited by Sterling P. Lamprecht. New York: Appleton-Century-Crofts, 1949.

Marx, Karl. *Das Kapital* (1867). *Capital*, Volume 1, translated by Ben Fowkes. London: Penguin Books, 1990. Volume 2, translated by David Fernbach. London: Penguin Books, 1992. Volume 3, translated by David Fernbach. London: Penguin Books, 1991.

Marx, Karl. *Grundrisse der politischen Oekonomie* (1939–1941). *Grundrisse*, translated by Martin Nicolaus. London: Penguin Books, 1973.

Marx, Karl. *Theorien über den Mehrwert* (1905). *Theories of Surplus-value*, translated by Emile Burns, edited by S. Ryazanskaya. Moscow: Progress Publishers, 1969.

Saussure, Ferdinand de. *Cours de linguistique générale* (1922). *Course in General Linguistics*, translated by Roy Harris, edited by Charles Bally and Albert Riedlinger. LaSalle, Illinois: Open Court, 1986.

Schneider, Michel. *Glenn Gould Piano Solo* (Paris: Gallimard, 1994)

Weber, Max. *Politik als Beruf* (1919). *Politics as a Vocation*, translated by H. H. Gerth and C. Wright Mills. Philadelphia: Fortress Press, 1965.

CHAPTER 13

AN EQUIVOCAL

CONCEPT BIOPOLITICS

Paolo Virno

Foucault introduced the term "bio-politics" in some courses he taught in the Seventies at the Collège de France (see Foucault). The term was applied to the changes which took place in the concept of "population" between the end of the eighteenth and the beginning of the nineteenth century. In Foucault's view, it is during this period that life, life as such, life as mere biological process, begins to be governed and administered politically. The concept of "bio-politics" has recently become fashionable: it is often, and enthusiastically, invoked in every kind of context. We should avoid this automatic and un-reflective use of the term. Let us ask ourselves, then, how and why life breaks through to the center of the public scene, how and why the State regulates and governs it.

In my opinion, to comprehend the rational core of the term "bio-politics," we should begin with a different concept, a much more complicated concept from a philosophical standpoint: that of *labor-power*. This is a concept discussed everywhere in the social sciences, where its harsh and paradoxical character is however, carelessly avoided. If professional philosophers were to get involved in something serious here, they would have to devote much effort and attention to it. What does "labor-power" mean? It means *potential* to produce. Potential, that is to say, aptitude, capacity, *dynamis*. Generic, undetermined potential: where one particular type of labor or another has not been designated, but *any* kind of labor is taking place, be it the manufacturing of a car door, or the harvesting of pears, the babble of someone calling in to a phone "party-line," or the work of a proofreader. Labor-power is "the aggregate of those mental and physical capabilities existing in the physical form, the living personality, of a human being" (*Capital*, Volume 1: 270). *All of those capabilities*, we should note well. By talking about labor-power we implicitly refer to every sort of faculty: linguistic competence, memory, motility, etc. Only in today's world, in the post-Ford era, is the reality of labor-power fully up to the task of realizing itself. Only in today's world, that is to say, can the notion of labor-power not be reduced (as it was at the time of Gramsci) to an aggregate of physical and mechanical attributes; now, instead, it encompasses within itself, and rightfully so, the "life of the mind."

But let us get to the point here. The capitalistic production relation is based on the difference between labor-power and effective labor. Labor-power, I repeat, is pure *potential*, quite distinct from its correspondent acts. Marx writes: "When we speak of capacity for labour, we do not speak of labour, any more than we speak of digestion when we speak of capacity for digestion" (*Capital*, Volume 1: 277). We are dealing here, however, with a potential which boasts of the extremely concrete prerogatives of commodities. Potential is something non-present, non-real; but in the case of labor-power, this non-present something is subject to the laws of supply and demand (Virno, *Il ricordo*: 121–3). Capitalists buy the *capacity* for producing as such ("the sum of all physical and intellectual aptitudes which exist in the material world"), and not simply one or more specific services. After the sale has occurred, capitalists can use as they please the commodity which has been acquired. "The purchaser of labour-power consumes it by setting the seller of it to work. By working, the latter becomes in actuality what previously he only was potentially" (*Capital*, Volume 1: 283). Labor which has actually been paid out does not simply reimburse the capitalist for the money spent previously in order to assure the other's potential for working; it continues for an additional period of time. Here lies the genesis of surplus-value, here lies the mystery of capitalistic accumulation.

Labor-power incarnates (literally) a fundamental category of philosophical thought: specifically, the potential, the *dynamis*. And "potential," as I have just said, signifies that which is *not* current, that which is *not* present. Well then, something which is not present (or real) becomes, with capitalism, an exceptionally important commodity. This potential, *dynamis*, non-presence, instead of remaining an abstract concept, takes on a pragmatic, empirical, socioeconomic dimension. The potential as such, when it still has not been applied, is at the core of the exchange between capitalist and worker. The object of the sale is not a real entity (labor services actually executed) but something which, in and of itself, does not have an autonomous spacial-temporal existence (the generic ability to work).

The paradoxical characteristics of labor-power (something unreal which is, however, bought and sold as any other commodity) are the premise of bio-politics. In order to understand it, however, we must go through another step in the argument. In the *Grundrisse* Marx writes that "the use value which the worker has to offer to the capitalist, which he has to offer to others in general, is not materialized in a product, does not exist apart from him at all, thus exists not really, but only in *potentiality*, as his *capacity*" (*Grundrisse*: 267; Virno's italics). Here is the crucial point: where something which exists only as *possibility* is sold, this something is not separable from the *living person* of the seller. The living body of the worker is the substratum of that labor-power which, in itself, has no independent existence. "Life," pure and simple *bios*, acquires a specific importance in as much as it is the tabernacle of *dynamis*, of mere potential.

Capitalists are interested in the life of the worker, in the body of the worker, only for an indirect reason: this life, this body, are what contains the faculty, the potential, the *dynamis*. The living body becomes an object to be governed not for its intrinsic value, but because it is the substratum of what really matters: labor-power as the aggregate of the most diverse human faculties (the potential for speaking, for thinking, for remembering, for acting, etc.). Life lies at the center of politics when the prize to be won is immaterial (and in itself non-present) labor-power. For this reason, and this reason alone, it is legitimate to talk about "bio-politics." The living body which is a concern of the administrative apparatus of the State, is the tangible sign of a yet unrealized potential, the semblance of labor not yet objectified; as Marx says eloquently, of "labor as subjectivity." The potential for working, bought and sold just like another commodity, is labor not yet objectified, "labor as subjectivity." One could say that while money is the universal representation of the value of exchange—or rather of the exchangeability itself of products—life, instead, takes the place of the productive potential, of the invisible *dynamis*.

The non-mythological origin of that mechanism of expertise and power which Foucault defines as bio-politics can be traced back, without hesitation, to the mode of being of the labor-power. The practical importance taken on by potential as potential (the fact that it is bought and sold as such), as well as its inseparability from the immediate corporeal existence of the worker, is the real foundation of bio-politics. Foucault mocks libertarian theoreticians like Wilhelm Reich (the heterodox psychiatrist), who claims that a spasmodic attention to life is the result of a repressive intention: disciplining the body in order to raise the level of productivity of labor. Foucault is totally right, but he is taking aim at an easy target. It is true: the government of life is extremely varied and articulated, ranging from the confinement of impulses to the most unrestrained laxity, from punctilious prohibition to the showy display of tolerance, from the ghetto for the poor to extravagant Keynesian incomes, from the high-security prison to the Welfare State. Having said this, we still have to address a crucial question: why is life, as such, managed and controlled? The answer is absolutely clear: because it acts as the substratum of a mere faculty, labor-power, which has taken on the consistency of a commodity. It is not a question, here, of the productivity of actual labor, but of the exchangeability of the potential to work. By the mere fact that it can be bought and sold, this potential calls into question the repository from which it is indistinguishable, that is, the living body. What is more, it sheds light on this repository as an object of innumerable and differentiated governmental strategies.

One should not believe, then, that bio-politics includes within itself, as its own distinct articulation, the management of labor-power. On the contrary: bio-politics is merely an effect, a reverberation, or, in fact, one articulation of that primary fact—both historical and philosophical—which consists of the commerce of potential as potential. Bio-politics exists wherever that which pertains to the potential dimension of human existence comes into the forefront, into immediate experience: not the spoken word, but the capacity for speaking as such; not the labor which has actually been completed, but the generic capability of producing. The potential dimension of existence becomes conspicuous only, and exclusively, under the guise of labor-power. In this potential we see the compendium of all the different faculties and potentials of the human animal. In fact, "labor-power" does not designate one specific faculty, but the *entirety* of human faculties in as much as they are involved in productive praxis. "Labor-power" is not a proper noun; it is a common noun.

References

Marx, Karl. *Das Kapital* (1867). *Capital*, Volume 1, translated by Ben Fowkes. London: Penguin Books, 1990. Volume 2, translated by David Fernbach. London: Penguin

Books, 1992. Volume 3, translated by David Fernbach. London: Penguin Books. 1991.

Marx, Karl. *Grundrisse der politischen Oekonomie* (1939–1941). *Grundrisse*, translated by Martin Nicolaus. London: Penguin Books, 1973.

Virno, Paolo. *Il ricordo del presente. Saggio sul tempo storico.* Torino: Bollati Boringhieri, 1999.

CHAPTER 14

THE BIOPOLITICS OF POSTMODERN BODIES CONSTITUTIONS OF SELF IN IMMUNE SYSTEM DISCOURSE

Donna Haraway

> If Koch's postulates must be fulfilled to identify a given microbe with a given disease, perhaps it would be helpful, in rewriting the AIDS text, to take 'Turner's postulates' into account (1984, p. 209): 1) disease is a language; 2) the body is a representation; and 3) medicine is a political practice.
>
> Treichler, 1987, p. 27

> Non-self: A term covering everything which is detectably different from an animal's own constituents.
>
> Playfair, 1984, p. 1

> [T]he immune system must *recognize* self in some manner in order to react to something foreign.
>
> Golub, 1987, p. 484

Lumpy Discourse and the Denatured Bodies of Biology and Medicine

It has become commonplace to emphasize the multiple and specific cultural dialects interlaced in any social negotiation of disease and sickness in the contemporary worlds marked by biological research, biotechnology, and scientific medicine. The language of biomedicine is never alone in the field of empowering meanings, and its power does not flow from a consensus about symbols and actions in the face of suffering. Paula Treichler's excellent phrase in the title of her essay on the constantly contested meanings of AIDS as an 'epidemic of signification' could be applied widely to the social text of sickness. The power of biomedical language—with its stunning artefacts, images, architectures, social forms, and technologies—for shaping the unequal experience of sickness and death for millions is a social fact deriving from ongoing heterogeneous social processes. The power of biomedicine and biotechnology is constantly re-produced, or it would cease. This power is not a thing fixed and permanent, embedded in plastic and ready to section for microscopic observation by the historian or critic. The cultural and material authority of biomedicine's productions of bodies and selves is more vulnerable, more dynamic, more elusive, and more powerful than that.

But if there has been recognition of the many non-, para-, anti-, or extra-scientific languages in company with biomedicine that structure the embodied semiosis of mortality in the industrialized world, it is much less common to find emphasis on the multiple languages *within* the territory that is often so glibly marked scientific. 'Science says' is represented as a univocal language. Yet even the spliced character of the potent words in 'science' hints at a barely contained and inharmonious heterogeneity. The words for the overlapping discourses and their objects of knowledge, and for the abstract corporate names for the concrete places where the discourse-building work is done, suggest both the blunt foreshortening of technicist approaches to communication and the uncontainable pressures and confusions at the boundaries of meanings within 'science'—biotechnology, biomedicine, psychoneuroimmunology, immunogenetics, immunoendocrinology, neuroendocrinology, monoclonal antibodies, hybridomas, interleukines, Genentech, Embrex, Immunetech, Biogen.

This chapter explores some of the contending popular and technical languages constructing biomedical, biotechnical bodies and selves in postmodern scientific culture in the United States in the 1980s. Scientific discourses are 'lumpy'; they contain and enact condensed contestations for meanings and practices. The chief object of my attention will be the potent and polymorphous object of belief, knowledge, and practice called the immune system. My thesis is that the immune system is an elaborate icon for principal systems of symbolic and material 'difference' in late capitalism. Pre-eminently a twentieth-century object, the immune system is a map drawn to guide recognition and misrecognition of self and other in the dialectics of Western biopolitics. That is, the immune system is a plan for meaningful action to construct and maintain the boundaries for what may count as self and other in the crucial realms of the normal and the pathological. The immune system is a historically specific terrain, where global and local politics; Nobel Prize–winning research; heteroglossic cultural productions, from popular dietary practices, feminist science fiction, religious imagery, and children's games, to photographic techniques and military strategic theory; clinical medical practice; venture capital investment strategies; world-changing developments in business and technology; and the deepest personal and collective experiences of embodiment, vulnerability, power, and mortality interact with an intensity matched perhaps only in the biopolitics of sex and reproduction.[1]

The immune system is both an iconic mythic object in high-technology culture and a subject of research and clinical practice of the first importance. Myth, laboratory, and clinic are intimately interwoven. This mundane point was fortuitously captured in the title listings in the 1986–87 *Books in Print*, where I was searching for a particular undergraduate textbook on immunology. The several pages of entries beginning with the prefix 'immuno-' were bounded, according to the English rules of alphabetical listing, by a volume called *Immortals of Science Fiction*, near one end, and by *The Immutability of God*, at the other. Examining the last section of the textbook to which *Books in Print* led me, Immunology: A Synthesis (Golub, 1987), I found what I was looking for: a historical progression of diagrams of theories of immunological regulation and an obituary for their draftsman, an important immunologist, Richard K. Gershon, who 'discovered' the suppressor T cell. The standard obituary tropes for the scientist, who 'must have had what the earliest explorers had, an insatiable desire to be the first person to see something, to know that you are where no man has been before', set the tone. The hero-scientist 'gloried in the layer upon interconnected layer of [the immune response's] complexity. He thrilled at seeing a layer of that complexity which no one had seen before' (Golub, 1987, pp. 531–2). It is reasonable to suppose that all the likely readers of this textbook have been reared within hearing range of the ringing tones of the introduction to the voyages of the federation starship *Enterprise* in *Star Trek*—to boldly go where no man has gone before. Science remains an important genre of Western exploration and travel literature. Similarly, no reader, no matter how literal-minded, could be innocent of the gendered erotic trope that figures the hero's probing into nature's laminated secrets, glorying simultaneously in the layered complexity and in his own techno-erotic touch that goes ever deeper. Science as heroic quest and as erotic technique applied to the body of nature are utterly conventional figures. They take on a particular edge in late twentieth-century immune system discourse, where themes of nuclear exterminism, space adventure, extra-terrestrialism, exotic invaders, and military high-technology are pervasive.

But Golub's and Gershon's intended and explicit text is not about space invaders and the immune system as a Star Wars prototype. Their theme is the love of complexity and the intimate natural bodily technologies for generating the harmonies of organic life. In four illustrations—dated 1968, 1974, 1977, and 1982—Gershon sketched his conception of 'the immunological orchestra' (Golub, 1987, pp. 533–6). This orchestra is a wonderful picture of the mythic and technical dimensions of the immune system. All the illustrations are about co-operation and control, the major themes of organismic biology since the late eighteenth century. From his commanding position in the root of a lymph node, the G.O.D. of the first illustration conducts the orchestra of T and B cells and macrophages as they march about the body and play their specific parts. The lymphocytes all look like Casper the ghost with the appropriate distinguishing nuclear morphologies drawn in the centre of their shapeless bodies. Baton in hand, G.O.D.'s arms are raised in quotation of a symphonic conductor. G.O.D. recalls the other 1960s bioreligious, Nobel Prize—winning 'joke' about the coded bodily text of post-DNA biology and medicine—the Central Dogma of molecular biology, specifying that 'information' flows only from DNA to RNA to protein. These three were called the Blessed Trinity of the secularized sacred body, and histories of the great adventures of molecular biology could be titled *The Eighth Day of Creation* (Judson, 1979), an image that takes on a certain irony in the venture capital and political environments of current biotechnology companies, like Genentech. In the technical-mythic systems of molecular biology, code rules embodied structure and function, never the reverse. Genesis is a serious joke, when the body is theorized as a coded text whose secrets yield only to the proper reading conventions, and when the laboratory seems best characterized as a vast assemblage of technological and organic inscription devices. The Central Dogma was about a master control system for information flow in the codes that determine meaning in the great technological communication systems that organisms progressively have become after the Second World War. The body is an artificial intelligence system, and the relation of copy and original is reversed and then exploded.

G.O.D. is the Generator of Diversity, the source of the awe-inspiring multiple specificities of the polymorphous system of recognition and misrecognition we call the immune system. By the second illustration (1974), G.O.D. is no longer in front of the immune orchestra, but is standing, arms folded, looking authoritative but not very busy, at the top of the lymph node, surrounded by the musical lymphocytes. A special cell, the T suppressor cell, has taken over the role of conductor. By 1977, the illustration no longer has a single conductor, but is 'led' by three mysterious subsets of T cells, who hold a total of twelve batons signifying their direction-giving surface identity markers; and G.O.D. scratches his head in patent confusion. But the immune band plays on. In the final illustration, from 1982, 'the generator of diversity seems resigned to the conflicting calls of the angels of help and suppression', who perch above his left and right shoulders (Golub, 1987, p. 536). Besides G.O.D. and the two angels, there is a T cell conductor and two conflicting prompters, 'each urging its own interpretation'. The joke of single masterly control of organismic harmony in the symphonic system responsible for the integrity of 'self' has become a kind of postmodern pastiche of multiple centres and peripheries, where the immune music that the page suggests would surely sound like nursery school space music. All the actors that used to be on the stage-set for the unambiguous and coherent biopolitical subject are still present, but their harmonies are definitely a bit problematic.

By the 1980s, the immune system is unambiguously a postmodern object—symbolically, technically, and politically. Katherine Hayles (1987b) characterizes postmodernism in terms of 'three waves of developments occurring at multiple sites within the culture, including literature and science'. Her archaeology begins with Saussurean linguistics, through which symbol systems were 'denaturalized'. Internally generated relational difference, rather than mimesis, ruled signification. Hayles sees the culmination of this approach in Claude Shannon's mid-century statistical theory of information, developed for packing the largest number of signals on a transmission line for the Bell Telephone Company and extended to cover communication acts in general, including those directed by the codes of bodily semiosis in ethology or molecular biology. 'Information' generating and processing systems, therefore, are postmodern objects, embedded in a theory of internally differentiated signifiers and remote from doctrines of representation as mimesis. A history-changing artefact, 'information' exists only in very specific kinds of universes.[2] Progressively, the world and the sign seemed to exist in incommensurable universes—there was literally no *measure* linking them, and the reading conventions for all texts came to resemble those required for science fiction.

What emerged was a global technology that 'made the separation of text from context an everyday experience'. Hayles's second wave, 'energized by the rapid development of information technology, made the disappearance of stable, reproducible context an international phenomenon . . . Context was no longer a natural part of every experience, but an artifact that could be altered at will.' Hayles's third wave of denaturalization concerned time. 'Beginning with the Special Theory of Relativity, time increasingly came to be seen not as an inevitable progression along a linear scale to which all humans were subject, but as a construct that could be conceived in different ways.'

Language is no longer an echo of the *verbum dei*, but a technical construct working on principles of internally generated difference. If the early modern natural philosopher or Renaissance physician conducted an exegesis of the text of nature written in the language of geometry or of cosmic correspondences, the postmodern scientist still reads for a living, but has as a text the coded systems of recognition—prone to the pathologies of mis-recognition—embodied in objects like computer networks and immune systems. The extraordinarily close tie of language and technology could hardly be overstressed in postmodernism. The 'construct' is at the centre of attention; making, reading, writing, and meaning seem to be very close to the same thing. This near-identity between technology, body, and semiosis suggests a particular edge to the mutually constitutive relations of political economy, symbol, and science that 'inform' contemporary research trends in medical anthropology.

The Apparatus of Bodily Production:
The Techno-biopolitics of Engagement

Bodies, then, are not born; they are made. Bodies have been as thoroughly denaturalized as sign, context, and time. Late twentieth-century bodies do not grow from internal harmonic principles theorized within Romanticism. Neither are they discovered in the domains of realism and modernism. One is not born a woman, Simone de Beauvoir correctly insisted. It took the political-epistemological terrain of postmodernism to be able to insist on a co-text to de Beauvoir's: one is not born an organism. Organisms are made; they are constructs of a world-changing kind. The constructions of an organism's boundaries, the job of the discourses of immunology, are particularly potent mediators of the experiences of sickness and death for industrial and post-industrial people.

In this over-determined context, I will ironically—and inescapably—invoke a constructionist concept as an analytic device to pursue an understanding of what kinds of units, selves, and individuals inhabit the universe structured by immune system discourse: Scientific bodies are not *ideological* constructions. Always radically historically specific, bodies have a different kind of specificity and effectivity, and so they invite a different kind of engagement and intervention. The notion of a 'material-semiotic actor' is intended to highlight the object of knowledge as an active part of the apparatus of bodily production, without *ever* implying immediate presence of such objects or, what is the same thing, their final or unique determination of what can count as objective knowledge of a biomedical body at a particular historical juncture. Bodies as objects of knowledge are material-semiotic generative nodes. Their boundaries materialize in social interaction; 'objects' like bodies do not pre-exist as such. Scientific objectivity (the siting/sighting of objects) is not about dis-engaged discovery, but about mutual and usually unequal structuring, about taking risks. The various contending biological bodies emerge at the intersection of biological research, writing, and publishing; medical and other business practices; cultural productions of all kinds, including available metaphors and narratives; and technology, such as the visualization technologies that bring colour-enhanced killer T cells and intimate photographs of the developing foetus into high-gloss art books for every middle-class home (Nilsson, 1977, 1987).

But also invited into that node of intersection is the analogue to the lively languages that actively intertwine in the production of literary value: the coyote and protean embodiments of a world as witty agent and actor. Perhaps our hopes for accountability in the techno-biopolitics in postmodern frames turn on revisioning the world as coding trickster with whom we must learn to converse. Like a protein subjected to stress, the world for us may be thoroughly denatured, but it is not any less consequential. So while the late twentieth-century immune system is a construct of an elaborate apparatus of bodily production, neither the immune system nor any other of bio-medicine's world-changing bodies—like a virus—is a ghostly fantasy. Coyote is not a ghost, merely a protean trickster.

The following chart abstracts and dichotomizes two historical moments in the biomedical production of bodies from the late nineteenth century to the 1980s. The chart highlights epistemological, cultural, and political aspects of possible contestations for constructions of scientific bodies in this century. The chart itself is a traditional little machine for making particular meanings. Not a description, it must be read as an argument, and one which relies on a suspect technology for the production of meanings—binary dichotomization.

Representation	Simulation
Bourgeois novel	Science fiction
Realism and modernism	Postmodernism
Organism	Biotic component, code
Work	Text
Mimesis	Play of signifiers
Depth, integrity	Surface, boundary
Heat	Noise
Biology as clinical practice	Biology as inscription
Physiology	Communications engineering
Microbiology, tuberculosis	Immunology, AIDS
Magic bullet	Immunomodulation
Small group	Subsystem
Perfection	Optimization
Eugenics	Genetic engineering
Decadence	Obsolescence
Hygiene	Stress management
Organic division of labour	Ergonomics, cybernetics
Functional specialization	Modular construction
Biological determinism	System constraints
Reproduction	Replication
Individual	Replicon
Community ecology	Ecosystem
Racial chain of being	United Nations humanism
Colonialism	Transnational capitalism
Nature/culture	Fields of difference
Co-operation	Communications enhancement
Freud	Lacan
Sex	Surrogacy
Labour	Robotics
Mind	Artificial intelligence
Second World War	Star Wars
White capitalist patriarchy	Informatics of domination

It is impossible to see the entries in the right-hand column as 'natural', a real-ization that subverts naturalistic status for the left-hand column as well. From the eighteenth to the mid-twentieth centuries, the great historical construc-tions of gender, race, and class were embedded in the organically marked bodies of woman, the colonized or enslaved, and the worker. Those inhabiting these marked bodies have been symbolically other to the fictive rational self of universal, and so unmarked, species man, a coherent subject. The marked or-ganic body has been a critical locus of cultural and political contestation, crucial both to the language of the liberatory politics of identity and to sys-tems of domination drawing on widely shared languages of nature as resource for the appropriations of culture. For example, the sexualized bodies of nineteenth-century middle-class medical advice literature in England and the United States, in their female form organized around the maternal function and the physical site of the uterus and in their male form ordered by the sper-matic economy tied closely to the nervous system, were part of an elaborate discourse of organic economy. The narrative field in which these bodies moved generated accounts of rational citizenship, bourgeois family life, and prophy-laxis against sexual pollution and inefficiency, such as prostitution, criminal-ity, or race suicide. Some feminist politics argued for the full inclusion of women in the body politic on grounds of maternal functions in the domestic economy extended to a public world. Late into the twentieth century, gay and lesbian politics have ironically and critically embraced the marked bodies constructed in nineteenth- and twentieth-century sexologies and gender identity medicines to create a complex humanist discourse of sexual libera-tion. Negritude, feminine writing, various separatisms, and other recent cul-tural movements have both drawn on and subverted the logics of naturalization central to biomedical discourse on race and gender in the histories of coloni-zation and male supremacy. In all of these various, oppositionally interlinked, political and biomedical accounts, the body remained a relatively unambiguous locus of identity, agency, labour, and hierarchicalized function. Both scientific humanisms and biological determinisms could be authorized and contested in terms of the biological organism crafted in post-eighteenth-century life sciences.

But how do narratives of the normal and the pathological work when the biological and medical body is symbolized and operated upon, not as a system of work, organized by the hierarchical division of labour, ordered by a privi-leged dialectic between highly localized nervous and reproductive functions, but instead as a coded text, organized as an engineered communications system, ordered by a fluid and dispersed command-control-intelligence network? From the mid-twentieth century, biomedical discourses have been progressively organized around a very different set of technologies and practices, which have destabilized the symbolic privilege of the hierarchical, localized, organic body. Concurrently—and out of some of the same historical matrices of decolonization, multinational capitalism, world-wide high-tech militarization, and the emergence of new collective political actors in local and global politics from among those persons previously consigned to labour in silence—the question of 'differences' has destabilized humanist discourses of liberation based on a politics of identity and substantive unity. Feminist theory as a self-conscious discursive practice has been generated in this post–Second World War period characterized by the translation of Western scientific and political languages of nature from those based on work, localization, and the marked body to those based on codes, dispersal and networking, and the fragmented postmodern subject. An account of the biomedical, biotechnical body must start from the multiple molecular interfacings of genetic, nervous, endocrine, and immune systems. Biology is about recognition and misrecognition, coding errors, the body's reading practices (for example, frameshift mutations), and billion-dollar projects to sequence the human genome to be published and stored in a national genetic 'library'. The body is conceived as a strategic system, highly militarized in key arenas of imagery and practice. Sex, sexuality, and reproduction are theorized in terms of local investment strategies; the body ceases to be a stable spatial map of normalized functions and instead emerges as a highly mobile field of strategic differences. The biomedical-biotechnical body is a semiotic system, a complex meaning-producing field, for which the discourse of immunology, that is, the central biomedical discourse on recognition/misrecognition, has become a high-stakes practice in many senses.

In relation to objects like biotic components and codes, one must think, not in terms of laws of growth and essential properties, but rather in terms of strategies of design, boundary constraints, rates of flows, system logics, and costs of lowering constraints. Sexual reproduction becomes one possible strategy among many, with costs and benefits theorized as a function of the system environment. Disease is a subspecies of information malfunction or communications pathology; disease is a process of misrecognition or transgression of the boundaries of a strategic assemblage called self. Ideologies of sexual reproduction can no longer easily call upon the notions of unproblematic sex and sex role as organic aspects in 'healthy' natural objects like organisms and families. Likewise for race, ideologies of human diversity have to be developed in terms of frequencies of parameters and fields of power-charged differences, not essences and natural origins or homes. Race and sex, like individuals, are artefacts sustained or undermined by the discursive nexus of knowledge and power. Any objects or persons can be reasonably thought of in terms of disassembly and reassembly; no 'natural' architectures constrain system design. Design is none the less highly constrained. What counts as a 'unit', a one, is highly problematic, not a permanent given. Individuality is a strategic defence problem.

One should expect control strategies to concentrate on boundary conditions and interfaces, on rates of flow across boundaries, not on the integrity of natural objects. 'Integrity' or 'sincerity' of the Western self gives way to decision procedures, expert systems, and resource investment strategies. 'Degrees of freedom' becomes a very powerful metaphor for politics. Human beings, like any other component or subsystem, must be localized in a system architecture whose basic modes of operation are probabilistic. No objects, spaces, or bodies are sacred in themselves; any component can be interfaced with any other if the proper standard, the proper code, can be constructed for processing signals in a common language. In particular, there is no ground for ontologically opposing the organic, the technical, and the textual.[3] But neither is there any ground for opposing the *mythical* to the organic, textual, and technical. Their convergences are more important than their residual oppositions. The privileged pathology affecting all kinds of components in this universe is stress—communications breakdown. In the body stress is theorized to operate by 'depressing' the immune system. Bodies have become cyborgs—cybernetic organisms—compounds of hybrid techno-organic embodiment and textuality (Haraway, 1985). The cyborg is text, machine, body, and metaphor—all theorized and engaged in practice in terms of communications.

Cyborgs for Earthly Survival[4]

However, just as the nineteenth- and twentieth-century organism accommodated a diverse field of cultural, political, financial, theoretic and technical contestation, so also the cyborg is a contested and heterogeneous construct. It is capable of sustaining oppositional and liberatory projects at

the levels of research practice, cultural productions, and political intervention. This large theme may be introduced by examining contrasting constructions of the late twentieth-century biotechnical body, or of other
contemporary postmodern communications systems. These constructs may
be conceived and built in at least two opposed modes: (1) in terms of master
control principles, articulated within a rationalist paradigm of language
and embodiment; or (2) in terms of complex, structurally embedded semiosis with many 'generators of diversity' within a counter-rationalist (*not*
irrationalist) or hermeneutic/situationist/constructivist discourse readily
available within Western science and philosophy. Terry Winograd and Fer-
nando Flores' (1986) joint work on *Understanding Computers and Cognition*
is particularly suggestive for thinking about the potentials for cultural/sci-
entific/political contestation over the technologies of representation and
embodiment of 'difference' within immunological discourse, whose object
of knowledge is a kind of 'artificial intelligence/language/communication
system of the biological body'.[5]

Winograd and Flores conduct a detailed critique of the rationalist paradigm
for understanding embodied (or 'structure-determined') perceptual and language systems and for designing computers that can function as prostheses in
human projects. In the simple form of the rationalist model of cognition,

> One takes for granted the existence of an objective reality made up of things
> bearing properties and entering into relations. A cognitive being gathers 'in-
> formation' about those things and builds up a mental 'model' which will be in
> some respects correct (a faithful representation of reality) and in other re-
> spects incorrect. Knowledge is a storehouse of representations that can be
> called upon to do reasoning and that can be translated into language. Think-
> ing is a process of manipulating those representations'. (Winograd, in Edwards
> and Gordon, forthcoming)

It is this doctrine of representation that Winograd finds wrong in many
senses, including on the plane of political and moral discourse usually suppressed in scientific writing. The doctrine, he continues, is also technically
wrong for further guiding research in software design: 'Contrary to common
consensus, the "commonsense" understanding of language, thought, and rationality inherent in this tradition ultimately *hinders* the fruitful application
of computer technology to human life and work'. Drawing on Heidegger,
Gadamer, Maturana, and others, Winograd and Flores develop a doctrine of

interdependence of interpreter and interpreted, which are not discrete and independent entities. Situated preunderstandings are critical to all communication and action. 'Structure-determined systems' with histories shaped through processes of 'structural-coupling' give a better approach to perception than doctrines of representation.

> Changes in the environment have the potential of changing the relative patterns of activity within the nervous system itself that in turn orient the organism's behavior, a perspective that invalidates the assumption that we acquire representations of our environment. Interpretation, that is, arises as a necessary consequence of the structure of biological beings. (Winograd, in Edwards and Gordon, forthcoming)

Winograd conceives the coupling of the inner and outer worlds of organisms and ecosystems, of organisms with each other, or of organic and technical structures in terms of metaphors of language, communication, and construction—but not in terms of a rationalist doctrine of mind and language or a disembodied instrumentalism. Linguistic acts involve shared acts of interpretation, and they are fundamentally tied to engaged location in a structured world. Context is a fundamental matter, not as surrounding 'information', but as co-structure or co-text. Cognition, engagement, and situation-dependence are linked concepts for Winograd, technically and philosophically. Language is not about description, but about commitment. The point applies to 'natural' language and to 'built' language.

How would such a way of theorizing the technics and biologics of communication affect immune system discourse about the body's 'technology' for recognizing self and other and for mediating between 'mind' and 'body' in postmodern culture? Just as computer design is a map of and for ways of living, the immune system is in some sense a diagram of relationships and a guide for action in the face of questions about the boundaries of the self and about mortality. Immune system discourse is about constraint and possibility for engaging in a world full of 'difference', replete with non-self. Winograd and Flores' approach contains a way to contest for notions of pathology, or 'breakdown', without militarizing the terrain of the body.

> Breakdowns play a central role in human understanding. A breakdown is not a negative situation to be avoided, but a situation of non-obviousness, in which

some aspect of the network of tools that we are engaged in using is brought forth to visibility . . . A breakdown reveals the nexus of relations necessary for us to accomplish our task . . . This creates a clear objective for design—to anticipate the form of breakdowns and provide a space of possibilities for action when they occur. (Winograd, in Edwards and Gordon, forthcoming)

This is not a Star Wars or Strategic Computing Initiative relation to vulnerability, but neither does it deny therapeutic action. It insists on locating therapeutic, reconstructive action (and so theoretic understanding) in terms of situated purposes, not fantasies of the utterly defended self in a body as automated militarized factory, a kind of ultimate self as Robotic Battle Manager meeting the enemy (not-self) as it invades in the form of bits of foreign information threatening to take over the master control codes.

Situated purposes are necessarily finite, rooted in partiality and a subtle play of same and different, maintenance and dissolution. Winograd and Flores' linguistic systems are 'denaturalized', fully constructivist entities; and in that sense they are postmodern cyborgs that do not rely on impermeable boundaries between the organic, technical, and textual. But their linguistic/communication systems are distinctly oppositional to the AI cyborgs of an 'information society', with its exterminist pathologies of final abstraction from vulnerability, and so from embodiment.[6]

The One and the Many: Selves, Individuals, Units, and Subjects

What is constituted as an individual within postmodern biotechnical, biomedical discourse? There is no easy answer to this question, for even the most reliable Western individuated bodies, the mice and men of a well-equipped laboratory, neither stop nor start at the skin, which is itself something of a teeming jungle threatening illicit fusions, especially from the perspective of a scanning electron microscope. The multi-billion-dollar project to sequence 'the human genome' in a definitive genetic library might be seen as one practical answer to the construction of 'man' as 'subject' of science. The genome project is a kind of technology of postmodern humanism, defining 'the' genome by reading and writing it. The technology required for this particular kind of literacy is suggested by the advertisment for MacroGene Workstation. The ad ties the mythical, organic, technical, and textual together in its graphic invocation of the 'missing link' crawling from the water on to the land, while the text reads, 'In the LKB MacroGene Workstation [for sequencing nucleic acids], there are no "missing links".' The monster *Ichthyostega* crawling out of the deep in one of earth's great transitions is a perfect figure for late twentieth-century bodily and technical metamorphoses. An act of canonization to make the theorists of the humanities pause, the standard reference work called the human genome would be the means through which human diversity and its pathologies could be tamed in the exhaustive code kept by a national or international genetic bureau of standards. Costs of storage of the giant dictionary will probably exceed costs of its production, but this is a mundane matter to any librarian (Roberts, 1987a,b,c; Kanigel, 1987). Access to this standard for 'man' will be a matter of international financial, patent, and similar struggles. The Peoples of the Book will finally have a standard genesis story. In the beginning was the copy.

The Human Genome Project might define postmodern species being (*pace* the philosophers), but what of *individual* being? Richard Dawkins raised this knotty problem in *The Extended Phenotype*. He noted that in 1912, Julian Huxley defined individuality in biological terms as 'literally indivisibility— the quality of being sufficiently heterogeneous in form to be rendered nonfunctional if cut in half' (Dawkins, 1982, p. 250). That seems a promising start. In Huxley's terms, surely you or I would count as an individual, while many worms would not. The individuality of worms was not achieved even at the height of bourgeois liberalism, so no cause to worry there. But Huxley's definition does not answer *which function* is at issue. Nothing answers that in the abstract; it depends on what is to be done.[7] You or I (whatever problematic address these pronouns have) might be an individual for some purposes, but not for others. This is a normal ontological state for cyborgs and women, if not for Aristotelians and men. Function is about action. Here is where Dawkins has a radical solution, as he proposes a view of individuality that is strategic at every level of meaning. There are many kinds of individuals for Dawkins, but one kind has primacy. 'The whole purpose of our search for a "unit of selection" is to discover a suitable actor to play the leading role in our metaphors of purpose' (1982, p. 91). The 'metaphors of purpose' come down to a single bottom line: replication. 'A successful replicator is one that succeeds in lasting, in the form of copies, for a very long time measured in generations, and succeeds in propogating many copies of itself (1982, pp. 87–8).

The replicator fragment whose individuality finally matters most, in the constructed time of evolutionary theory, is not particularly 'unitary'. For all that it serves, for Dawkins, as the 'unit' of natural selection, the replicator's boundaries are not fixed and its inner reaches remain mutable. But still, these units must be a bit smaller than a 'single' gene coding for a protein. Units are only good enough to sustain the technology of copying. Like the replicons' borders, the boundaries of other strategic assemblages are not fixed either—it all has to do with the broad net cast by strategies of replication in a world where self and other are very much at stake.

> The integrated multi-cellular organism is a phenomenon which has emerged as a result of natural selection on primitively selfish replicators. It has paid replicators to behave gregariously [so much for 'harmony', in the short run]. The phenotypic power by which they ensure their survival is in principle extended and unbounded. In practice the organism has arisen as a partially bounded local concentration, a shared knot of replicator power. (Dawkins, 1982, p. 264)

'In principle extended and unbounded'—this is a remarkable statement of interconnectedness, but of a very particular kind, one that leads to theorizing the living world as one vast arms race. '[P]henotypes that extend outside the body do not have to be inanimate artefacts: they themselves can be built of living tissue . . . I shall show that it is logically sensible to regard parasite genes as having phenotypic expression in host bodies *and behaviour*' (1982, p. 210, emphasis mine). But the being who serves as another's phenotype is itself populated by propagules with their own replicative ends. '[A]n animal will not necessarily submit passively to being manipulated, and an evolutionary "arms race" is expected to develop' (1982, p. 39). This is an arms race that must take account of the stage of the development of the means of bodily production and the costs of maintaining it:

> The many-celled body is a machine for the production of single-celled propagules. Large bodies, like elephants, are best seen as heavy plant and machinery, a temporary resource drain, invested so as to improve later propagule production. In a sense the germ-line would 'like' to reduce capital investment in heavy machinery . . . (1982, p. 254)

Large capital is indeed a drain; small is beautiful. But you and I have required large capital investments, in more than genetic terms. Perhaps we should keep an eye on the germ-line, especially since 'we'—the non-germ-line components of adult mammals (unless you identify with your haploid gametes and their contents, and some do)—cannot be copy units. 'We' can only aim for a defended self, not copy fidelity, the property of other sorts of units. Within 'us' is the most threatening other—the propagules, whose phenotype we, temporarily, are.

What does all this have to do with the discourse of immunology as a map of systems of 'difference' in late capitalism? Let me attempt to convey the flavour of representations of the curious bodily object called the human immune system, culled from textbooks and research reports published in the 1980s. The IS is composed of about 10 to the 12th cells, two orders of magnitude more cells than the nervous system has. These cells are regenerated throughout life from pluripotent stem cells that themselves remain undifferentiated. From embryonic life through adulthood, the immune system is sited in several relatively amorphous tissues and organs, including the thymus, bone marrow, spleen, and lymph nodes; but a large fraction of its cells are in the blood and lymph circulatory systems and in body fluids and spaces. There are two major cell lineages to the system. The first is the *lymphocytes*, which include the several types of T cells (helper, suppressor, killer, and variations of all these) and the B cells (each type of which can produce only one sort of the vast array of potential circulating antibodies). T and B cells have particular specificities capable of recognizing almost any molecular array of the right size that can ever exist, no matter how clever industrial chemistry gets. This specificity is enabled by a baroque somatic mutation mechanism, clonal selection, and a polygenic receptor or marker system. The second immune cell lineage is the *mononuclear phagocyte system*, including the multi-talented macrophages, which, in addition to their other recognition skills and connections, also appear to share receptors and some hormonal peptide products with neural cells. Besides the cellular compartment, the immune system comprises a vast array of circulating acellular products, such as antibodies, lymphokines, and complement components. These molecules mediate communication among components of the immune system, but also between the immune system and the nervous and endocrine systems, thus linking the body's multiple control and co-ordination sites and functions. The genetics of the immune system cells, with their high rates of somatic mutation and gene product splicings and rearrangings to make finished surface receptors and antibodies, makes a mockery of the notion of a constant genome even within 'one' body. The hierarchical body of old has given way to a network-body of truly amazing complexity and specificity. The immune system is everywhere and nowhere.

Its specificities are indefinite if not infinite, and they arise randomly; yet these extraordinary variations are the critical means of maintaining individual bodily coherence.

In the early 1970s, the Nobel Prize–winning immunologist, Niels Jerne, proposed a theory of immune system self-regulation, called the network theory, that must complete this minimalist account (Jerne, 1985; Golub, 1987, pp. 379–92). 'The network theory differs from other immunological thinking because it endows the immune system with the ability to regulate itself using only itself' (Golub, 1987, p. 379). Jerne's basic idea was that any antibody molecule must be able to act functionally as both antibody to some antigen *and* as antigen for the production of an antibody to itself, albeit at another region of 'itself.' All these sites have acquired a nomenclature sufficiently daunting to keep popular understanding of the theory at bay indefinitely, but the basic conception is simple. The concatenation of internal recognitions and responses would go on indefinitely, in a series of interior mirrorings of sites on immunoglobulin molecules, such that the immune system would always be in a state of dynamic internal responding. It would never be passive, 'at rest', awaiting an activating stimulus from a hostile outside. In a sense, there could be no *exterior* antigenic structure, no 'invader', that the immune system had not already 'seen' and mirrored internally. 'Self' and 'other' lose their rationalistic oppositional quality and become subtle plays of partially mirrored readings and responses. The notion of the *internal image* is the key to the theory, and it entails the premise that every member of the immune system is capable of interacting with every other member. As with Dawkins's extended phenotype, a radical conception of *connection* emerges unexpectedly at the heart of postmodern moves.

> This is a unique idea, which if correct means that all possible reactions that the immune system can carry out with epitopes in the world outside of the animal are already accounted for in the internal system of paratopes and idiotopes already present inside the animal. (Golub, 1987, pp. 382–3)

Jerne's conception recalls Winograd and Flores' insistence on structural coupling and structure-determined systems in their approach to perception. The internal, structured activity of the system is the crucial issue, not formal representations of the 'outer' world within the 'inner' world of the communications system that is the organism. Both Jerne's and Winograd's formulations resist the means of conceptualization facilitated most readily by a rationalist theory of recognition or representation. In discussing what he called the deep structure and generative grammar of the immune system, Jerne argued that 'an identical structure can appear on many structures in many contexts and be reacted to by the reader or by the immune system' (quoted in Golub, 1987, p. 384).[8]

Does the immune system—the fluid, dispersed, networking techno-organic-textual-mythic system that ties together the more stodgy and localized centres of the body through its acts of recognition—represent the ultimate sign of altruistic evolution towards wholeness, in the form of the means of co-ordination of a coherent biological self? In a word, no, at least not in Leo Buss's (1987) persuasive postmodern theoretic scheme of *The Evolution of Individuality*.

Constituting a kind of technological holism, the earliest cybernetic communications systems theoretic approaches to the biological body from the late 1940s through the 1960s privileged co-ordination, effected by 'circular causal feedback mechanisms'. In the 1950s, biological bodies became technological communications systems, but they were not quite fully reconstituted as sites of 'difference' in its postmodern sense—the play of signifiers and replicators in a strategic field whose significance depended problematically, at best, on a world outside itself. Even the first synthetic proclamations of sociobiology, particularly E.O. Wilson's *Sociobiology: The New Synthesis* (1975), maintained a fundamentally techno-organicist or holist ontology of the cybernetic organism, or cyborg, repositioned in evolutionary theory by post–Second World War extensions and revisions of the principle of natural selection. This 'conservative' dimension of Wilson and of several other sociobiologists has been roundly criticized by evolutionary theorists who have gone much further in denaturing the co-ordinating principles of organismic biology at every level of biotic organization, from gene fragments through ecosystems. The sociobiological theory of inclusive fitness maintained a kind of envelope around the organism and its kin, but that envelope has been opened repeatedly in late 1970s' and 1980s' evolutionary theory.

Dawkins (1976, 1982) has been among the most radical disrupters of cyborg biological holism, and in that sense he is most deeply informed by a postmodern consciousness, in which the logic of the permeability among the textual, the technic, and the biotic and of the deep theorization of all possible texts and bodies as strategic assemblages has made the notions of 'organism' or 'individual' extremely problematic. He ignores the mythic, but it pervades his texts. 'Organism' and 'individual' have not disappeared; rather, they have been fully denaturalized. That is, they are ontologically contingent constructs from the point of view of the biologist, not just in the loose ravings of a cultural critic or feminist historian of science.

Leo Buss reinterpreted two important remaining processes or objects that had continued to resist such denaturing: (1) embryonic development, the very process of the construction of an individual; and (2) immune system interactions, the iconic means for maintaining the integrity of the one in the face of the many. His basic argument for the immune system is that it is made up of several variant cell lineages, each engaged in its own replicative 'ends'. The contending cell lineages serve somatic function because

> the receptors that ensure delivery of growth-enhancing mitogens also compel somatic function. The cytotoxic T-cell recognizes its target with the same receptor arrangement used by the macrophage to activate that cell lineage. It is compelled to attack the infected cell by the same receptor required for it to obtain mitogens from helper cells . . . The immune system works by exploiting the inherent propensity of cells to further their own rate of replication. (Buss, 1987, p. 87)

The individual is a constrained accident, not the highest fruit of earth history's labours. In metazoan organisms, at least two units of selection, cellular and individual, pertain; and their 'harmony' is highly contingent. The parts are not *for* the whole. There is no part/whole relation at all, in any sense Aristotle would recognize. Pathology results from a conflict of interests between the cellular and organismic units of selection. Buss has thereby recast the multi-cellular organism's means of self-recognition, of the maintenance of 'wholes', from an illustration of the priority of co-ordination in biology's and medicine's ontology to a chief witness for the irreducible vulnerability, multiplicity, and contingency of every construct of individuality.

The potential meanings of such a move for conceptualizations of pathology and therapeutics within Western biomedicine are, to say the least, intriguing. Is there a way to turn the discourse suggested by Jerne, Dawkins, and Buss into an oppositional/alternative/liberatory approach analogous to that of Winograd and Flores in cognition and computer research? Is this postmodern body, this construct of always vulnerable and contingent individuality, *necessarily* an automated Star Wars battlefield in the now extra-terrestrial space of the late twentieth-century Western scientific body's intimate interior? What might we learn about this question by attending to the many contemporary representations of the immune system, in visualization practices, self-help doctrines, biologists' metaphors, discussions of immune system diseases, and science fiction? This is a large enquiry, and in the paragraphs that follow I only begin to sketch a few of the sometimes promising but more often profoundly disturbing recent cultural productions of the postmodern immune system-mediated body.[9] At this stage, the analysis can only serve to sharpen, not to answer, the question.

Immune Power: Images, Fictions, and Fixations

This chapter opened with a reminder that science has been a travel discourse, intimately implicated in the other great colonizing and liberatory readings and writings so basic to modern constitutions and dissolutions of the marked bodies of race, sex, and class. The colonizing and the liberatory, and the constituting and the dissolving, are related as internal images. So I continue this tour through the science museum of immunology's cultures with the 'land, ho!' effect described by my colleague, James Clifford, as we waited in our university chancellor's office for a meeting in 1986. The chancellor's office walls featured beautiful colour-enhanced photographic portraits of the outer planets of earth's solar system. Each 'photograph' created the effect for the viewer of having been there. It seemed some other observer must have been there, with a perceptual system like ours and a good camera; somehow it must have been possible to *see* the land masses of Jupiter and Saturn coming into view of the great ships of *Voyager* as they crossed the empty reaches of space. Twentieth-century people are used to the idea that all photographs are constructs in some sense, and that the appearance that a photograph gives of being a 'message without a code', that is, what is pictured being simply *there*, is an effect of many layers of history, including prominently, technology (Barthes, 1982; Haraway, 1984–5; Petchesky, 1987). But the photographs of the outer planets up the ante on this issue by orders of magnitude. The wonderful pictures have gone through processes of construction that make the metaphor of the 'eye of the camera' completely misleading. The chancellor's snapshot of Jupiter is a postmodern photographic portrait—a denatured construct of the first order, which has the effect of utter naturalistic realism. *Someone* was there. Land, ho! But that some*one* was a spaceship that sent back digitalized signals to a whole world of transformers and imagers on a distant place called 'earth', where art photographs could be produced to give a reassuring sense of the *thereness* of Jupiter, and, not incidentally, of *spacemen*, or at least virtual space-men, whose eyes would see in the same colour spectrum as an earthly primate's.

The same analysis must accompany any viewing of the wonderful photo-graphs and other imaging precipitates of the components of the immune sys-tem. The cover of *Immunology: A Synthesis* (Golub, 1987) features an iconic replication of its title's allusion to synthesis: a multi-coloured computer graphic of the three-dimensional structure of insulin showing its antigenic determi-nants clustered in particular regions. Golub elicits consciousness of the *con-structed* quality of such images in his credit: 'Image created by John A. Tainer and Elizabeth D. Getzoff'. Indeed, the conventional trope of scientist as artist runs throughout Golub's text, such that scientific construction takes on the particular resonances of high art and genius, more than of critical theories of productions of the postmodern body. But the publications of Lennart Nils-son's photographs, in the coffee table art book *The Body Victorious* (Nilsson, 1987) and in the *National Geographic* (Jaret, 1986), allow the 'land, ho!' effect unmediated scope. The blasted scenes, sumptuous textures, evocative colours, and ET monsters of the immune landscape are simply *there*, inside us. A white extruding tendril of a pseudopodinous macrophage ensnares a bacterium; the hillocks of chromosomes lie flattened on a blue-hued moonscape of some other planet; an infected cell buds myriads of deadly virus particles into the reaches of inner space where more cells will be victimized; the auto-immune-disease-ravaged head of a femur glows in a kind of sunset on a non-living world; can-cer cells are surrounded by the lethal mobil squads of killer T cells that throw chemical poisons into the self's malignant traitor cells.

The equation of Outer Space and Inner Space, and of their conjoined dis-courses of extra-terrestrialism, ultimate frontiers, and high technology war, is quite literal in the official history celebrating 100 years of the National Geo-graphic Society (Bryan, 1987). The chapter that recounts the *National Geograph-ic*'s coverage of the Mercury, Gemini, Apollo, and Mariner voyages is called 'Space' and introduced with the epigraph, 'The Choice is the Universe—or Nothing'. The final chapter, full of Nilsson's and other biomedical images, is entitled 'Inner Space' and introduced with the epigraph, 'The Stuff of the Stars Has Come Alive' (Bryan, 1987, pp. 454, 352). It is photography that convinces the viewer of the fraternal relation of inner and outer space. But curiously, in outer space, we see spacemen fitted into explorer craft or floating about as in-dividuated cosmic foetuses, while in the supposed earthy space of our own interiors, we see non-humanoid strangers who are supposed to be the means by which our bodies sustain our integrity and individuality, indeed our humanity in the face of a world of others. We seem invaded not just by the threatening 'non-selves' that the immune system guards against, but more fundamentally by our own strange parts. No wonder auto-immune disease carries such awful significance, marked from the first suspicion of its existence in 1901 by Morgenroth and Ehrlich's term, *horror autotoxicus.*

The trope of space invaders evokes a particular question about directionality of travel: in which direction is there an invasion? From space to earth? From outside to inside? The reverse? Are boundaries defended symmetrically? Is inner/outer a hierarchicalized opposition? Expansionist Western medical discourse in colonizing contexts has been obsessed with the notion of contagion and hostile penetration of the healthy body, as well as of terrorism and mutiny from within. This approach to disease involved a stunning reversal: the colonized was perceived as the invader. In the face of the disease genocides accompanying European 'penetration' of the globe, the 'coloured' body of the colonized was constructed as the dark source of infection, pollution, disorder, and so on, that threatened to overwhelm white manhood (cities, civilization, the family, the white personal body) with its decadent emanations. In establishing the game parks of Africa, European law turned indigenous human inhabitants of the 'nature reserves' into poachers, invaders in their own terrain, or into part of the wildlife. The residue of the history of colonial tropical medicine and natural history in late twentieth-century immune discourse should not be underestimated. Discourses on parasitic diseases and AIDS provide a surfeit of examples.

The tones of colonial discourse are also audible in the opening paragraphs of *Immunology: The Science of Non-Self Discrimination*, where the dangers to individuality are almost lasciviously recounted. The first danger is 'fusion of individuals':

> In a jungle or at the bottom of the sea, organisms—especially plants, but also all kinds of sessile animals—are often in such close proximity that they are in constant danger of losing their individuality by fusion . . . But only in the imagination of an artist does all-out fusion occur; in reality, organisms keep pretty much separate, no matter how near to one another they live and grow. (Klein, 1982, p. 3)

In those exotic, allotropic places, any manner of contact might occur to threaten proper mammalian self-definition. Harmony of the organism, that favourite theme of biologists, is explained in terms of the aggressive defence of individuality; and Klein advocates devoting as much time in the undergraduate biology curriculum to defence as to genetics and evolution. It reads a bit like the defence department fighting the social services budget for federal funds. Immunology for Klein is 'intraorganismic defense reaction', proceding by *recognition, processing,* and *response.'* Klein defines *'self'* as 'everything constituting an integral part of a given individual' (1982, p. 5; emphasis in original). What counts as an individual, then, is the nub of the matter. Everything else is *'not-self'* and elicits a defence reaction if boundaries are crossed. But this chapter has repeatedly tried to make problematic just what does count as self, within the discourses of biology and medicine, much less in the postmodern world at large.

A diagram of the 'Evolution of Recognition Systems' in a recent immunology textbook makes clear the intersection of the themes of literally 'wonderful' diversity, escalating complexity, the self as a defended stronghold, and extra-terrestrialism. Under a diagram culminating in the evolution of the mammals, represented without comment by a mouse and a *fully-suited spaceman,*[10] who appears to be stepping out, perhaps on the surface of the moon, is this explanation:

> From the humble amoeba searching for food . . . to the mammal with its sophisticated humoral and cellular immune mechanisms . . . the process of **'self versus non-self recognition'** shows a steady development, keeping pace with the increasing need of animals to maintain their integrity in a hostile environment. The decision at which point 'immunity' appeared is thus a purely semantic one'. (Playfair, 1984, p. 3; emphasis in original)

These are the semantics of defence and invasion. When is a self enough of a self that its boundaries become central to entire institutionalized discourses in medicine, war, and business? Immunity and invulnerability are intersecting concepts, a matter of consequence in a nuclear culture unable to accommodate the experience of death and finitude within available liberal discourse on the collective and personal individual. Life is a window of vulnerability. It seems a mistake to close it. The perfection of the fully defended, 'victorious' self is a chilling fantasy, linking phagocytotic amoeba and moon-voyaging man cannibalizing the earth in an evolutionary teleology of post-apocalypse extra-terrestrialism. It is a chilling fantasy, whether located in the abstract spaces of national discourse, or in the equally abstract spaces of our interior bodies.

Images of the immune system as battlefield abound in science sections of daily newspapers and in popular magazines, for example, *Time* magazine's 1984 graphic for the AIDS virus's 'invasion' of the cell-as-factory. The virus is imaged as a tank, and the viruses ready for export from the expropriated cells are lined up as tanks ready to continue their advance on the body as a productive force. The *National Geographic* explicitly punned on Star Wars in its graphic entitled 'Cell Wars' in Jaret's 'The Wars Within' (1986, pp. 708–9). The battle imagery is conventional, not unique to a nuclear and Cold War era, but it has taken on all the specific markings of those particular historical crises. The militarized, automated factory is a favourite convention among immune system illustrators and photographic processors. The specific historical markings of a Star Wars–maintained individuality[11] are enabled in large measure by high-technology visualization technologies, which are also critical to the material means of conducting postmodern war, science, and business, such as computer-aided graphics, artificial intelligence software, and many kinds of scanning systems.

'Imaging' or 'visualization' has also become part of therapeutic practice in both self-help and clinical settings, and here the contradictory possibilities and potent ambiguities over biomedical technology, body, self, and other emerge poignantly. The immune system has become a lucrative terrain of self-development practices, a scene where contending forms of power are evoked and practised. In *Dr. Berger's Immune Power Diet*, the 'invincible you' is urged to 'put immune power to work for you' by using your 'IQ (Immune Quotient)' (Berger, 1985, p. 186). In the great tradition of evangelical preaching, the reader is asked if 'You are ready to make the immune power commitment?' (1985, p. 4). In visualization self-help, the sufferer learns in a state of deep relaxation to image the processes of disease and healing, in order both to gain more control in many senses and to engage in a kind of meditation on the meanings of living and dying from an embodied vantage point in the microplaces of the postmodern body. These visualization exercises need not be prototypes for Star Wars, but they often are in the advice literature. The *National Geographic* endorses this approach in its description of one such effort: 'Combining fun and therapy, a young cancer patient at the M. D. Anderson Hospital in Houston, Texas, zaps cancer cells in the "Killer T Cell" video game' (Jaret, 1987, p. 705). Other researchers have designed protocols to determine if aggressive imagery is effective in mediating the healing work of visualization therapies, or if the relaxation techniques and non-aggressive imagery would 'work'. As with any function, 'work' for *what* cannot remain unexamined, and not just in terms of the statistics of cancer survival. Imaging is one of the vectors in the 'epidemics of signification' spreading in the cultures of postmodern therapeutics. What is at stake is the kind of collective and personal selves that will be constructed in this organic-technical-mythic-textual semiosis. As cyborgs in this field of meanings, how can 'we', late-twentieth-century Westerners, image our vulnerability as a window on to life?

Immunity can also be conceived in terms of shared specificities; of the semi-permeable self able to engage with others (human and non-human, inner and outer), but always with finite consequences; of situated possibilities and impossibilities of individuation and identification; and of partial fusions and dangers. The problematic multiplicities of postmodern selves, so potently figured *and* repressed in the lumpy discourses of immunology, must be brought into other emerging Western and multi-cultural discourses on health, sickness, individuality, humanity, and death.

The science fictions of the black American writer, Octavia Butler, invite both sobering and hopeful reflections on this large cultural project. Drawing on the resources of black and women's histories and liberatory movements, Butler has been consumed with an interrogation into the boundaries of what counts as human and into the limits of the concept and practices of claiming 'property in the self' as the ground of 'human' individuality and selfhood. In *Clay's Ark* (1984) Butler explores the consequences of an extra-terrestrial disease invading earth in the bodies of returned spacemen. The invaders have become an intimate part of all the cells of the infected bodies, changing human beings at the level of their most basic selves. The invaders have a single imperative that they enforce on their hosts: replication. Indeed, *Clay's Ark* reads like *The Extended Phenotype;* the invaders seem disturbingly like the 'ultimate' unit of selection that haunts the biopolitical imaginations of postmodern evolutionary theorists and economic planners. The humans in Butler's profoundly dystopic story struggle to maintain their own areas of choice and self-definition in the face of the disease they have become. Part of their task is to craft a transformed relation to the 'other' within themselves and to the children born to infected parents. The offsprings' quadruped form archetypically marks them as the Beast itself, but they are also the future of what it will mean to be human. The disease will be global. The task of the multi-racial women and men of *Clay's Ark* comes to be to reinvent the dialectics of self and other within the emerging epidemics of signification signalled by extra-terrestrialism in inner and outer space. Success is not judged in this book; only the naming of the task is broached.

In *Dawn*, the first novel of Butler's series on *Xenogenesis*, the themes of global holocaust and the threateningly intimate other as self emerge again. Butler's is a fiction predicated on the natural status of adoption and the un-natural violence of kin. Butler explores the interdigitations of human, ma-chine, non-human animal or alien, and their mutants, especially in relation to the intimacies of bodily exchange and mental communication. Her fic-tion in the opening novel of *Xenogenesis* is about the monstrous fear and hope that the child will not, after all, be like the parent. There is never one parent. Monsters share more than the word's root with the verb 'to demon-strate'; monsters signify. Butler's fiction is about resistance to the imperative to recreate the sacred image of the same (Butler, 1978). Butler is like 'Doris Lessing, Marge Piercy, Joanna Russ, Ursula LeGuin, Margaret Atwood, and Christa Wolf, [for whom] reinscribing the narrative of catastrophe engages them in the invention of an alternate fictional world in which the other (gender, race, species) is no longer subordinated to the same' (Brewer, 1987, p. 46).

Catastrophe, survival, and metamorphosis are Butler's constant themes. From the perspective of an ontology based on mutation, metamorphosis, and the diaspora, restoring an original sacred image can be a bad joke. Origins are precisely that to which Butler's people do not have access. But patterns are an-other matter. At the end of *Dawn*, Butler has Lilith—whose name recalls her original unfaithful double, the repudiated wife of Adam—pregnant with the child of five progenitors, who come from two species, at least three genders, two sexes, and an indeterminate number of races. Preoccupied with marked bodies, Butler writes not of Cain or Ham, but of Lilith, the woman of colour whose confrontations with the terms of selfhood, survival, and reproduction in the face of repeated ultimate catastrophe presage an ironic salvation history, with a salutary twist on the promise of a woman who will crush the head of the serpent. Butler's salvation history is not utopian, but remains deeply furrowed by the contradictions and questions of power within all communication. Therefore, her narrative has the possibility of figuring something other than the Second Coming of the sacred image. Some other order of difference might be possible in *Xenogenesis*—and in immunology.

In the story, Lilith Iyapo is a young American black woman rescued with a motley assortment of remnants of humanity from an earth in the grip of nuclear war. Like all the surviving humans, Lilith has lost everything. Her son and her second-generation Nigerian-American husband had died in an accident before the war. She had gone back to school, vaguely thinking she might become an anthropologist. But nuclear catastrophe, even more radically and comprehensively than the slave trade and history's other great genocides, ripped all rational and natural connections with past and future from her and everyone else. Except for intermittent periods of questioning, the human remnant is kept in suspended animation for 250 years by the Oankali, the alien species that originally believed humanity was intent on committing suicide and so would be far too dangerous to try to save. Without human sensory organs, the Oankali are primatoid Medusa figures, their heads and bodies covered with multi-talented tentacles like a terran marine invertebrate's. These humanoid serpent people speak to the woman and urge her to touch them in an intimacy that would lead humanity to a monstrous metamorphosis. Multiply stripped, Lilith fights for survival, agency, and choice on the shifting boundaries that shape the possibility of meaning.

The Oankali do not rescue human beings only to return them unchanged to a restored earth. Their own origins lost to them through an infinitely long series of mergings and exchanges reaching deep into time and space, the Oankali *are* gene traders. Their essence is embodied commerce, conversation, communication—with a vengeance. Their nature is always to be midwife to themselves as other. Their bodies themselves are immune and genetic technologies, driven to exchange, replication, dangerous intimacy across the boundaries of self and other, and the power of images. Not unlike us. But unlike us, the hydra-headed Oankali do not build non-living technologies to mediate their self-formations and reformations. Rather, they are complexly webbed into a universe of living machines, all of which are partners in their apparatus of bodily production, including the ship on which the action of *Dawn* takes place. But deracinated captive fragments of humanity packed into the body of the aliens' ship inescapably evoke the terrible Middle Passage of the Atlantic slave trade that brought Lilith's ancestors to a 'New World'. There also the terms of survival were premised on an unfree 'gene trade' that permanently altered meanings of self and other for all the 'partners' in the exchange. In Butler's science fictional 'middle passage' the resting humans sleep in tamed carnivorous plant-like pods, while the Oankali do what they can to heal the ruined earth. Much is lost for ever, but the fragile layer of life able to sustain other life is restored, making earth ready for recolonization by large animals. The Oankali are intensely interested in humans as potential exchange partners partly because humans are built from such beautiful and dangerous genetic structures. The Oankali believe humans to be fatally, but reparably, flawed by their genetic nature as simultaneously intelligent and hierarchical. Instead, the aliens live in the postmodern geometries of vast webs and networks, in which the nodal points of individuals are still intensely important. These webs are hardly innocent of power and violence; hierarchy is not power's only shape—for aliens or humans. The Oankali make 'prints' of all their refugees, and they can print out replicas of the humans from these mental-organic-technical images. The replicas allow a great deal of gene trading. The Oankali are also fascinated with Lilith's 'talent' for cancer, which killed several of her relatives, but which in Oankali 'hands' would become a technology for regeneration and metamorphoses. But the Oankali want more from humanity; they want a full trade, which will require the intimacies of sexual mingling and embodied pregnancy in a shared colonial venture in, of all places, the Amazon valley. Human individuality will be challenged by more than the Oankali communication technology that translates other beings into themselves as signs, images, and memories. Pregnancy raises the tricky question of consent, property in the self, and the humans' love of themselves as the sacred image, the sign of the same. The Oankali intend to return to earth as trading partners with humanity's remnants. In difference is the irretrievable loss of the illusion of the one.

Lilith is chosen to train and lead the first party of awakened humans. She will be a kind of midwife/mother for these radically atomized peoples' emergence from their cocoons. Their task will be to form a community. But first Lilith is paired in an Oankali family with the just pre-metamorphic youngster, Nikanj, an ooloi. She is to learn from Nikanj, who alters her mind and body subtly so that she can live more freely among the Oankali; and she is to protect it during its metamorphosis, from which they both emerge deeply bonded to each other. Endowed with a second pair of arms, an adult ooloi is the third gender of the Oankali, a neuter being who uses its special appendages to mediate and engineer the gene trading of the species and of each family. Each child among the Oankali has a male and female parent, usually sister and brother to each other, and an ooloi from another group, race, or moitié. One translation in Oankali languages for ooloi is 'treasured strangers'. The ooloi will be the mediators among the four other parents of the planned cross-species children. Heterosexuality remains unquestioned, if more complexly mediated. The different social subjects, the different genders that could emerge from another embodiment of resistance to compulsory heterosexual reproductive politics, do not inhabit this *Dawn*.

The treasured strangers can give intense pleasure across the boundaries of group, sex, gender, and species. It is a fatal pleasure that marks Lilith for the other awakened humans, even though she has not yet consented to a pregnancy. Faced with her bodily and mental alterations and her bonding with Nikanj, the other humans do not trust that she is still human, whether or not she bears a human-alien child. Neither does Lilith. Worrying that she is none the less a Judas-goat, she undertakes to train the humans with the intention that they will survive and run as soon as they return to earth, keeping their humanity as people before them kept theirs. In the training period, each female human pairs with a male human, and then each pair, willing or not, is adopted by an adult ooloi. Lilith loses her Chinese-American lover, Joseph, who is murdered by the suspicious and enraged humans. At the end, the first group of humans, estranged from their ooloi and hoping to escape, are ready to leave for earth. Whether they can still be fertile without their ooloi is doubtful. Perhaps it is more than the individual of a sexually reproducing species who always has more than one parent; the species too might require multiple mediation of its replicative biopolitics. Lilith finds she must remain behind to train another group, her return to earth indefinitely deferred. But Nikanj has made her pregnant with Joseph's sperm and the genes of its own mates. Lilith has not consented, and the first book of *Xenogenesis* leaves her with the ooloi's uncomprehending comfort that 'The differences will be hidden until metamorphosis' (Butler, 1987, p. 263). Lilith remains unreconciled: 'But they won't be human. That's what matters. You can't understand, but that is what matters.' The treasured stranger responds, 'The child inside you matters' (p. 263). Butler does not resolve this dilemma. The contending shapes of sameness and difference in any possible future are at stake in the unfinished narrative of traffic across the specific cultural, biotechnical, and political boundaries that separate and link animal, human, and machine in a contemporary global world where survival is at stake. Finally, this is the contested world where, with or without our consent, we are located. '[Lilith] laughed bitterly. "I suppose I could think of this as fieldwork—but how the hell do I get out of the field?"' (1987, p. 91).

From this field of differences, replete with the promises and terrors of cyborg embodiments and situated knowledges, there is no exit. Anthropologists of possible selves, we are technicians of realizable futures. Science *is* culture.

Notes

Special thanks to Scott Gilbert, Rusten Hogness, Jaye Miller, Rayna Rapp, and Joan Scott. Research and writing for this project were supported by the Alpha Fund and the Institute for Advanced Study, Princeton, NJ; Academic Senate Faculty Research Grants of the University of California Santa Cruz; and the Silicon Valley Research Project, UCSC. Crystal Gray was an excellent research assistant. Benefiting from many people's comments, this paper was first presented at the Wenner Gren Foundation's Conference on Medical Anthropology, Lisbon, Portugal, 5–13 March 1988.

1. Even without taking much account of questions of consciousness and culture, the extensive importance of immunological discourse and artefacts has many diagnostic signs: (1) The first Nobel Prize in medicine in 1901 was given for an originary development, namely, the use of diphtheria anti-toxin. With many intervening awards, the pace of Nobel awards in immunology since 1970 is stunning, covering work on the generation of antibody diversity, the histocompatibility system, monoclonal antibodies and hybridomas, the network hypothesis of immune regulation, and development of the radioimmunoassay system. (2) The products and processes of immunology enter into present and projected medical, pharmaceutical, and other industrial practices. This situation is exemplified by monoclonal antibodies, which can be used as extremely specific tools to identify, isolate, and manipulate components of production at a molecular scale and then gear up to an industrial scale with unheard-of specificity and purity, for a wide array of enterprises—from food flavouring technology, to design and manufacture of industrial chemicals, to delivery systems in chemotherapy (see figure on 'Applications of monoclonal antibodies in immunology and related disciplines', Nicholas, 1985, p. 12). The *Research Briefings* for 1983 for the federal Office of Science and Technology Policy and various other federal departments and agencies identified immunology, along with artificial intelligence and cognitive science, solid earth sciences, computer design and manufacture, and regions of chemistry, as research areas 'that were likely to return the highest scientific dividends as a result of incremental federal investment' (Committee on Science, Engineering, and Public Policy, 1983). The dividends in such fields are hardly expected to be simply 'scientific'. 'In these terms the major money spinner undoubtedly is hybridoma technology, and its chief product the monoclonal antibody' (Nicholas, 1985, Preface). (3) The field of immunology is itself an international growth industry. The First International Congress of Immunology was held in 1971 in Washington, DC, attended by most of the world's leading researchers in the field, about 3500 people from 45 countries. Over 8000 people attended the Fourth International Congress in 1980 (Klein, 1982, p. 623). The number of journals in the field has been expanding since 1970 from around twelve to over eighty by 1984. The total of books and monographs on the

subject reached well over 1000 by 1980. The industrial-university collaborations characteristic of the new biotechnology pervade research arrangements in immunology, as in molecular biology, with which it cross-reacts extensively, for example, the Basel Institute for Immunology, entirely financed by Hoffman-La Roche but featuring all the benefits of academic practice, including publishing freedoms. The International Union of Immunological Societies began in 1969 with ten national societies, increased to thirty-three by 1984 (Nicholas, 1985). Immunology will be at the heart of global biotechnological inequality and 'technology transfer' struggles. Its importance approaches that of information technologies in global science politics. (4) Ways of writing about the immune system are also ways of determining which diseases—and which interpretations of them—will prevail in courts, hospitals, international funding agencies, national policies, memories and treatment of war veterans and civilian populations, and so on. See for example the efforts of oppositional people, like labour and consumer advocates, to establish a category called 'chemical AIDS' to call attention to widespread and unnamed ('amorphous') sickness in late industrial societies putatively associated with its products and environments and to link this sickness with infectious AIDS as a political strategy (Hayes, 1987; Marshall, 1986). Discourse on infectious AIDS is part of mechanisms that determine what counts as 'the general population', such that over a million infected people in the US alone, not to mention the global dimensions of infection, can be named in terms that make them *not* part of the general population, with important national medical, insurance, and legal policy implications. Many leading textbooks of immunology in the United States give considerably more space to allergies or auto-immune diseases than to parasitic diseases, an allocation that might lead future Nobel Prize–winners into some areas of research rather than others and that certainly does nothing to lead undergraduates or medical students to take responsibility for the differences and inequalities of sickness globally. (Contrast Golub [1987] with Desowitz [1987] for the sensitivities of a cellular immunology researcher and a parasitologist.) Who counts as an individual is not unrelated to who counts as the general population.

2. Like the universe inhabited by readers and writer of this essay.

3. This ontological continuity enables the discussion of the growing practical problem of 'virus' programs infecting computer software (McLellan, 1988). The infective, invading information fragments that parasitize their host code in favour of their own replication and their own program commands are more than metaphorically like biological viruses. And like the body's unwelcome invaders, the software viruses are discussed in terms of pathology as communications terrorism, requiring therapy in the form of strategic security measures. There is a kind of epidemiology of virus infections of artificial intelligence systems, and neither the large corporate or military systems nor the personal computers have good immune defences. Both are extremely vulnerable to terrorism and rapid proliferation of the foreign code that multiplies silently and subverts their normal functions. Immunity programs to kill the viruses, like Data Physician sold by Digital Dispatch, Inc., are being marketed. More than half the buyers of Data Physician in 1985 were military. Every time I start up my Macintosh, it shows the icon for its vaccine program—a hypodermic needle.

4. Thanks to Elizabeth Bird for creating a political button with this slogan, which I wore as a member of an affinity group called Surrogate Others at the Mothers and Others Day Action at the Nevada Nuclear Test Site in May 1987.

5. The relation of the immune and nervous systems conceived within contemporary neuroimmunology or psychoneuroimmunology would be the ideal place to locate a fuller argument here. With the discovery of receptors and products shared by cells of the neural, endocrine, and immune systems, positing the dispersed and networking immune system as the mediator between mind and body began to make sense to 'hard' scientists. The implications for popular and official therapeutics are legion, for example, in relation to the polysemic entity called 'stress'. See Barnes (1986, 1987); Wechsler (1987); Kanigel (1986). The biological metaphors invoked to name the immune system also facilitate or inhibit notions of the IS as a potent mediator, rather than a master control system or hyper-armed defence department. For example, developmental biologist and immunologist, Scott Gilbert, refers in his teaching to the immune system as an ecosystem and neuroimmunology researcher, Edwin Blalock, calls the immune system a sensory organ. These metaphors can be oppositional to the hyper-rationalistic AI immune body in Star Wars imagery. They can also have multiple effects in research design, as well as teaching and therapeutics.

6. When I begin to think I am paranoid for thinking anyone *really* dreams of transcendent disembodiment as the telos of life and mind, I find such things as the following quote by the computer designer W. Daniel Hillis in the Winter 1988 issue of *Daedalus* on artificial intelligence: 'Of course, I understand that this is just a dream, and I will admit that I am propelled more by hope than by the probability of success. But if this artificial mind can sustain itself and grow of its own accord, then for the first time human thought will live free of bones and flesh, giving this child of mind an earthly immortality denied to us' (Hillis, 1988, p. 180). Thanks to Evelyn Keller for pointing me to the quote. See her 'From secrets of life, secrets of death' (1990). I am indebted to Zoe Sofia (1984; Sofoulis, 1988) for analysis of the iconography and mythology of nuclear exterminism, extraterrestrialism, and cannibalism.

7. That, of course, is why women have had so much trouble counting as individuals in modern Western discourses. Their personal, bounded individuality is compromised by their bodies' troubling talent for making other bodies, whose individuality can take precedence over their own, even while the little bodies are fully contained and invisible without major optical technologies (Petchesky, 1987). Women can, in a sense, be cut in half and retain their maternal function—witness their bodies maintained after death to sustain the life of another individual. The special ambiguity of female individuality—perhaps more resistant, finally, than worms to full liberal personhood—extends into accounts of immune function during pregnancy. The old biomedical question has been, why does the mother not reject the little invader within as foreign? After all, the embryo and foetus are quite well marked as 'other' by all the ordinary immunological criteria; and there is intimate contact between foetal and maternal tissue at the site of certain cells of the placenta, called trophoblasts. Counter-intuitively, it turns out that it is women with 'underactive immune systems' who end up rejecting their foetuses immunologically by forming anti-

bodies against their tissues. Normally, women make special antibodies that mask the tell-tale foreign signals on the foetal trophoblasts, so that the mother's immune surveillance system remains blind to the foetus's presence. By immunizing the 'rejecting' women with cells taken from their 'husbands' or other genetically unrelated donors, the women's immune systems can be induced to make blocking antibodies. It appears that most women are induced to make this sort of antibody as a result of 'immunization' from their 'husband's' sperm during intercourse. But if the 'husband' is too genetically close to the potential mother, some women won't recognize the sperm as foreign, and their immune systems won't make blocking antibodies. So the baby gets recognized as foreign. But even this hostile act doesn't make the female a good invidivual, since it resulted from her failure to respond properly to the original breach of her boundaries in intercourse (Kolata, 1988a, b). It seems pretty clear that the biopolitical discourses of individuation have their limits for feminist purposes!

8. Jerne's debt to Chomsky's structuralism is obvious, as are the difficulties that pertain to any such version of structuralist internal totality. My argument is that there is more to see here than a too rapid criticism would allow. Jerne's and Chomsky's internal image of each other does not constitute the first time theories of the living animal and of language have occupied the same epistemic terrain. See Foucault, *The Order of Things* (1970). Remember that Foucault in *Archaeology of Knowledge* defined discourses as 'practices that systematically form the objects of which they speak' (Foucault, 1972, p. 49). The family relation between structuralism and rationalism is something I will avoid for now.

9. Emily Martin has begun a three-year fieldwork project on networks of immunological discourse in laboratories, the media, and among people with and without AIDS.

10. Mice and 'men' are constantly associated in immune discourse because these sibling animal bodies have been best characterized in the immunological laboratory. For example, the Major Histocompatibility Complex (MHC), a complex of genes that encodes a critical array of surface markers involved in almost all of the key immune response recognition events, is well characterized for each species. The complex is called the H2 locus in the mouse and the HLA locus in humans. The MHC codes for what will be recognized as 'self'. The locus is critically involved in 'restriction' of specificities. Highly polygenic and polyallelic, the MHC may be the main system allowing discrimination between self and non-self. 'Non-self' must be presented to an immune system cell 'in the context of self'; that is, associated with the surface markers coded by the MHC. Comparative studies of the antigens of the MHC with the molecular structures of other key actors in the immune response (antibodies, T cell differentiation antigens) have led to the concept of the 'immunoglobulin superfamily', characterized by its extensive sequence homologies that suggest an evolutionary elaboration from a common genie ancestor (Golub, 1987, pp. 202–33). The conceptual and laboratory tools developed to construct knowledge of the MHC are a microcosm for understanding the apparatus of production of the bodies of the immune system. Various antigens coded by the MHC confer 'public' or 'private' specificities, terms which designate degrees of shared versus differentiating antigens against a background of close genetic similarity, but not identity. Immunology could be approached as the science constructing such language-like

'distinguishing features' of the organic communications system. Current research on 'tolerance' and the ways thymic cells (T cells) 'educate' other cells about what is and is not 'self' led the biologist, Scott Gilbert, to ask if that is immunology's equivalent of the injunction to know 'thy-self' (personal communication). Reading immunological language requires both extreme literal-mindedness and a taste for troping. Jennifer Terry examined AIDS as a 'trop(olog)ical pandemic' (unpublished paper, UCSC).

11. It is not just imagers of the immune system who learn from military cultures; military cultures draw symbiotically on immune system discourse, just as strategic planners draw directly from and contribute to video game practices and science fiction. For example, in *Military Review* Colonel Frederick Timmerman argued for an élite corps of special strike force soldiers in the army of the future in these terms: The most appropriate example to describe how this system would work is the most complex biological model we know—the body's immune system. Within the body there exists a remarkably complex corps of internal bodyguards. In absolute numbers they are small—only about one percent of the body's cells. Yet they consist of reconnaissance specialists, killers, reconstitution specialists, and communicators that can seek out invaders, sound the alarm, reproduce rapidly, and swarm to the attack to repel the enemy . . . In this regard, the June 1986 issue of *National Geographic* contains a detailed account of how the body's immune system functions (Timmerman, 1987, p. 52).

References

Barnes, Deborah M. (1986) "Nervous and Immune System Disorders Linked in a Variety of Diseases," *Science* 232: 160–1.

Barnes, Deborah M. (1987) "Neuroimmunology Sites on Broad Research Base," *Science* 237:1568–9.

Brewer, Mária Minich (1987) "Surviving Fictions: Gender and Difference in Postmodern and Postnuclear Narrative," Discourse 9: 37–52.

Bryan, C. D. B. (1987) *The National Geographic Society: 100 Years of Adventure and Discovery.* New York: Abrams.

Butler, Octavia (1987) *Dawn.* New York: Warner.

Committee on Science, Engineering, and Public Policy of the National Academy of Sciences, the National Academy of Medicine, and the Institute of Medicine (1983) *Research Briefings 1983.* Washington: National Academy Press.

Dawkins, Richard (1982) *The Extended Phenotype: The Gene as the Unit of Selection.* Oxford: Oxford University Press.

Desowitz, Robert S. (1987) *The Immune System and How It Works.* New York: Norton.

Foucault, Michel (1972) *The Archaeology of Knowledge,* Alan Sheridan, trans. New York: Pantheon.

Foucault, Michel (1970) *The Order of Things.* New York: Random House.

Golub, Edward S. (1987) *Immunology: A Synthesis.* Sunderland, MA: Sinauer Associates.

Haraway, Donna (1985) "Manifesto for cyborgs: science, technology, and socialist feminism in the 1980s," *Socialist Review* 80: 65–108.

Hayles, Katherine (1987b) "Denaturalizing Experience: Postmodern Literature and Science," (abstract), Meetings of the Society for Literature and Science, 8–11 October, Worcester Polytechnic Institute.

Hayes, Dennis (1987) "Making Chips with Dust-free Poison," *Science as Culture*: I:89–104.

Hillis, W. Daniel (1988) "Intelligence as Emergent Behavior, or, the Songs of Eden," *Daedalus* Winter, 175–89.

Jaret, Peter (1986) "Our Immune System: The Wars Within," National Geographic 169(6): 701–35.

Jerne, Niels. K. (1985) "The Generative Grammar of the Immune System," Science 229: 1057–9.

Kanigel, Robert (1986) "Where Mind and Body Meet," *Mosaic* 17(2): 52–60.

Kanigel, Robert (1987) "The Genome Project," *New York Times Sunday Magazine* 13 December, pp. 44, 98–101, 106.

Keller, Evelyn Fox (1990) "From Secrets of Life to Secrets of Death," in M. Jacobus, E. F. Keller, and S. Shuttleworth, eds. *Body/Politics: Women and the Discourses of Science*. New York: Routledge, 177–91.

Klein, Jan (1982) *Immunology: The Science of Non-Self Discrimination*. New York: Wiley-Interscience.

Marshall, Eliot (1986) "Immune System Theories on Trial," *Science* 234:1490–2.

McLellan, Vin (1988) "Computer Systems Under Siege," *New York Times* 31 January, Sec. 3:1, 8.

Nicholas, Robin (1985) *Immunology: An Information Profile*. London: Mansell.

Nilsson, Lennart (1977) *A Child is Born*. New York: Dell.

Petchesky, Rosalind Pollack (1987) "Fetal Images: The Power of Visual Culture in the Politics of Reproduction," Feminist Studies 13(2): 263–92.

Playfair, J. H. L. (1984) *Immunology at a Glance*, 3rd ed. Oxford: Blackwell.

Roberts, Leslie (1987a) "Who Owns the Human Genome?" Science 237: 358–61.

_____ (1987b) "Human Genome: Questions of Cost," Science 238: 1411–12.

_____ (1987c) "New Sequencers Take on the Genome," Science 238: 271–3.

Sofia, Zoe (1984) "Exterminating Fetuses: Abortion, Disarmament, and the Sexo-Semiotics of Extra-Terrestrialism," *Diacritics* 14(2): 47–59.

Soufoulis, Zoe (1988) "Through the Lumen: Frankenstein and the Optics of Re-Origination," University of California at Santa Cruz, PhD thesis.

Timmerman, Colonel Frederick W., Jr. (1987, September) "Future Warriors," *Military Review*, pp. 44–55.

Treichler, Paula (1987) "AIDS, homophobia, and biomedical discourse: an epidemic of signification," *October* 43: 31–70.

Wechsler, Rob (1987, February) "A New Prescription: Mind over Malady," *Discover*: 51–61.

CHAPTER 15

THE IMMUNOLOGICAL TRANSFORMATION ON THE WAY TO THIN-WALLED "SOCIETIES"

Peter Sloterdijk

From the noisy monotony of the current sociological and political literature on globalization, a number of patterns can be abstracted that have good chances of becoming journalistic universals of a sort for the coming decades, perhaps even centuries. The first of these almost timeless themes is the claim that a new *modus vivendi* between the local and the global must be negotiated time and again; the second is that political communities "after modernity" have entered a new constellation "beyond the nation-state.[1] The third is that the gaping divide between rich and poor has brought the globalized world to a state of political and moral tension; and the fourth is that the progressive consumption of the biosphere along with the pollution of water, air and soil changes "humanity" willy-nilly into an ecological community of interests whose reflection and dialogue must bring forth a new, far-sighted culture of reason. It is not hard to perceive a common tendency in all these themes: the blurring of traditional notions of political subjects and social units. Wherever one looks, one notes that the most important trends have slipped from the hands of those responsible for them, and that the problem-solvers of yesterday and the problems of today (let alone the problem-solvers of today and the problems of tomorrow) make a poor match.

We intend to translate these perceptions from the sociological debate into our own context: a political poetics of space or "macrospherology."[2] After this shift of perspective, all questions of social and personal identity pose themselves in morphological and immunological terms, which is to say in terms of how something resembling liveable forms of "dwelling" or being-with-oneself-and-one's-own can be accommodated in historically active macro-worlds.

Contemporary nervousness about globalization mirrors the fact that with the nation-state, what was previously the largest possible scale of political dwelling—the living and conference room of democratic (or imagined) peoples, as it were—is now subject to negotiation, and that this national living room already has some very unpleasant draughts—most of all in those places where high unemployment rates converge with routines of lamentation at high standards. Looking back, we can see more clearly the extraordinary achievement of the nation-state, which was to offer the majority of those dwelling there, a form of domesticity, a simultaneously imaginary and real immune structure, that could be experienced as a convergence of place and self, or as a regional identity in the most favourable sense of the word. This service was performed most impressively where the welfare state had successfully tamed the power state.

The immunological construction of political-ethnic identity has been set in motion and it is clear that the connection between place and self is not always as stable as the political folklores of territorialism (from ancient agrarian cultures to the modern welfare state) had demanded and pretended. Weakening or dissolving the link of places and selves can allow us to see the two extreme positions that reveal the structure of the social field in an almost experimental state of disintegration: a self without a place and a place without a self. It is clear that all actually existing societies have always had to seek their *modus vivendi* somewhere between the poles—ideal-typically at the most favourable distance from each extreme position, and one can easily understand that in the future too, every genuine political community will have to give an answer to the double imperative of self-determination and place-determination.

The first extreme of dissolution—the *self without a place*—is probably approached most closely by the diaspora Judaism of the previous two millennia, which has been described not unjustly as a people without a land—a fact that Heinrich Heine put in a nutshell when he stated that the Jews are not at home in a country, but rather in a book: the Torah, which they carried with them like a "portative fatherland" [*portatives Vaterland*].[3] This profound and elegant comment illuminates a fact that is frequently passed over: "nomadizing" or "deterritorialized" groups construct their symbolic immunity and ethnic coherence not—or only marginally—from a supporting soil; rather, their communications among themselves act directly as an "autogenous vessel"[4] in which the participants are enclosed and stay in shape [in *Form bleiben*], while the group moves through external landscapes. A landless people rooted in a scriptural tradition, therefore, cannot fall prey to the misconception that has imposed itself on virtually all settled groups throughout human history: understanding the land itself as the container of the people, and viewing their native soil as the *a priori* of their life's meaning or their identity. This territorial fallacy endures as one of the most effective and problematic heirlooms of the sedentary age, as the basic reflex underlying all seemingly legitimate applications of political force. Indeed what is termed "national defense" relates directly to it. National defense is based on the obsessive equation of place and self, the axiomatic logical error of territorialized reason (which struck the great majority of Israeli citizens after 1948) as a desirable one to make. This error has increasingly been exposed after an unprecedented wave of transnational mobility began to ensure that peoples and territories everywhere qualify their liaison. The trend towards a multi-local self is characteristic of advanced modernity—like the trend towards a polyethnic or denationalized place.

The Indo-American cultural anthropologist Arjun Appadurai has drawn attention to this state of affairs with his conceptual creation of the "ethnoscape," allowing us to examine issues like the progressive deterritorialization of ethnic connections, or the formation of "imaginary communities" outside nation-states and the imaginary sharing of the images of life forms from other cultures among countless individuals.[5] As far as Judaism during its period of exile is concerned, its provocation lay in the fact that it constantly reminded the peoples of the western hemisphere of the seeming paradox and actual scandal of a factually existing self without a place.

At the other extreme, the phenomenon of the *place without a self* becomes increasingly clear. The earth's uninhabitable regions—the white deserts (polar world), the grey ones (high mountains), the green ones (jungles), the yellow ones (sand deserts) and the blue deserts (oceans)—are paradigmatic of this extreme "selflessness": the secondary man-made deserts can be placed alongside them. In the context of our investigation of spheric conditions, the latter are of interest by way of contrast as they constitute places with which people do not usually develop any cultivating relationship, let alone attempt any identification. This applies to all transit spaces, both in the narrower and wider sense of the term, be they facilities intended for traffic such as train stations, docks and airports, roads, squares and shopping centres, or complexes designed for limited stays such as holiday villages and tourist cities, factory premises or night shelters. Such places may have their own atmospheres—but these do not depend on a populace or collective self that would be at home in them. By definition, they do not hold on to those who pass through them. They are the alternately overrun or empty no man's lands; the transit deserts that proliferate in the enucleated centres and hybrid peripheries of contemporary "societies."

It does not require much analytical effort to see that in these "societies," globalizing tendencies work against a prior normality—life in massive, ethnic or national containers (along with their specific phantasms of origin and mission) and the unendangered licence to confuse land with self—is decisively infringed upon by globalizing tendencies. On one hand, such "societies" loosen their regional ties through large populations acquiring unprecedented mobility. On the other hand, there is an increasing number of transit places with which those who frequent them are unable to inhabit them. Thus globalizing and mobilizing "societies" simultaneously approach both the "nomadic" pole, a self without a place, and the desert pole, a place without a self—with a shrinking middle ground of regional cultures and grounded contentments.

The formal crisis of modern "mass societies," which is now seen chiefly as a loss of meaning for the nation-state, thus results from the advanced erosion of ethnic container functions. What was previously understood as "society" and invoked with it was usually, in fact, nothing other than the content of a thick-walled, territorially grounded, symbol-assisted and generally monolingual container—that is, a collective which found its self-assurance in a certain national hermeticism and flourished in redundancies of its own (that could never be entirely understood by strangers).[6] Because of their self-containing qualities, such historical communities—known as peoples—stayed on the point of intersection between self and place and usually relied on a considerable asymmetry between inside and outside; this usually manifested itself in pre-political cultures as naïve ethnocentrism, and at the political level in the substantive difference between inner (domestic) and outer (foreign) policy. The effects of globalization increasingly evened out this difference and asymmetry; the immunity offered by the national container is perceived as increasingly endangered by those who profit from it. Certainly no one who has tasted the advantages of free transnational movement is likely to desire a return to the militant enclosures of older nation-states in earnest, much less the totalitarian self-hypnoses that often characterized tribal life forms. Yet for numerous people today, the purpose and risk of the trend towards a world of thin-walled and mixed "societies" are neither clear nor welcome. Globalization, Roland Robertson rightly observes, is a "basically contested process."[7] The protest against globalization is *also* globalization itself—it is part of the inevitable and indispensable immune reaction of local organs to infections through the larger format of the world.

The psychopolitical challenge of the Global Age, which Martin Albrow aptly describes as a wilful result stage of the Modern Age, lies in the fact that the weakening of container immunities must not be dealt with simply as decadence and loss of form, that is to say as an ambivalent or cynical abetment of self-destruction. What is at stake for the postmoderns are successful new designs for liveable, immune relationships, and these are precisely what can and will develop anew in the "societies" with permeable walls—albeit, as has always been the case, not among all and not for all.

In this context the epochal trend towards individualistic life forms reveals its immunological significance: today, in advanced "societies," it is the individuals who—perhaps for the first time in the history of hominid coexistence—break away from their group bodies as carriers of immune competencies, groups which had to that point functioned primarily as protection. They seek in great numbers to disconnect their happiness and unhappiness from the being-in-shape [in *Form sein*] of the political commune. We are now experiencing what is probably the irreversible transformation of political security collectives into groups with individualistic immune designs. This trend would remain in force even if a purported or genuine "return of war" were to lead to a renewed primacy of the political. Such a returned war would certainly have a therapeutic, defensive and immunitary character; the re-militarized individualistic group could only relapse into collectivist moods episodically.

This tendency manifests itself most clearly in the pilot nation of the Western world, the USA, where the concept of the pursuit of happiness has nominally been the foundation for the "social contract" since the Declaration of Independence. The centrifugal effects of making individual happiness the guiding concept have thus far been balanced out by the combined energies of communities and and civil-societies such that the traditional immunological precedence of the group over its members also seemed embodied in that synthetic people, United States Americans. Meanwhile, the tables have been turned: no country, population or culture on earth practises as much biological, psychotechnic and religioid self-concern in parallel with a growing abstinence from political commitments. In the 1996 presidential election, the USA saw its first voter turnout of under 50% (Clinton's re-election). In the November 1998 elections to the House of Representatives and the Senate in 1998, roughly two out of three voters stayed at home (though experts did not view the 38% turn-out as a particularly bad result).[8] It was only through an exceptionally hard-fought election campaign that some 60% of eligible voters were mobilized to cast their votes in the re-election of George W. Bush in November 2004. This testifies to a situation in which the majority feel sure that they can largely abandon solidarity with the fates of their political commune—guided by the highly plausible notion that the individual will, in future, no longer (or only in exceptional cases) find their immunological optimum in the national collective, but at best in the solidary system of their own community, or more precisely the victimological collective, though most clearly in the private insurance arrangements.

The axiom of the individualistic immune order gained currency in populations of self-centred individuals like some new vital insight: that, ultimately, no one would do for them what they do not do for themselves. The new immunity techniques (in their institutional centre, private insurances and pension funds, and at their individual periphery, dietetics and biotechnology) presented themselves as existential strategies for "societies" of individuals in which the long way to flexibilization [in *die Flexibilisierung*], the weakening of "object relationships" and the general authorization of unfaithful disloyal or reversible inter-human relationships had led to the "goal," to what Spengler rightly prophesized as the final stage of every culture: the state in which it is impossible to determine whether individuals are diligent or decadent (but diligent in what respect, and decadent in relation to which height?[9]). It is the state in which individuals have lost their ability of exemplary world-formation. The individualized humans behaved as if they had realized that the optimum immunization cannot be attained by absorbing "the world" in a multi-faceted way, but rather by defining one's contact with it very narrowly. As a result, the last metaphorical difference, namely the distinction between noble and common, lost its meaning. The end of the heroic age of discovery and creation was also the end of the great men, those all-encompassing individuals who seemed capable of unifying their respective epochs and collectives in themselves. They were followed by the individualistic cycle in which everyone made themselves their own speciality [*Spezialgebiet*]. The consequences are well-known. One of them was that the anthropological phantom of the Modern Age, *l'homme monde*—the microcosmic, the variously receptive and expressive, the complete human—disappeared like a face drawn in the sand at the seashore.

Notes

1. See Martin Albrow, *The Global Age* and Jürgen Habermas, *The Postnational Constellation: Political Essays*, trans. Max Pensky (Cambridge: Polity, 2001).

2. We use this term to encompass the reflections with which the theory of intimate spheres (microspherology) is "elevated" to the level of a theory of large immune structures (states, realms, "worlds"). See Peter Sloterdijk, *Bubbles, Spheres 1: Microspherology*, trans. Wieland Hoban (Los Angeles: Semiotext(e), 2011) and *Sphären II, Globen, Makrosphärologie* (Frankfurt: Editions Suhrkamp, 1999).

3. Concerning the imaginative complex of the "portable God," see Régis Debray, *God: An Itinerary*, trans. Jeffrey Mehlman (London & New York: Verso, 2007), pp. 83f.

4. For an elaboration on this phrase, see *Bubbles*, 59f.

5. See Arjun Appadurai, "Global Ethnoscapes—Notes and Queries for a Transnational Anthropology," in Richard G. Fox (ed.), *Recapturing Anthropology: Working in the Present* (Santa Fe: School of American Research Press, 1991), pp. 191–210.

6. For the anthropological explanation of deeper layers of the feeling of belonging via the concepts of the "uterotope" (or sphere of election) and the "uterotope" (or sphere of pampering), see *Sphären III, Schäume*, pp. 386–405.

7. Roland Robertson, *Globalization: Social Theory and Global Culture* (London/Thousand Oaks/New Delhi: SAGE, 1992), p. 182.

8. Walter Lippmann, admittedly, already pointed out similar abstinence rates among the (non-)voters damned to passivity and incompetence in 1927, in his democracy-sceptical masterpiece, *The Phantom Public* (New York: MacMillan Co., 1927).

9. *Translator's Note*: in referring to height, the author invokes the original implication of the word "decadence" (from Lat. *decadere*, "to fall away").

CHAPTER 16

BIOPOLITICS

Roberto Esposito

1. *Incorporations*

It is all too evident that politics enters fully into the immune paradigm the moment life becomes the immediate content of its action. When this occurs, all formal mediation disappears: the object of politics is no longer a "life form," its own specific way of being, but rather, life itself—all life and only life, in its mere biological reality. Whether an individual life or the life of the species is involved, life itself is what politics is called upon to make safe, precisely by immunizing it from the dangers of extinction threatening it. When "biopolitics" is talked about as a form of politics in which the existence and very possibility of the living being is at stake, this radical reduction in meaning is what points to the original, most general sense of the term. And yet, this approach only brings into view one facet of the matter—its most obvious. To infuse it with greater significance, it needs to be examined from another angle as well, focusing not just on the object of biopolitics, but also on the way that object is grasped: to be able to save life from its tendency toward self-dissolution, politics has to lead life back to the realm of the body. What appeared to be a relation between two terms—politics and life—must instead be interpreted as a more complex game that includes a third term upon which it depends: the bodily dimension is where life lends itself to being preserved as such by political immunization.

After all, in order to be conceived in the first place, life needs some type of organic representation binding it to reality, or at least the potential of a bodily structure. When looked at from the point of view of its protection from a danger that imperils it, whether endogenous or exogenous, the need for life to be included within the confines of the body is all the more pressing. Bodily confines are exactly what act as lines of defense against whatever threatens to take life away from itself, expel it to its outside, or reverse it into its opposite. It is in the body and only in the body that life can remain what it is and even grow, be strengthened, and reproduce. Of course, this works equally both ways: if the body is the privileged locus for the unfolding of life, it is also the place where the presence of death is most noticeable; and even before that, the effects of illness, aging, and deterioration. But this constitutive binarism—between life and death, growth and decay—is precisely what makes the body the liminal zone where the immunitary intention of politics is carried out, namely, to delay the passage from life to death as long as possible, to drive death to the farthest point from the presentness of life. The body is both the instrument and terrain of this battle. As long as it holds out, there will be no death. When death arrives on the scene, the body is what vanishes: not only its physiological activity, but also, shortly thereafter, its very material substance, doomed to rapid decomposition. The fact is, death and the body do not go together for very long. Their encounter is only momentary: once dead, the body does not endure. To be a body, it must keep itself alive. It is the frontline, both symbolic and material, in life's battle against death.

This explains why it has been by far the most influential metaphor used in political discourse to represent life in society. Even a rough outline of the complex history of the analogy between the body natural and the body politic—touched on in the second chapter—is out of the question in this context. However, we may recall that for centuries it was the most common figural *topos* through which political authorities and men of letters represented the constitution and functioning of the body political. Each part was compared to an organ of the human body, with all the normative consequences that a correspondence of this sort naturally gave rise to, both in terms of the ensuing hierarchy that was established between the king/head and subjects/limbs, and between the different estates and orders of the kingdom. This point, which has received a great deal of scholarly attention, is not my focus here, though. My interest lies instead in the immunitary character that the metaphor of the body politic lends to the modern political lexicon as a whole. True, this would seem to be belied by the chronological limit that has been set to its development around the mid-seventeenth century, beyond which it seems to fade out in favour of the mechanistic and individualistic paradigm established by Hobbes.[1] But even apart from the essential lack of distinction between organicism and mechanism that persisted at least until the eighteenth century—to which we owe the extensive contamination between body and machine culminating in Hobbes's reference to "the artificial animal"[2]—it is clear that the metaphor did not disappear at all, but simply adapted to the changed historical and conceptual context.

Indeed, it can be argued that the gradual predominance of mechanistic metaphysics and the individualistic model was precisely what signaled a growth in the immune-oriented significance of the State-body analogy. The key to this step lay in the increasing complexity of the relation between life and body politic. The naturalness of the relation began to fade when the body politic was subjected to increasingly violent environmental pressures—uprisings, wars, revolutions. But this intractability was exactly what made the relationship between life and body politic even more necessary: precisely because the life of the body politic was constitutively fragile, it needed to be preventively protected from what threatened it. Nobody grasped the mortal precariousness of the body politic better than Hobbes, who no longer ascribed it to the natural decay of all forms of government envisaged by the traditional Polybian model, but rather to the destructive powers [*potenze*] latent in its organism.[3] But this fact—that death was not natural so much as induced, and as such, avoidable or at least deferrable—was precisely what made an immune strategy of containment indispensable for Hobbes:

> Though nothing can be immortal which mortals make; yet, if men had the use of reason they pretend to, their Commonwealths might be secured, at least, from perishing by internal diseases. For by the nature of their institution, they are designed to live as long as mankind, or as the laws of nature, or as justice itself, which gives them life. Therefore when they come to be dissolved, not by external violence, but intestine disorder, the fault is not in men as they are the *matter*, but as they are the *makers* and orderers of them.[4]

If the causes that expose the body politic to the catastrophic possibility of its dissolution are attributable to human error rather than being natural, they can be tackled through a type of order that takes the impending risks into account beforehand. Following this line of reasoning, the machine lexicon is adopted by Hobbes not to oppose the body lexicon, but to supplement it. The machine metaphor is meant to strengthen the connection—otherwise precarious—between life and body, like a sort of metal skeleton designed to keep the body alive beyond its natural capacity. This does not mean eliminating the possibility of death: on the contrary, death is meant to be kept in mind at all times to avoid being taken by surprise. Nor does it mean indefinitely postponing the death of each of the individuals who together make up the body of the State, depicted in the famous frontispiece of the first edition of *Leviathan*. The idea rather is to establish a functional relationship between the inevitable deaths of the individuals and the duration of the artificial body of the State, ensured by the ununinterrupted continuity of sovereign power: "Of all these forms of government, the matter being mortal, so that not only monarchs, but also whole assemblies die, it is necessary for the conservation of the peace of men that as there was order taken for an artificial man, so there be order also taken for an artificial eternity of life."[5] That this life is artificial— just like the "great Leviathan" to which it inheres—is the most unmistakeable sign that a body has been immunized rather than replaced: not only does it survive the death of its members, it even periodically derives its reproductive energy from them, like an organism first nourished with the life of all the parts that compose it and then additionally with their death. Or like a body capable of incorporating its own discorporation, exactly like what happens to the organismic metaphor with respect to its own artificial counterpart. The body-machine, the machine-body, is a body that can no longer be undone, because it is already undone and rebuilt, as if embalmed, in its bodily armor. As a body that is permanently such as it is—because it has no gaps, no openings, no wounds—it is entirely coincident with itself and therefore everlasting: all body, one body, forever body. And because it is accustomed to living with the death that lives inside it, this is a body that does not die—at least until death is roused one day with so many lethal effects that it explodes into a thousand pieces.

The fact that contractualist language far from dismisses the metaphor of the body politic, moreover, can be illustrated even more effectively in Rousseau, who, after having declared it to be "inaccurate" in the *Discourse on Political Economy*,[6] in *The Social Contract* then goes on to reinstate it in all its salvific powers:

"Each of us puts his person and all his power in common under the supreme direction of the general will, and, in our corporate capacity, we receive each member as an indivisible part of the whole." At once, in place of the individual personality of each contracting party, this act of association creates a moral and collective body, composed of as many members as the assembly contains votes, and receiving from this act its unity, its common identity, its life and its will.[7]

What we have here is a double incorporation, a reciprocal cross-incorporation, between the body of each individual and the collective body, derived from the incorporation of each individual body into a common body. But for this to happen, each individual body must have incorporated each of its parts, beforehand, as a member of a single body. The middle term in this passage from body to body—in this doubling of the body—lies of course in the concept of "general will," which founds and at the same time deconstructs the individualistic logic of the contract when it assumes incorporation as a premise that should be its outcome and yet is instead its precondition. This is because, unlike the Hobbesian model, the immune mechanism of this body politic has no need of artificial support; it is, so to speak, inside the same corporeal (meaning, intrinsically unitary) constitution of the body: "As soon as this multitude is so united in one body, it is impossible to offend against one of the members without attacking the body, and still more to offend against the body without the members resenting it."[8] From this point of view, the ancient hierarchy between the different parts of the body—and between the corresponding organs of the State—ceases to be meaningful, because what makes it so is the correspondence between the subject and object of the sovereign function inherent to a body without a head, or to a head extending over the entire surface of the body.

This reinstatement of the head within the body politic is the strategic move that allowed the ancient metaphor to survive and even regenerate itself from its apparent demise, during and after the revolution, when the royal beheading should have done away with its semantic force forever. The reason it did not is because, even before falling, the head had been dissolved as such and incorporated into the collective body of the nation. By then, through the representation of the National Assembly, it had become the new subject of the analogy, now transposed from the ancient king's body to that of the citizens united together in a single population. When Emmanuel Joseph Sieyès's texts are read from this perspective, not only is it clear that the metaphor of the body stubbornly remains the centerpiece of his argument, it actually acts as the rhetorical and figurative go-between through which the revolutionary rupture, far from putting the life of the nation into danger, is actually portrayed as necessary to it. If revolution is viewed as the nation's only possible salvation, the reason is because it does not split the body into parts, but rather regroups it, contrary to the divisive threat represented by the ancient privileges. This body—in seeking to be such, namely, the principle and safeguard of the nation's life—can only be one. Hence, it cannot host any other privileged body inside itself, as is stated in no uncertain terms at the end of *"What is the Third Estate?"*:

> In the end it is not worth asking what kind of place there should be for the privileged classes in the social order. It is like asking what kind of place a malignant tumor should have in the body of someone who is ill, as it devours and ruins his health. It is essential to restore every organ to health and activity so that any malign combination able to vitiate the most essential principles of life can no longer occur.[9]

What most stands out in this passage is not only the thorough overlapping between the political lexicon and the medical lexicon, once again connoted by the metaphor of the body, but also the immunitary consequence that directly follows from it: in order for the body to heal permanently, the power of the illness afflicting it must be leveraged, and, precisely for this reason, drastically eliminated. Only if it is assumed in all its negativity can it be fought through and through. On these lines Sieyès can claim that healing takes place through an excess of disease, and that only when the disease is taken to its extreme pathogenic consequences does regeneration becomes possible: because in reality it is essential to the process. The concept of "regeneration" is said to have taken on a specifically political meaning in addition to its medical and religious ones only after its negative antonym, the concept of "degeneration," had been firmly established.[10] But what we have here is not a simple chronological antecedence: as is implicit to the turn taken by the immune metaphor of the body politic, there can be no regeneration that does not begin from, and within, a prior degeneration. After all, what would health be without the nuisance of illness?

How can we explain this irresistible tendency of political philosophy—and political practice as well—to incorporate social plurality? What is the source of this veritable repetition compulsion that drives it to continuously incorporate

what so doggedly resists it? Jacob Rogozinski traces its origin back to the dialectical backlash engendered through opposition from the phantasmic methods adopted by this resistance; whence the oscillating movement between a
drive toward incorporation and a symmetrically opposed drive toward "discorporation."[11] To understand this explanation, we have to go back to the
phenomenological horizon that constitutes its premise and conceptual framework: to be specific, to the theme of *carne* (flesh), specifically in the version
provided by Husserl and later by Merleau-Ponty. For both, albeit stressing
different aspects, the semantics of the flesh (German *Leib*, French *chair*) do
not coincide with those of the body (German *Körper*, French *corps*) to which it
is nevertheless linked by a close relation of implication. Whether involving a
singular or potentially plural experience—such as what Merleau-Ponty referred to with the terms "flesh of the world" or "flesh of history"—the process
of mutual incorporation of two members of the same body or between several
different bodies can never be fully achieved because it is interrupted by an
original difference which the author calls "carnal difference" *(différence char-
nelle)*. This impossibility of essential co-belonging, or simultaneous co-
givenness, which keeps suspended the chiasm between the hand that touches
and the hand that is touched, has the effect of undoing any possible identification between flesh and body. There is something about the flesh, like a hiatus
or an original break, which resists incorporation, reversing it into the opposing movement of disincorporation. But, as we were saying, this stubborn resistance of the flesh to being made body cannot come about without aporetic
consequences. It generates a series of phantasmic figures of laceration and
dislocation that return to the flesh, threatening to drive it back into a place of
absence resembling a true disembodiment: as if the crisis of the chiasm—
affecting the body proper or the body of others—gives rise to a non-flesh
within the flesh, an abject object, destined to suck it into a deadly maelstrom
or prompt it to self-expulsion. It is at this point that the phantasm of necrotic
decomposition—ensuing from the imaginary intensification of the distance
toward the body—by contrast produces a new and stronger process of incorporation. This prohibits the obsessive fantasies of stripping the flesh, recom-
posing the scattered fragments into a new identificatory synthesis, until it,
too, is dismantled in its turn and its demand for fusion is negated by the irreducible carnal difference.

The most important instances of political self-interpretation in the modern
era can be traced back to this reading grid. From this point of view, despite

their liberating capacity, the return to the organismic metaphor of Rousseau and Marxist opposition to the alienation of the social body created by capital actually represent a counter-reaction to the modern processes of individualistic disincorporation. This does not mean that political thought oriented to the celebration of the individual is able to represent instances of the flesh free from totalizing hypostases. Indeed, the self-centering concept of the individual is itself born from a corporeal hypostasis that overlaps onto the pluralistic character of carnal existence. Moreover, it is precisely the incapacity of the concept of the individual to grasp the unquenchable need for social bonding that produces the totalitarian reaction, in which the will to incorporation and the phantasm of stripped flesh are redoubled in the most catastrophically destructive way. The collapse of totalitarian regimes, however, brings this seemingly inexhaustible dialectic of discorporation and re-incorporation to a point of no return beyond which a new horizon of meaning opens up. What finally comes into view is the possibility of bringing to the surface that "primal flesh" no philosophy has yet been able to name, except by negatively deducing it from the element that negated it. When this happens, out of the final dismemberment of the body politic and its organismic metaphors, instead of the neurotic obsession for new incorporations there will emerge the silhouette of a "flesh that rebels against the One, always already divided, polarized into the Two of the chiasm, but such as to ignore all hierarchies, all irreversible separations between one part that controls and the other that obeys."[12]

Although this perspective is highly intriguing, the conclusion leaves some question marks. Without going into the more technical issue—which, I believe, remains to be resolved—regarding the political-historical translatability of transcendental categories (at least as far as Husserl is concerned, but also in part for Merleau-Ponty), I have some reservations about the interpretation of "primordial flesh." How are we to understand "primordial"? As an original background, covered and disfigured by the dynamics we have described, and which can therefore only come into view when it has been exhausted? Or as something which that same dynamic brings inside as its own antinomic opposite? Are we to understand it as an ontological alternative that opposes the hegemony of the body from the outside—or the void inside which inhabits it and exposes it to its otherness? More pointedly: is there another flesh beyond the body, or is this not the locus of its constitutive non-belonging—the differential limit that separates it from itself by opening it up to its outside? I think that Rogozinski vacillates between these two hermeneutic possibilities without opting for one or the other, and that this indecision should be attributed to the Utopian and even slightly eschatological tone that transpires from the sentence quoted above. There is no doubt that the category of "body" no longer responds to questions posed by a world with no internal borders; and therefore it should be deconstructed through a different lexicon, one in which "flesh" is the most meaningful term.[13] However, this must be done without losing sight of their connection, and also of the fact that we are talking about *the same thing.* Flesh is nothing but the unitary weave of the difference between bodies. It is the non-belonging, or rather the intra-belonging, which allows what is different to not hermetically seal itself up within itself, but rather, to remain in contact with its outside. What we are talking about is not just an externalization of the body, but also the internal cleavage that prevents its absolute immanence. To fully grasp the meaning of the flesh requires that we be capable of simultaneously conceiving the outside and the inside of the body: one in the other and one for the other. It is the internal threshold that everts the inverted; and which therefore makes the individual body no longer such. No longer exclusively proper (which, in the end, makes the translation of *Leib* as "the body proper" untenable),[14] it is at the same time "improper," as Didier Franck also words it: "The flesh as originally proper and the origin of the proper is originally improper and the origin of the improper."[15] But if the flesh is the expropriation of the proper, then it is also what makes the proper common. This is why both Husserl and Heidegger, in a different way, associate it from the outset with the semantics of givenness: "*Bodily presence is a superlative mode of the self-givenness of an entity (Leibhaftigkeit ist ein ausgezeichneter Modus der Selbstgegebenheit eines Seienden).*"[16] The originary relationship between the figure of the flesh and that of the *munus* suddenly leaps out at us. The flesh is neither another body nor the body's other: it is simply the way of being in common of that which seeks to be immune.

2. The *Phármakon*

If the organological metaphor is at the heart of political treatises, at the heart of the metaphor lies disease. True, the point of intersection between political knowledge and medical knowledge is the common problem of preserving the body. But this preservation takes on a central role precisely from the perspective opened up by disease. Of course, logically speaking, the physiological—or morphological—determination of the body precedes its pathology. But, in point of fact, its physiology and morphology derive their meaning from the layout of the pathological condition: what is healthy is only defined through contrast by the "decision" about what is diseased—the origin, development and outcome of the illness. If, for example, the ultimate evil is identified in the threat of insurrections and rioting, the health of the State will be viewed as residing in an order guaranteed by the control of the head over the other parts of the body. If, on the contrary, what we fear instead is the tyranny of a despotic ruler, the salvation of the body politic will be located in a balanced equilibrium between its different members.

So far, however, we have remained with the traditional sources that seem to resurface essentially unchanged throughout the centuries, from classical and Christian antiquity to the Renaissance and Modernity, along a line that arrives at the organismic sociology of Comte, Spencer and Durkheim. In reality, following this approach we end up losing sight of those very steps, or epistemological leaps, that imbue the metaphor with a specifically immune tonality. It is undeniable that even the simple figurative superimposition of the biomedical on top of the legal-political language in the representation of the body implicitly points to the question of its immunity. But for it to acquire a more specific connotation, the advent of two changes in the metaphor of the body were required, initially regarding the location of the disease and, subsequently, its relation to health. As for the first question, the two causes of decay and subsequent collapse of the body politic were traditionally attributed firstly to natural aging—in accord with the ancient Polybian principle that all living entities necessarily decline—and secondly, to a violent shock due to a civil war or coup d'etat. In both cases, therefore, disease was endogenous, generated from within the body politic, and could be addressed by treatment methods aimed at gently restoring the shattered equilibrium, or surgically, by cutting out the diseased part.[17] It is precisely this topological order that gradually, but more and more clearly, came to show cracks at the beginning of the modern period, in association with intensified interstate conflict and the transformation of medical knowledge. There remains, of course, the classic pairing of disease with discord, with all its retinue of signs, symptoms, and remedies, but whose center of gravity faced more outwardly than inwardly. The pathogenic matrix of the disease that attacked the body politic—whether a foreign invasion or civil war—lay outside the body, and the pathogen was transmitted through the infiltration of a contagious element that was not engendered by the body.

It may be useful to recall that, in conjunction with the increasingly catastrophic spread of major epidemics—especially syphilis and the plague—between 1536 and 1546, Girolamo Fracastoro published his two treatises *Syphilis sive Morbus Gallicus* and *De Contagione et Contagiosis Morbis*. For the first time, the traditional Galenic humoral theory was flanked and then opposed by the theory that disease is communicated through contamination caused by the body's intake of tiny infectious agents *(semina)* of an exogenous nature, and therefore by means of a mechanism structurally different from the endogenous processes involved with the putrefaction of bodies. During this same phase—of course without any direct connection, but within a common horizon of meaning—in political treatises as well attention shifted from the overall state of health of the body politic, to preventive prophylactic measures to keep it safe from the infiltration of allogenous elements. Hence the need, increasingly emphasized, for immunitary barriers, protection and apparatuses aimed at reducing, if not eliminating, the porosity of external borders against contaminating toxic germs. How much actual or threatened invasions contributed to this obsession with self-protection, such as the Spanish one in England, or even contact with unfamiliar cultures and ethnicities such as the Native American, not to mention the growing Jewish immigration to Western Europe, is not difficult to imagine: the greater the vulnerability of the body politic must have appeared, the more urgent the need became to hermetically seal the orifices that had opened up in its frontiers. The images of besieged cities, fortified castles, and territories surrounded by potential invaders that filled the pages of English, French and Italian political treatises between the sixteenth and seventeenth centuries offer tangible evidence of this point.

But even more important than the external origin of the pathogenic germ—in keeping with the immunitary character of the bodily metaphor—is the dialectical function assumed by the disease in relation to the therapy intended to treat it. While an entirely negative portrayal of illness, understood as the absolute opposite of health, predominated until a given time, at a certain stage—which can be pinpointed to the second half of the sixteenth century—an appreciable change occurred in the semantics. Of course, illness continued to be mentioned as the cause that weakens the body politic to the point of endangering its life. But this did not exhaust its function, which gradually even assumed a positive value. To begin with, disease is seen as strengthening or even creating the diseased organism's self-defense through opposition. From this point of view, we should not underestimate the indirect influence of Machiavelli's conception of the political productivity of social conflicts.[18] But political treatises from the sixteenth and seventeenth centuries draw another, more sinister teaching from Machiavelli as well, according to which political power can use insurrections and tumults to legitimize and strengthen its repressive apparatus, or even use its art to create them, by infiltrating potentially subversive groups with government agents, for example. Nothing reinforces the host body politic better than an ill that has been dominated and turned against itself.[19]

But this is only one axis of the immune character assumed by the metaphor, which is doubled when the dialectic function—neither purely negative nor purely positive, but rather one in the other and one arising from the other—transmigrates from the political sphere of conflict into the same interpretation of disease and its treatment. To fully elucidate this latest twist, Jonathan Harris brings up the figure of Paracelsus and the epistemic break which he makes with the Galenic medical paradigm (leaving aside his unresolved relation with the tradition of medieval magic and alchemy).[20] While Fracastoro still places his theory of infectious *semina* within the framework of the classical conception of the humors, Lucretian atomism, and the Hippocratic miasma theory, Paracelsus, on the other hand, without breaking with the Neoplatonic assumption of the microcosm-macrocosm analogy, introduces a new perspective based on chemical principles. As we were saying, this is not only because it situates the origin of disease outside the body—transmitted contagiously into the openings of the body through the penetration of mineral or gaseous elements—but because he interprets it explicitly in ontological terms: disease is no longer the simple effect of a disruption to the overall balance of the body, but a separate entity located in a determined part of the body. What resulted from this new localistic approach to diagnosis—the overall condition of the body is not what causes the disease, but rather, the converse—was also a drastic transformation of the treatment. For traditional medicine to heal the body's imbalance from the lack or excess of one of the four humors of the body meant to add or subtract what was missing or in excess, in accord with a compensatory type of logic. Paracelsus initiated an approach that was diametrically opposed: what heals is not the allopathic principle of the contrary, but rather the homeopathic principle of the similar.[21] Contrary to the Galenic assumption that *"contraria a contrariis curantur*," that heat cures cold and vice versa, he asserted the isopathic rule that "like cures like":

> You should be able to recognize diseases according to their anatomy, for it is in its anatomy that the remedy is identical with the agent that caused the disease. Hence a scorpion cures scorpion poisoning, because it has the same anatomy; [thus to the anatomy of the outer man corresponds that of the inner man, the one thing always corresponds to the other]. Arsenic cures arsenic poisoning, the heart the heart, the lungs the lungs, the spleen the spleen; not ox spleen, nor is the brain of a pig any good for the brain of man, but that which corresponds to the brain in the outside world can cure the human brain.[22]

Even in the highly imaginative lexicon of astral correspondences, we come closer to the heart of the matter: if the cure against a poison is poison, then disease and health no longer lie along the axis of a frontal opposition, but in a dialectical relationship which naturally makes one the opposite of the other, but also and above all, the instrument of the other. Along these lines, Paracelsus can say that "... every single thing is double. Where there is disease, there is medicine, where there is medicine, there is sickness,"[23] since "at any one time, a medicine is often a poison and often a drug for a disease."[24] The way to remedy a disease is by administering it in forms and doses capable of bringing about permanent immunization. Of course, Paracelsus does not express himself in these terms, but the entire tenor of his iatrochemical medicine goes exactly in this direction.

True, the philosophical principle that associates a disease with its remedy has a long history rooted in the classical world, continued through Montaigne, Shakespeare and Rousseau, by which providence has placed "salutary simples beside noxious plants, and [made] poisonous animals contain their own antidote."[25] But up until a certain moment it remained essentially a literary motif: the fire extinguished by another fire (Tertullian, *De pudicitia*, 1.16), the wound healed by the same hand that inflicted it (Ovid, *Remedia amoris*, 43–48), the spear that heals the gash it opened up (Macedonius, *Greek Anthology*, 5.225). In Paracelsus's etiology it becomes not only a hermeneutical principle, but also a principle of active intervention in the face of disease: what Paracelsus advanced, far ahead of the microbiological theories of the nineteenth century, is none other than therapeutic inoculation using a portion of the same poison from which one seeks to be protected. This is exactly the same prescription that the political treatises of the Tudor and Stuart period absorbed and translated through a bodily metaphor now very distant from its canonical formulation, one that was capable of giving expression to a profound change in the discursive order.

If read in chronological order, the most important political texts of the period constructed around the State-body analogy—*A Mervailous Combat of Contrareties* (1588) by William Averell, *A Comparative Discourse of the Bodies Naturall and Politique* (1606) by Edward Forset, and *The Whore of Babylon* (1606) by Thomas Dekker—provide a sort of diagram of the era's growing immunitary bent. Beyond their marked ideological differences, what unifies these texts is the proto-functional principle that all parts of the body, including toxic germs that come to infect it from the outside, when looked at a little farther away, ultimately contribute to the body's health and safety. Unlike the old concept of the body as a structure differentiated according to a clear hierarchy between its members—still active in the *Dialogue Between Reginald Pole and Thomas Lupset* (1535) by Thomas Starkey, for example—what we have now is its representation as an integrated system of functions, in which even the potentially destructive elements can be used productively to strengthen the whole of which they are a part. For this reason, enemy infiltrators—Catholic or Jewish—are depicted as purgative medicines designed to promote healthy expulsion, or even as a poison necessary for the preventive vaccination of the body. Just as governments often make legitimate use of agents provocateurs or encourage sedition to ferret out potential conspirators, disease can also produce good and therefore be artificially reproduced for this purpose, at least if there is someone who is able "to make even poysons medicinable" as Forset expresses it.[26] The result is a true dialectical exchange between a good that comes from an evil and an evil that is transformed into good, in a sort of progressive indistinctiveness comparable to the structurally double-edged character of the Platonic *phármakon* (but also of the Latin *medicamentum* or High-German and Anglo-Saxon *Gift*).

As Derrida has argued in a form that reinstates the logic and semantics of the immune lexicon, the *phármakon* is what is opposed to its other not by excluding it, but, on the contrary, by incorporating and vicariously substituting it.[27] The other resists the *phármakon* by imitating it, and confronts it by obeying it, like the ancient *katéchon* in the face of anomy. The *phármakon* is both the evil and what opposes it, by bowing to its logic. It is itself to the extent it is other, and it is other to the extent it is itself; the point at which one passes away into two while remaining one; the one-two which is neither one nor two, yet both, overlapping across their line of opposition. This difference remains ungraspable by any identity, including the contradictory one of the *coincidentia oppositorum*. Disease and antidote, poison and cure, potion and counter potion: the *phármakon* is not a substance but rather a non-substance, a non-identity, a non-essence. But above all, it is something that relates to life from the ground of its reverse. More than affirm life, it negates its negation, and in the process ends up doubling it: *"Morte mortuos liberavit" (De doctrina Christiana*, 1.14.13), wrote Augustine in an expression that contained the nucleus of the modern immune *pharmacy*. The secret movement of the *phármakon* is thus revealed: it is a gentle power that draws death into contact with life and exposes life to the test of death.

3. *Zellenstaat*

Before we can make out this dialectic at the nerve center of contemporary biopolitics, we need to focus our attention on one further metamorphosis the organismic metaphor underwent. We have discussed the semantic turn it took during the eighteenth century at the same time the concepts of machine and body, which had remained closely linked until then, became autonomous. As a result of this divergence, and fostered by the new Romantic climate, an opposite reaction arose starting from the early nineteenth century. It was precisely at this point that the legal and political treatises began once again to speak the language of the body, regardless of their different, often conservative but sometimes liberal, and even revolutionary ideological bents. This occurred in England and France, but especially in Germany, where the works of Karl Salomo Zachariä, Johann Caspar Bluntschli and Lorenz Stein are the most well known of many that reworked the theme of the *Staatsorganismus*. Once again, the categories used by political theory to think about the form of the State organism and its internal organization were borrowed from the life sciences, especially from medicine. Just as the philosophies of the time tended to absorb images and conceptual terms from the embryological conceptions of preformism and epigenesis, similarly, administrative and economic doctrines came to represent themselves modeled on the physiological systems of the circulation of the blood. It was a seamless transfer from the natural sciences to what were known as the sciences of the spirit, a process that continued throughout the course of the century and beyond, shaping a plethora of important works including those by Trendelenburg, Spencer, Dilthey, Nietzsche, Scheler, and Simmel.[28]

But what is even more relevant to our discussion is the opposite transfer that took place over the same years: namely, instead of the influence of biological and natural sciences on sociopolitical thought that we have examined until now, the reverse tendency to import suggestions from the legal and political lexicon into the analytical framework of biomedical knowledge. This always took place within the confines of the State-body analogy, but along a line that went from the State to the body instead of from the body to the State. An example of this striking reversal between the sender and the recipient of the metaphor is already detectable in the Malthusian theory of population. This interpreted the natural sciences question of the species in sociopolitical terms, based on a process partly taken from Darwin through the theory of natural selection, which was obviously influenced in its turn by the Hobbesian *bellum omnium contra omnes*. Something similar can be said about how Adam Smith's concept of the division of labor was transposed from the field of zoology, conceived by Henri Milne-Edwards to explain the functional differences of animal organs.

However, the most emblematic case—because of the breadth and accuracy of the terms of comparison in this exchange of parts in the metaphoric process—can be found in the work of the great pathologist Rudolf Virchow in Berlin, best known as the greatest proponent of cell theory in the field of medicine. It was Virchow who was responsible for this linguistic and conceptual turn allowing the simile between the State and body to be moved onto a whole new terrain. He did this by shifting the comparison from the parts of the body (the orders or classes of the absolutist State) or its totality (the peoplenation of the later phase), to the individual elements composing it. As we know, the central premise of *Cellulartheorie*, which grew out of the work of Theodor Schwann in the late 1840s, is the thesis that the body is not an indivisible whole, but rather a set composed of elementary particles defined as cells. In them is contained the main driving force of life, namely, the function of nutrition and growth. This means that a body is not based on a single life force *(Lebenskraft)* aimed at specific ends, but on a multiplicity of discrete entities that interact with each other and mutually influence each other. However, although Schwann built on the work of Matthias Jacob Schleiden by extending to animals the cellular structure that Schleiden had identified in plants,[29] neither made use of the analogy between the body natural and the body politic. In both their works, it is true, cells are modeled as "individuals," each of which are endowed with an independent vital principle. And it is also true that some steps in Schwann employ expressions with possible political origins such as, for example, the "autocracy of the organism" *(Autokratie des Organismus)*.[30] But by no means is this accompanied by explicit use of the organismic metaphor. This was used at the end of the eighteenth century by Johann Christian Reil, from a perspective that highlighted the mutual autonomy of the individual parts of the body potentially affected by disease, but on a lexical horizon related to the concept of fiber rather than to that of the cell. François-Vincent Raspail also used a number of similarities when defining primary nuclei in plant and animal bodies, but he did not go so far as to represent them in terms of political assemblies.

The first to do so was undoubtedly Virchow. How much weight should be given to his intense participation in the Prussian democratic movement—which took him from the barricades of 1848 to a firm decision to oppose Bismarck during the years of constitutional conflict *(Verfassungskonflikt)*—is difficult to establish. Probably, as Renato Mazzolini observes in a wide-ranging, well-documented essay on the subject,[31] there was a sort of dialectical circuit between political position and scientific research which projected conceptual references from one sphere onto the other and vice versa. Georges Canguilhem, when discussing Haeckel, Virchow's student who radicalized the metaphorical device, goes so far as to argue that "a biological theory holds sway over a political philosophy. Who could tell whether one is a republican because one is a partisan of cell theory, or rather a partisan of cell theory because one is a republican?"[32] The fact remains that when the decisive moment came for Virchow to present his cell theory to the general public, he did not hesitate to use an analogy with social institutions:

> The characteristics and unity of life cannot be limited to any one particular spot in a highly developed organism (for example, to the brain of man), but are to be found only in the definite, constantly recurring structure, which every individual element displays. Hence it follows that the structural composition of a body of considerable size, a so-called individual, always represents a kind of social arrangement of parts, an arrangement of a social kind, in which a number of individual existences are mutually dependent, but in such a way, that every element has its own special action, and, even though it derive its stimulus to activity from other parts, yet alone effect the actual performance of its duties.[33]

This famous passage from *Cellularpathologie* seems to tie together all the different threads we have laid out thus far. First of all, it reproduces all the figurative traits of the body politic metaphor, and secondly, it reverses the meaning by removing it from the conservative semantics of the *Staatsorganismus*, sending it into an ideological orbit that turns in the opposite direction. But even more remarkable is the fact that this changeover of the metaphor is accomplished through the same analytical tools which led to its development during its classical phase. When Virchow argues against the perspective that assigns the brain the primary role as source and distributor of life over all other parts of the body, he is picking up again and embracing the "localist" and "territorial" position of Paracelsus versus the "generalist" approach of Galenic medicine. Of course, while an abyss divides the scientific methodology of the Berlin physician from the magical-alchemical language of his distant predecessor, it is not so wide that Virchow feels no compunction to repeatedly refer to the doctrines of Paracelsus, or to those of his successor van Helmont, as well as to others coming later who argued for the autonomy of individual existences.[34] Virchow's two-pronged attack against hemopathology, which attributed diseases to a defect in the blood circulation as a whole, and against neuropathology, which attributed them to a disorder in the entire nervous system, should be interpreted in the same vein. The opposing thesis that he advances against both is that the cells are not just a substrate of the blood and nerves, but its constitutive components endowed with a specific identity. It is true that blood and nerves are the parts of the body most likely to affect the others, but this is not in the form of a hegemony of the center over the periphery; rather, it is a mutual dependence. Not only does each stimulus generate a local response which affects the body in its turn, the more its individual components behave independently with respect to each other, the more effectively the body is regulated. In short, there are no parts of the body in which life is concentrated more than any other because life, as such, resides in each individual cell.

This is simultaneously a point of continuity and rupture with the entire biopolitical horizon: life—its preservation and development—remains connected to the figure of the body, but multiplied by the number of elementary entities that compose it. It is as if a body contained infinite lives within it, or as if life distributed itself into each of the individual particles that "make" the body. If we recall the absolutist and hierarchical connotations that the primacy of the heart and brain gave to the organismic metaphor, the significance that Virchow's cellular theory has for the same political paradigm from which he drew his inspiration is obvious:

> A historian is inclined to forget, secluded in his room, the living individuals that make up a State or a people. He speaks about the life of peoples, about the character of nations, as if a unitary power animated and pervaded every individual people, every individual nation, and he is easily persuaded to place the total action of the nation as a whole into the broader context of the history of mankind, without regard to the individual actions which make up that action. Yet every action consists in its instances, and the life of a people is nothing more than the sum of the lives of its individual citizens.[35]

Virchow's *Zellenstaat* differs from Bismarckian theories of *Staatsorganismus* with respect to where life is situated: neither in the unitary power of the body nor in the point of command that unifies it, but rather, divided and distributed among the individual elements which form it. These do not constitute an organic whole, but a structured assembly, a complex of independent, intertwined relations that recall a "unity based on community and not a despotic or oligarchic unity as the humoral and solidist schools would have it,"[36] or even a "federal arrangement of the body" since "unity, not federation, is an axiom."[37]

This is an extremely important step for the establishment of the biopolitical language. It goes so far as to assume an explicitly communitarian connotation. This is because, in Virchow's formulation, the metaphor of the body politic seems to refer to a societal institution, or even to a community open to the constitutive difference of its members, rather than to a fully-fledged State. When Virchow argues against scientists who model their theories on a "monarchical principle of the body" or on the "aristocracy" and "hierarchy" of the blood and the nervous system, opposing them to a conception of the body whose members are "dependent on each other and connected by the solidarity of their mutual need,"[38] what he ultimately does is dismantle the very principle of sovereignty which the organismic metaphor had always employed as its vehicle. The body is neither an absolutist kingdom nor a nation unified by its general will, but rather a community constituted by the equal difference of all of its members. A few years after the publication of Virchow's *Cellularpathologie*, Claude Bernard, the greatest French physiologist of the century, again using the metaphor of the political city to describe the structure of the living body, remarks about its inhabitants that "everyone has their own craft, work, attitude and talent through which they participate in the social life and on which they depend. The builder, the baker, the butcher, the industrialist and the artisan provide different products that are more varied, numerous and diversified the higher the degree of development attained by the society we are describing."[39] What emerges is a veritable deconstruction of the idea of the individual, understood etymologically as that which cannot be further divided. Nothing like the individual—a subject that would soon be taken up and radicalized by Nietzsche—is divided into a thousand fragments united solely by their difference: the "I" of the philosopher, says Virchow, is just a consequence of the "we" of the biologist.[40] Rather than being a part of the community, the individual is itself an infinitely plural community.

Once the originality of Virchow's perspective in the history of the organic metaphor is recognized, we must be cautious about extending its scope beyond the specific context of the late nineteenth century. I am not referring only to the next stage—during which the exhaustion, or the radical transformation, of cell theory would undermine the very possibility of using the analogy—but also to the previous stage, when the terms of the comparison between State and biological organism are arranged in a semantic constellation that is difficult to reduce to Virchow's conceptual apparatus. This applies particularly to the controversy he engaged in against a model of the body internally unified by the circulation of the blood and nerve ramifications. If this organic body appeared to Virchow as metaphorically proximate to a monarchical and conservative conception—versus the republican, democratic one he supported—this latter model was exactly the kind of organic body that had been associated with the monarchical conception in revolutionary France. Antoine de Baecque reconstructs the phenomenology of this conception in a frame of reference in which the metapolitical associations established by Virchow turn out to be diametrically reversed. While these associations juxtapose a localist taxonomy against the principle of corporeal unification—which Virchow identified with that of authority and hierarchy—the authors of the revolution sought precisely in the unity of the body politic, represented by the third estate, the point of rupture with the traditional theory of anatomical distinction between classes, organs and functions of the monarchy. No matter which organ is given the power to command the other parts of the body—the brain, heart, or stomach—what is asserted in all the treatises with monarchical and aristocratic roots is actually the non-equivalence of each individual in relation to the governance of the all. It is precisely to counter this—its anti-egalitarian political consequences—that the democratic pamphleteers opposed the image of one big body replenished by the blood and nerves of all the citizens reunited into one.[41]

But even more interesting for our investigation into biopolitics is the homology created between this polemical front and the controversy that during the same decades divided the exponents of the two great French medical schools: the classical clinical tradition that went from Valsalva to Morgagni passing through Bonet, and the new anatomical pathology which culminated in the teaching of Bichat. A comparison of *De causis et sedibus morborum* by Morgagni (1760) with the *Traité des membranes* by Bichat, published at a distance of forty years, provides the clearest evidence of this. While the first—in line with the regional and localist conception just described—located the origin and cause of disease in a specific area of the body, the second situated them in a wider, more complex scenario, defined by the vital relationship that connects the various body parts to the inseparable unity of a single organism. In this case, in accordance with the Jacobin unification of the body politic, the different organs are nothing but functional tributary tools of the general system of tissues which compose them. As Foucault points out, providing the most vivid representation of the epistemological contrast between the two schools,[42] the principle of diversification in organs that dominated the anatomy of Morgagni was replaced by Bichat with an isomorphic criterion of tissues based on "the same in parts distinct in their external conformation, their vital properties, and their functions."[43] Starting from this premise, the physician Cabanis, a leading exponent of the revolutionary front, was able to conclude almost in *ante litteram* opposition to the autonomist and federalistic theses later advanced by Virchow that "whole, perfect little lives exist only in the totality of one single life accompanied by all the great organs."[44]

Of course, Foucault himself points out that Bichat, Pinel and Corvisart do not exclude the nosological division made by the great anatomists of the past from the new clinical knowledge. Rather, they incorporate this division into a spatial and temporal sequence that acknowledges the entire development of the disease. This is exactly when the decisive difference arose that made it impossible for the two perspectives to be assimilated: to reinstate the life course of the disease, it was necessary to expose the body that contained it to a gaze informed by the knowledge of death. While in eighteenth-century medicine death was nothing but the end of life and of the disease that interrupted it, for the medicine beginning in the following century, death took on an independent status which detached it from the preceding pathological stages. By being removed from its indistinguishability with illness in this way, death could now shed a light on disease that made it possible to a provide a detailed reconstruction of all its different stages, including the last one which may—although not necessarily—have caused it. Death thus became an essential structure of medical perception: just as pathology illuminated physiology through contrast, beginning with Bichat, death became the starting point from which medical knowledge was able to grasp the truth of life.

4. *The Governance of Life*

It was Foucault who connected the crisis in sovereignty to the birth of biopolitics in the same epochal transition: while sovereignty was still exercised through the right to put to death, the focus of biopolitics was centered on the care of life. However, Foucault also cautioned against an overly mechanical interpretation of this opposition: in neither case are life and death placed in an alternation that entirely excludes one another. Certainly this is not the case in the classic framework of sovereign power, in which the right to put subjects to death was limited to defending the State and the person of the king, and hence directed toward the need to keep the body politic alive. But nor is it the case in the context of modern biopower either, which was established for the purpose of developing life, certainly, but in a form that did not lose all contact with the presence of death. One could say that if the ancient sovereign right looked at life from the perspective of distributing death, the new biopolitical order subordinated even death to the demands of reproducing life. This stubborn persistence of death within a politics of life was confirmed early on by the singular fact that the greatest international effort made toward setting up a health organization—the Beveridge Plan—took place in 1942, in the midst of a war destined to kill fifty million people, almost as if the right to health could temporarily substitute the right to life, or even be deduced from its opposite. But so far death still remained outside the life-producing mechanism, like a non-metabolized residue or one term in a dialectical opposition. What takes on even greater importance, though, is the way death enters into the enclosure that seemed to exclude it. This is where Foucault seeks out the black box of biopolitics: in the liminal space where death is not solely the archaic figure against which life defines itself, nor the tragic price that life must pay in order to expand, but rather one of its inner folds, a mode—or tonality—of its own preservation.

This is the mechanism that we have thus far traced back to the logic of immunity. To recognize its most typical movements at work in biopolitical practices, we must go back to the particular place where it operates—at the juncture between the spheres of the individual and the species. When Foucault identifies the object of biopower as the population, he does not refer to individual holders of certain rights, nor to their confluence in a people defined as the collective subject of a nation, but rather to the living being in the *specificity* of its constitution.[45] In other words, he is referring to the only element that groups all individuals into the same species: namely, the fact that they have a body. Biopolitics addresses itself to this body—an individual one because it belongs to each person, and at the same time a general one because it relates to an entire genus—with the aim of protecting it, strengthening it, and reproducing it, in line with an objective that goes beyond the old disciplinary apparatus because it concerns the very existence of the State in its economic, legal and political "interest." This explains Foucault's comment about the Prussian health system that ". . . the workers' body was not what interested this public health administration, but rather the body of the individuals themselves who, by reuniting, constituted the State."[46] As we noted in the metaphorical device used by Virchow, just as individuals are an integral part of the State, in the same way, the State does not exist outside the body of the individuals who compose it. These bodies—each and every one—have to be cared for, stimulated, and multiplied as the absolute good from which the State derives its legitimacy. From this point of view, rather than viewing the shift from the sovereign to the biopolitical as a further development of the organismic metaphor, it actually signals the effective realization of the body politic metaphor in the material body of the individuals who constitute a population. It is as if the metaphor of the body finally took on its own body: "The social 'body' ceased to be a simple juridico-political metaphor (like the one in the *Leviathan*) and became a biological reality and a field for medical intervention."[47] While the bodies of the subjects inscribed in the great body of *Leviathan* were necessary for its life, to the point that one could sacrifice one's own life to it, following the sovereign logic of an appropriative and subtractive power, these bodies are now one with the larger body, in the sense that the power of the State coincides literally with the survival of the individuals who bear it in their bodies.

This explains the growing political importance that medical knowledge assumed starting from the middle of the eighteenth century: when the body of citizens became the real rather than simply metaphoric place where the exercise of power was concentrated, the issue of public health—understood in its widest and most general sense as the "welfare" of the nation—clearly became the pivot around which the entire economic, administrative and political affairs of the state revolved. This perspective brings into view another difference between biopolitical governance versus the traditional procedures of sovereign rule.[48] These, too, were set up and arranged to defend the State from both internal and external threats to its survival, of course, but in a form that was only indirectly related to the actual life of individual citizens, in a way that was institutionally mediated. On the contrary, what characterizes the horizon of biopower is rather the way the whole sphere of politics, law and economics becomes a function of the qualitative welfare and quantitative increase of the population, considered purely in its biological aspect: life becomes government business, in all senses of the word, just as government becomes first and foremost the governance of life. This is when the institution of health care began to undergo progressive expansion into spheres that had previously fallen strictly under political and administrative competence. Foucault describes these using the term "noso-politics": meaning not so much mandatory State intervention in the domain of medical knowledge as the emergence of health care and related practices on the scene of every public sector. The resulting limitless process of medicalization thus extended well beyond the health sector in a growing interplay between the biological, legal and political. It is well represented by the semantic passage from the sovereign language of the law to the biopolitical language of norms: while law still subjected life to an order that presupposed it, norms are based on an absolute implication between biology and right. By establishing the boundaries of medical competency, norm allows the physician to define the threshold of criminal liability for illegal behavior through the distinction between criminality and abnormality. Moreover, current law-making on matters of life and death—such as artificial insemination, eugenics, and euthanasia—demonstrates that the sphere of the living being has been effectively superimposed onto that of the political, as summed up by Foucault in a justly famous observation: "For millennia, man remained what he was for Aristotle: a living animal with the additional capacity for a political existence; modern man is an animal whose politics place his existence as a living being into question."[49]

But what does it mean to say that politics is enclosed within the boundaries of life? That life is the primary object—and purpose—of politics? What is the horizon of meaning that is given to biopolitics as a result of this cobelonging? In my view, the answer to this question should not be sought in the folds of a sovereign power that includes life by excluding it. Rather, what I believe it should point to is an epochal conjuncture out of which the category of sovereignty makes room for, or at least intersects with, that of immunization. This is the general procedure through which the intersection between politics and life is realized. The purpose of biopolitics is not to distinguish life along a line which sacrifices one part of it to the violent domination of the other—although that possibility can never be completely ruled out—but on the contrary, to save it, protect it, develop it as a whole. But the point we have focused on from the outset is that this objective involves the use of an instrument that is bound to it through the negative, as if the very doubling that life experiences of itself through the political imperative that "makes it live" contained something that internally contradicted it. A look at the process of generalized, undefined medicalization described by Foucault over the last two centuries provides a powerful confirmation of this notion.[50] He describes it as taking place through three different parallel scansions which he traces back to the medicine of the German State, the medicine of urban France, and English occupational medicine. Without reconstructing the entire dynamic, the element that unifies them is the leading role given to the fight against the risk of infection in each of these experiments. Connected with this prophylactic need is the importance granted to public hygiene as a prerequisite of sanitary practice, but also the function of social control that was associated with it from the outset.

The first step is to isolate places where infectious germs may develop more easily due to the storage of bodies, whether dead or alive: ports, prisons, factories, hospitals, cemeteries. But the entire territory is gradually divided into strictly separate zones based on the need for both medical and social surveillance. The original model from medieval times is that of quarantine, separated in its turn into the two pathogenic archetypes of leprosy and the plague: while the first led to the expulsion of the sick outside the city walls, the second provided for their placement into individual settings that would allow them to be numbered, registered and assiduously controlled. Overlapping onto this more archaic model, over time there arose another variation coming from the worlds of the military and schools, also tending toward spatial division, first by conglomerates or classes and then by individual places. What is formed at the confluence of both these dispositifs is a kind of *quadrillage*, or pigeonholing, that placed individuals in an extensive system of institutional segments—family, school, army, factory, hospital—prohibiting, or at least controlling, circulation in the name of public safety. All the urbanization that developed in Europe starting in the middle of the eighteenth century took on the appearance of a dense network of fences between places, zones, and territories protected by boundaries established according to political and administrative rules that went well beyond sanitary needs. The impression we get is actually of a continuous passage—and mutual reinforcement—between sanitary measures, such as compulsory vaccination, and inclusionary/exclusionary ones of a socio-economic nature. For example, the separation between rich neighborhoods and poor neighborhoods that was carried out in many nineteenth-century English cities was the direct consequence of the cholera epidemic of 1832, just as the formation of large urban safety systems was parallel to the discovery of antibiotics against endemic and epidemic infectious diseases.

The immune framework inside of which lies this general process of superimposition between therapeutic practice and political order is all too obvious: to become the object of political "care," life had to be separated off and closed up inside progressively desocialized spaces that were meant to immunize it against anything arising from community. This first form of coercion against any external excess of the life force was flanked by another that penetrated to its interior as well. Foucault draws attention to it primarily in a text written in 1976 on the potentially lethal nature of medicine: "It was not necessary to wait for Illich or the disciples of anti-medicine to know that one of the capabilities of medicine is killing. Medicine kills, it has always killed, and it has always been aware of this."[51] What Foucault is trying to draw our attention to here is how the premise he began with has been transformed from being attributable to the ignorance of medicine to the skill of medicine. As in Paracelsus's poisonous pharmacopia, the potential danger of treatment arises not from lack of medical knowledge, but from its progress:

> what one might call positive iatrogenicity, rather than iatrogenicity: the harmful effects of medication due not to errors of diagnosis or the accidental inges-

tion of those substances, but to the action of medical practice itself, in so far as it has a rational basis. At present, the instruments that doctors and medicine in general have at their disposal cause certain effects, precisely because of their efficacy. Some of these effects are purely harmful and others are unable to be controlled, which leads the human species into a perilous area of history, into a field of probabilites and risks, the magnitude of which cannot be precisely measured.[52]

The methods causing these adverse effects in the history of medicine are various. One of the main culprits is immunotherapy, which in acting to defend the body ends up weakening it, thereby lowering its sensitivity threshold to aggressors. As in all areas of contemporary social systems, neurotically haunted by a continuously growing need for security, this means that the risk from which the protection is meant to defend is actually created by the protection itself.[53] The risk, in short, requires protection to the same degree that the protection creates the risk: "Bacterial and viral protection, which represent both a risk and a protection for the organism, with which it has functioned until then, undergoes a change as a result of the therapeutic intervention, thus becoming exposed to attacks against which the organism had previously been protected."[54] This potential outcome, inscribed at the heart of modern biopolitics, becomes less and less hypothetical when physicians and biologists "are no longer working at the level of the individual and his descendants, but are beginning to work at the level of life itself and its fundamental events."[55] This is obviously a limit-point beyond which the entire horizon of biopower is likely to come into deadly conflict with itself. This does not mean that we can go back, by re-establishing the old figures of sovereign power, for instance. Any form of politics not directed toward life as such, which does not regard citizens from the point of view of their living body, is inconceivable today. But this can happen in mutually opposing forms that bring into play the very meaning of biopolitics: either the self-destructive revolt of immunity against itself or an opening to its converse, community.

For Foucault, as we have noted, the biopolitical horizon is defined by the passage from the sovereign order of the law to the disciplinary order of the norm. But what exactly is a norm? And how does it statutorily differ from the law? The answers Foucault provides in historical terms would seem to leave this question unanswered from a strictly conceptual point of view. Beginning with his *Maladie mentale et personnalité*[56] a system of norms is defined as a set of social, institutional, and linguistic rules that structure human life according to given orders of control and power.[57] In this sense, even if different from the law in terms of its effect—which is not only repressive but also productive—a norm reiterates the way law relates to its object, which remains by way of a presupposed anticipation. Although based on different objectives, both in the case of the law and the norm, the subjects are preconstituted by something which both exceeds them and precedes them. Or, as we have seen, it exceeds them in the form of precedence: life is already included in its normative decision, just as in the sovereign model life was already pre-judged by the efficacy of the legal system. It is this structural homology that maintains the disciplinary norm in the immunitary circle of the law. What unites them, though in inverted form, is the negative connection that both establish between the singularity of the living being and the preservation of life: the conditions of preservation, or reproduction, of life are located outside and before the living being's natural line of development.

To force this interpretive grid into a different conception of the norm, we must look to the work of Georges Canguilhem. Without tracing out the entire course of his reflection on the normal and the pathological, the point we need to focus on, because it gives an indication of the extent to which it differs from Foucault's lexicons,[58] is precisely his attempt to remove the norm from the transcendental presupposition of the law. Rather than presupposed, and therefore outside the sphere of deployment of the living being, the biological norm is intrinsic and immanent. It is not prescribed, as is the law, but inscribed in the matter through which it exerts itself: "an organism's norm of life is furnished by the organism itself, contained in its existence . . . the norm of a human organism coincides with the organism itself."[59] What Canguilhem accomplishes—in the double wake of Leriche and Goldstein's physiological research and the psychiatric experiments by Lagache, Blondel and Minkowski—is a true reversal of the relations between precedence and succession: while the law is what establishes the threshold of the infraction by sanctioning it, the infraction is what determines the need as well as the possibility of the norm. Thus, if the illegal is preceded by the legal both on the historical and logical planes, "the abnormal, while logically second, is existentially first."[60] Not only that but, in addition to pre-existing and then resisting the normativization that invests it, the abnormal somehow gets inside it, to the point of changing it. This dynamic issues not only from the individual and differentiating, rather than general and homologizing, character of the norm, but also, more deeply, from its tendency toward permanent self-deconstruction. Since every norm can only establish itself through the infraction of, or deviation from, the one that precedes it, it follows that the organism that is most "normal" is able to break and change its own norms more often. The norm for an organism, in short, is the ability to change its own norms. This means, firstly, that biological normality coincides with normativity, namely, the power to create new norms; and secondly, that normativity, far from being reducible to a form of preventive or even subsequent normalization, is a measure of the vital force of existence.

Without now probing more generally into Canguilhem's vitalism, let us go directly to where we want to arrive: unlike the law, the norm he refers to is not situated in the boundary of separation between the living being and life, but at their point of tangency. This conceptual difference is what removes it from the immune paradigm: not only is the preservation of life not based, as Walter Benjamin said, on the sacrifice of the living, it no longer constitutes the original motive of living things. If anything, preservation is the residual commitment life assumes when it has already lost some of its vitality. As Kurt Goldstein already noted, the survival instinct is not a general law of life, but that of a life that has retracted into diseases.[61] By contrast, the healthy organism is measured by its capacity and willingness to experience the unexpected, with all the risks this entails, including the extreme risk of a catastrophic reaction. One might say that for the organism, disease represents the risk of not being able to take risks: not a lack, but an excess of preservation. This is where the main axis of Canguilhem's perspective joins up. To say that the pathological is not just a quantitative change in physiology is to assert that disease, like health, has its own norm, but a norm that lacks the ability to modify itself, to produce new norms. It is a non-normative norm. To return to how it differs from sovereign law, "bare life" is not the object or effect of the norm, but the place of its invariance. It is not the sphere of anomy or anomaly; nor is it the contrary of *nómos* or *omalós* but, rather, the entropic contrary of anormativity.

Notes

1. This is the thesis put forward by D. G. Hale in *The Body Politic: A Political Metaphor in Renaissance English Literature*, Mouton, The Hague-Paris 1971; and then essentially

reworked by E. M. W. Tillyard, in *The Elizabethan World Picture*, Pelican, Harmondsworth 1972 and by L. Barkan, in *Nature's Work of Art: The Human Body as Image of the World*, Yale University Press, New Haven 1975. Finally, see J. Sawday, *The Body Emblazoned: Dissection and the Human Body in Renaissance Culture*, Routledge, London 1995.

2. See P. Becchi, "Meccanicismo e organicismo. Gli antecedenti di un'opposizione," in *Filosofia politica* (1999), no. 3, pp. 457–72. But see the entire section on the "body politic" in *Filosofia politica* (1993), no. 3, which includes essays by A. Cavarero, D. Panizza and S. Mezzadra.

3. See A. Cavarero, *Corpo in figure*, Feltrinelli, Milan 1995, pp. 187–217 (although it supports the thesis we argue against on the logocentric marginalization of the body in modernity).

4. Thomas Hobbes, *Leviathan (1651)*, Chapter 29.

5. Ibid., Chapter 19.

6. Jean-Jacques Rousseau, *Economie politique*, in *Oeuvres Complètes*, Gallimard, Paris 1959–69, III.

7. Jean-Jacques Rousseau, *The Social Contract*, Section 6, "The Social Compact".

8. Ibid., Section 7, "The Sovereign".

9. Emmanuel Joseph Sieyès, "What is the Third Estate?" in *Political Writings*, ed. and trans. Michael Sonenscher, Hackett Publishing, Indianapolis IN 2003, p. 162.

10. I am alluding to the important work by Antoine de Baecque, *The Body Politic. Corporeal Metaphor in Revolutionary France, 1770–1800*, Stanford UP, Stanford CA 1997.

11. Rogozinski, " 'Comme les paroles d'un homme ivre . . .': chair de l'histoire et corps politique," *Les Cahiers de Philosophic*, 1994–95, no. 18, pp. 71–102.

12. Ibid., p. 101.

13. M. Carbone appears to take a similar approach in an essay entitled appropriately "Carne," appearing in *Aut Aut*, 2001, no. 304, pp. 99–119. The political significance of the theme of "flesh" is also well delineated by E. Lisciani-Petrini in "La passione impolitica della politica. Merleau-Ponty tra 'filosofia e non filosofia'," in *Nichilismo e politica*, op. cit. pp. 55–73.

14. This is what Jacques Derrida also winds up admitting, although with many reservations, in *Le Toucher, Jean-Luc Nancy*, Galilée, Paris 2000, pp. 262 ff.

15. D. Franck, *Chair et corps. Sur la phenoménologie de Husserl*, Minuit, Paris 1981, p. 167.

16. Martin Heidegger, *History of the Concept of Time*, Indiana UP, Bloomington IN 1992, p. 41.

17. See J. Schlanger, *Les métaphores de l'organisme*, l'Harmattan (earlier ed. Vrin 1971), Paris 1995, pp. 182 ff.

18. For more on this topic, see S. D'Alessio, "Tra la vita e la morte: declinazioni della libertà in Machiavelli e Hobbes," in *Tolleranza e libertà*, ed. V. Dini, Elèuthera, Milan 2001, pp. 41–66.

19. See S. Greenblatt, "Invisible Bullets: Authority and its Subversion," in *Shakespeare's 'Rough Magic': Renaissance Essays in Honor of C. L. Barber*, ed. P. Erickson and C. Kahn, U of Delaware P, Newark 1985, pp. 276–302.

20. J. G. Harris, *Foreign Bodies and the Body Politic*, Cambridge University Press, Cambridge 1998, pp. 23 ff.

21. For more on this, see also W. Pagel, *Paracelsus: An Introduction to Philosophical Medicine in the Era of Renaissance*, Kargel, Basel 1968.

22. Paracelsus, *Paragranum*, trans. Nicholas Goodrick-Clarke, North Atlantic Books, Berkeley CA, Section 5.7, pp. 74–75 [Sentence in square brackets quoted from Italian version: *Paragrano*, trans. F. Masini, Laterza, Bari 1973, p. 105.]

23. Ibid, *Paragrano*, Italian version, p. 105.

24. Ibid., p. 121.

25. Jean-Jacques Rousseau, *Rousseau's Social Contract, Etc.*, trans. G. D. H. Cole, J. M. Dent, Dutton, London-NY 1920, p. 149.

26. J. G. Harris, *Foreign Bodies and the Body Politic*, p. 73.

27. Jacques Derrida, "La pharmacie de Platon," in *La dissémination*, Seuil, Paris 1972. For a discussion on this aspect of Derrida—between *communitas* and *immunitas*—see the monograph by C. Resta, *L'evento dell'altro. Etica e politica in Jacques Derrida*, Bollati Boringhieri (coll. Saggi), Torino 2003.

28. For a look at this relationship see the very helpful study by A. Orsucci, *Dalla biologia cellulare alle scienze dello spirito*, il Mulino, Bologna 1992.

29. The reconstruction of this question by V. Cappelletti, *Entelechia. Saggi sulle dottrine biologiche del secolo decimonono*, Sansoni, Florence 1965 is still useful.

30. T. Schwann, *Mikroskopische Untersuchungen über die Übereinstimmung in der Struktur und dem Wachsthum der Thiere und Pflanzen*, Verlag der Sander'schen Buchhandlung, Berlin 1839, p. 223.

31. R. G. Mazzolini, "Stato e organismo, individui e cellule nell'opera di Rudolf Virchow negli anni 1845–1860," in *Annali dell'Istituto storico italo-germanico*, IX, 1983, pp. 153–293. But for more on Virchow's role see equally A. Bauer, *Rudolph Virchow—der politische Arzt*, Stopp, Berlin 1982.

32. Georges Canguilhem, *Knowledge of Life*, Fordham UP, New York 2008, p 48.

33. Rudof Virchow, *Cellular Pathology: as based upon physiological and pathological history*, John Churchill, London 1860, p. 14.

34. See A. Orsucci, *Dalla biologia cellulare alle scienze dello spirito*, p. 76.

35. Rudof Virchow, *Alter und neuer Vitalismus*, in *Archiv für pathologische Anatomie und Physiologie und für klinische Medicin*, IX (1856) [Quoted from Italian version: *Vecchio e nuovo vitalismo*, Laterza, Bari 1969, p. 137].

36. Ibid., pp. 163–64.

37. Ibid., pp. 167–68.

38. The texts by Virchow that are cited here are collected in an appendix to the essay by Mazzolini, cited above, pp. 282–90.

39. C. Bernard, *Leçons sur les phénomènes de la vie communs aux animaux et aux végétaux*, Librairie J.-B. Baillière et Fils, Paris 1885, p. 356.

40. Virchow, *Die Cellularpathologie*, pp. 72–73.

41. Antoine de Baecque, *The Body Politic. Corporeal Metaphor in Revolutionary France, 1770–1800*, Stanford UP, Stanford CA 1997, p. 93.

42. Michel Foucault, *The Birth of the Clinic*, Routledge Classics, London 2003, p. 157.

43. X. Bichat, *A Treatise On the Membranes in General: and on different membranes in particular*, Cummings and Hillliard, Boston 1813, p. 22–23.

44. P.-J.-G. Cabanis, *Note touchant le supplice de la guillotine*, in *Oeuvres complètes de Cabanis*, Bosange Frères, Paris 1823, II, pp. 161–83.

45. For an overview of the concept see the article "Biopolitica" by L. Bazzicalupo, in *Enciclopedia del pensiero politico*, ed. R. Esposito and C. Galli, Laterza, Rome-Bari 2000, p. 70. More specifically on biopolitics in Foucault, see the issue of *Cités*, 2000, no. 2, *Michel Foucault: de la guerre des races au biopouvoir*.

46. M. Foucault, "The Birth of Social Medicine," in *Power, Essential Works of Foucault, Vol. 3*, Penguin Books, London 2002, pp. 134–156 [Quoted from the Italian version: "La nascita della medicina sociale," in *Archivio Foucault 2. 1971–1977. Poteri, saperi, strategie*, ed. A. Dal Lago, Feltrinelli, Milan 1997, p. 227].

47. Michel Foucault, "About the Concept of the 'Dangerous Individual' in 19th Century Legal Psychiatry," *Politics, philosophy, culture: interviews and other writings, 1977–1984*, ed. M. Morris and P. Patton, Routledge, London 1988, p. 134.

48. On the phenomenology and crisis of the paradigm of sovereignty, see E. Balibar, "Prolégomènes à la souveraineté," in *Nous, citoyens d'Europe?*, La Découverte, Paris 2001, pp. 257–85.

49. Michel Foucault, *Will to Knowledge, History of Sexuality Vol. 1*, Penguin Books, London 1998, p. 143.

50. Among the many works that Foucault dedicated to the process of medicalization of modern society, in addition to the above-cited "Birth of Social Medicine" see also "La politique de la santé au XVIII siècle," in *Les Machines à guérir. Aux origines de l'hôpital moderne; dossiers et documents*, Institut de l'environnement, Paris 1976.

51. Michel Foucault, "The Crisis of Medicine or the Crisis of Anti-medicine?" in *Foucault Studies Journal*, 2004, no. 1, p. 9. On this topic see also *Reassessing Foucault. Power, Medicine and the Body*, ed. C. Jones and R. Porter, Routledge, London 1994.

52. Foucault, "Crisis of Medicine," pp. 9–10.

53. This aporetic dialectic between risk and protection is central to interpreters of contemporaneity as well, among critics from such widely divergent schools as J. Delumeau (*Rassurer et proteger*, Fayard, Paris 1989), Niklas Luhmann (*Soziologie des Risikos*, De Gruyter, Berlin 1991), U. Beck (*Risikogesellschaft. Auf dem Weg in eine andere Moderne*, Suhrkamp, Frankfurt am Main 1986) and Z. Bauman (*In Search of Politics*, Polity Press, Cambridge 1999).

54. Foucault, "Crisis of Medicine," p. 10.

55. Ibid., p. 11.

56. Michel Foucault, *Maladie mentale et personnalité*, Puf, Paris 1954.

57. See G. Le Blanc, *Foucault et le contournement du normal et du pathologique* and B. Cabestan, *Du régime: normativité et subjectivité*, entrambi in *Michel Foucault et la médecine*, ed. Ph. Artières and E. Da Silva, Kimé, Paris 2001, respectively, pp. 29–48 and 60–83.

58. For a comparison of the two thinkers, see P. Macherey, "De Canguilhem à Canguilhem en passant par Foucault," in *Georges Canguilhem, Philosophe, historien des sciences*, Albin Michel, Paris 1993, pp. 286–94. On the topic of norm see also G. Le Blanc, *Canguilhem et les normes*, Puf, Paris 1998.

59. Georges Canguilhem, *On the Normal and the Pathological*, D. Reidal Pub. Co., 1978, p. 159.

60. Ibid., p. 149.

61. See K. Goldstein, *Der Aufbau des Organismus*, Nijhoff, Den Haag 1934 (especially Chapter X on *norm, health and disease* and the section in it on the tendency toward preservation as the expression of a life in decline).

CHAPTER 17

THE ENIGMA OF BIOPOLITICS

Roberto Esposito

Bio/politics

Recently, not only has the notion of "biopolitics" moved to the center of international debate, but the term has opened a completely new phase in contemporary thought. From the moment that Michel Foucault reproposed and redefined the concept (when not coining it), the entire frame of political philosophy emerged as profoundly modified. It wasn't that classical categories such as those of "law" *[diritto]*, "sovereignty," and "democracy" suddenly left the scene—they continue to organize current political discourse—but that their effective meaning always appears weaker and lacking any real interpretive capacity. Rather than explaining a reality that everywhere slips through their analytic grip, these categories themselves demand to be subjected to the scrutiny of a more penetrating gaze that both deconstructs and explains them. Let's consider, for instance, law *[legge]*. Differently from what many have argued, there is nothing that suggests that such a domain has somehow been reduced. On the contrary, the impression is that the domain of law is gaining terrain both domestically and internationally; that the process of normativization is investing increasingly wider spaces. Nevertheless, this doesn't mean that juridical language per se reveals itself to be incapable of illuminating the profound logic of such a change. When one speaks of "human rights," for example, rather than referring to established juridical subjects, one refers to individuals defined by nothing other than the simple fact of being alive. Something analogous can be said about the political *dispositif* of sovereignty. Anything but destined to weaken as some had rashly forecast (at least with regard to the world's greatest power), sovereignty seems to have extended and intensified its range of action—beyond a repertoire that for centuries had characterized its relation to both citizens and other state structures. With the clear distinction between inside and outside weakened (and therefore also the distinction between war and peace that had characterized sovereign power for so long), sovereignty finds itself directly engaged with questions of life and death that no longer have to do with single areas, but with the world in all of its extensions. Therefore, if we take up any perspective, we see that something that goes beyond the customary language appears to involve directly law and politics, dragging them into a dimension that is outside their conceptual apparatuses. This "something"—this element and this substance, this substrate and this upheaval—is precisely the object of biopolitics.

Yet there doesn't appear to be an adequate categorical exactitude that corresponds to the epochal relevance of biopolitics. Far from having acquired a definitive order, the concept of biopolitics appears to be traversed by an uncertainty, by an uneasiness that impedes every stable connotation. Indeed, I would go further. Biopolitics is exposed to a growing hermeneutic pressure that seems to make it not only the instrument but also the object of a bitter philosophical and political fight over the configuration and destiny of the current age. From here its oscillation (though one could well say its disruption) between interpretations, and before that even its different, indeed conflicting tonalities. What is at stake of course is the nature of the relation that forces together the two terms that make up the category of biopolitics. But even before that its definition: what do we understand by *bíos* and how do we want to think of a politics that directly addresses it? The reference to the classic figure of *bíos politikos* doesn't help, since the semantics in question become meaningful precisely when the meaning of the term withdraws. If we want to remain with the Greek (and in particular with the Aristotelian) lexicon, biopolitics refers, if anything, to the dimension of *zōē*, which is to say to life in its simple biological capacity *[tenuta]*, more than it does to *bíos*, understood as "qualified life" or "form of life," or at least to the line of conjugation along which *bíos* is exposed to *zōē*, naturalizing *bíos* as well. But precisely with regard to this terminological exchange, the idea of biopolitics appears to be situated in a zone of double indiscernibility, first because it is inhabited by a term that does not belong to it and indeed risks distorting it. And then because it is fixed by a concept, precisely that of *zōē*, which is stripped of every formal connotation. *Zōē* itself can only be defined problematically: what, assuming it is even conceivable, is an absolutely natural life? It's even more the case today, when the human body appears to be increasingly challenged and also literally traversed by technology *[tecnica]*.[1] Politics penetrates directly in life and life becomes other from itself. Thus, if a natural life doesn't exist that isn't at the same time technological as well; if the relation between *bíos* and *zōē* needs by now (or has always needed) to include in it a third correlated term, *technē*— then how do we hypothesize an exclusive relation between politics and life?

Here too the concept of biopolitics seems to withdraw or be emptied of content in the same moment in which it is formulated. What remains clear is its negative value, what it is *not* or the horizon of sense that marks its closing. Biopolitics has to do with that complex of mediations, oppositions, and dialectical operations that in an extended phase made possible the modern political order, at least according to current interpretation. With respect to these and the questions and problems to which they correspond relative to the definition of power, to the measure of its exercise and to the delineation of its limits, it's indisputable that a general shift of field, logic, and the object of politics has taken place. At the moment in which on one side the modern distinctions between public and private, state and society, local and global collapse, and on the other that all other sources of legitimacy dry up, life becomes encamped in the center of every political procedure. No other politics is conceivable other than a politics of life, in the objective and subjective sense of the term. But it is precisely with reference to the relation between the subject and object of politics that the interpretive divergence to which I alluded earlier appears again: How are we to comprehend a political government of life? In what sense does life govern politics or in what sense does politics govern life? Does it concern a governing *of* or *over* life? It is the same conceptual alternative that one can express through the lexical bifurcation between the terms, used indifferently sometimes, of "biopolitics" and "biopower." By the first is meant a politics in the name of life and by the second a life subjected to the command of politics. But here too in this mode the paradigm that seeks a conceptual linking between the terms emerges as split, as if it had been cut in two by the very same movement. Compressed (and at the same time destabilized) by competing readings and subject to continuous rotations of meaning around its own axis, the concept of biopolitics risks losing its identity and becoming an enigma.

To understand why, it isn't enough to limit our perspective simply to Foucault's observations. Rather, we need to return to those texts and to authors (often not cited) that Foucault's discussion derives from, and against which he repositions himself, while critically deconstructing them. These can be cataloged in three distinct and successive blocks in time (at least those that explicitly refer to the concept of biopolitics). They are characterized, respectively, by an approach that is organistic, anthropological, and naturalistic. In the first instance, they refer to a substantial series of essays, primarily German, that are joined by a vitalistic conception of the state, such as Karl Binding's *Zum Werden und Leben der Staaten* (1920), of which we will have occasion to speak later; Eberhard Dennert's *Der Staat als lebendiger Organismus* (1920); and Edward Hahn's *Der Staat, ein Lebenwesen* (1926).[2] Our attention will be focused, however, most intently on the Swede Rudolph Kjellén, probably because he was the first to employ the term "biopolitics" (we also owe him the expression "geopolitics" that Friedrich Ratzel and Karl Haushofer will later elaborate in a decidedly racist key). With respect to such a racist propensity, which will shortly thereafter culminate in the Nazi theorization of a "vital space" *(Lebensraum)* we should note that Kjellén's position remains less conspicuous, despite his proclaimed sympathy for Wilhelminian German as well as a certain propensity for an aggressive foreign policy. As he had previously argued in his book of 1905 on the great powers, vigorous states, endowed with a limited territory, discover the need for extending their borders through the conquest, fusion, and colonialization of other lands.[3] But it's in the volume from 1916 titled *The State as Form of Life* that Kjellén sees this geopolitical demand as existing in close relation to an organistic conception that is irreducible to constitutional theories of a liberal framework.[4] While these latter represent the state as the artificial product of a free choice of individuals that have created it, he understands it to be a "living form" *(som livsform* in Swedish or *als Lebensform* in German), to the extent that it is furnished with instincts and natural drives. Already here in this transformation of the idea of the state, according to which the state is no longer a subject of law born from a voluntary contract but a whole that is integrated by men and which behaves as a single individual both spiritual and corporeal, we can trace the originary nucleus of biopolitical semantics. In *Outline for a Political System*, Kjellén brings together a compendium of the preceding theses:

> This tension that is characteristic of life itself . . . pushed me to denominate such a discipline *biopolitics*, which is analogous with the science of life, namely, biology. In so doing we gain much, considering that the Greek word *bíos* designates

not only natural and physical life, but perhaps just as significantly cultural life. Naming it in this way also expresses that dependence of the laws of life that society manifests and that promote, more than anything else, the state itself to that role of arbiter or at a minimum of mediator.[5]

These are expressions that take us beyond the ancient metaphor of the body-state with all its multiple metamorphoses of post-Romantic inspiration. What begins to be glimpsed here is the reference to a natural substrate, to a substantial principle that is resistant and that underlies any abstraction or construction of institutional character. The idea of the impossibility of a true overcoming of the natural state in that of the political emerges in opposition to the modern conception derived from Hobbes that one can preserve life only by instituting an artificial barrier with regard to nature, which is itself incapable of neutralizing the conflict (and indeed is bound to strengthen it). Anything but the negation of nature, the political is nothing else but the continuation of nature at another level and therefore destined to incorporate and reproduce nature's original characteristics.

If this process of the naturalization of politics in Kjellén remains inscribed within a historical-cultural apparatus, it experiences a decisive acceleration in the essay that is destined to become famous precisely in the field of comparative biology. I am referring to *Staatsbiologie*, which was also published in 1920 by Baron Jakob von Uexküll with the symptomatic subtitle *Anatomy, Physiology, and Pathology of the State*.[6] Here, as with Kjellén, the discourse revolves around the biological configuration of a state-body that is unified by harmonic relations of its own organs, representative of different professions and competencies, but with a dual (and anything but irrelevant) lexical shift with respect to the preceding model. Here what is spoken about is not any state but the German state with its peculiar characteristics and vital demands. What makes the difference, however, is chiefly the emphasis that pathology assumes with respect to what is subordinated to it, namely, anatomy and physiology. Here we can already spot the harbinger of a theoretical weaving—that of the degenerative syndrome and the consequent regenerative program—fated to reach its macabre splendors in the following decades. Threatening the public health of the German body is a series of diseases, which obviously, referring to the revolutionary traumas of the time, are located in subversive trade unionism, electoral democracy, and the right to strike: tumors that grow in the tissues of the state, causing anarchy and finally the state's dissolution. It would be "as if the majority of the cells in our body (rather than those in our brain) decided which impulses to communicate to the nerves."[7] But even more relevant, if we consider the direction of future totalitarian developments, is the biopolitical reference to those "parasites" which, having penetrated the political body, organize themselves to the disadvantage of other citizens. These are divided between "symbionts" from different races who under certain circumstances can be useful to the state and true parasites, which install themselves as an extraneous living body within the state, and which feed off of the same vital substance. Uexküll's threateningly prophetic conclusion is that one needs to create a class of state doctors to fight the parasites, or to confer on the state a medical competency that is capable of bringing it back to health by removing the causes of the disease and by expelling the carriers of germs. He writes: "What we are still lacking is an academy with a forward-looking vision not only for creating a class of state doctors, but also for instituting a state system of medicine. We possess no organ to which we can trust the hygiene of the state."[8]

The third text that should hold our attention—because it is expressly dedicated to the category in question—is *Bio-politics*. Written by the Englishman Morley Roberts, it was published in London in 1938 with the subtitle *An Essay in the Physiology, Pathology and Politics of the Social and Somatic Organism*.[9] Here too the underlying assumption, which Roberts sets forth immediately in the book's introduction, is the connection, not only analogical, but real, between politics and biology, and particularly medicine. His perspective is not so distant fundamentally from that of Uexküll. If physiology is indivisible from the pathology from which it derives its meaning and emphasis, the state organism cannot be truly known or guided except by evaluating its actual and potential diseases. More than a simple risk, these diseases represent the ultimate truth because it is principally a living entity that in fact can die. For this reason, biopolitics has the assignment on the one hand of recognizing the organic risks that jeopardize the body politic and on the other of locating and predisposing mechanisms of defense against them; these too are rooted in the same biological terrain. The most innovative part of Roberts's book is connected precisely to this ultimate demand and is constituted by an extraordinary comparison between the defensive apparatus of the state and the immunitary system that anticipates an interpretive paradigm to which we will return:

> The simplest way to think of immunity is to look on the human body as a complex social organism, and the national organism as a simpler functional

individual, or "person," both of which are exposed to dangers of innumerable kinds for which they must continually provide. This provision is immunity in action.[10]

Beginning with this first formulation, Roberts develops a parallel between the state and the human body involving the entire immunological repertoire—from antigens to antibodies, from the function of tolerance to the reticuloendothelial system—and finds in each biological element its political equivalent. The most significant step, however, one that moves in the direction previously taken by Uexküll, is perhaps constituted by the reference to mechanisms of immunitary repulsion and expulsion of the racial sort:

> The student of political biology should study national mass attitudes and their results as if they were actual secretions or excretion. National or international repulsions may rest on little. To put the matter at once on the lowest physiological level, it is well known that the smell of one race may offend as much or even more than different habits and customs.[11]

That Roberts's text closes with a comparison between an immunitary rejection of the Jews by the English and an anaphylactic shock of the political body in the year in which the Second World War begins is indicative of the increasingly slippery slope that the first biopolitical elaboration takes on: a politics constructed directly on *bíos* always risks violently subjecting *bíos* to politics.

The second wave of interest in the thematic of biopolitics is registered in France in the 1960s. The difference from the first wave is all too obvious and it couldn't be otherwise in a historical frame that was profoundly modified by the epochal defeat of Nazi biocracy. The new biopolitical theory appeared to be conscious of the necessity of a semantic reformulation even at the cost of weakening the specificity of the category in favor of a more domesticated neohumanistic declension, with respect not only to Nazi biocracy, but also to organistic theories that had in some way anticipated their themes and accents. The volume that in 1960 virtually opened this new stage of study was programmatically titled *La biopolitique: Essai d'interprétation de l'histoire de l'humanité et des civilisations* [Biopolitics: An Essay on the Interpretation and History of Humanity and Civilization], and it takes exactly this step.[12] Already the double reference to history and humanity as the coordinates of a discourse intentionally oriented toward *bíos* expresses the central direction and conciliatory path of Aroon Starobinski's essay. When he writes that "biopolitics is an attempt to explain the history of civilization on the basis of the laws of cellular life as well as the most elementary biological life," he does not in fact intend to push his treatment toward a sort of naturalistic outcome.[13] On the contrary, the author argues (sometimes even acknowledging the negative connotations that the natural powers *[potenze]* of life enjoy), for the possibility as well as the necessity that politics incorporate spiritual elements that are capable of governing these natural powers in function of metapolitical values:

> Biopolitics doesn't negate in any way the blind forces of violence and the will to power, nor the forces of self-destruction that exist in man and in human civilization. On the contrary, biopolitics affirms their existence in a way that is completely particular because these forces are the elementary forces of life. But biopolitics denies that these forces are fatal and that they cannot be opposed and directed by spiritual forces: the forces of justice, charity, and truth.[14]

That the concept of biopolitics thus risks being whittled down to the point of losing its meaning, that is, of being overturned into a sort of traditional humanism, is also made clear in a second text published nine years later by an author destined for greater fortune. I am referring to Edgar Morin's *Introduction à une politique de l'homme*.[15] Here the "fields" that are truly "biopolitical of life and of survival" are included in a more sweeping aggregate of the "anthropolitical" type, which in turn refers to the project of a "multidimensional politics of man."[16] Rather than tightening the biological-political nexus, Morin situates his perspective on the problematic connection in which the infrapolitical themes of minimal survival are productively crossed with those that are suprapolitical or philosophical, relative to the sense of life itself. The result, more than a biopolitics in the strict sense of the expression, is a sort of "onto-politics," which is given the task of circumscribing the development of the human species, limiting the tendency to see it as economic and productive. "And so all the paths of life and all the paths of politics begin to intersect and then to penetrate one another. They announce an onto-politics that is becoming ever more intimately and globally man's being."[17] Although Morin, in the following book dedicated to the paradigm of human nature, contests in a partially self-critical key the humanistic mythology that defines man in opposition to the animal, culture in opposition to nature, and order in opposition to disorder, there doesn't seem to emerge from all of this an idea of biopolitics endowed with a convincing physiognomy.[18]

Here we are dealing with a theoretical weakness as well as a semantic uncertainty to which the two volumes of *Cahiers de la biopolitique*, published in Paris at the end of the 1960s by the Organisation au Service de la Vie, certainly do not put an end. It is true that with respect to the preceding essay we can recognize in them a more concrete attention to the real conditions of life of the world's population, exposed to a double checkmate of neocapitalism and socialist realism—both incapable of guiding productive development in a direction that is compatible with a significant increase in the quality of life. And it is also true that in several of these texts criticism of the current economic and political model is substantiated in references concerning technology, city planning, and medicine (or better the spaces and the material forms of living beings). Still, not even here can we say that the definition of biopolitics avoids a categorical genericness that will wind up reducing its hermeneutic scope: "Biopolitics was defined as a science by the conduct of states and human collectives, determined by laws, the natural environment, and ontological givens that support life and determine man's activities."[19] There is, however, no suggestion in such a definition of what the specific statute of its object or a critical analysis of its effects might be. Much like the "Days of Biopolitical Research" held in Bordeaux in December 1966, so too these works have difficulty freeing the concept of biopolitics from a mannerist formulation into a meaningful conceptual elaboration.[20]

The third resumption of biopolitical studies took place in the Anglo-Saxon world and it is one that is still ongoing. We can locate its formal introduction in 1973, when the International Political Science Association officially opened a research site on biology and politics. After that various international conventions were organized, the first of which took place in Paris in 1975 at the École des Hautes Études en Sciences Humaines and another at Bellagio, in Warsaw, Chicago, and New York. In 1983, the Association for Politics and the Life Sciences was founded, as was the journal *Politics and Life Sciences* two years later, as well as the series *Research in Biopolitics* (of which a number of volumes were published).[21] But to locate the beginning of this sort of research we need to return to the middle of the 1960s when two texts appeared that elaborated the biopolitical lexicon. If Lynton K. Caldwell was the first to adopt the term in question in his 1964 article "Biopolitics: Science, Ethics, and Public Policy," the two polarities within which is inscribed the general sense of this new biopolitical thematization can be traced to the previous year's *Human Nature in Politics* by James C. Davies.[22] It is no coincidence that when Roger D. Masters attempts to systematize the thesis in a volume (dedicated, however, to Leo Strauss) twenty years later, he will eventually give it a similar title, *The Nature of Politics*.[23] These are precisely the two terms that constitute both the object and the perspective of a biopolitical discourse, which after its organistic declension in the 1920s and 1930s and its neohumanistic one of the 1960s in France, now acquires a marked naturalistic character. Leaving aside the quality of this production, which in general is admittedly mediocre, its symptomatic value resides precisely in the direct and insistent reference made to the sphere of nature as a privileged parameter of political determination. What emerges—not always with full theoretical knowledge on the part of the authors—is a considerable categorical shift with respect to the principal line of modern political philosophy. While political philosophy presupposes nature as the problem to resolve (or the obstacle to overcome) through the constitution of the political order, American biopolitics sees in nature its same condition of existence: not only the genetic origin and the first material, but also the sole controlling reference. Politics is anything but able to dominate nature or "conform" *[formare]* to its ends and so itself emerges "informed" in such a way that it leaves no space for other constructive possibilities.

At the origin of such an approach can be distinguished two matrices: on the one side, Darwinian evolution (or more precisely social Darwinism), and, on the other, the ethological research, developed principally in Germany at the end of the 1930s. With regard to the first, the most important point of departure is to be sought in *Physics and Politics* by Walter Bagehot within a horizon that includes authors as diverse as Spencer and Sumner, Ratzel and Gumplowitz.[24] The clear warning, however, is that the emphasis of the biopolitical perspective resides in the passage from a physical paradigm to one that is exactly biological, something that Thomas Thorson underscores forcefully in his book from 1970 with the programmatic title *Biopolitics*.[25] What matters, therefore, is not so much conferring the label of an exact science on politics as referring it back to its natural domain, by which is understood the vital terrain from which it emerges and to which it inevitably returns.[26] Above all, we are dealing with the contingent condition of our body, which keeps human action within the limits of a determinate anatomical and physical possibility, but also the biological or indeed genetic baggage of the subject in question (to use the lexicon of a nascent sociobiology). Against the thesis that social events require complex historic explanations, they refer here finally to dynamics that are tied to evolutive demands of a species such as ours, different quantitatively but not qualitatively from the animal that precedes and comprises our species. In this way, not only does the predominantly aggressive behavior of man (as well as the cooperative) refer to an instinctive modality of the animal sort, but insofar as it inheres in our feral nature, war ends up taking on a characteristic of inevitability.[27] All political behavior that repeats itself with a certain frequency in history—from the control of territory to social hierarchy to the domination of women—is deeply rooted in a prehuman layer not only to which we remain tied, but which is usually bound to resurface. In this interpretive framework, democratic societies are not impossible in themselves, but appear in the form of parentheses that are destined to be quickly closed (or that at least allow one to see the dark depths out of which they contradictorily emerge). The implicit and often explicit conclusion of the reasoning is that any institution or subjective option that doesn't conform, or at least adapt, to such a given is destined to fail.

The biopolitical notion that emerges at this point is sufficiently clear, as Somit and Peterson, the most credentialed theoreticians of this interpretive line express it.[28] What remains problematic, however, is the final point, which is to say the relation between the analytic-descriptive relation and that of the propositional-normative (all because it is one thing to study, explain, and forecast and another to prescribe). Yet it is precisely in this postponement from the first to the second meaning, that is, from the level of being to that of requirement, that the densest ideological valence is concentrated in the entire discourse.[29] The semantic passage is conducted through the double versant of fact and value in the concept of nature. It is used as both a given and a task, as the presupposition and the result, and as the origin and the end. If political behavior is inextricably embedded in the dimension of *bíos* and if *bíos* is what connects human beings [*l'uomo*] to the sphere of nature, it follows that the only politics possible will be the one that is already inscribed in our natural code. Of course, we cannot miss the rhetorical short-circuit on which the entire argument rests: no longer does the theory interpret reality, but reality determines a theory that in turn is destined to corroborate it. The response is announced even before the analysis is begun: human beings cannot be other than what they have always been. Brought back to its natural, innermost part, politics remains in the grip of biology without being able to reply. Human history is nothing but our nature repeated, sometimes misshapen, but never really different. The role of science (but especially of politics) is that of imped-ing the opening of too broad a gap between nature and history; making our nature, in the final analysis, our only history. The enigma of biopolitics appears resolved, but in a form that assumes exactly what needs to be "researched."

Politics, Nature, History

From a certain point of view it's understandable that Foucault never gestured to the different biopolitical interpretations that preceded his own—from the moment in which his extraordinary survey is born precisely from the distance he takes up with regard to his predecessors. This doesn't mean that no points of contact exist, if not with their positive contents, then with the critical de-mand that follows from them, which refers more broadly to a general dissatis-faction with how modernity has constructed the relation among politics, nature, and history. It is only here that the work begun by Foucault in the middle of the 1970s manifests a complexity and a radicality that are utterly incomparable with the preceding theorizations. It isn't irrelevant that Fou-cault's specific biopolitical perspective is indebted in the first place to Nietz-schean genealogy. This is because it is precisely from genealogy that Foucault derives that oblique capacity for disassembly and conceptual reelaboration that gives his work the originality that everyone has recognized. When Fou-cault, returning to the Kantian question surrounding the meaning of the En-lightenment, establishes a contemporary point of view, he doesn't simply allude to a different mode of seeing things that the past receives from the pres-ent, but also to the interval that such a point of view of the present opens be-tween the past and its self-interpretation. From this perspective, Foucault doesn't think of the end of the modern epoch—or at least the analytic block of its categories highlighted by the first biopolitical theorizations—as a point or a line that interrupts an epochal journey, but rather as the disruption of its trajectory produced by a different sort of gaze: if the present isn't what (or only what) we have assumed it to be until now; if its meanings begin to cluster around a different semantic epicenter; if something novel or ancient emerges from within that contests the mannerist image; this means, then, that the past, which nonetheless the present derives from, is no longer necessarily the same. This can reveal a face, an aspect, or a profile that before was obscured or perhaps hidden by a superimposed (and at times imposed) narrative; not necessarily a false narrative, but instead functional to its prevailing logic, and for this reason partial, when not tendentious.

Foucault identifies this narrative, which compresses or represses with increasing difficulty something that is heterogeneous to its own language, with the discourse on sovereignty. Despite the infinite variations and transformations to which it has been subjected in the course of modernity on the part of those who have made use of it, sovereignty has always been based on the same figural schema: that of the existence of two distinct entities, namely, the totality of individuals and power that at a certain point enters into relation between individuals in the modalities defined by a third element, which is constituted by the law. We can say that all modern philosophies, despite their heterogeneity or apparent opposition, are arranged within this triangular grid, now one, now the other, of its poles. That these affirm the absolute character of sovereign power according to the Hobbesian model or that, on the contrary, they insist on its limits in line with the liberal tradition; that they subtract or subject the monarch with respect to the laws that he himself has promulgated; that they subject or distinguish the principles of legality and of legitimacy— what remains common to all these conceptions is the *ratio* that subtends them, which is precisely the one characterized by the preexistence of subjects to sovereign power that these conceptions introduce and therefore by the rights *[diritto]* that in this mode they maintain in relation to subjects. Even apart from the breadth of such rights—one that moves from the minimum of the preservation of life and the maximum of participation in political government—the role of counterweight that is assigned to subjects in relation to sovereign decision is clear. The result is a sort of a zero-sum relation: the more rights one has, the less power there is and vice versa. The entire modern philosophical-juridical debate is inscribed to varying degrees within this topological alternative that sees politics and law *[legge]*, decision and the norm as situated on opposite poles of a dialectic that has as its object the relation between subjects *[sudditi]* and the sovereign.[30] Their respective weight depends on the prevalence that is periodically assigned to the two terms being compared. When, at the end of this tradition, Hans Kelsen and Carl Schmitt will argue (the one, normativism, armed against the other, decisionism), they do nothing but replicate the same topological contrast that from Bodin on, indeed in Bodin, seemed to oppose the versant of law to that of power.

It is in the breaking of this categorical frame that Foucault consciously works.[31] Resisting what he himself will define as a new form of knowledge (or better, a different order of discourse with that of all modern philosophical-political theories) doesn't mean, of course, erasing the figure or reducing the decisively objective role of the sovereign paradigm, but rather recognizing the real mechanism by which it functions. It isn't that of regulating relations between subjects or between them and power, but rather their subjugation *at the same time* to a specific juridical and political order. On the one side, rights will emerge as nothing other than the instrument that the sovereign uses for imposing his own domination. Correspondingly, the sovereign can dominate only on the basis of the right that legitimates the whole operation. In this way, what appeared as split in an alternative bipolarity between law and power, legality and legitimacy, and norm and exception finds its unity in a same regime of sense. Yet this is nothing but the first effect of the reversal of perspective that Foucault undertakes, one that intersects with another effect relative to the line of division no longer internal to the categorical apparatus of the sovereign *dispositif*, but now immanent to the social body. This perspective claimed to unify it through the rhetorical procedure of polar oppositions. It is as if Foucault undertook the dual work of deconstructing or outflanking the modern narration, which, while suturing an apparent divergence, located a real distinction. It is precisely the recomposition of the duality between power and right, excavated by the sovereign paradigm that makes visible a conflict just as real that separates and opposes groups of diverse ethnicity in the predominance over a given territory. The presumed conflict between sovereignty and law is displaced by the far more real conflict between potential rivals who fight over the use of resources and their control because of their different racial makeup. This doesn't mean in any way that the mechanism of juridical legitimation fails, but rather than preceding and regulating the struggle under way, it constitutes the result and instrument used by those who now and again emerge as victorious. It isn't that the discourse of rights [*diritto*] determines war, but rather that war adopts the discourse of rights in order to consecrate the relation of forces that war itself defines.

Already this unearthing of the constituitive character of war—not its background or its limit, but instead its origin and form of politics—inaugurates an analytic horizon whose historical import we can only begin to see today. But the reference to the conflict between races, a topic to which Foucault dedicated his course in 1976 at the Collège de France, indicates something else, which brings us directly to our underlying theme. That such a conflict concerns so-called populations from an ethnic point of view refers to an element that is destined to disrupt in a much more radical way the modern political and philosophical apparatus. I am referring to *bíos*, a life presupposed simultaneously in its general and specific dimension of biological fact. This is both the object and the subject of the conflict and therefore of the politics that it forms:

> It seems to me that one of the basic phenomena of the nineteenth century was what might be called power's hold over life. What I mean is the acquisition of power over man insofar as man is a living being, that the biological came under State control, that there was at least a certain tendency that leads to what might be termed State control of the biological.[32]

This phrase that opens the lecture of March 17, 1976, and appears to be a new formulation, is in fact already the point of arrival of a trajectory of thought that was inaugurated at least a biennial before. That the first utilization of the term in Foucault's lexicon can be traced directly back to the conference in Rio in 1974, in which Foucault said that "for capitalist society it is the biopolitical that is important before everything else; the biological, the somatic, the corporeal. The body is a biopolitical reality; medicine is a biopolitical strategy" doesn't have much importance.[33] What counts is that all his texts from those years seem to converge in a theoretical step within which every discursive segment comes to assume a meaning that isn't completely perceptible if it is analyzed separately or outside of a biopolitical semantics.

Already in *Discipline and Punish*, the crisis of the classical model of sovereignty, which was represented by the decline of its deadly rituals, is marked by the emergence of a new disciplinary power, which is addressed rather to the life of the subjects that it invests.[34] Although capital punishment through the dismemberment of the convicted responds well to the individual's breaking of the contract (making him guilty of injuring the Majesty), from a certain moment every individual death now is assumed and interpreted in relation to a vital requirement of society in its totality. Yet it is in the course Foucault offered simultaneously titled *Abnormal* that the process of deconstruction of the sovereign paradigm in both its state-power declination and its juridical identity of subject culminates: the entrance and then the subtle colonization of medical knowledge in what was first the competence of law *[diritto]* establishes a true shift in regime, one that pivots no longer on the abstraction of juridical relations but on the taking on of life in the same body of those who are its carriers.[35] In the moment in which the criminal act is no longer to be charged to the will of the subject, but rather to a psychopathological configuration, we enter into a zone of indistinction between law and medicine in whose depths we can make out a new rationality centered on the question of life—of its preservation, its development, and its management. Of course, we must not confuse levels of discourse: such a problematic was always at the center of sociopolitical dynamics, but it is only at a certain point that its centrality reaches a threshold of awareness. Modernity is the place more than the time of this transition and turning [svolta]. By this I mean that while, for a long period of time, the relation between politics and life is posed indirectly—which is to say mediated by a series of categories that are capable of distilling or facilitating it as a sort of clearinghouse—beginning at a certain point these partitions are broken and life enters directly into the mechanisms and dispositifs of governing human beings.

Without retracing the steps that articulate this process of the governmentalization of life in Foucauldian genealogy—from "pastoral power" to the reason of state to the expertise of the "police"—let's keep our attention on the outcome: on the one side, all political practices that governments put into action (or even those practices that oppose them) turn to life, to its process, to its needs, and to its fractures. On the other side, life enters into power relations not only on the side of its critical thresholds or its pathological exceptions, but in all its extension, articulation, and duration. From this perspective, life everywhere exceeds the juridical constraints used to trap it. This doesn't imply, as I already suggested, some kind of withdrawal or contraction of the field that is subjected to the law. Rather, it is the latter that is progressively transferred from the transcendental level of codes and sanctions that essentially have to do with subjects of will to the immanent level of rules and norms that are addressed instead to bodies: "these power mechanisms are, at least in part, those that, beginning in the eighteenth century, took charge of men's existence, men as living bodies."[36] It is the same premise of the biopolitical regime. More than a removal of life from the pressure that is exercised upon it by law, it is presented rather as delivering their relation to a dimension that both determines and exceeds them both. It is with regard to this meaning that the apparently contradictory expression needs to be understood according to which "it was life more than the law that became the issue of political struggles, even if the latter were formulated through affirmations concerning rights."[37] What is in question is no longer the distribution of power or its subordination to the law, nor the kind of regime nor the consensus that is obtained, but something that precedes it because it pertains to its "primary material." Behind the declarations and the silences, the mediations and the conflicts that have characterized the dynamics of modernity—the dialectic that up until a certain stage we have named with the terms of liberty, equality, democracy (or, on the contrary, tyranny, force, and domination)—Foucault's analysis uncovers in *bíos* the concrete power from which these terms originate and toward which they are directed.

Regarding such a conclusion, Foucault's perspective would seem to be close to that of American biopolitics. Certainly, he too places life at the center of the frame and he too, as we have seen, does so polemically vis-à-vis the juridical subjectivism and humanistic historicism of modern political philosophy. But the *bíos* that he opposes to the discourse of rights and its effects on domination is also configured in terms of a historical semantics that is also symmetrically reversed with respect to the legitimating one of sovereign power. Nothing more than life—in the lines of development in which it is inscribed or in the vortexes in which it contracts—is touched, crossed, and modified in its innermost being by history. This was the lesson that Foucault drew from the Nietzschean genealogy, when he places it within a theoretical frame that substituted a search for the origin (or the prefiguration of the end) with that of a force field freed from the succession of events and conflict between bodies. Yet he also was influenced by Darwinian evolution, whose enduring actuality doesn't reside in having substituted "the grand old biological metaphor of life and evolution" for history, but, on the contrary, in having recognized in life the marks, the intervals, and the risks of history.[38] It is precisely from Darwin, in fact, that the knowledge comes that "life evolved, that the evolution of the species is determined, by a certain degree, by accidents of a historical nature."[39] And so it makes little sense to oppose a natural paradigm to a historical one within the frame of life, or locate in nature the hardened shell in which life is immobilized or loses its historical content. This is because, contrary to the underlying presupposition of Anglo-Saxon *biopolitics*, something like a definable and identifiable human nature doesn't exist as such, independent from the meanings that culture and therefore history have, over the course of time, imprinted on it. And then because the same knowledges that have thematized it contain within them a precise historical connotation outside of which their theoretical direction risks remaining indeterminate. Biology itself is born around the end of the eighteenth century, thanks to the appearance of new scientific categories that gave way to a concept of life that is radically different from what was in use before. "I would say," Foucault will say in this regard, "that the notion of life is not a *scientific concept;* it has been an *epistemological indicator* of which the classifying, delimiting, and other functions had an effect on scientific discussions, and not on what they were talking about."[40]

It is almost too obvious the shift (though one could also rightly say the reversal) that such an epistemological deconstruction impresses on the category of biopolitics. That it is always historically qualified according to a modality that Foucault defines with the term "biohistory" as anything but limited to its simple, natural casting implies a further step that to this point has been excluded from all the preceding interpretations. Biopolitics doesn't refer only or most prevalently to the way in which politics is captured—limited, compressed, and determined—by life, but also and above all by the way in which politics grasps, challenges, and penetrates life:

> If one can apply the term *bio-history* to the pressures through which the movements of life and processes of history interfere with one another, one would have to speak of *bio-power* to designate what brought life and its mechanisms into the realm of explicit calculations and made knowledge-power an agent of transformation of human life.[41]

We can already glimpse in this formulation the radical novelty of the Foucauldian approach. What in the preceding declensions of biopolitics was presented as an unalterable given—nature or life, insofar as it is human—now becomes a problem; not a presupposition but a "site," the product of a series of causes, forces, and tensions that themselves emerge as modified in an incessant game of action and reaction, of pushing and resisting. History and nature, life and politics cross, propel, and violate each other according to a rhythm that makes one simultaneously the matrix and the provisional outcome of the other. But it is also a sagittal gaze that deprives it of its presumed fullness, as well as of every presumption of mastery of the entire field of knowledge. Just as Foucault adopts the category of life so as to break apart the modern discourse of sovereignty and its laws from within, so too in turn does that of history remove from life the naturalistic flattening to which the American biopolitical exposes it:

It is history that designs these complexes [the genetic variations from which the various populations arise] before erasing them; there is no need to search for brute and definitive biological facts that from the depths of "nature" would impose themselves on history.[42]

It is as if the philosopher makes use of a conceptual instrument that is necessary for taking apart a given order of discourse in order to give it other meanings, at the moment in which it tends to assume a similarly pervasive behavior. Or additionally that it is separated from itself, having been placed in the interval in such a way as to be subject to the same effect of knowledge that it allows externally. From here we can see the continual movement, the rotation of perspective, along a margin that, rather than distinguishing concepts, dismantles and reassembles them in topologies that are irreducible to a monolinear logic. Life as such doesn't belong either to the order of nature or to that of history. It cannot be simply ontologized, nor completely historicized, but is inscribed in the moving margin of their intersection and their tension. The meaning of biopolitics is sought "in this dual position of life that placed it at the same time outside history, in its biological environment, and inside human historicity, penetrated by the latter's techniques of knowledge and power."[43]

The complexity of Foucault's perspective, that is, of his biopolitical *cantiere*, doesn't end here. It doesn't only concern his own position, which is situated precisely between what he calls "the threshold of modernity," on the limit in which modern knowledge folds upon itself, carried in this way outside itself.[44] Rather, it is also the effect of meaning that from an undecidable threshold communicates with the notion defined thusly: once the dialectic between politics and life is reconstructed in a form that is irreducible to every monocausal synthesis, what is the consequence that derives for each of the two terms and for their combination? And so we return to the question with which I opened this chapter on the ultimate meaning of biopolitics. What does biopolitics mean, what outcomes does it produce, and how is a world continually more governed by biopolitics configured? Certainly, we are concerned with a mechanism or a productive *dispositif*, from the moment that the reality that invests and encompasses it is not left unaltered. But productive of what? What is the *effect* of biopolitics? At this point Foucault's response seems to diverge in directions that involve two other notions that are implicated from the outset in the concept of *bíos*, but which are situated on the extremes of its semantic extension: these are *subjectivization* and *death*. With respect to life, both constitute more than two possibilities. They are at the same time life's form and its background, origin, and destination; in each case, however, according to a divergence that seems not to admit any mediation: it is either one or the other. Either biopolitics produces subjectivity or it produces death. Either it makes the subject its own object or it decisively objectifies it. Either it is a politics of life or a politics over life. Once again the category of biopolitics folds in upon itself without disclosing the solution to its own enigma.

Politics of Life

In this interpretive divergence there is something that moves beyond the simple difficulty of definition, which touches the profound structure of the concept of biopolitics. It is as if it were traversed initially and indeed constituted by an interval of difference or a semantic layer that cuts and opens it into two elements that are not constituted reciprocally. Or that the elements are constituted only at the price of a certain violence that subjects one to the domination of the other, conditioning their superimposition to an obligatory positioning-under [sotto-posizione]. It is as if the two terms from which biopolitics is formed (life and politics) cannot be articulated except through a modality that simultaneously juxtaposes them. More than combining them or even arranging them along the same line of signification, they appear to be opposed in a long-lasting struggle, the stakes of which are for each the appropriation and the domination of the other. From here the never-released tension, that lacerating effect from which the notion of biopolitics never seems to be able to liberate itself because biopolitics produces the effect in the form of an alternative between the two that cannot be bypassed. Either life holds politics back, pinning it to its impassable natural limit, or, on the contrary, it is life that is captured and prey to a politics that strains to imprison its innovative potential. Between the two possibilities there is a breach in signification, a blind spot that risks dragging the entire category into a vacuum of sense. It is as if biopolitics is missing something (an intermediary segment or a logical juncture) that is capable of unbinding the absoluteness of irreconcilable perspectives in the elaboration of a more complex paradigm that, without losing the specificity of its elements, seizes hold of the internal connection or indicates a common horizon.

Before attempting a definition, it is to be noted that not even Foucault is able to escape completely from such a deadlock, and this despite working in a profoundly new framework with respect to the preceding formulations. Foucault too ends up reproducing the stalemate in the form of a further "indecisiveness"—no longer relative to the already acquired impact of power on life, but relative to its effects, measured along a moving line that, as was said, has at one head the production of new subjectivity and at the other its radical destruction. That these contrastive possibilities cohabit within the same analytic axis, the logical extremes of which they constitute, doesn't detract from the fact that their different accentuations determine an oscillation in the entire discourse in opposite directions both from the interpretive and the stylistic point of view. Such a dyscrasia is recognizable in a series of logical gaps and of small lexical incongruences or of sudden changes in tonality, on which it is not possible to linger in detail here. When taken together, however, they mark a difficulty that is never overcome—or, more precisely, an underlying hesitation between two orientations that tempt Foucault equally. Yet he never decisively opts for one over the other. The most symptomatic indication of such an uncertainty is constituted by the definitions of the category, which he from time to time puts into play. Notwithstanding the significant distortions (owing to the different contexts in which they appear), the definitions are mostly expressed indirectly. This was already the case for perhaps Foucault's most celebrated formulation, according to which "for millennia, man remained what he was for Aristotle: a living animal with the additional capacity for a political existence; modern man is an animal whose politics places his existence as a living being in question."[45] This is even more the case where the notion of biopolitics is derived from the contrast with the sovereign paradigm. In this case too a negative modality prevails: biopolitics is primarily that which is *not* sovereignty. More than having its own source of light, biopolitics is illuminated by the twilight of something that precedes it, by sovereignty's advance into the shadows.

Nevertheless, it is precisely here in the articulation of the relation between the two regimes that the prospective splitting to which I gestured previously reappears, a split that is destined in this case to invest both the level of historical reconstruction and that of conceptual determination. How are sovereignty and biopolitics to be related? Chronologically or by a differing superimposition? It is said that one emerges out of the background of the other, but what are we to make of such a background? Is it the definitive withdrawal of a preceding presence, or rather is it the horizon that embraces and holds what newly emerges within it? And is such an emergence really new or is it already inadvertently installed in the categorical framework that it will also modify? On this point too Foucault refuses to respond definitively. He continues to oscillate between the two opposing hypotheses without opting conclusively for either one or the other. Or better: he adopts both with that characteristic, optical effect of splitting or doubling that confers on his text the slight dizziness that simultaneously seduces and disorients the reader.

The steps in which discontinuity seems to prevail are at first sight univocal. Not only is biopolitics other than sovereignty, but between the two a clear and irreversible caesura passes. Foucault writes of that disciplinary power that constitutes the first segment of the *dispositif* that is truly biopolitical: "An important phenomenon occurred in the seventeenth and eighteenth centuries: the appearance—one should say the invention—of a *new* mechanism of power which had very specific procedures, completely *new* instruments, and *very different* equipment. It was, I believe, *absolutely incompatible* with relations of sovereignty."[46] It is new because it turns most of all on the control of bodies and of that which they do, rather than on the appropriation of the earth and its products. From this side, the contrast appears frontally and without any nuances: "It seems to me that this type of power is the exact, point-for-point opposite of the mechanics of power that the theory of sovereignty described or tried to transcribe."[47] For this reason, it "can therefore *no longer* be transcribed in terms of sovereignty."[48]

What is it that makes biopolitics completely unassimilable to the sovereign? Foucault telescopes such a difference in a formula, justifiably famous for its synthetic efficacy, which appears at the end of *The History of Sexuality*: "One might say that the ancient right to *take* life or *let* live was replaced by a power to *foster* life or *disallow* it to the point of death."[49] The opposition couldn't be any plainer: whereas in the sovereign regime life is nothing but the residue or the remainder left over, saved from the right of taking life, in biopolitics life encamps at the center of a scenario of which death constitutes the external limit or the necessary contour. Moreover, whereas in the first instance life is seen from the perspective opened by death, in the second death acquires importance only in the light radiated by life. But what precisely does affirming life mean? *To make* live, rather than limiting oneself to allowing to live? The internal articulations of the Foucauldian discourse are well known: the distinction—here too defined in terms of succession and a totality of copresence—between the disciplinary apparatus and *dispositifs* of control; the techniques put into action by power with regard first to individual bodies and then of populations as a whole; the sectors—school, barracks, hospital, factory—in which they drill and the domains—birth, disease, mortality—that they affect. But to grasp in its complexity the affirmative semantics that—at least in this first declension of the Foucauldian lexicon—the new regime of power connotes, we need to turn again to the three categories of *subjectivization, making immanent,* and *production* that characterize it. Linked between them by the same orientation of sense, they are distinctly recognizable in three genealogical branches in which the biopolitical code is born and then develops, which is to say those that Foucault defines as the pastoral power, the art of government, and the police sciences.

The first alludes to that modality of government of men that in the Jewish-Christian tradition especially moves through a strict and one-to-one relation between shepherd and flock. Unlike the Greek or the Roman models, what counts is not so much the legitimacy of power fixed by law or the maintenance of the harmony between citizens, but the concern that the shepherd devotes to protecting his own flock. The relation between them is perfectly unique: as the sheep follow the will of him who leads them without hesitation, in the same way the shepherd takes care of the life of each of them, to the point, when necessary, of being able to risk his own life. But what connotes the pastoral practice even more is the mode in which such a result is realized: that of a capillary direction, that is both collective and individualized, of the bodies and souls of subjects. At the center of such a process is that durable *dispositif* constituted by the practice of confession on which Foucault confers a peculiar emphasis, precisely because it is the channel through which the process of subjectivization is produced of what remains the object of power.[50] Here for the first time the fundamental meaning of the complex figure of subjection is disclosed. Far from being reduced to a simple objectivization, confession refers rather to a movement that conditions the domination over the object to its subjective participation in the act of domination. Confessing—and in this way placing oneself in the hands of the authority of him who will apprehend and judge its truth—the object of pastoral power is subjugated to its own objectivization and is objectivized in the constitution of its subjectivity. The medium of this criss-crossing effect is the construction of the individual. Forcing him into exposing his subjective truth, controlling the most intimate sounds of his conscience, power singles out the one that it subjects as its own object, and so doing recognizes him as an individual awarded with a specific subjectivity:

It is a form of a power that makes individuals subjects. There are two meanings of the word "subject": subject to someone else by control and dependence; and tied to his own identity by a conscience or self-knowledge. Both meanings suggest a form of power which subjugates and makes subject to.[51]

If the direction of the conscience by the pastors of souls opens the movement of the subjectivization of the object, the conduct of government, which was theorized and practiced in the form of the reason of state, translates and determines the progressive shift of power from the outside to within the confines of that on which it is exercised. Although the Machiavellian principle still preserves a relation of singularity and of transcendence with regard to its own principality, the art of governing induces a double movement of making immanent and pluralization. On the one side, power is no longer in circular relation with itself, which is to say to the preservation or the amplification of its own order, but in relation to the life of those that it governs, in the sense that its ultimate end is not simply that of obedience but also the welfare of the governed. Power, more than dominating men and territories from on high, adheres to their demands, inscribes its own operation in the processes that the governed establish, and draws forth its own force from that of the subjects [sudditi]. But to do so, that is, to collect and satisfy all the requests that arrive from the body of the population, power is forced into multiplying its own services for the areas that relate to subjects—from that of defense, to the economy, to that of public health. From here there is a double move that intersects: the first is a vertical sort that moves from the top toward the bottom, placing in continuous communication the sphere of the state with that of the population and families, reaching finally that of single individuals; the other the horizontal, which places in productive relation the practices and the languages of life in a form that amplifies the horizons, improves the services, and intensifies the performance. With respect to the inflection of sovereign power that is primarily negative, the difference is obvious. If sovereign power was exercised in terms of subtraction and extraction of goods, services, and blood from its own subjects, governmental power, on the contrary, is addressed to the subjects' lives, not only in the sense of their defense, but also with regard to how to deploy, strengthen, and maximize life. Sovereign power removed, extracted, and finally destroyed. Governmental power reinforces, augments, and stimulates. With respect to the salvific tendency of the pastoral power, governmental power shifts decisively its attention onto the secular level of health, longevity, and wealth.

Yet in order that the genealogy of biopolitics can be manifested in all its breadth, a final step is missing. This is represented by the science of the police. Police science is not to be understood in any way as a specific technology within the apparatus of the state as we understand it today. It is rather the productive modality that its government assumes in all sectors of individual and collective experience—from justice, to finance, to work, to health care, to pleasure. More than avoiding harm *[mali]*, the police need to produce goods *[beni]*. Here the process of the positive reconversion of the ancient sovereign right of death reaches its zenith. If the meaning of the term *Politik* remains the negative one of the defense from internal and external enemies, the semantics of *Polizei* is absolutely positive. It is ordered to favor life in all its magnitude, along its entire extension, through all its articulations. And, as Nicolas De Lamare wrote in his compendium, there is even more to be reckoned with. The police are given the task of doing what is necessary as well as what is opportune and pleasurable: "In short, life is the object of the police: the indispensable, the useful, and the superfluous. That people survive, live, and even do better than just that: this is what the police have to ensure."[52] In his *Elements of Police*, Johann Heinrich Gottlob von Justi aims the lens even further ahead: if the object of the police is defined here too as "live individuals living in society," a more ambitious understanding is that of creating a virtuous circle between the vital development of individuals and the strengthening of the forces of the state:[53]

> [T]he police has to keep the citizens happy—happiness being understood as survival, life, and improved living . . . to develop those elements constituitive of individuals' lives in such a way that their development also fosters the strength of the state.[54]

The affirmative character is already fully delineated above, those features (at least from this perspective) that Foucault seems to assign to biopolitics in contrast to the commanding tendency of the sovereign regime. In opposition to it, biopolitics does not limit or coerce *[violenta]* life, but expands it in a manner proportional to its development. More than two parallel flows, we ought to speak of a singular expansive process in which power and life constitute the two opposing and complementary faces. To strengthen itself, power is forced at the same time into strengthening the object on which it discharges itself; not only, but, as we saw, it is also forced to render it subject to its own subjugation *[assoggettamento]*. Moreover, if it wants to stimulate the action of subjects, power must not only presuppose but also produce the conditions of freedom of the subjects to whom it addresses itself. But—and here Foucault's discourse tends toward the maximum point of its own semantic extension—if we are free *for* power, we are also free *against* power. We are able not only to support power and increase it, but also to resist and oppose power. In fact, Foucault concludes that "where there is power, there is resistance, and yet, or rather consequently, this resistance is never in a position of exteriority in relation to power."[55] This doesn't mean, as Foucault quickly points out, that resistance is always already subjected to power against which it seems to be opposed, but rather that power needs a point of contrast against which it can measure itself in a dialectic that doesn't have any definitive outcome. It is as if power, in order to reinforce itself, needs continually to divide itself and fight against itself, or to create a projection that pulls it where it wasn't before. This line of fracture or protrusion is life itself. It is the place that is both the object and the subject of resistance. At the moment in which it is directly invested by power, life recoils against power, against the same striking force that gave rise to it:

> Moreover, against this power that was still new in the nineteenth century, the forces that resisted relied for support on the very thing it invested, that is, on life and man as a living being . . . life as a political object was in a sense taken at face value and turned back against the system that was bent on controlling it.[56]

Simultaneously within and outside of power, life appears to dominate the entire scenario of existence; even when it is exposed to the pressure of power—and indeed, never more than in such a case—life seems capable of taking back what had deprived it before and of incorporating it into its infinite folds.

Politics over Life

This, however, isn't Foucault's entire response, nor is it his only. Certainly, there is an internal coherence therein, as is testified by an entire interpretive line, which not only has made itself the standard-bearer of Foucault's position, but which has pushed Foucault's response well beyond his own manifest intentions.[57] Be that as it may, this doesn't eliminate an impression of insufficiency, or indeed of an underlying reservation concerning a definitive outcome. It is as if Foucault himself wasn't completely satisfied by his own historical-conceptual reconstruction or that he believed it to be only partial and incapable of exhausting the problem; indeed, it is bound to leave unanswered a decisive question: if life is stronger than the power that besieges it, if its resistance doesn't allow it to bow to the pressure of power, then how do we account for the outcome obtained in modernity of the mass production of death?[58] How do we explain that the culmination of a politics of life generated a lethal power that contradicts the productive impulse? This is the paradox, the impassable stumbling block that not only twentieth-century totalitarianism, but also nuclear power asks philosophy with regard to a resolutely affirmative declension of biopolitics. How is it possible that a power of life is exercised against life itself? Why are we not dealing with two parallel processes or simply two simultaneous processes? Foucault accents the direct and proportional relation that runs between the development of biopower and the incremental growth in homicidal capacity. There have never been so many bloody and genocidal wars as have occurred in the last two centuries, which is to say in a completely biopolitical period. It is enough to recall that the maximum international effort for organizing health, the so-called Beveridge Plan, was elaborated in the middle of a war that produced 50 million dead: "One could symbolize such a coincidence by a slogan: Go get slaughtered and we promise you a long and pleasant life. Life insurance is connected with a death command."[59] Why? Why does a power that functions by insuring, protecting, and augmenting life express such a potential for death? It is true that wars and mass destruction are no longer perpetrated in the name of a politics of power [potenza]—at least according to the declared intentions of those who conduct these wars—but in the name of the survival itself of populations that are involved. But it is precisely what reinforces the tragic aporia of a death that is necessary to preserve life, of a life nourished by the deaths of others, and finally, as in the case of Nazism, by its own death.[60]

Once again we are faced with that enigma, that terrible unsaid, that the "bio" placed before politics holds for the term's meaning. Why does biopolitics continually threaten to be reversed into thanatopolitics? Here too the response to such an interrogative seems to reside in the problematic point of intersection between sovereignty and biopolitics. But seen now from an angle of refraction that bars an interpretation linearly in opposition to the two types of regime. The Foucauldian text marks a passage to a different representation of their relation by the slight but meaningful semantic slip between the verb "to substitute" (which still connotes discontinuity) and the verb "to complement," which alludes differently to a process of progressive and continuous mutation:

> And I think that one of the greatest transformations that the political right underwent in the nineteenth century was precisely that, I wouldn't say exactly that sovereignty's old right—to take life or let live—was *replaced*, but it came to be *complemented* by a new right which does not erase the old right but which does penetrate it, permeate it.[61]

It isn't that Foucault softens the typological distinction as well as the opposition between the two kinds of power: these are defined as they were previously. It is only that, rather than deploying the distinction along a single sliding line, he returns it to a logic of copresence. From this point of view, the same steps that were read before in a discontinuous key now appear to be articulated according to a different argumentative strategy:

> This power cannot be described or justified in terms of the theory of sovereignty. It is radically heterogeneous and should logically have led to the complete disappearance of the great juridical edifice of the theory of sovereignty. In fact, the theory of sovereignty not only continued to exist as, if you like, an ideology of right; it also continued to organize the juridical codes that nineteenth-century Europe adopted after the Napoleonic codes.[62]

Foucault furnishes an initial explanation of the ideological-functional kind vis-à-vis such a persistence, in the sense that the use of the theory of the sovereign, once it has been transferred from the monarch to the people, would have allowed both a concealment and a juridicization of the *dispositifs* of control put into action by biopower. From here the institution of a double level is intertwined between an effective practice of the biological kind and a formal representation of juridical character. Contractualist philosophies would have constituted from this point of view the natural terrain of contact between the old sovereign order and the new governmental apparatus, applied this time not only to the individual sphere, but also to the area of population in its totality. And yet, this reconstruction, insofar as it is plausible on the historical level, doesn't completely answer the question on the theoretical level. It is as if between the two models, sovereignty and biopolitics, there passes a relation at once more secret and essential, one that is irreducible both to the category of analogy and to that of contiguity. What Foucault seems to refer to is rather a copresence of opposing vectors superimposed in a threshold of originary indistinction that makes one both the ground and the projection, the truth and the surplus of the other. It is this antinomic crossing, this aporetic knot, that prevents us from interpreting the association of sovereignty and biopolitics in a monolinear form or in the sense of contemporaneity or succession. Neither the one nor the other restores the complexity of an association that is much more antithetical. In their mutual relation, different times are compressed within a singular epochal segment constituted and simultaneously altered by their reciprocal tension. Just as the sovereign model incorporates the ancient pastoral power—the first genealogical incunabulum of biopower—so too biopolitics carries within it the sharp blade of a sovereign power that both crosses and surpasses it. If we consider the Nazi state, we can say indifferently, as Foucault himself does, that it was the old sovereign power that adopts biological racism for itself, a racism born in opposition to it. Or, on the contrary, that it is the new biopolitical power that made use of the sovereign right of death in order to give life to state racism. If we have recourse to the first interpretive model, biopolitics becomes an internal articulation of sovereignty; if we privilege the second, sovereignty is reduced to a formal schema of biopolitics. The antinomy emerges more strongly with regard to nuclear equilibrium. Do we need to look at it from the perspective of life that, notwithstanding everything, has been able to ensure it or from the perspective of total and mass death that continues to threaten us?

> So the power that is being exercised in this atomic power is exercised in such a way that it is capable of suppressing life itself. And, therefore, to suppress itself insofar as it is the power that guarantees life. Either it is sovereign and uses the atomic bomb, and therefore cannot be power, biopower, or the power to guarantee life, as it has been ever since the nineteenth century. Or, at the opposite extreme, you no longer have a sovereign right that is in excess of biopower, but a biopower that is in excess of sovereign right.[63]

Once again, after having defined the terms of an alternating hermeneutic between two opposing theses, Foucault never opts decisively for one or the other. On the one hand, he hypothesizes something like a return to the sovereign paradigm within a biopolitical horizon. In that case, we would be dealing with a literally phantasmal event, in the technical sense of a reappearance of death—of the destitute sovereign decapitated by the grand revolution—on the scene of life; as if a tear suddenly opened in the reign of immunization (which is precisely that of biopolitics), from which the blade of transcendence once again vibrates, the ancient sovereign power of taking life. On the other hand, Foucault introduces the opposing hypothesis, which says that it was precisely the final disappearance of the sovereign paradigm that liberates a vital force so dense as to overflow and be turned against itself. With the balancing constituted by sovereign power diminished in its double orientation of absolute power and individual rights, life would become the sole field in which power that was otherwise defeated is exercised:

> The excess of biopower appears when it becomes technologically and politically possible for man not only to manage life but to make it proliferate, to create living matter, to build the monster, and ultimately, to build viruses that cannot be controlled and that are universally destructive. This formidable extension of biopower, unlike what I was just saying about atomic power, will put it beyond all human sovereignty.[64]

Perhaps we have arrived at the point of maximum tension, as well as at the point of potential internal fracture of the Foucauldian discourse. At the center remains the relation (not only historical, but conceptual and theoretical) between sovereignty and politics, or more generally between modernity and what precedes it, between present and past. Is that past truly past or does it extend as a shadow that reaches up to the present until it covers it entirely? In this irresolution there is something more than a simple exchange between a topological approach of the horizontal sort and another, more epochal, of the vertical kind; or we are dealing with both a retrospective and a prospective gaze.[65] There is indecision concerning the underlying meaning of secularization. Is it nothing other than the channel, the secret passage through which death has returned to capture "life" again? Or, on the contrary, was it precisely the absolute disappearance of death, its conclusive death without remainder that sparks in the living a lethal battle against itself? Once again, how do we wish to think the sovereign paradigm within the biopolitical order, and then what does it represent? Is it a residue that is delayed in consuming itself, a spark that doesn't go out, a compensatory ideology or the ultimate truth, because it is prior to and originary of its own installation, its own profound subsurface, its own underlying structure? And when it pushes with greater force so as to resurface (or, on the contrary, when it ultimately collapses), does death rise again in the heart of life until it makes it burst open?

What remains suspended here isn't only the question of the relation of modernity with its "pre," but also that of the relation with its "post." What was twentieth-century totalitarianism with respect to the society that preceded it? Was it a limit point, a tear, a surplus in which the mechanism of biopower broke free, got out of hand, or, on the contrary, was it society's sole and natural outcome? Did it interrupt or did it fulfill it? Once again the problem concerns the relation with the sovereign paradigm: does Nazism (but also, true [reale] communism) stand on the outside or inside vis-à-vis it? Do they mark the end or the return? Do they reveal the most intimate linking or the ultimate disjunction between sovereignty and biopolitics? It isn't surprising that Foucault's response is split into lines of argument that are substantially at odds with each other. Totalitarianism and modernity are at the same time continuous and discontinuous, not assimilable and indistinguishable:

> One of the numerous reasons why [fascism and Stalinism] are, for us, so puzzling is that in spite of their historical weakness they are not quite original. They used and extended mechanisms already present in most other societies. More than that: in spite of their internal madness, they used to a large extent the ideas and the devices of our political rationality.[66]

The reason Foucault is prevented from responding less paradoxically is clear: if the thesis of indistinction between sovereignty, biopolitics, and totalitarianism were to prevail—the continuist hypothesis—he would be forced to assume genocide as the constituitive paradigm (or at least as the inevitable outcome) of the entire parabola of modernity.[67] Doing so would contrast with his sense of historical distinctions, which is always keen. If instead the hypothesis of difference were to prevail—the discontinuist hypothesis—his conception of biopower would be invalidated every time that death is projected inside the circle of life, not only during the first half of the 1900s, but also after. If totalitarianism were the result of what came before it, power would always have to enclose and keep watch over life relentlessly. If it were the temporary and contingent displacement, it would mean that life over time is capable of beating back every power that wants to violate it. In the first case, biopolitics would be an absolute power over life; in the second, an absolute power of life. Held between these two opposing possibilities and blocked in the aporia that is established when they intersect, Foucault continues to run simultaneously in both directions. He doesn't cut the knot, and the result is to keep his ingenious intuitions unfinished on the link between politics and life.

Evidently, Foucault's difficulty and his indecision move well beyond a simple question of historical periodization or genealogical articulation between the paradigms of sovereignty and biopolitics to invest the same logical and semantic configuration of the latter. My impression is that such a hermeneutic impasse is connected to the fact that, notwithstanding the theorization of their reciprocal implication, or perhaps because of this, the two terms of life and politics are to be thought as originally distinct and only later joined in a manner that is still extraneous to them. It is precisely for this reason that politics and life remain indefinite in profile and in qualification. What, precisely, are "politics" and "life" for Foucault? How are they to be understood and in what way does their definition reflect on their relationship? Or, on the contrary, how does their relation impact on their respective definitions? If one begins to think them separately in their absoluteness, it becomes difficult and even contradictory to condense them in a single concept. Not only, but one risks blocking a more profound understanding, relating precisely to the originary and elemental character of that association. It has sometimes been said that Foucault, absorbed for the most part in the question of power, never sufficiently articulated the concept of politics—to the point of substantially superimposing the expressions of "biopower" and "biopolitics." But an analogous observation—a conceptual elaboration that is lacking or insufficient—could be raised as well in relation to the other term of the relation, which is to say that of life; that despite describing the term analytically in its historical-institutional, economic, social, and productive nervature, life remains, nevertheless, little problematized with regard to its epistemological constitution. What is life in its essence and even before that, does life have an essence—a recognizable and describable designation outside of the relation with other lives and with what is not life? Does there exist a simple life—a bare life—or does it emerge from the beginning as formed, as put into form by something that pushes it beyond itself? From this perspective as well, the category of biopolitics seems to demand a new horizon of meaning, a different interpretive key that is capable of linking the two polarities together in a way that is at the same time more limited and more complex.

Notes

1. See in this regard the collection *Biopolitik*, ed. Christian Geyer (Frankfurt, Suhrkamp, 2001).

2. Karl Binding, *Zum Werden und Leben der Staaten: Zehn Staatsrechtliche Abhandlungen* (Munich and Leipzig: Duncker & Humblot, 1920); Eberhard Dennert, *Der Staat als lebendiger Organismus: Biologische Betrachtungen zum Aufbau der neuen Zeit* (Halle [Saale]: C. E. Müller, 1920); and Edward Hahn, *Der Staat, ein Lebenwesen* (Munich: Dt. Volksverlag, 1926).

3. Rudolph Kjellén, *Stormakterna: Konturer kring samtidens storpolitik* (Stockholm: Gebers, 1905).

4. Rudolph Kjellén, *Staten som Lifsform* (Stockholm: Hugo Geber, 1916).

5. Rudolph Kjellén, *Grundriss zu einem System der Politik* (Leipzig: Rudolf Leipzig Hirzel, 1920), 3–4.

6. Jakob von Uexküll, *Staatsbiologie: Anatomie, Phisiologie, Pathologie des Staates* (Berlin: Verlag von Gebrüder Paetel, 1920).

7. Ibid., 46.

8. Ibid., 55.

9. Morley Roberts, *Bio-politics: An Essay in the Physiology, Pathology and Politics of the Social and Somatic Organism* (London: Dent, 1938).

10. Ibid., 153.

11. Ibid., 160.

12. Aroon Starobinski, *La biopolitique: Essai d'interprétation de l'histoire de l'humanité et des civilisations* (Geneva: Imprimerie des Arts, 1960).

13. Ibid., 7.

14. Ibid., 9.

15. Edgar Morin, *Introduction à une politique de l'homme* (Paris: Éditions du Seuil, 1969).

16. Ibid., 11.

17. Ibid., 12.

18. Edgar Morin, *Le paradigme perdu: La nature humaine* (Paris: Éditions du Seuil, 1973).

19. André Birré, "Introduction: Si l'Occident s'est trompé de conte?" *Cahiers de la biopolitique* 1:1 (1968): 3.

20. Antonella Cutro also discusses this first French production in biopolitics in her *Michel Foucault. Tecnica e vita. Biopolitica e filosofia del "Bios"* (Naples: Bibliopolis, 2004), which constitutes the first, useful attempt to systematize Foucauldian biopolitics. More generally on biopolitics, see *Politica della vita*, eds. Laura Bazzicalupo and Roberto Esposito (Milan: Laterza, 2003), as well as *Biopolitica minore*, ed. Paolo Petricari (Rome: Manifestolibri, 2003).

21. *Research in Biopolitics*, eds. Stephen A. Peterson and Albert Somit (Greenwich, Conn.: JAI Press). The volumes, in order, are *Sexual Politics and Political Feminism* (1991); *Biopolitics in the Mainstream* (1994); *Human Nature and Politics* (1995); *Research in Biopolitics* (1996); *Recent Explorations in Biology and Politics* (1997); *Sociology and Politics* (1998); *Ethnic Conflicts Explained by Ethnic Nepotism* (1999); and *Evolutionary*

Approaches in the Behavioral Sciences: Toward a Better Understanding of Human Nature (2001).

22. Lynton K. Caldwell, "Biopolitics: Science, Ethics, and Public Policy," *Yale Review*, no. 54 (1964): 1–16; and James C. Davies, *Human Nature in Politics: The Dynamics of Political Behavior* (New York: Wiley, 1963).

23. Roger D. Masters, *The Nature of Politics* (New Haven and London: Yale University Press, 1989).

24. Walter Bagehot, *Physics and Politics, or, Thoughts on the Application of the Principles of "Natural Selection" and "Inheritance" to Political Society* (Kitchener, Ont.: Batoche, 2001).

25. Thomas Thorson, *Biopolitics* (Washington, D.C.: University Press of America, 1970).

26. See, on this point, D. Easton, "The Relevance of Biopolitics to Political Theory," in *Biology and Politics*, ed. Albert Somit (The Hague: Mouton, 1976), 237–47, as well as before that William James Miller Mackenzie, *Politics and Social Science* (Baltimore: Johns Hopkins University Press, 1967), and H. Lasswell, *The Future of the Comparative Method*, in *Comparative Politics* 1 (1968): 3–18.

27. Warder C. Allee's volumes on the animal are classic: *Animal Life and Social Growth* (Baltimore: Williams & Wilkins Company and Associates in Cooperation with the Century of Progress Exposition, 1932) and *The Social Life of Animals* (Boston: Beacon Press, 1958). Also of interest are Lionel Tiger, *Men in Groups* (New York: Vintage Books, 1970) and Desmond Morris, *The Human Zoo* (New York: Dell, 1969). For this "natural" conception of war, see especially Quincy Wright, *A Study of War* (Chicago: University of Chicago Press, 1942), and Hans J. Morgenthau, *Politics among Nations: The Struggle for Power and Peace* (New York: Alfred A. Knopf, 1948). More recently there is V. S. E. Falger, *Biopolitics and the Study of International Relations: Implication, Results, and Perspectives*, in *Research in Biopolitics* 2: 115–34.

28. Albert Somit and Stephen A. Peterson, *Biopolitics in the Year 2000, Research in Biopolitics* 8: 181.

29. In this direction, compare Carlo Galli, "Sul valore politico del concetto di 'natura,'" in *Autorità e natura: Per una storia dei concetti filosofico-politici* (Bologna: Centro stampa Baiesi, 1988), 57–94, and Michela Cammelli, "Il darwinismo e la teoria politica," *Filosofia politica*, no. 3 (2000): 489–518.

30. An acute historical-conceptual analysis of sovereignty, if from another perspective, is that proposed by Biagio De Giovanni, "Discutere la sovranità," in Bazzicalupo and Esposito, *Politica della vita*, 5–15. See as well Luigi Alfieri's "Sovranità, morte, e politica," in the same volume (16–28).

31. For an analytic reconstruction of the problem, see Alessandro Pandolfi, "Foucault pensatore politico postmoderno," in *Tre studi su Foucault* (Naples: Terzo Millennio Edizioni, 2000), 131–246. On the relation between power and law, I refer the reader to Lucio D'Alessandro, "Potere e pena nella problematica di Michel Foucault," in *La verità e le forme giuridiche* (Naples: La città del sole, 1994), 141–60.

32. Michel Foucault, *"Society Must Be Defended": Lectures at the Collège de France, 1975–1976*, ed. Mauro Bertani and Alessandro Fontana, trans. David Macey (New York: Picador, 2003), 239–40.

33. Michel Foucault, "Crisis de un modelo en la medicina?" in *Dits et Écrits*, vol. 3 (Paris: Gallimard, 2001), 222.

34. Michel Foucault, *Discipline and Punish: The Birth of the Prison*, trans. Alan Sheridan (New York: Vintage Books, 1977).

35. Michel Foucault, *Abnormal: Lectures at the Collège de France 1974–1975*, trans. Graham Burchell (New York: Picador, 2003).

36. Michel Foucault, *The History of Sexuality*, vol. 1: *An Introduction*, trans. Robert Hurley (New York: Vintage Books, 1978), 89.

37. Ibid., 145.

38. Michel Foucault, "Return to History," in *Aesthetics, Method, and Epistemology*, ed. J. Faubion (New York: New Press, 1998), 430–31.

39. Michel Foucault, "The Crises of Medicine or the Crises of Anti-Medicine," *Foucault Studies*, no. 1 (December 2004): 11.

40. Michel Foucault, "Human Nature: Justice versus Power" (Noam Chomsky and Michel Foucault), in *Michel Foucault and His Interlocutors*, ed. A. I. Davidson (Chicago: University of Chicago Press, 1997), 110. Cf. Stefano Catucci's *La 'natura' della natura umana: Note su Michel Foucault*, in Noam Chomsky and Michel Foucault, *Della natura umana: Invariante biologico e potere politico* (Rome: Derive Approdi, 2004), 75–85.

41. Foucault, *History of Sexuality*, 143.

42. Michel Foucault, "Bio-histoire et bio-politique," in *Dits et Écrits, 1954–1988*, vol. 3 (Paris: Gallimard, 1994), 97.

43. Foucault, *History of Sexuality*, 143.

44. Ibid.

45. Ibid.

46. Foucault, *"Society Must Be Defended,"* 35; my emphasis.

47. Ibid., 36.

48. Ibid.; my emphasis.

49. Foucault, *History of Sexuality*, 138.

50. On the processes of subjectivization, cf. Mariapaola Fimiani, "Le véritable amour et le souci commun du monde," in *Foucault: Le courage de la vérité*, ed. Frédéric Gros (Paris: Presses universitaires de France, 2002), 87–127, and Yves Michaud, "Des modes de subjectivationaux techniques de soi: Foucault et les identités de notre temps," *Cités*, no. 2 (2000): 11–39. Fundamental for the theme remains Gilles Deleuze, *Foucault*, trans. Seán Hand (Minneapolis: University of Minnesota Press, 1988).

51. Michel Foucault, "The Subject and Power," *Critical Inquiry* 8:4 (summer 1982): 781.

52. Michel Foucault, "'Omnes et Singulatim': Towards a Critique of Political Reason," in *Power*, ed. James Faubion (New York: New Press, 1997), 321.

53. Ibid., 322.

54. Ibid.

55. Foucault, *History of Sexuality*, 95.

56. Ibid., 144–45.

57. I am alluding to Michael Hardt and Antonio Negri's *Empire* (Cambridge: Harvard University Press, 2000), esp. 22–41, but also to the group headed by the French journal

Multitudes. See in particular the first issue of 2000, dedicated precisely to *Biopolitique et biopouvoir,* with contributions by Maurizio Lazzarato, Éric Alliez, Bruno Karsenti, Paolo Napoli, and others. It should be said that the theoretical-political perspective is in itself interesting, but only weakly linked to that of Foucault, who inspires it.

58. See, on this point, Valerio Marchetti, "La naissance de la biopolitique," in *Au risque de Foucault* (Paris: Éditions du Centre Georges Pompidou: Centre Michel Foucault, 1997), 237–47.

59. Michel Foucault, "The Political Technology of Individuals," in Faubion, *Power,* 405.

60. Marco Revelli has recently discussed the relation between politics and death in a vigorously ethical and theoretical essay, *La politica perduta* (Turin: Einaudi, 2003). See as well his earlier *Oltre il Novecento* (Turin: Einaudi, 2001).

61. Foucault, "*Society Must Be Defended*," 241; my emphasis.

62. Ibid., 36.

63. Ibid., 253–54.

64. Ibid., 254.

65. Cf. Michael Donnelly, "On Foucault's Uses of the Notion 'Biopower,'" in *Michel Foucault Philosopher,* ed. Timothy Armstrong (New York: Routledge, 1992), 199–203, as well as Jacques Rancière, "Biopolitique ou politique?" *Multitudes* 1 (March 2000): 88–93.

66. Foucault, "The Subject and Power," 779.

67. This is the outcome that Giorgio Agamben coherently arrives at in *Homo Sacer: Sovereign Power and Bare Life,* trans. Daniel Heller-Roazen (Stanford, Calif.: Stanford University Press, 1998).

CHAPTER 18

THE DIFFICULT LEGACY

OF MICHEL FOUCAULT

Jacques Rancière

In this very month, Michel Foucault will have been dead for 20 years. A new occasion has thus arisen for a commemoration, popular as they are in France. This anniversary, however, is more problematic than that of Sartre's 4 years ago. For this latter occasion, it was necessary to produce a major operation of reconciliation in order to extricate the provocative philosopher from the 'extremist' causes in which he had compromised himself, so that he could be introduced into the national pantheon of writers and thinkers, the friends of liberty. The case of Foucault is more complex. The philosopher and activist has no excesses that must be pardoned in the name of his virtues. For, precisely, one does not know what the activist should be reproached for, nor with what the philosopher should be credited. More radically, there is a serious uncertainty in understanding the relation between the one and the other.

This uncertainty receives expression in the debates over Foucault's legacy. One of them concerns his relation to the cause of sexual minorities. In *La Volonté de savoir*,[1] in fact, Foucault put forward a provocative argument: the notion of 'sexual repression' actually works to mask the inverse operation, the efforts of power to get us to speak about sex, to oblige individuals to over-invest in the secrets and the promises that it detained. Some were keen, notably in the United States, to infer from this an invalidation of the forms of identity politics to which sexual minorities were committed. Conversely, with David Halperin's *Saint Foucault*,[2] the philosopher was enthroned as the patron saint of the *queer* movement for his denouncing of the game of sexual identities that the homophobic tradition had set up. In France the polemic developed on another terrain. Indeed, one of the editors of Foucault's *Dits et*

Écrits,[3] François Ewald, is today the appointed theoretician of a bosses union, and is committed, in the name of the morality of risk, to continuing the struggle against the French system of social protection. Hence, the question that worked the polemicists: can a programme of struggle against social security be drawn from the Foucauldian critique of the 'society of control'?

Some have aimed to rise above these debates and attempted to draw out the philosophical foundations of Foucault's politics. These are generally sought for in the analysis of biopower that he once sketched. Others, with Michael Hardt and Toni Negri, have equipped him with the substratum of a philosopher of life, which he himself never took the time to elaborate, in a bid to assimilate biopolitics to the movement of the multitudes breaking open the shackles of Empire. Others still, like Giorgio Agamben, have assimilated Foucault's description of 'the power over life' to a generalized regime of the state of exception, common to democracies and totalitarian regimes alike. And still others see Foucault as a theoretician of ethics and enjoin us to discover— between his scholarly studies on asceticism in antiquity and his small confidences in the contemporary pleasures of the sauna—the principles of a new morality of the subject.

All these enterprises have one point in common. They hope to ascertain in Foucault's trajectory a principle of finality that would assure the coherence of the whole and provide a solid basis for a new politics or a novel ethics. They want to see in him a confirmation of the idea of the philosopher who synthesizes knowledge and teaches us the rules of action.

Now, this idea of the philosopher and of the concordance between knowledge, thought, and life is precisely the one that Foucault challenged, through his approach even more than his statements. What he foremost invented was an original way of doing philosophy. When phenomenology was promising us—at the end of its abstractions—access to the 'things themselves' and to the 'world of life', and when some were dreaming of making this promised world coincide with the one that Marxism promised the workers, he practiced a maximum distance. He did not promise life. He was fully in it, in the decisions of the police, the cries of the imprisoned or the examination of the bodies of the ill. But he did not say to us what we could do with this 'life' and with its knowledge. Much rather, he saw it as the refutation in act of discourses of consciousness [*conscience*] and of the human that back then underpinned the hopes of liberated tomorrows. More than any other 'structuralist' theoretician, Foucault was accused of being a thinker of technocratism, of turning our society and our thought into a machine defined by ineluctable and anonymous functionings.

We know how the year(s) of 1968 would overturn things. Between the creation of the *Université de Vincennes* and the founding of the Group of Information on Prisons, the structuralist 'technocrat' figured among the top rung of intellectuals in which the anti-authoritarian movement recognized itself. Everything suddenly became obvious: he who had analysed the birth of medical power and the great confinement of the mad and the marginal was perfectly predisposed to symbolize a movement which attacked not only the relations of production and the visible institutions of the state, but all the forms of power that are disseminated throughout the social body. One photograph would sum up this logic: in it we see Foucault, armed with a microphone, alongside his old enemy Sartre, rousing some demonstrators who had gathered together to condemn a racist crime. The photo is titled 'the philosophers are in the street.'

But a philosopher's being in the street does not suffice for his philosophy to ground the movement, nor even his own presence there. The philosophical displacement operated by Foucault implied precisely upsetting the relations between positive knowledge, philosophical consciousness and action. In abandoning itself to the examination of the real functioning by which effective thought acts on bodies, philosophy abdicates its central position. But the knowledge that it yields does not thus form any weapon of the masses in the Marxist manner. It simply constitutes a new map on the terrain of this effective and decentered thought. It does not provide the revolt with a consciousness. But it permits the network of its reasons to find the network of reasons of those who, here or there, exploit their knowledge and their own reason to introduce the grain of sand that jams the machine.

The archaeology of the relations of power and of the workings of thought, then, founds revolt no more than it does subjugation. It redistributes the maps and the territories. In subtracting thought from its royal place, it gives right to that of each and all of us, that notably of the 'infamous men' whose lives Foucault had undertaken to write. By the same token, however, it prohibits thought, *restored to all*, from taking any central position in the encounter between knowledge and power. This does not mean that politics loses itself in the multiplicity of power relations everywhere disseminated. It means, first of all, that it is always a leap that no knowledge justifies and which no knowledge administers. The passage from knowledge to an intervention supposes a singular relay, the sentiment of something intolerable.

'The situation in the prisons is intolerable', Foucault declared in 1971 with the founding of the Groups of Information on Prisons. This 'intolerable' did not come from some self-evidence piece of knowledge and was not addressed to some universal consciousness that would be compelled to accept it. It was only a 'sentiment', the same one, no doubt, that had pushed the philosopher to commit himself to the unknown terrain of archives without knowing where it would lead him, and still less where it might lead others. Some months later, however, the intolerable sentiment of the philosopher would be forced to encounter that which the prisoners in revolt in several French prisons declared with their own weapons based upon their own knowledge. Thought does not transmit itself to action. Instead thought transmits itself to a thought and action which provokes another. Thought acts insofar as it accepts not to know very well what is pushing it and renounces to assert control over its effects.

The paradox is that Foucault himself seems to have found it difficult to accept this entirely. We know that he stopped writing for a long while. It occurred right after *La Volonté de savoir*, the book around which today's exegetes vie. This book aimed in principle to be an introduction to a *Histoire de la sexualité*, whose signification it summed up in advance. It seems that Foucault came to fear the path that he had mapped out in advance. Before the imminence of death pushed him to publish *L'Usage des plaisirs* and *Le Souci de soi*, he had not published anything save interviews.[4] In these interviews, of course, he was asked to say what it was that linked his patient investigations in the archives with his interventions on the repression in Poland, his delving into the Greek techniques of subjectivation and his work with a union confederation. All his responses, as we clearly sense, comprise so many deceptions that reintroduce a place of mastery which his very own work had undermined. The same holds for all those rationalizations that purport to draw from his writings either the principle of the queer revolution, that of the emancipation of the multitudes or that of a new ethics of the individual. There is not a body of Foucauldian thought that founds a new politics or a new ethics. There are books which produce effects to the very extent that they do not say to us what we must do with them. The embalmers are going to have a tough time of it.

Notes

1. Michel Foucault, *History of Sexuality, Volume 1: An Introduction*, trans. Robert Hurley, Harmondsworth: Penguin books, 1978 (French original, 1976).

2. David M. Halperin, *Saint Foucault: Toward a Gay Hagiography,* New York: Oxford University Press, 1995.

3. Michel Foucault, *The Essential Works of Michel Foucault 1954–84* (in 4 volumes), edited by Robert Hurley, James D. Faubion and Paul Rabinow, New York: The New Press, 2000–2006.

4. Michel Foucault, *The Use of Pleasure: The History of Sexuality, Volume 2,* trans. Robert Hurley, Harmondsworth: Penguin books, 1992 (French original, 1984) and *Care of the Self: The History of Sexuality, Volume 3,* trans. Robert Hurley, Harmondsworth: Penguin books, 1990 (French original, 1984).

CHAPTER 19

FROM POLITICS TO BIOPOLITICS

. . . AND BACK

Slavoj Žižek

In our Western tradition, the exemplary case of a traumatic Real is the Jewish Law. In the Jewish tradition, the divine Mosaic Law is experienced as something externally imposed, contingent, and traumatic—in short, as an impossible/real Thing that "makes the law." What is arguably the ultimate scene of religious-ideological interpellation—the pronouncement of the Decalogue on Mount Sinai—is the very opposite of something that emerges "organically" as the outcome of the path of self-knowing and self-realization. The Judeo-Christian tradition is thus to be strictly opposed to the New Age gnostic problematic of self-realization or self-fulfillment: when the Old Testament enjoins you to love and respect your neighbor, this does not refer to your imaginary semblable/double, but to the neighbor qua traumatic Thing. In contrast to the New Age attitude that ultimately reduces my Other/Neighbor to my mirror image or to the means on the path to self-realization (like the Jungian psychology in which other persons around me are ultimately reduced to the externalizations/projections of the different disavowed aspects of my personality), Judaism opens up a tradition in which an alien traumatic kernel forever persists in my Neighbor—the Neighbor remains an inert, impenetrable, enigmatic presence that hystericizes me.

The Jewish commandment that prohibits images of God is the obverse of the statement that relating to one's neighbor is the *only* terrain of religious practice, of where the divine dimension is present in our lives—"no images of God" does not point toward a gnostic experience of the divine beyond our reality, a divine that is beyond any image; on the contrary, it designates a kind of ethical *hic Rhodus, hic salta*: You want to be religious? Okay, prove it here, in the "works of love," in the way you relate to your neighbors. . . . We have here a nice case of the Hegelian reversal of reflexive determination into determinate reflection: instead of saying "God is love," we should say "Love is divine" (and, of course, the point is not to conceive of this reversal as the standard humanist platitude. It is for this precise reason that Christianity, far from standing for a regression toward an image of God, only draws the consequence of the Jewish iconoclasm through asserting the identity of God and man).

If, then, the modern topic of human rights is ultimately grounded in this Jewish notion of the Neighbor as the abyss of Otherness, how did we reach the weird contemporary negative link between Decalogue (the traumatically imposed divine Commandments) and human rights? That is to say, within our postpolitical, liberal-permissive society, human rights are ultimately, in their innermost, simply the rights to violate the Ten Commandments. "The right to privacy"—the right to adultery, done in secret, where no one sees me or has the right to probe into my life. "The right to pursue happiness and to possess private property"—the right to steal (to exploit others). "Freedom of the press and of the expression of opinion"—the right to lie. "The right of the free citizens to possess weapons"—the right to kill. And, ultimately, "freedom of religious belief"—the right to celebrate false gods.[1] Of course, human rights do not directly condone the violation of the Commandments—the point is just that they keep open a marginal "gray zone," which should remain out of reach of (religious or secular) power: in this shady zone, I can violate the commandments, and if the power probes into it, catching me with my pants down and trying to prevent my violations, I can cry, "Assault on my basic human rights!" The point is thus that it is structurally impossible, for the Power, to draw a clear line of separation and prevent only the "misuse" of the Right, while not infringing on the proper use—that is, the use that does *not* violate the Commandments. The first step in this direction was accomplished by the Christian notion of grace. In Mozart's *La Clemenza di Tito*, just before the final pardon, Tito himself is exasperated by the proliferation of treasons that oblige him to proliferate acts of clemency:

The very moment that I absolve one criminal, I discover another. / . . . / I believe the stars conspire to oblige me, in spite of myself, to become cruel. No: they shall not have this satisfaction. My virtue has already pledged itself to continue the contest. Let us see, which is more constant, the treachery of others or my mercy. / . . . / Let it be known to Rome that I am the same and that I know all, absolve everyone, and forget everything.

One can almost hear Tito complaining: "Uno per volta, per carita!"—"Please, not so fast, one after the other, in the line for mercy!" Living up to his task, Tito forgets everyone, but those whom he pardons are condemned to remember it forever:

SEXTUS: It is true, you pardon me, Emperor; but my heart will not absolve me; it will lament the error until it no longer has memory.

TITUS: The true repentance of which you are capable, is worth more than constant fidelity.

This couplet from the finale blurts out the obscene secret of *Clemenza*: the pardon does not really abolish the debt, it rather makes it infinite—we are *forever* indebted to the person who pardoned us. No wonder Tito prefers repentance to fidelity: in fidelity to the Master, I follow him out of respect, while in repentance, what attaches me to the Master is the infinite indelible guilt. In this, Tito is a thoroughly Christian master.

Usually, Judaism is conceived as the religion of the superego (of man's subordination to the jealous, mighty, and severe God), in contrast to the Christian God of Mercy and Love—one opposes the Jewish rigorous Justice and the Christian Mercy, the inexplicable gesture of undeserved pardon: we, humans, were born in sin, we cannot ever repay our debts and redeem ourselves through our own acts—our only salvation lies in God's Mercy, in His supreme sacrifice. However, in this very gesture of breaking the chain of Justice through the inexplicable act of Mercy, of paying our debt, Christianity imposes on us an even stronger debt: we are forever indebted to Christ, we cannot ever repay him for what he did for us. The Freudian name for such an excessive pressure that we cannot ever remunerate is, of course, superego. It is precisely through *not* demanding from us the price for our sins, through paying this price for us Himself, that the Christian God of Mercy establishes itself as the supreme superego agency: I paid the highest price for your sins, and you are thus indebted to me *forever*. Is this God as the superego agency, whose very Mercy generates the indelible guilt of believers, the ultimate horizon of Christianity? One should effectively correlate the unconditional guilt of superego and the mercy of love—two figures of excess, the excess of guilt without proportion to what I effectively did, and the excess of mercy without proportion to what I deserve on account of my acts.

As such, the dispensation of mercy is the most efficient constituent of the exercise of power. That is to say: Is the relationship between law (legal justice) and mercy really the one between necessity and choice? Is it really that one *has* to obey the law, while mercy is by definition dispensed as a free and excessive act, as something that the agent of mercy is free to do or not to do—mercy under compulsion is no mercy but, at its best, a travesty of mercy? What if, at a deeper level, the relationship is the opposite one? What if, with regard to law, we have the freedom to choose (to obey or violate it)? While mercy is obligatory, we *have* to display it—mercy is an unnecessary excess that, as such, *has* to occur. (And does the law not always take into account this freedom of ours, not only by punishing us for its transgression, but by providing escapes to being punished by its ambiguity and inconsistency?) Is it not that showing mercy is the *only* way for a Master to demonstrate his supralegal authority? If a Master were merely to guarantee the full application of the law, of legal regulations, he would be deprived of his authority and turn into a mere figure of knowledge, the agent of the discourse of university. (This is why even a great judge is a Master figure: he always somehow twists the law in its application by way of interpreting it creatively.) This goes even for Stalin himself, a figure we definitely do not associate with mercy: one should never forget that, as the (now-available) minutes of the meetings of the Politburo and Central Committee (CC) from the 1930s demonstrate, Stalin's direct interventions, as a rule, displayed mercy. When younger CC members, eager to prove their revolutionary fervor, demanded the instant death penalty for Bukharin, Stalin always intervened and said "Patience! His guilt is not yet proven!" or something similar. Of course this was a hypocritical attitude—Stalin was well aware that he himself generated the destructive fervor, that the younger members were eager to please him—but, nonetheless, the appearance of mercy is necessary here.

We encounter the same "unity of opposites" in the new capitalist ethics, where the ruthless pursuit of profit is counteracted by charity: charity is, today, part of the game: it serves as a humanitarian mask hiding the underlying economic exploitation. In a superego blackmail of gigantic proportions, the developed countries are constantly "helping" the undeveloped (with aid, credits, and so on), thereby avoiding the key issue, namely, their *complicity* in and coresponsibility for the miserable situation of the undeveloped. Which discursive shift underlies this new form of domination?

Lacan provides the answer in *L'envers de la psychanalyse*, his Seminar XVII (1969–1970) on the four discourses, Lacan's response to the events of 1968—its premise is best captured in his reversal of the well-known anti-structuralist graffiti from the Paris walls of 1968, "Structures do not walk on the streets!"—if anything, this seminar endeavors to demonstrate how structures *do* walk on the streets, that is, how structural shifts *can* account for the social outbursts like that of 1968. Instead of the one symbolic Order with its set of a priori rules that guarantee social cohesion, we get the matrix of the passages from one to another discourse: Lacan's interest is focused on the passage from the discourse of the Master to the discourse of the university as the hegemonic discourse in contemporary society. No wonder that the revolt was located at the universities: as such, it merely signaled the shift to the new forms of domination in which the scientific discourse serves to legitimize the relations of domination. Lacan's underlying premise is skeptic-conservative— Lacan's diagnosis is best captured by his famous retort to the student revolutionaries: "As hysterics, you demand a new master. You will get it!" This passage can also be conceived in more general terms, as the passage from the prerevolutionary ancien régime to the postrevolutionary new Master who does not want to admit that he is one, but proposes himself as a mere "servant" of the People—in Nietzsche's terms, it is simply the passage from Master's ethics to slave morality, and this fact, perhaps, enables a new approach to Nietzsche: when Nietzsche scornfully dismisses "slave morality," he is not attacking lower classes as such, but, rather, the new masters who are no longer ready to assume the title of the Master—*slave* is Nietzsche's term for a fake master. How, then, more closely, are we to read the University Discourse?

$$\frac{S_2}{S_1} \begin{matrix} \rightarrow \\ \leftarrow \end{matrix} \frac{a}{\$}$$

The University Discourse is enunciated from the position of "neutral" Knowledge; it addresses the remainder of the real (say, in the case of pedagogical knowledge, the "raw, uncultivated child"), turning it into the subject ($). The "truth" of the University Discourse, hidden beneath the bar, of course, is power, that is, the Master-Signifier: the constitutive lie of the University Discourse is that it disavows its performative dimension, presenting what effectively amounts to a political decision based on power as a simple insight into the factual state of things. What one should avoid here is the Foucauldian misreading: the produced subject is not simply the subjectivity that arises as the result of the disciplinary application of knowledge-power, but its remainder, that which eludes the grasp of knowledge-power. *Production* (the fourth term in the matrix of discourses) does not stand for the result of the discursive operation, but rather for its "indivisible remainder," for the excess that resists being included in the discursive network—that is, for what the discourse itself produces as the foreign body in its very heart.

Perhaps the exemplary case of the Master's position that underlies the University Discourse is the way in which medical discourse functions in our everyday lives: at the surface level, we are dealing with pure objective knowledge, which desubjectivizes the subject-patient, reducing him to an object of research, of diagnosis and treatment; however, beneath it, one can easily discern a worried hystericized subject, obsessed with anxiety, addressing the doctor as his Master and asking for reassurance from him. At a more common level, suffice it to recall the market expert who advocates strong budgetary measures (cutting welfare expenses, and the like) as a necessity imposed by his neutral expertise devoid of any ideological biases: what he conceals is the series of power relations (from the active role of state apparatuses to ideological beliefs) that sustain the "neutral" functioning of the market mechanism.

In the University Discourse, is not the upper level ($-a$) that of biopolitics (in the sense deployed from Foucault to Agamben)? Of the expert knowledge dealing with its object which is a—not subjects, but individuals reduced to bare life? And does the lower not designate what Eric Santner called the "crisis of investiture"—the impossibility of the subject to relate to S_1, to identify with a Master-Signifier, to assume the imposed symbolic mandate?[2] The key point here is that the expert rule of "biopolitics" is grounded in and conditioned by the crisis of investiture; this crisis generated the "postmetaphysical" survivalist stance of the Last Men, which ends up in an anemic spectacle of life dragging on as its own shadow. It is within this horizon that one should appreciate today's growing rejection of the death penalty: what one should be able to discern is the hidden "biopolitics" that sustains this rejection. Those who assert the "sacredness of life," defending it against the threat of transcendent powers that parasitize on it, end up in a world in which, on behalf of its very official goal—long pleasurable life—all effective pleasures are prohibited or strictly controlled (smoking, drugs, food, etc.). Spielberg's *Saving Private Ryan* is the latest example of this survivalist attitude toward dying, with its "demystifying" presentation of war as a meaningless slaughter which nothing can really justify—as such, it provides the best possible justification for Colin Powell's "no-casualties-on-our-side" military doctrine.

In today's market, we find a whole series of products deprived of their malignant property: coffee without caffeine, cream without fat, beer without alcohol. And the list goes on: what about virtual sex as sex without sex, the Colin Powell doctrine of war with no casualties (on our side, of course) as war without warfare, the contemporary redefinition of politics as the art of expert administration as politics without politics, up to today's tolerant liberal multiculturalism as an experience of Other deprived of its Otherness (the idealized Other who dances fascinating dances and has an ecologically sound holistic approach to reality, while features like wife-beating remain out of sight)? Virtual Reality simply generalizes this procedure of offering a product deprived of its substance: it provides reality itself deprived of its substance, of the resisting hard kernel of the Real—in the same way decaffeinated coffee smells and tastes like real coffee without being real, Virtual Reality is experienced as reality without being one.

Is this not the attitude of the hedonistic Last Man? Everything is permitted, you can enjoy everything, *but* deprived of the substance that makes it dangerous. (This is also the Last Man's revolution—"revolution without revolution.") Is this not one of the two versions of Lacan's anti-Dostoyevsky motto, "If God doesn't exist, everything is prohibited": 1) God is dead, we live in a permissive universe, you should strive for pleasures and happiness—but, in order to have a life full of happiness and pleasures, you should avoid dangerous excesses, so everything is prohibited if it is not deprived of its substance; 2) If God is dead, superego enjoins you to enjoy, but every determinate enjoyment is already a betrayal of the unconditional one, so it should be prohibited. The nutritive version of this is to enjoy directly the Thing Itself: Why bother with coffee? Inject caffeine directly into your blood! Why bother with sensual perceptions and excitations by external reality? Take drugs that directly affect your brain! And if there is God, then everything is permitted—to those who claim to act directly on behalf of God, as the instruments of His will; clearly, a direct link to God justifies our violation of any "merely human" constraints and considerations (as in Stalinism, where the reference to the big Other of historical Necessity justifies absolute ruthlessness).

Today's hedonism combines pleasure with constraint—it is no longer the old notion of the "right measure" between pleasure and constraint, but a kind of pseudo-Hegelian immediate coincidence of the opposites: action and reaction should coincide, the very thing that causes damage should already be the medicine. The ultimate example of it is arguably a *chocolate laxative*, available in the United States, with the paradoxical injunction to eat *more* chocolate—the very thing that causes constipation—to alleviate constipation. Do we not find here a weird version of Wagner's famous "Only the spear which caused the wound can heal it" from *Parsifal*? And is not a negative proof of the hegemony of this stance the fact that true unconstrained consumption (in all its main forms: drugs, sex, smoking, etc.) is emerging as the main danger? The fight against these dangers is one of the main investments of today's "biopolitics." Solutions are desperately sought that would reproduce the paradox of the chocolate laxative. The main contender is *safe sex*, a phrase that makes one appreciate the truth of the saying, "Is having sex with a condom not like taking a shower with a raincoat on?" The ultimate goal here would be along the lines of decaf coffee, to invent "opium without opium": no wonder marijuana is so popular among liberals who want to legalize it—it already *is* a kind of "opium without opium."

The structure of a product containing the agent of its own containment can be discerned throughout today's ideological landscape. There are two topics that determine today's liberal tolerant attitude toward Others: the respect of Otherness, openness toward it, *and* the obsessive fear of harassment—in short, the Other is okay insofar as its presence is not intrusive, insofar as the Other is not really Other. This is emerging as the central "human right" in late-capitalist society: *the right not to be harassed*, to be kept at a safe distance from others. A similar structure is clearly present in how we relate to capitalist profiteering: it is okay *if* it is counteracted with charitable activities—first you amass billions, then you return (part of) them to the needy. And the same goes for war, for the emerging logic of humanitarian or pacifist militarism: war is okay insofar as it really serves to bring about peace, democracy, or to create conditions for distributing humanitarian help. And does not the same hold true even for democracy and human rights? It is okay if human rights are "rethought" to include torture and a permanent emergency state, if democracy is cleansed of its populist "excesses."

However, what I am describing cannot but appear as two opposite ideological spaces: that of the reduction of humans to bare life, to *homo sacer* as the disponible object of the expert caretaking knowledge; and that of the respect for the vulnerable Other brought to an extreme, of the attitude of narcissistic subjectivity that experiences itself as vulnerable, constantly exposed to a multitude of potential "harassments." Is there a stronger contrast than the one between the respect for the Other's vulnerability and the reduction of the Other to "mere life" regulated by the administrative knowledge?

But what if these two stances nonetheless rely on the same root, what if they are the two aspects of one and the same underlying attitude, what if they coincide in what one is tempted to designate as the contemporary case of the Hegelian "infinite judgement," which asserts the identity of opposites? What the two poles share is precisely the underlying refusal of any higher Causes, the notion that the ultimate goal of our lives is life itself. Nowhere is the complicity of these two levels clearer as in the case of the opposition to the death penalty—no wonder, since (violently putting another human being to) death is, quite logically, the ultimate traumatic point of biopolitics, the politics of the administration of life. To put it in Foucauldian terms, is the abolition of the death penalty not part of a certain biopolitics that considers crime as the result of social, psychological, ideological, and like circumstances: the notion of the morally/legally responsible subject is an ideological fiction whose function is to cover up the network of power relations; individuals are not responsible for the crimes they commit, so they should not be punished? Is, however, the obverse of this thesis not that those who control the circumstances control the people? No wonder the two strongest industrial complexes today are the military and the medical, that of destroying and that of prolonging life.

Superego is thus not directly S_2: it is rather the S_1 of the S_2 itself, the dimension of an unconditional injunction that is inherent to knowledge itself. Recall the messages about health we are bombarded with all the time: "Smoking is dangerous! Too much fat may cause a heart attack! Regular exercise leads to a longer life!" and so on, and so on. It is impossible not to hear beneath it the unconditional injunction, "You should enjoy a long and healthy life!" What this means is that the discourse of the university is thoroughly mystifying, concealing its true foundation, obfuscating the unfreedom on which it relies.

Within this horizon, the concept of radical, "irrepresentable" Evil, be it holocaust or gulag, plays the central role, that of the constitutive limit and point of reference of today's predominant notion of democracy: *democracy* means avoiding the "totalitarian" extreme; it is defined as a permanent struggle against the "totalitarian" temptation to close the gap, to (pretend to) act on behalf of the Thing Itself. Ironically, it is thus as if one should turn around the well-known Augustinian notion of Evil as having no positive substance or force of its own, but being just the absence of Good: Good itself is the absence of Evil, the distance toward the Evil Thing.

It is this liberal blackmail of dismissing every radical political act as evil that one should thoroughly reject—even when it is coated in Lacanian colors, as is the case in Ioannis Stavrakakis's recent critical reply to my reading of *Antigone*, which focuses on the danger of what he calls the "absolutization" of the event, which then leads to a totalitarian *desastre*. When Stavrakakis writes that "fidelity to an event can flourish and avoid absolutization only as an infidel fidelity, only within the framework of another fidelity, fidelity to the openness of the political space and to the awareness of the constitutive impossibility of a final suture of the social," he thereby surreptitiously introduces a difference, which can be given different names, between the unconditional-ethical and the pragmatico-political: the original fact is the lack, opening, which pertains to human finitude, and all positive acts always fall short of this primordial lack; we have thus what Derrida calls the unconditional ethical injunction, impossible to fulfill, and positive acts, interventions, which remain strategic interventions. One should evoke two arguments against this position:

First, "Acts" in Lacan's sense precisely *suspend* this gap—they are "impossible" not in the sense of "impossible *to* happen," but in the sense of "impossible *that* happened." *This* is why Antigone was of interest to me: her act is not a strategic intervention that maintains the gap toward the impossible Void—it rather tends to "absolutely" enact the Impossible. I am well aware of the "lure" of such an act, but I claim that, in Lacan's later versions of the act, this moment of "madness" beyond strategic intervention remains. In this precise sense, the notion of act not only does not contradict the "lack in the Other," which, according to Stavrakakis, I neglect; it directly presupposes it: it is only through an act that I effectively assume the big Other's inexistence, that is, I enact the impossible, namely what appears as impossible within the coordinates of the existing sociosymbolic order.

Second, there *are* (also) political acts: politics cannot be reduced to the level of strategic-pragmatic interventions. In a radical political act, the opposition between a "crazy" destructive gesture and a strategic political decision momentarily breaks down—which is why it is theoretically and politically wrong to oppose strategic political acts, as risky as they can be, to radical "suicidal" gestures à la Antigone, gestures of pure self-destructive ethical insistence with, apparently, no political goal. The point is not simply that, once we are thoroughly engaged in a political project, we are ready to put everything at stake for it, inclusive of our lives, but, more precisely, that *only such an "impossible" gesture of pure expenditure can change the very coordinates of what is strategically possible within a historical constellation.* This is the key point: an act is neither a strategic intervention *into* the existing order, nor its "crazy" destructive *negation*; an act is an "excessive," trans-strategic, intervention that redefines the rules and contours of the existing order.

So what about the reproach that Antigone not only risks death or suspends symbolic order—my determination of a political act—but that she actively strives for death, for symbolic and real death, thereby displaying a purity of desire beyond any sociopolitical transformative action? First, is Antigone's act really outside politics, "apolitical"? Is not her defiance of the order of the supreme power (Creon, who acts on behalf of the common good) political, albeit in a negative way? Is not, in certain extreme circumstances, such "apolitical" defiance on behalf of "decency" or "old customs" even the very model of heroic political resistance? Second, her gesture is not simply pure desire for death—to do that, she could have directly killed herself and spared the people around her all the fuss . . . hers was not a pure symbolic striving for death, but an unconditional insistence on a particular symbolic ritual.

And this brings us to the key dilemma: the reference to democracy involves the rejection of the radical attempts to "step outside," to risk a radical break, to pursue the trend of self-organized collectives in areas outside the law. Arguably the greatest literary monument to such a utopia comes from an unexpected source—Mario Vargas Llosa's *The War of the End of the World* (1981), the novel about Canudos, an outlaw community deep in the Brazilian backlands that was home to prostitutes, freaks, beggars, bandits, and the most wretched of the poor. Canudos, led by an apocalyptic prophet, was a utopian space without money, property, taxes, and marriage. In 1897, it was destroyed by the military forces of the Brazilian government. The echoes of Canudos are clearly discernible in today's *favelas* in Latin American megalopolises: Are they, in some sense, not the first "liberated territories," the cells of futural self-organized societies? Are institutions like community kitchens not a model of "socialized" communal local life? The Canudos liberated territory in Bahia will remain forever the model of a liberated space, of an alternative community that thoroughly negates the existing state space. Everything is to be endorsed here, up to the religious "fanaticism." It is as if, in such communities, *the Benjaminian other side of the historical Progress, the defeated ones, acquires a space of its own.* Utopia *existed* here for a brief period of time—this is the only way to account for the "irrational," excessive, violence of the destruction of these communities (in 1897 Brazil, *all* inhabitants of Canudos, children and women included, were slaughtered, as if the very memory of the possibility of freedom had to be erased—and this by a government that presented itself as "progressive" liberal-democratic-republican). Until now, such communities exploded from time to time as passing phenomena, a site of eternity that interrupted the flow of temporal progress—one should have the courage to recognize them in the wide span from the Jesuit *reduciones* in eighteenth-century Paraguay (brutally destroyed by the joint action of Spanish and Portuguese armies) up to the settlements controlled by Sendero Luminoso in 1990s Peru. There is a will to accomplish the "leap of faith" and *step out* of the global circuit that is at work here, the will whose extreme and terrifying expression is the well-known accident from the Vietnam war: after the United States Army occupied a local village, their doctors vaccinated the children on their left arm in order to demonstrate their humanitarian care; when, a day later, the village was retaken by the Vietcong, they cut off the left arm of all vaccinated children. Although difficult to sustain as a literal model to follow, this thorough rejection of the Enemy precisely in its helping "humanitarian" aspect, no matter what the costs, has to be endorsed in its basic intention. In a similar way, when Sendero Luminoso took over a village, they did not focus on killing the soldiers or policemen stationed there, but more on the UN or U.S. agricultural consultants or health workers trying to help the local peasants—after lecturing them for hours and then forcing them to confess publicly their complicity with imperialism, the Sendero Luminoso shot them. Brutal as this procedure was, it was sustained by the correct insight: they, not the police or the army, were the true danger, the enemy at its most perfidious, since they were "lying in the guise of truth"—the more they were "innocent" (they "really" tried to help the peasants), the more they served as a tool of the United States. It is only such a strike against the enemy at his best, at the point where the enemy "indeed helps us," that displays a true revolutionary autonomy and "sovereignty" (to use this term in its Bataillean meaning). If one adopts the attitude of "let us take from the enemy what is good and reject or even fight against what is bad," one is already caught in the liberal trap of "humanitarian help."

Since today capitalism defines and structures the totality of the human civilization, every "Communist" territory was and is—again, in spite of its horrors and failures—a kind of "liberated territory," as Fred Jameson put it apropos of Cuba. What we are dealing with here is the old structural notion of the gap between the Space and the positive content that fills it in: although, as to their positive content, the Communist regimes were mostly a dismal failure, generating terror and misery, at the same time they opened up a certain space, the space of utopian expectations, which, among other things, enabled us to measure the failure of the really existing Socialism itself. (What the anti-Communist dissidents as a rule tend to overlook is that the very space from which they themselves criticized and denounced the everyday terror and misery was opened and sustained by the Communist breakthrough, by its attempt to escape the logic of the Capital.) This is how one should understand Alain Badiou's *mieux vaut un desastre qu'un desetre*, so shocking for the liberal sensitivity: better the worst Stalinist terror than the most liberal capitalist democracy. Of course, the moment one compares the positive content of the two, the Welfare State capitalist democracy is incomparably better—what redeems the Stalinist "totalitarianism" is the formal aspect, the *space* it opens up. Can one imagine a Utopian point at which this subterranean level of the Utopian Other Space would unite with the positive space of "normal" social life? The key political question is here: Is there in our "postmodern" time still a space for such communities? Are they limited to the undeveloped outskirts (*favelas*, ghettos), or is a space for them emerging in the very heart of the "postindustrial" landscape? Can one make a wild wager that the dynamics of "postmodern" capitalism with its rise of new eccentric geek communities provides a new chance here, that, perhaps for the first time in history, the logic of alternative communities can be grafted onto the latest state of technology?

The main form of such alternative communities in the twentieth century were so-called councils ("Soviets")—(almost) everybody in the West loved them, up to liberals like Hannah Arendt who perceived in them the echo of the old Greek life of *polis*. Throughout the age of the Really Existing Socialism (RES), the secret hope of "democratic socialists" was the direct democracy of the "soviets," the local councils as the form of self-organization of the people; and it is deeply symptomatic how, with the decline of RES, this emancipatory shadow that haunted it all the time also disappeared. Is this not the ultimate confirmation of the fact that the council version of "democratic socialism" was just a spectral double of the "bureaucratic" RES, its inherent transgression with no substantial positive content of its own, unable to serve as the permanent basic organizing principle of a society? What both RES and council democracy shared is the belief in the possibility of a self-transparent organization of society that would preclude political "alienation" (state apparatuses, institutionalized rules of political life, legal order, police, and so on) and is the basic experience of the end of RES not precisely the rejection of this *shared* feature, the resigned "postmodern" acceptance of the fact that society is a complex network of "subsystems," which is why a certain level of "alienation" is constitutive of social life, so that a totally self-transparent society is a utopia with totalitarian potentials?[3] (In this sense, it is Habermas who is "postmodern," in contrast to Adorno who, in spite of all his political compromises, to the end remained attached to a radically utopian vision of revolutionary redemption.)

Are, however, things really so simple? First, direct democracy is not only still alive in many places like *favelas*, it is even being "reinvented" and given a new boost by the rise of the "postindustrial" digital culture (do the descriptions of the new "tribal" communities of computer hackers not often evoke the logic of council democracy?). Second, the awareness that politics is a complex game in which a certain level of institutional alienation is irreducible should not lead us to ignore the fact that there is still a line of separation that divides those who are "in" from those who are "out," excluded from the space of the *polis*—there are citizens, and there is the specter of *homo sacer* haunting them all. In other words, even the "complex" contemporary societies still rely on the basic divide between included and excluded. The fashionable notion of "multitude" is insufficient precisely insofar as it cuts across this divide: there is a multitude *within* the system and the multitude of those *excluded*, and to simply encompass them within the scope of the same notion amounts to the same obscenity as equating starvation with dieting. And those excluded do not simply dwell in a psychotic nonstructured Outside—they have (and are forced into) their own self-organization, one of the names (and practices) of which was precisely the council democracy.

But should we still call it democracy? At this point, it is crucial to avoid what one cannot but call the "democratic trap." Many "radical" leftists accept the legalistic logic of "transcendental guarantee": they refer to democracy as the ultimate guarantee of those who are aware that there is no guarantee. That is to say, since no political act can claim a direct foundation in some transcendent figure of the big Other (of the "we are just instruments of a higher Necessity or Will" type), since every such act involves the risk of a contingent decision, nobody has the right to impose his choice on others—which means that every collective choice has to be democratically legitimized. From this perspective, democracy is not so much the guarantee of the right choice as a kind of opportunistic insurance against possible failure: if things turn out wrong, I can always say we are all responsible. Consequently, this last refuge must be dropped; one should fully assume the risk. The only adequate position is the one advocated already by Lukacs in his *History and Class Consciousness*: democratic struggle should not be fetishized; it is one of the forms of struggle, and its choice should be determined by a global strategic assessment of circumstances, not by its ostensibly superior intrinsic value. Like the Lacanian analyst, a political agent has to commit acts that can only be authorized by himself, for which there is no external guarantee.

An authentic political act can be, as to its form, a democratic one as well as a nondemocratic one. There are some elections or referendums in which "the impossible happens"—recall, decades ago in Italy, a referendum on divorce where, to the great surprise also of the Left which distrusted the people, the prodivorce side convincingly won, so that even the Left, privately skeptical, was ashamed of its distrust. (There were elements of the event even in the unexpected first electoral victory of François Mitterand.) It is only in *such* cases that one is justified in saying that, beyond and above the mere numeral majority, people effectively have spoken in a substantial sense of the term. On the other hand, an authentic act of popular will can also occur in the form of a violent revolution, of a progressive military dictatorship, and so on. In this precise sense, Khrushchev's 1956 speech denouncing Stalin's crimes was a true political act—as William Taubman put it, after this speech, "the Soviet regime never fully recovered, and neither did he."[4] Although the opportunist motives for this daring move are plain enough, there was clearly more than mere calculation to it, a kind of reckless excess that cannot be accounted for by strategic reasoning. After this speech, things were never the same again, the fundamental dogma of the infallible leadership was undermined, so no wonder that, as a reaction to the speech, the entire nomenklatura sank into temporary paralysis.

The present crisis thus compels us to rethink democracy itself as today's Master-Signifier. Democracy is not merely the "power of, by, and for the people." It is not enough just to claim that, in democracy, the will and interests (the two in no way automatically coincide) of the large majority determine the state decisions. *Democracy*—in the way this term is used today—concerns, above all, formal legalism: its minimal definition is the unconditional adherence to a certain set of formal rules which guarantee that antagonisms are fully absorbed into the agonistic game. *Democracy* means that, whatever electoral manipulation took place, every political agent will unconditionally respect the results. In this sense, the U.S. presidential elections of 2000 were effectively democratic: in spite of obvious electoral manipulations, and of the patent meaninglessness of the fact that a couple hundred Floridian voices will determine who will be president, the Democratic candidate accepted his defeat. In the weeks of uncertainty after the elections, Bill Clinton made an appropriate acerbic comment: "The American people have spoken; we just don't know what they said." This comment should be taken more seriously than it was meant: even now, we don't know it—and, maybe, because there was no substantial "message" behind the result at all.

Those old enough still remember the boring attempts of "democratic Socialists" to oppose to the miserable RES the vision of authentic socialism—to such attempts, the standard Hegelian answer is quite sufficient: the failure of reality to live up to its notion always bears witness to the inherent weakness of this notion itself. But why should the same also not hold for democracy itself? Is it also not all too simple to oppose to the "really-existing" liberal capitalo-democracy a more true "radical" democracy?

Interestingly enough, there is at least one case in which formal democrats themselves (or, at least, a substantial part of them) would tolerate the suspension of democracy: What if the formally free elections are won by an antidemocratic party whose platform promises the abolition of formal democracy? (This did happen, among other places, in Algeria a couple of years ago.) In such a case, many a democrat would concede that the people were not yet "mature" enough to be allowed democracy, and that some kind of enlightened despotism whose aim will be to educate the majority into proper democrats is preferable. A crucial component of any populism is also the dismissal of the formal democratic procedure: even if these rules are still respected, it is always made clear that they do not provide the crucial legitimacy to political agents—populism rather evokes the direct pathetic link between the charismatic leadership and the crowd, verified through plebiscites and mass gatherings. Consequently, it seems politically much more productive and theoretically much more adequate to limit "democracy" to the translation of antagonism into agonism: while democracy acknowledges the irreducible plurality of interests, ideologies, narratives, and the like, it excludes those who, as we put it, reject the democratic rules of the game—liberal democrats are quite right in claiming that populism is inherently "antidemocratic."

This is the sense in which one should render problematic democracy: Why should the Left always and unconditionally respect the formal democratic "rules of the game"? Why should it not, in some circumstances, at least, put in question the legitimacy of the outcome of a formal democratic procedure? All democratic leftists venerate Rosa Luxembourg's famous "Freedom is freedom for those who think differently." Perhaps, the time has come to shift the accent from "differently" to "think": "Freedom is freedom for those who think differently"—*only* for those who *really think*, even if differently, not for those who just blindly (unthinkingly) act out their opinions. In his famous short poem "The Solution" from 1953 (published in 1956), Bertolt Brecht mocks the arrogance of the Communist nomenklatura when faced with the workers' revolt:

> After the uprising of the 17th June
> The Secretary of the Writers Union
> Had leaflets distributed in the Stalinallee
> Stating that the people
> Had forfeited the confidence of the government
> And could win it back only
> By redoubled efforts.
> Would it not be easier
> In that case for the government
> To dissolve the people and elect another?[5]

However, this poem is not only politically opportunistic, the obverse of his letter of solidarity with the East German Communist regime published in *Neues Deutschland*—to put it brutally, Brecht wanted to cover both his flanks, to profess his support for the regime as well as to hint at his solidarity with the workers, so that whoever wins, he will be on the winning side—but also simply *wrong* in the theoretico-political sense: one should bravely admit that it effectively *is* a duty—*the* duty even—of a revolutionary party to "dissolve the people and elect another," that is, to bring about the transubstantiation of the "old" opportunistic people (the inert "crowd") into a revolutionary body aware of its historical task. Far from being an easy task, to "dissolve the people and elect another" is the most difficult of them all. What this means is that one should gather the courage to question radically today's predominant attitude of antiauthoritarian tolerance. It was, surprisingly, Bernard Williams who, in his perspicuous reading of David Mamet's *Oleanna*, outlined the limits of this attitude:

> A complaint constantly made by the female character is that she has made sacrifices to come to college, in order to learn something, to be told things that

she did not know, but that she has been offered only a feeble permissiveness. She complains that her teacher . . . does not control or direct her enough: he does not tell her what to believe, or even, perhaps, what to ask. He does not exercise authority. At the same time, she complains that he exercises power over her. This might seem to be a muddle on her part, or the playwright's, but it is not. The male character has power over her (he can decide what grade she gets), but just because he lacks authority, this power is mere power, in part gender power.[6]

Power appears (is experienced) "as such" at the very point where it is no longer covered by "authority." There are, however, further complications to Williams's view. First, "authority" is not simply a direct property of the master figure, but an effect of the social relationship between the master and his subjects: even if the master remains the same, it may happen, because of the change in the sociosymbolic field, that his position is no longer perceived as legitimate authority, but as mere illegitimate power (is such a shift not the most elementary gesture of feminism: male authority is all of a sudden unmasked as mere power?). The lesson of all revolutions from 1789 to 1989 is that such a disintegration of authority, its transformation into arbitrary power, always precedes the revolutionary outbreak. Where Williams is right is in his emphasis on how the very permissiveness of the power-figure, its restraining from exercising authority by directing, controlling, his subject, enables authority to appear as illegitimate power. Therein resides the vicious cycle of today's academia: the more professors renounce "authoritarian" active teaching, imposing knowledge and values, the more they are experienced as figures of power. And, as every parent knows, the same goes for parental education: a father who exerts true transferential authority will never be experienced as "oppressive"—it is, on the contrary, a father who tries to be permissive, who does not want to impose on his children his views and values, but allows them to discover their own way, that is denounced as exerting power, as being "oppressive."

The paradox to be fully endorsed here is that the only way to effectively abolish power relations leads through freely accepted relations of authority: the model of a free collective is not a group of libertines indulging in their pleasures, but the extremely disciplined revolutionary collective. The injunction that holds together such a collective is best encapsulated by the logical form of double negation (prohibition), which, precisely, is *not* the same as the direct positive assertion. Toward the end of Brecht's *Die Massnahme*, the Four Agitators declare:

It is a terrible thing to kill.
But not only others would we kill, but ourselves too if need be
Since only force can alter this
Murderous world, as
Every living creature knows.
It is still, we said
Not given to us not to kill.[7]

The text does *not* say "we are allowed to kill," but "it is still not permitted (an adequate paraphrase of *vergönnen*) to us not to kill"—or, simply, it is still *prohibited* to us not to kill. Brecht's precision is here admirable: the double negation is crucial. "It is allowed to kill" would amount to simple immoral permissivity; "it is ordered to kill" would transform killing into an obscene-perverse superego injunction that is the truth of the first version (as Lacan put it, the permitted *jouissance* inexorably turned into a prescribed one). The only correct way is thus the reversal of the biblical prohibition, the prohibition *not* to kill, which goes to the end, to the anti-Antigonean prohibition to provide for the proper funeral ritual: the young comrade has to "vanish, and vanish entirely"—that is, his disappearance (death) itself should disappear, should not leave any (symbolic) traces. This radical stance is the logical conclusion of the self-erasure of the revolutionary agent who is denied not only public recognition, but even posthumous recognition after his death; in the "Praise of Illegal Activity," the Control Chorus sings:

Speaking, but
Without betraying the speaker.
Winning, but
Without betraying the winner.
Dying, but
Without declaring the death.
Who would not do a lot for fame? Who
Would do as much for silence?[8]

This is revolutionary activity performed from the stance of "subjective destitution": not "authentically displaying one's position of enunciation," but erasing oneself behind the enunciated, in an act without subject. What the immortal Martha Argerich said about her piano playing ("I love piano playing, I just hate to be a pianist") also goes for the revolutionary: he loves the revolution, but hates to be a revolutionary.

Bernard Williams can again be of some help here, when he elaborates what forever separates *must* from *ought*: "*Ought* is related to *must* as *best* is related to *only*."[9] We arrive at what we must do after a long and anxious consideration of alternatives, and "can have that belief while remaining uncertain about it, and still very clearly seeing the powerful merits of alternative courses."[10] This difference between *must* and *ought* also relies on temporality: we can reproach somebody for not having done what he "ought to have done," while we cannot say to someone "You must have done it" if he did not do it—we use the expression "You must have done it" to console somebody who *did* a thing he found distasteful (like "Do not blame yourself, even if you loved him, you must have punished him!"), while the standard use of the expression "You ought to have done it" implies, on the contrary, that you did *not* do it.

This reference to a "must" also opens up the space of manipulation, like when a bargaining partner or outright blackmailer says that, "deplorably," this leaves him with no alternative to taking an unpleasant action—and, we may add, like the ruthless Stalinist who "cannot but" engage in terror. The falsity of this position resides in the fact that, when we "must" do something, it is not only that, within the limits that our situation sets to deliberation, we "cannot do otherwise but this": the character of a person is not only revealed in that he does what he must, but also "in the location of those limits, and in the very fact that one can determine, sometimes through deliberation itself, that one cannot do certain things, and must do others."[11] And one *is* responsible for one's character, for the choice of coordinates that prevent me from doing some things and impel me to do others. This brings us to the Lacanian notion of act: in an act, I precisely redefine the very coordinates of what I cannot and must do.

Must and *ought* thus relate as the Real and the Symbolic: the Real of a drive whose injunction cannot be avoided (which is why Lacan says that the status of a drive is ethical); the Ought as a symbolic ideal caught in the dialectic of desire (if you ought not to do something, this very prohibition generates the desire to do it). When you "must" do something, it means you have no choice but to do it, even if is terrible: in Wagner's *Die Walkure*, Wotan is cornered by Fricka and he "must" ("cannot but") allow the murder of Siegmund, although his heart bleeds for him; he "must" ("cannot but") punish Brunhilde, his dearest child, the embodiment of his own innermost striving. And, incidentally, the same goes for Wagner's *Tristan und Isolde,* the Bayreuth staging of which was Mueller's last great theatrical achievement: they *must,* they *cannot but,* indulge in their passion, even if this goes against their *Sollen,* their social obligations. In Wotan's forced exercise of punishment, Wagner encounters here the paradox of the "killing with *pietà*" at work from the Talmud (which calls us to dispense Justice with Love) to Brecht's two key *Lehrstücke, Der Jasager* and *Die Massnahme,* in which the young comrade is killed by his companions with loving tenderness. And this is what today, in our time in which the abstract humanitarian rejection of violence is accompanied by its obscene double, the anonymous killing *without pietà,* we need more than ever.

Notes

1. I owe this point to Ken Rinehard, UCLA.
2. See Eric Santner, *My Own Private Germany* (Princeton: Princeton University Press, 1996), 26.
3. For a clear articulation of this stance, see Martin Jay, "No Power to the Soviets," in his *Cultural Semantics* (Amherst: University of Massachusetts Press, 1998).
4. William Taubman, *Khrushchev: The Man and His Era* (London: Free Press, 2003), 493.
5. Bertolt Brecht, *Gedichte in einem Band* (Frankfurt: Suhrkamp, 1982), 1009–10.
6. Bernard Williams, *Truth and Truthfulness* (Princeton: Princeton University Press, 2002), 7–8.
7. Bertolt Brecht, *Collected Plays: Three* (London: Methuen, 1997), 87.
8. Brecht, *Collected Plays,* 68.
9. Williams, *Truth and Truthfulness,* 125.
10. Ibid., 126.
11. Ibid., 130.

CHAPTER 20

WHAT IS IT TO LIVE?

Alain Badiou

0. We are now in a position to propose a response to what has always been the 'daunting' question—as one of Julien Gracq's characters has it—the question that, however, great its detour, philosophy must ultimately answer: what is it to live? 'To live' obviously not in the sense of democratic materialism (persevering in the free virtualities of the body), but rather in the sense of Aristotle's enigmatic formula: to live 'as an Immortal'.

To begin with, we can reformulate the exacting system of conditions for an affirmative response of the type: 'Yes! The true life is present'.

1. It is not a world, as given in the logic of its appearing (the infinite of its objects and relations), which induces the possibility of living—at least not if life is something other than existence. The induction of such a possibility depends on that which acts in the world as the trace of the fulgurating disposition that has befallen that world. That is, the trace of a vanished event. Within worldly appearing, such a trace is always a maximally intense existence. Through the incorporation of the world's past to the present opened up by the trace, it is possible to learn that prior to what happened and is no longer, the ontological support of this intense existence was an inexistent of the world. The birth of a multiple to the flash of appearing, to which it previously only belonged in an extinguished form, makes a trace in the world and signals towards life.

For those who ask where the true life is, the first philosophical directive is thus the following: 'Take care of what is born. Interrogate the flashes, probe into their past without glory. You can only put your hope in what in-appears.'

2. It is not enough to identify a trace. One must incorporate oneself into what the trace authorizes in terms of consequences. This point is crucial. Life is the creation of a present, but just like the world vis-à-vis God in Descartes, this creation is a continuous creation. The cohesion of a hitherto impossible body constitutes itself around the trace, around the anonymous flash of a birth to the world of being-there. To accept and declare this body is not enough if one wishes to be the contemporary of the present of which this body is the material support. It is necessary to enter into its composition, to become an active element of this body. The only real relation to the present is that of incorporation: the incorporation into this immanent cohesion of the world which springs from the becoming existent of the evental trace, as a new birth beyond all the facts and markers of time.

3. The unfolding of the consequences linked to the evental trace—consequences that create a present—proceeds through the treatment of the points of the world. It does not take place through the continuous trajectory of a body's efficacy, but in sequences, point by point. Every present has a kind of fibre. The points of the world in which the infinite appears before the Two of choice are like the fibres of the present, its intimate constitution in its worldly becoming. In order for a living present to open up, it is thus required that the world not be atonic, that it contain points which guarantee the efficacy of a body, thus lending creative time its fibre.

4. Life is a subjective category. A body is the materiality that life requires, but the becoming of the present depends on the disposition of this body in a subjective formalism, whether it be produced (the formalism is faithful, the body is directly placed 'under' the evental trace), erased (the formalism is reactive, the body is held at a double distance by the negation of the trace), or occulted (the body is denied). Neither the reactive deletion of the present, which denies the value of the event, nor, a fortiori, its mortifying occultation, which presupposes a 'body' transcendent to the world, sanction the affirmation of life, which is the incorporation, point by point, to the present.

To live is thus an incorporation into the present under the faithful form of a subject. If the incorporation is dominated by the reactive form, one will not speak of life, but of mere conservation. It is a question of protecting oneself from the consequences of a birth, of not relaunching existence beyond itself. If incorporation is dominated by the obscure formalism, one will instead speak of mortification.

Ultimately life is the wager, made on a body that has entered into appearing, that one will faithfully entrust this body with a new temporality, keeping at a distance the conservative drive (the ill-named 'life' instinct) as well as the mortifying drive (the death instinct). Life is what gets the better of the drives.

5. Because it prevails over the drives, life engages in the sequential creation of a present, and this creation both constitutes and absorbs a new type of past.

For democratic materialism, the present is never created. Democratic materialism affirms, in an entirely explicit manner, that it is important to maintain the present within the confines of an atonic reality. That is because it regards any other view of things as submitting the body to the despotism of an ideology, instead of letting it roam freely among the diversity of languages. Democratic materialism proposes to call 'thought' the pure algebra of appearing. This atonic conception of the present results in the fetishization of the past as a separable 'culture'. Democratic materialism has a passion for history; it is truly the only authentic historical materialism.

Contrary to what transpires in the Stalinist version of Marxism—a version that Althusser inherited, though he disrupted it from within—it is crucial to disjoin the materialist dialectic, the philosophy of emancipation through truths, from historical materialism, the philosophy of alienation through language-bodies. To break with the cult of genealogies and narratives means restoring the past as the amplitude of the present.

I already wrote it more than twenty years ago, in my *Theory of the Subject*: History does not exist. There are only disparate presents whose radiance is measured by their power to unfold a past worthy of them.

In democratic materialism, the life of language-bodies is the conservative succession of the instants of the atonic world. It follows that the past is charged with the task of endowing these instants with a fictive horizon, with a cultural density. This also explains why the fetishism of history is accompanied by an unrelenting discourse on novelty, perpetual change, and the imperative of modernization. The past of cultural depths is matched by a dispersive present, an agitation which is itself devoid of any depth whatsoever. There are monuments to visit and devastated instants to inhabit. Everything changes at every instant, which is why one is left to contemplate the majestic historical horizon of what does not change.

For the materialist dialectic, it is almost the opposite. What strikes one first is the stagnant immobility of the present, its sterile agitation, the violently imposed atonicity of the world. There have been few, very few, crucial changes in the nature of the problems of thought since Plato, for instance. But, on the basis of some truth-procedures that unfold subjectivizable bodies, point by point, one reconstitutes a different past, a history of achievements, discoveries, breakthroughs, which is by no means a cultural monumentality but a legible succession of fragments of eternity. That is because a faithful subject creates the present as the being-there of eternity. Accordingly, to incorporate oneself into this present amounts to perceiving the past of eternity itself.

To live is therefore also, always, to experience in the past the eternal amplitude of a present. We concur with Spinoza's famous formula from the scholium to Proposition XXIII of Book V of the *Ethics*: 'We feel and know by experience that we are eternal'.

6. Yet it remains important to give a name to this experience [*expérimentation*]. It belongs neither to the order of lived experience, nor to that of expression. It is not the finally attained accord between the capacities of a body and the resources of a language. It is the incorporation into the exception of a truth. If we agree to call 'Idea' what both manifests itself in the world—what sets forth the being-there of a body—and is an exception to its transcendental logic, we will say, in line with Platonism, that to experience in the present the eternity that authorizes the creation of this present is to experience an Idea. We must therefore accept that for the materialist dialectic, 'to live' and 'to live for an Idea' are one and the same thing.

In what it would instead call an ideological conception of Life, democratic materialism sees nothing but fanaticism and the death instinct. It is true that, if there is nothing but bodies and languages, to live for an Idea necessarily implies the arbitrary absolutization of one language, which bodies must comply with. Only the material recognition of the 'except that' of truths allows us to declare, not that bodies are submitted to the authority of a language, far from it, but that a new body is the organization in the present of an unprecedented subjective life. I maintain that the real experience of such a life, the comprehension of a theorem or the force of an encounter, the contemplation of a drawing or the momentum of a meeting, is irresistibly universal. This means that, for the form of incorporation that corresponds to it, the advent of the Idea is the very opposite of a submission. Depending on the type of truth that we are dealing with, it is joy, happiness, pleasure or enthusiasm.

7. Democratic materialism presents as an objective given, as a result of historical experience, what it calls 'the end of ideologies'. What actually lies behind this is a violent subjective injunction whose real content is: 'Live without Idea'. But this injunction is incoherent.

That this injunction pushes thought into the arms of sceptical relativism has long been obvious. We are told this is the price to be paid for tolerance and the respect of the Other. But each and every day we see that this tolerance is itself just another fanaticism, because it only tolerates its own vacuity. Genuine scepticism, that of the Greeks, was actually an absolute theory of exception: it placed truths so high that it deemed them inaccessible to the feeble intellect of the human species. It thus concurred with the principal current in ancient philosophy, which argues that attaining the True is the calling of the immortal part of men, of the inhuman excess that lies in man. Contemporary scepticism—the scepticism of cultures, history and self-expression—is not of this calibre. It merely conforms to the rhetoric of instants and the politics of opinions. Accordingly, it begins by dissolving the inhuman into the human, then the human into everyday life, then everyday (or animal) life into the atonicity of the world. It is from this dissolution that stems the negative maxim 'Live without Idea', which is incoherent because it no longer has any idea of what an Idea could be.

That is the reason why democratic materialism in fact seeks to destroy what is external to it. As we have noted, it is a violent and warmongering ideology. Like every mortifying symptom, this violence results from an essential inconsistency. Democratic materialism regards itself as humanist (human rights, etc.). But it is impossible to possess a concept of what is 'human' without dealing with the (eternal, ideal) inhumanity which authorizes man to incorporate himself into the present under the sign of the trace of what changes. If one fails to recognize the effects of these traces, in which the inhuman commands humanity to exceed its being there, it will be necessary, in order to maintain a purely animalistic, pragmatic notion of the human species, to annihilate both these traces and their infinite consequences.

The democratic materialist is a fearsome and intolerant enemy of every human—which is to say inhuman—life worthy of the name.

8. The banal objection says that if to live depends on the event, life is only granted to those who have the luck [*chance*] of welcoming the event. The democrat sees in this 'luck' the mark of an aristocratism, a transcendent arbitrariness—of the kind that has always been linked to the doctrines of Grace. It is true that several times I have used the metaphor of grace, in order to indicate that what is called living always involves agreeing to work through the (generally unprecedented) consequences of what happens.

The advocates of the divine, rather than of God, have long strived to rectify the apparent injustice of this gift, of this incalculable supplement from which stems the sublation of an inexistent. In order to fulfil this task, the most recent, talented and neglected among these advocates, Quentin Meillassoux, is developing an entirely new theory of the 'not yet' of divine existence, accompanied by a rational promise concerning the resurrection of bodies. This goes to show that new bodies and their birth are inevitably at stake in this affair.

9. I believe in eternal truths and in their fragmented creation in the present of worlds. My position on this point is entirely isomorphic with that of Descartes: truths are eternal because they have been created and not because they have been there forever. For Descartes, 'eternal truths'—which, as we recalled in the preface, he posed in exception of bodies and ideas—cannot transcend divine will. Even the most formal of these, the truths of mathematics or logic, like the principle of non-contradiction, depend on a free act of God:

> God cannot have been determined to make it true that contradictories cannot be true together and, therefore, he could have done the opposite.

Of course, the process of creation of a truth, whose present is constituted by the consequences of a subjectivated body, is very different from the creative act of a God. But, at bottom, the idea is the same. That it belongs to the essence of a truth to be eternal does not dispense it in the least from having to appear in a world and to be inexistent prior to this appearance. Descartes proposes a truly remarkable formula with regard to this point:

> Even if God has willed that some truths should be necessary, this does not mean that he willed them necessarily.

Eternal necessity pertains to a truth in itself: the infinity of prime numbers, the pictorial beauty of the horses in the Chauvet cave, the principles of popular war or the amorous affirmation of Héloïse and Abelard. But its process of creation does not—since it depends on the contingency of worlds, the aleatory character of a site, the efficacy of the organs of a body and the constancy of a subject.

Descartes is indignant that one could consider truths as separate from other creatures, turning them, so to speak, into the fate of God:

> The mathematical truths which you call eternal have been laid down by God and depend on him entirely no less than the rest of his creatures. Indeed to say that these truths are independent of God is to talk of him as if he were Jupiter or Saturn and to subject him to the Styx and the Fates.

I too affirm that all truths without exception are 'established' through a subject, the form of a body whose efficacy creates point by point. But, like Descartes, I argue that their creation is but the appearing of their eternity.

10. I am indignant then, like Descartes, when the True is demoted to the rank of the Styx and the Fates. Truth be told, I am indignant twice over. And life's worth also stems from this double quarrel. First of all against those, the culturalists, relativists, people preoccupied with immediate bodies and available languages, for whom the historicity of all things excludes eternal truths. They fail to see that a genuine creation, a historicity of exception, has no other criterion than to establish, between disparate worlds, the evidence of an eternity. And that what appears only shines forth in its appearance to the extent that it subtracts itself from the local laws of appearing. A creation is trans-logical, since its being upsets its appearing. Second, against those for whom the universality of the truth takes the form of a transcendent Law, before which we must bend our knee, to which we must conform our bodies and our words. They do not see that every eternity and every universality must appear in a world and, 'patiently or impatiently', be created within it. Since a truth is an appearance of being, a creation is logical.

11. But I need neither God nor the divine. I believe that it is here and now that we rouse or resurrect ourselves as Immortals.

Man is this animal to whom it belongs to participate in numerous worlds, to appear in innumerable places. This kind of objectal ubiquity, which makes him shift almost constantly from one world to another, on the background of the infinity of these worlds and their transcendental organization, is in its own right, without any need for a miracle, a grace: the purely logical grace of innumerable appearing. Every human animal can tell itself that it is ruled out that it will encounter always and everywhere atonicity, the inefficiency of the body or the dearth of organs capable of treating its points. Incessantly, in some accessible world, something happens. Several times in its brief existence, every human animal is granted the chance to incorporate itself into the subjective present of a truth. The grace of living for an Idea, that is of living as such, is accorded to everyone and for several types of procedure.

The infinite of worlds is what saves us from every finite disgrace. Finitude, the constant harping on of our mortal being, in brief, the fear of death as the only passion—these are the bitter ingredients of democratic materialism. We overcome all this when we seize hold of the discontinuous variety of worlds and the interlacing of objects under the constantly variable regimes of their appearances.

12. We are open to the infinity of worlds. To live is possible. Therefore, to (re)commence to live is the only thing that matters.

13. I am sometimes told that I see in philosophy only a means to reestablish, against the contemporary apologia of the futile and the everyday, the rights of heroism. Why not? Having said that, ancient heroism claimed to justify life through sacrifice. My wish is to make heroism exist through the affirmative joy which is universally generated by following consequences through. We could say that the epic heroism of the one who gives his life is supplanted by the mathematical heroism of the one who creates life, point by point.

14. In *Man's Fate*, Malraux makes the following remark about one of his characters: 'The heroic sense had given him a kind of discipline, not a kind of justification of life'. In effect, I place heroism on the side of discipline, the only weapon both of the True and of peoples, against power and wealth, against the insignificance and dissipation of the mind. But this discipline demands to be invented, as the coherence of a subjectivizable body. Then it can no longer be distinguished from our own desire to live.

15. We will only be consigned to the form of the disenchanted animal for whom the commodity is the only reference-point if we consent to it. But we are shielded from this consent by the Idea, the secret of the pure present.

CHAPTER 21

IMMANENCE A LIFE

Gilles Deleuze

What is a transcendental field? It can be distinguished from experience in that
it doesn't refer to an object or belong to a subject (empirical representation). It
appears therefore as a pure stream of a subjective consciousness, a pre-
reflexive impersonal consciousness, a qualitative duration of consciousness
without a self. It may seem curious that the transcendental be defined by such
immediate givens: we will speak of a transcendental empiricism in contrast to
everything that makes up the world of the subject and the object. There is
something wild and powerful in this transcendental empiricism that is of
course not the element of sensation (simple empiricism), for sensation is only
a break within the flow of absolute consciousness. It is, rather, however close
two sensations may be, the passage from one to the other as becoming, as increase or decrease in power (virtual quantity). Must we then define the transcendental field by a pure immediate consciousness with neither object nor
self, as a movement that neither begins nor ends? (Even Spinoza's conception
of this passage or quantity of power still appeals to consciousness.)

But the relation of the transcendental field to consciousness is only a conceptual one. Consciousness becomes a fact only when a subject is produced at
the same time as its object, both being outside the field and appearing as
"transcendents." Conversely, as long as consciousness traverses the transcendental field at an infinite speed everywhere diffused, nothing is able to reveal
it.[1] It is expressed, in fact, only when it is reflected on a subject that refers it to
objects. That is why the transcendental field cannot be defined by the consciousness that is coextensive with it, but removed from any revelation.

The transcendent is not the transcendental. Were it not for consciousness, the transcendental field would be defined as a pure plane of immanence, because it eludes all transcendence of the subject and of the object.[2] Absolute immanence is in itself: it is not in something, to something; it does not depend on an object or belong to a subject. In Spinoza, immanence is not immanence to substance; rather, substance and modes are in immanence. When the subject or the object falling outside the plane of immanence is taken as a universal subject or as any object to which immanence is attributed, the transcendental is entirely denatured, for it then simply redoubles the empirical (as with Kant), and immanence is distorted, for it then finds itself enclosed in the transcendent. Immanence is not related to Some Thing as a unity superior to all things or to a Subject as an act that brings about a synthesis of things: it is only when immanence is no longer immanence to anything other than itself that we can speak of a plane of immanence. No more than the transcendental field is defined by consciousness can the plane of immanence be defined by a subject or an object that is able to contain it.

We will say of pure immanence that it is A LIFE, and nothing else. It is not immanence to life, but the immanent that is in nothing is itself a life. A life is the immanence of immanence, absolute immanence: it is complete power, complete bliss. It is to the degree that he goes beyond the aporias of the subject and the object that Johann Fichte, in his last philosophy, presents the transcendental field as a life, no longer dependent on a Being or submitted to an Act—it is an absolute immediate consciousness whose very activity no longer refers to a being but is ceaselessly posed in a life.[3] The transcendental field then becomes a genuine plane of immanence that reintroduces Spinozism into the heart of the philosophical process. Did Maine de Biran not go through something similar in his "last philosophy" (the one he was too tired to bring to fruition) when he discovered, beneath the transcendence of effort, an absolute immanent life? The transcendental field is defined by a plane of immanence, and the plane of immanence by a life.

What is immanence? A life . . . No one has described what a life is better than Charles Dickens, if we take the indefinite article as an index of the transcendental. A disreputable man, a rogue, held in contempt by everyone, is found as he lies dying. Suddenly, those taking care of him manifest an eagerness, respect, even love, for his slightest sign of life. Everybody bustles about to save him, to the point where, in his deepest coma, this wicked man himself senses something soft and sweet penetrating him. But to the degree that he comes back to life, his saviors turn colder, and he becomes once again mean and crude. Between his life and his death, there is a moment that is only that of *a* life playing with death.[4] The life of the individual gives way to an impersonal and yet singular life that releases a pure event freed from the accidents of internal and external life, that is, from the subjectivity and objectivity of what happens: a "Homo tantum" with whom everyone empathizes and who attains a sort of beatitude. It is a haecceity no longer of individuation but of singularization: a life of pure immanence, neutral, beyond good and evil, for it was only the subject that incarnated it in the midst of things that made it good or bad. The life of such individuality fades away in favor of the singular life immanent to a man who no longer has a name, though he can be mistaken for no other. A singular essence, a life . . .

But we shouldn't enclose life in the single moment when individual life confronts universal death. *A* life is everywhere, in all the moments that a given living subject goes through and that are measured by given lived objects: an immanent life carrying with it the events or singularities that are merely actualized in subjects and objects. This indefinite life does not itself have moments, close as they may be one to another, but only between-times, between-moments; it doesn't just come about or come after but offers the immensity of an empty time where one sees the event yet to come and already happened, in the absolute of an immediate consciousness. In his novels, Alexander Lernet-Holenia places the event in an in-between time that could engulf entire armies. The singularities and the events that constitute *a* life coexist with the accidents of *the* life that corresponds to it, but they are neither grouped nor divided in the same way. They connect with one another in a manner entirely different from how individuals connect. It even seems that a singular life might do without any individuality, without any other concomitant that individualizes it. For example, very small children all resemble one another and have hardly any individuality, but they have singularities: a smile, a gesture, a funny face—not subjective qualities. Small children, through all their sufferings and weaknesses, are infused with an immanent life that is pure power and even bliss. The indefinite aspects in a life lose all indetermination to the degree that they fill out a plane of immanence or, what amounts to the same thing, to the degree that they constitute the elements of a transcendental field (individual life, on the other hand, remains inseparable from empirical determinations). The indefinite as such is the mark not of an empirical indetermination but of a determination by immanence or a transcendental determinability. The indefinite article is the indetermination of the person only because it is determination of the singular. The One is not the transcendent that might contain immanence but the immanent contained within a transcendental field. One is always the index of a multiplicity: an event, a singularity, a life . . . Although it is always possible to invoke a transcendent that falls outside the plane of immanence, or that attributes immanence to itself, all transcendence is constituted solely in the flow of immanent consciousness that belongs to this plane.[5] Transcendence is always a product of immanence.

A life contains only virtuals. It is made up of virtualities, events, singularities. What we call virtual is not something that lacks reality but something that is engaged in a process of actualization following the plane that gives it its particular reality. The immanent event is actualized in a state of things and of the lived that make it happen. The plane of immanence is itself actualized in an object and a subject to which it attributes itself. But however inseparable an object and a subject may be from their actualization, the plane of immanence is itself virtual, so long as the events that populate it are virtualities. Events or singularities give to the plane all their virtuality, just as the plane of immanence gives virtual events their full reality. The event considered as non-actualized (indefinite) is lacking in nothing. It suffices to put it in relation to its concomitants: a transcendental field, a plane of immanence, a life, singularities. A wound is incarnated or actualized in a state of things or of life; but it is itself a pure virtuality on the plane of immanence that leads us into a life. My wound existed before me: not a transcendence of the wound as higher actuality, but its immanence as a virtuality always within a milieu (plane or field).[6] There is a big difference between the virtuals that define the immanence of the transcendental field and the possible forms that actualize them and transform them into something transcendent.

Notes

1. "As though we reflected back to surfaces the light which emanates from them, the light which, had it passed unopposed, would never have been revealed" (Henri Bergson, *Matter and Memory* [New York: Zone Books, 1988], p. 36).

2. Cf. Jean-Paul Sartre, who posits a transcendental field without a subject that refers to a consciousness that is impersonal, absolute, immanent: with respect to it, the subject and the object are "transcendents" (*La transcendance de l'Ego* [Paris: Vrin, 1966], pp. 74–87). On James, see David Lapoujade's analysis, "Le Flux intensif de la conscience chez William James," *Philosophie* 46 (June 1995).

3. Already in the second introduction to *La Doctrine de la science*: "The intuition of pure activity which is nothing fixed, but progress, not a being, but a life" (*Oeuvres choisies de la philosophie première* [Paris: Vrin, 1964], p. 274). On the concept of life according to Fichte, see *Initiation à la vie bienheureuse* (Paris: Aubier, 1944), and Martial Guéroult's commentary (p. 9).

4. Dickens, *Our Mutual Friend* (New York: Oxford University Press, 1989), p. 443.

5. Even Edmund Husserl admits this: "The being of the world is necessarily transcendent to consciousness, even within the originary evidence, and remains necessarily transcendent to it. But this doesn't change the fact that all transcendence is constituted solely in the *life of consciousness*, as inseparably linked to that life . . ." (*Méditations cartésiennes* [Paris: Vrin, 1947], p. 52). This will be the starting point of Sartre's text.

6. Cf. Joë Bousquet, *Les Capitales* (Paris: Le Cercle du Livre, 1955).

ACKNOWLEDGMENT OF COPYRIGHT

INDEX

Abnormal (Foucault), 364

academia, authoritarian teaching in, 408

action: Arendt on, 103–5, 107, 112–15, 119, 123, 125, 126n1; collective, 204–5; communicative, 225; intentions vs. consequences of, 197; vs. thought, 110, 126, 128n16 (*see also* labor, political action, and intellect)

acts and the existing order, 400–401

Adorno, Theodor, 254–55, 404

advertising/consumption theories, 234–35n22

Agamben, Giorgio: on bare life, 146; on the biological threshold of modernity, 156; on biopolitics, overview of, 25–26, 32; on biopolitics and thanatopolitics, 148; on birth/nativity, 154, 156–59; on concentration camps, 141–42, 146, 148, 157, 162, 200; on *de homine replegiando*, 149; on *habeas corpus*, 148–50; on *homo sacer* (sacred man), 26, 149–50, 200; on humanitarianism vs. politics, 158–59; on human life as sacred, 6; on human rights, 152–60; on inoperative activity, 238–39; on the politicization of life, 145–51 (*see also* biopolitics); on racism, 148; on refugees, 156–59; on resistance, 238; on Sade, 159–60; on sadomasochism, 159; on *zoē* (natural life), 10, 134, 149. See also *Homo Sacer: Sovereign Power and Bare Life*

aging, 326

Albrow, Martin, 314

Althusser, Louis, 193, 201, 414

American Revolution, 84

Amnesty International, 226–27

analytic-descriptive vs. propositional-normative relation, 360

anarchism, 80, 143

anatomo-politics, 14, 44–46, 64

Anatomy, Physiology, and Pathology of the State (Uexküll), 354–56

The Ancient City (Coulanges), 129–30n27, 131n37, 131–32n43

aneu logon (without word), 112

animality vs. humanity, 16, 37n44

animal laborans, 113, 122–26

Antelme, Robert, 141–42

antiauthoritarian tolerance, 407–8

antibiotics, 342

Antigone, 114, 130n29, 400–401

anti-pastoral revolution, 21, 38n60

Apache helicopters, 177

apartheid regime, 170–71, 174

Appadurai, Arjun, 312

apparatus, 10–12, 23, 36n31. See also *dispositifs*

Aquinas, Saint Thomas, 113, 116, 127n9, 128nn11–13, 129n24

Arato, Andrew, 235n28

Arendt, Hannah: on the Cave parable, 112; on civil death, 97n8; on civilization, 93–94, 95–96; on colonialism, 171; on concentration camps, 88, 96n4, 162; on excommunication, 97n8; on human rights of stateless people, 23–24, 159 (*see also* Declaration of the Rights of Man and Citizen; human rights); on outlawry, 96–97n8; on political